Register for Free Membership

solutions@syngr

MW01057187

Over the last few years, Syngress has published many best-selling and critically acclaimed books, including Tom Shinder's *Configuring ISA Server 2004*, Brian Caswell and Jay Beale's *Snort 2.1 Intrusion Detection*, and Angela Orebaugh and Gilbert Ramirez's *Ethereal Packet Sniffing*. One of the reasons for the success of these books has been our unique **solutions@syngress.com** program. Through this site, we've been able to provide readers a real time extension to the printed book.

As a registered owner of this book, you will qualify for free access to our members-only solutions@syngress.com program. Once you have registered, you will enjoy several benefits, including:

- Four downloadable e-booklets on topics related to the book. Each booklet is approximately 20-30 pages in Adobe PDF format. They have been selected by our editors from other best-selling Syngress books as providing topic coverage that is directly related to the coverage in this book.

- A comprehensive FAQ page that consolidates all of the key points of this book into an easy-to-search web page, providing you with the concise, easy-to-access data you need to perform your job.

- A "From the Author" Forum that allows the authors of this book to post timely updates links to related sites, or additional topic coverage that may have been requested by readers.

Just visit us at **www.syngress.com/solutions** and follow the simple registration process. You will need to have this book with you when you register.

Thank you for giving us the opportunity to serve your needs. And be sure to let us know if there is anything else we can do to make your job easier.

SYNGRESS®

YNGRESS®

Network Security Evaluation

Using the
NSA IEM

Bryan Cunningham   Chuck Little

Ted Dykstra   Greg Miles

Ed Fuller   Travis Schack

Matthew Hoagberg

Russ Rogers Technical Editor and Contributor

Syngress Publishing, Inc., the author(s), and any person or firm involved in the writing, editing, or production (collectively "Makers") of this book ("the Work") do not guarantee or warrant the results to be obtained from the Work.

There is no guarantee of any kind, expressed or implied, regarding the Work or its contents. The Work is sold AS IS and WITHOUT WARRANTY. You may have other legal rights, which vary from state to state.

In no event will Makers be liable to you for damages, including any loss of profits, lost savings, or other incidental or consequential damages arising out from the Work or its contents. Because some states do not allow the exclusion or limitation of liability for consequential or incidental damages, the above limitation may not apply to you.

You should always use reasonable care, including backup and other appropriate precautions, when working with computers, networks, data, and files.

Syngress Media®, Syngress®, "Career Advancement Through Skill Enhancement®," "Ask the Author UPDATE®," and "Hack Proofing®," are registered trademarks of Syngress Publishing, Inc. "Syngress: The Definition of a Serious Security Library"™, "Mission Critical™," and "The Only Way to Stop a Hacker is to Think Like One™" are trademarks of Syngress Publishing, Inc. Brands and product names mentioned in this book are trademarks or service marks of their respective companies.

KEY	SERIAL NUMBER
001	HJIRTCV764
002	PO9873D5FG
003	829KM8NJH2
004	HJBN743999
005	CVPLQ6WQ23
006	VBP965T5T5
007	HJJJ863WD3E
008	2987GVTWMK
009	629MP5SDJT
010	IMWQ295T6T

PUBLISHED BY
Syngress Publishing, Inc.
800 Hingham Street
Rockland, MA 02370

Network Security Evaluation Using the NSA IEM

Copyright © 2005 by Syngress Publishing, Inc. All rights reserved. Printed in the United States of America. Except as permitted under the Copyright Act of 1976, no part of this publication may be reproduced or distributed in any form or by any means, or stored in a database or retrieval system, without the prior written permission of the publisher, with the exception that the program listings may be entered, stored, and executed in a computer system, but they may not be reproduced for publication.

Printed in the United States of America
1 2 3 4 5 6 7 8 9 0
ISBN: 1-597490-35-0

Publisher: Andrew Williams
Acquisitions Editor: Jaime Quigley
Technical Editor: Russ Rogers
Cover Designer: Michael Kavish

Page Layout and Art: Patricia Lupien
Copy Editor: Darlene Bordwell
Indexer: Julie Kawabata

Distributed by O'Reilly Media, Inc. in the United States and Canada.
For information on bulk sales, rights, and translations, contact Matt Pedersen, Director of Sales and Rights, at Syngress Publishing; email matt@syngress.com or fax to 781-681-3585.

Acknowledgments

Syngress would like to acknowledge the following people for their kindness and support in making this book possible.

A special thank you to Michele Fincher for her support of our publishing program and being a good friend to the Syngress family.

Syngress books are now distributed in the United States and Canada by O'Reilly Media, Inc. The enthusiasm and work ethic at O'Reilly are incredible, and we would like to thank everyone there for their time and efforts to bring Syngress books to market: Tim O'Reilly, Laura Baldwin, Mark Brokering, Mike Leonard, Donna Selenko, Bonnie Sheehan, Cindy Davis, Grant Kikkert, Opol Matsutaro, Steve Hazelwood, Mark Wilson, Rick Brown, Tim Hinton, Kyle Hart, Sara Winge, C. J. Rayhill, Peter Pardo, Leslie Crandell, Regina Aggio, Pascal Honscher, Preston Paull, Susan Thompson, Bruce Stewart, Laura Schmier, Sue Willing, Mark Jacobsen, Betsy Waliszewski, Kathryn Barrett, John Chodacki, Rob Bullington, Aileen Berg, and Wendy Patterson.

The incredibly hardworking team at Elsevier Science, including Jonathan Bunkell, Ian Seager, Duncan Enright, David Burton, Rosanna Ramacciotti, Robert Fairbrother, Miguel Sanchez, Klaus Beran, Emma Wyatt, Chris Hossack, Krista Leppiko, Marcel Koppes, Judy Chappell, Radek Janousek, and Chris Reinders for making certain that our vision remains worldwide in scope.

David Buckland, Marie Chieng, Lucy Chong, Leslie Lim, Audrey Gan, Pang Ai Hua, Joseph Chan, and Siti Zuraidah Ahmad of STP Distributors for the enthusiasm with which they receive our books.

David Scott, Tricia Wilden, Marilla Burgess, Annette Scott, Andrew Swaffer, Stephen O'Donoghue, Bec Lowe, Mark Langley, and Anyo Geddes of Woodslane for distributing our books throughout Australia, New Zealand, Papua New Guinea, Fiji, Tonga, Solomon Islands, and the Cook Islands.

Security Horizon would like to personally thank Wilbur, Diann, Paul, and Harley at the National Security Agency for their continued support and guidance.

Lead Author and Technical Editor

Russ Rogers (CISSP, CISM, IAM, IEM, HonScD), author of the popular *Hacking a Terror Network* (Syngress Publishing, ISBN 1-928994-98-9), co-author on multiple other books including the best selling *Stealing the Network: How to Own a Continent*(Syngress Publishing, ISBN 1-931836-05-1), and Editor in Chief of *The Security Journal;* is Co-Founder, Chief Executive Officer, and Chief Technology Officer of Security Horizon; a veteran-owned small business based in Colorado Springs, Colorado. Russ has been involved in information technology since 1980 and has spent the last 15 years working professionally as both an IT and INFOSEC consultant. Russ has worked with the United States Air Force (USAF), National Security Agency (NSA), and the Defense Information Systems Agency (DISA). Mr. Rogers is a globally renowned security expert, speaker, and author who has presented at conferences around the world including Amsterdam, Tokyo, Singapore, Sao Paulo, and cities all around the United States.

Mr. Rogers has an Honorary Doctorate of Science in Information Technology from the University of Advancing Technology, a Masters Degree in Computer Systems Management from the University of Maryland, a Bachelor of Science in Computer Information Systems from the University of Maryland, and an Associate Degree in Applied Communications Technology from the Community College of the Air Force. He is a member of both ISSA and ISACA and Co-Founded the Global Security Syndicate (gssyndicate.org), the Security Tribe (securitytribe.com), and acts in the role of Professor of Network Security for the University of Advancing Technology (uat.edu).

Russ would like to thank his father for his lifetime of guidance, his kids (Kynda and Brenden) for their understanding, and Michele for her constant support. A great deal of thanks goes to Andrew Williams and Jaime Quigley from Syngress Publishing for the abundant opportunities and trust they give me. Shouts go out to UAT, Security Tribe, the GSS, the Defcon Groups, and the DC Forums. I'd like to also thank my friends, Chris, Greg, Michele, Ping, Pyr0, and everyone in #dc-forums that I don't have room to list here.

Contributing Authors

Greg Miles, (Ph.D., CISSP#24431, CISM#0300338, IAM, IEM) co-author of *Security Assessment: Case Studies for implementing the NSA IAM* (Syngress Publishing, ISBN 1-932266-96-8) is a Co-Founder, President, and Chief Financial Officer of Security Horizon, Inc. Security Horizon is a global veteran-owned small business headquartered in Colorado Springs, Colorado. Security Horizon provides global information security professional service, training, and publishes *The Security Journal.* Greg is an U.S. Air Force Veteran and has been supporting the technology and security community for the last 18 years. Greg's background includes work with NSA, NASA, and DISA. Greg has supported efforts covering security assessments, evaluations, policy, penetration testing, incident response, and computer forensics.

Greg holds a Ph.D. in Engineering Management from Kennedy Western University, a master's degree in Management Administration from Central Michigan University, and a bachelor's degree in Electrical Engineering from the University of Cincinnati. Greg is a member of the Information System Security Association (ISSA) and the Information System Audit and Control Association (ISACA). He is also a co-founder of the Global Security Syndicate and teaches network security for the University of Advancing Technology.

Greg would like to thank his family and friends for the incredible support provided to him. Without the support of his loving children, Kirstin and Justin, nothing is possible. He would like to thank the friends that have supported him through challenging times: Mom, Bob, Russ, Michele, and Tim. Greg would like to dedicate his contribution to this book to Dad.

Special report from Bryan Cunningham of **Morgan & Cunningham LLC**: Why the White House Cares about Your Information Security

Bryan Cunningham (JD, Certified in NSA IAM, Top Secret security clearance) has extensive experience in information security, intelligence, and homeland security matters, both in senior U.S. Government posts and the private sector. Cunningham, now a corporate information and homeland security consultant and Principal at the Denver law firm of Morgan & Cunningham LLC, most recently served as Deputy Legal Adviser to National Security Advisor Condoleezza Rice. At the White House, Cunningham drafted key portions of the Homeland Security Act, and was deeply involved in the formation of the National Strategy to Secure Cyberspace, as well as numerous Presidential Directives and regulations relating to cybersecurity. He is a former senior CIA Officer, federal prosecutor, and founding co-chair of the ABA CyberSecurity Privacy Task Force, and, in January 2005, was awarded the National Intelligence Medal of Achievement for his work on information issues. Cunningham has been named to the National Academy of Science Committee on Biodefense Analysis and Countermeasures, and is a Senior Counselor at APCO Worldwide Consulting, as well as a member of the Markle Foundation Task Force on National Security in the Information Age. Cunningham counsels corporations on information security programs and other homeland security-related issues and, working with information security consultants, guides and supervises information security assessments and evaluations.

 **Travis Schack** (CISSP) is the founder and CEO of Vitalisec Inc., a Denver-based information security research and services company. Prior to founding Vitalisec, Travis worked in the network communications and financial industries, where he has performed numerous security application reviews as well as network attack and penetration tests against Unix, Linux, Windows, network, and communication systems. He has extensive knowledge in attack methodologies, intrusion detection, wireless networking, VoIP, security tools, physical security, fraud detection and investigation, incident response, and computer security standards. He maintains his own test laboratory for researching the latest system vulnerabilities, attack methods/trends, and how to defend against them.

Travis has been published in multiple publications and has been a featured speaker at numerous security events around the world. He is an adjunct instructor for Denver University, teaching a technical hands-on Security Testing course for DU's Master program in Information Security. In his spare time, he organizes DC303, contributes to the Open Source Vulnerability Database (OSVDB) and Voice over IP Security Alliance (VOIPSA), and is a co-founder of the Global Security Syndicate (GSS).

Travis currently resides in Arvada, Colorado with his wife Kendra and 5 children, Kelsea, Austin, Gavin, Olivia, and Vivienne.

Chuck Little (CCSA, NSA IAM, NSA IEM) is a Senior Security Consultant for Security Horizon Inc. Security Horizon is a small veteran-owned business focused on INFOSEC, headquartered in Colorado Springs, Colorado. His specialties include Checkpoint FW-1, NetScreen Firewall/IDS/IPS, Perl coding, Linux, Solaris, Mac OS X, compliance auditing, network security architecture and design, and snowboarding.

Chuck is a veteran of the US Army, having spent over seven years on active duty. Chuck holds a bachelor's degree in Applied Computer Science from Illinois State University, with a minor in Philosophy. He is an occasional contributor to the MIND Project, a research venture into cognitive sciences, at Illinois State University. Chuck currently resides in Denver, Colorado; with winter weekends spent at Loveland Ski Area.

Chuck would like to thank Karmen for her constant support and confidence, his parents for their guidance and wisdom, his friends Patrick, Russ, Matt, Ben, Sean, and "…everyone else I don't have room to list here." Thank you for everything. Shouts go out to DFT (Dead Fish Technologies), the Security Tribe, BeFunk, RangerRick, Mantis, the DC303 group, and #fink on Freenode.

Matthew Paul Hoagberg is an information technology and security professional with diverse experience in IT, personnel management, technology training, and business development support with Security Horizon, Inc., a Colorado-based professional security services and training provider. Matthew contributes to the security training, assessments, and evaluation that Security Horizon offers.

He currently serves as a Security Consultant, along with guidance from the Department of the Interior (DOI) and National Institute of Standards and Technology (NIST), to enhance the Bureau of Reclamation's (BOR) IT security management processes with a goal of improving the BOR's compliance with the Federal Information Security Management Act (FISMA) requirements.

Matthew holds a bachelor's degree from Northwestern College and is a member of the Information Systems Security Association (ISSA), and co-author of *Security Assessment: Case Studies for Implementing the NSA IAM* (Syngress Publishing, ISBN 1-932266-96-8). Matthew currently resides in Monument, Colorado with his family.

Ed Fuller (CISSP, GIAC GSEC) is the Chief Operating Officer and Principle Security Consultant with Security Horizon, Inc., a Colorado-based professional security services and training provider. He currently is the lead instructor for the NSA IAM and IEM courses and leads assessments and evaluations as well leading the IA-CMM appraisals. His specialties include implementation of the NSA IAM and IEM into commercial environments and the IA-CMM. Ed's background includes positions as a senior consultant for Titan Systems, and JAWZ, Inc, and Averstar, Inc.

Ed is a retired United States Navy Chief Petty Officer and later participated on the development of System Security Engineering Capability Maturity Model (SSE-CMM). Ed has also been involved in the development of the Information Assurance Capability Maturity Model (IA-CMM). Ed is a frequent contributor to *The Security Journal* and co-author of *Security Assessment: Case Studies for Implementing the NSA IAM*. Ed holds a Bachelor of Science in Information Management from the University of Maryland. He lives in Colorado with his family Patience and Leila, who patiently put up with his distractions during the writing of this book.

Ted Dykstra (CISSP, CISA, CCNP, MCSE, IAM/IEM) is a Security Consultant for Security Horizon, Inc., a Colorado-based professional security services and training provider. Ted is a key contributor in the technical security efforts and service offerings for Security Horizon, and an instructor for the National Security Agency (NSA) Information Assurance Methodology (IAM). Ted's background is in both commercial and government support efforts, focusing on secure architecture development and deployment, INFOSEC assessments and audits, as well as attack and penetration testing. His areas of specialty are Cisco networking products, Check Point and Symantec Enterprise Security Products, Sun Solaris, Microsoft, and Linux systems. Ted is a regular contributor to *The Security Journal*, as well as a member of the Information System Security Association (ISSA) and Information Systems Audit and Control Association (ISACA).

Additional Contributors

C. Forrest Morgan (JD (1987), Trained in NSA IAM) has extensive experience in corporate practice and structure including contracting, corporate formation, and operations. Mr. Morgan advises information security consultants on drafting and negotiating contracts with their customers to best protect them against potential legal liability. Mr. Morgan's practice also has emphasized commercial contract drafting and reorganization, and corporate litigation, providing in-depth understanding of the business and legal environment. He has represented both national corporations and regional firms in state and federal courts and administrative agencies in matters of litigation, creditors' rights, bankruptcy, administrative law and employment issues. Mr. Morgan served as the Regional Editor of the Colorado Bankruptcy Court Reporter from 1989 to 1992, and he co-authored the Bankruptcy section of the Annual Survey of Colorado from 1991 to 1997. As a Principal of the Denver law firm of Morgan & Cunningham, LLC, Mr. Morgan's practice also includes corporate information and security consulting. He counsels corporations on information security programs, including development of corporate policies and procedures to minimize business risks and litigation exposure

Amanda Hubbard [JD] is a Trial Attorney assigned to the Computer Crime and Intellectual Property Section of the U.S. Department of Justice working on national security and computer intrusion issues. Prior to this assignment, Ms. Hubbard worked as an attorney for the Intelligence Community and the military on issues of computer forensics, electronic evidence, encryption, network security, vulnerability assessments, criminal law, and information sharing. She also serves as an Adjunct Professor for the Columbus School of Law at Catholic University where she co-teaches the seminar "National Security Law in Cyberspace," and a guest lecturer at: the Naval Postgraduate School Information Warfare Workshops; the Air Force Judge Advocate General School Information Warfare Course; the U.S. Secret Service; Federal Bureau of Investigation, and the United States Department of Justice National Advocacy Center. Ms. Hubbard regularly speaks to international audiences on cybersecurity and cybercrime. Prior works include portions of the 2002 ABA Committee on Cyberspace publication, *Patriot 'Games' No Longer: The Business Community's Role in Cybersecurity*, and submissions to the International Telecommunications Union and the United Nations. She has been named as a 2005-06 Fulbright Scholar to the Norwegian Research Center for Computers and Law at the University of Oslo to research and write on transnational cybercrime issues.

Contents

Why the IEM?

By Russ Rogers

Taking a Look Back

Welcome to the National Security Agency's INFOSEC Evaluation Methodology, also lovingly known as the IEM. In April 2000, I was working as a contractor for the Defense Information Systems Agency (DISA) when the client asked me to sit in on a National Security Agency (NSA) developed course called the INFOSEC Assessment Methodology (IAM). At the time, my background was primarily in the technical areas surrounding information security. My job entailed technical research and development, along with a smattering of penetration testing. Although I wasn't aware of it at the time, that two-day course was going to change the way I thought about information security for the rest of my career.

Individuals who work the technical side of information security aren't normally tuned in to the other areas that are considered more mundane. During penetration testing I never really cared what a company's mission was or what information was critical to that mission. I wasn't sitting back in my computer chair staring blankly at the screen wondering what the actual impact would be to your organization if my network intrusions had been real. The IAM was created to address that part of the equation.

The idea of involving the customer in the security process at such an intimate level was new to me. But as I began using the methodology in real-life situations, I began to see its true value. My experience is as a security professional; the customer could be an expert at researching, developing, and manufacturing widgets. If I'm being truly honest with myself, I don't know squat about widgets. I know about information security.

A great many pieces of the IAM provide a tremendous amount of value to the information security life cycle. How many of your customers can sit down and tell you specifically the mission of the organization? Let's assume they've managed to get that far. Can they relate to you, specifically, the types of information that are most critical to their organization or where those pieces of information are stored, processed, or transmitted? What is the impact to their organization if they lose the confidentiality, integrity, availability, accountability, or nonrepudiation of those pieces of information?

During the IAM course, there was a short discussion on the NSA's view of the information security or information assurance life cycle (see Figure P.1). It was a three-phase approach consisting of an organizational assessment (IAM), a technical evaluation of the network and hosts (IEM), and a penetration test or Red Team Methodology (RTM).

Figure P.1 The NSA View of Information Security

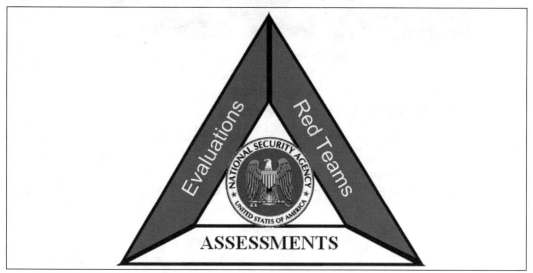

The IAM is often called a *white team* activity. The assessment is looking for vulnerabilities that exist within the organizational structure. This means that we're considering all relevant policies, procedures, regulations, and processes. Where are the policies in place at the organization not meeting federal requirements? What standards are the customer liable to comply with—HIPAA, FERPA, GLBA, Sarbanes-Oxley? Where are these policies not being enforced or utilized?

For more information on the IAM, see *Security Assessment: Case Studies for Implementing the NSA IAM*, also from Syngress Publishing.

Useful Information

Common Standards and Regulations

British Standard 7799 (BS7799), eventually evolved into ISO17799 (see below)

Child Online Protection Act (COPA), www.copacommission.org

Health Insurance Portability and Accountability Act (HIPAA), www.cms.hhs.gov/hipaa/hipaa1/content/more.asp

Family Educational Rights and Privacy Act (FERPA), www.ed.gov/policy/gen/guid/fpco/ferpa/index.html

Federal Information Security Mgmt Act (FISMA), csrc.nist.gov/sec-cert/

Gramm-Leach Bliley Act (GLBA), www.ftc.gov/privacy/glbact/

Homeland Security Presidential Directive 7 (HSPD-7), www.whitehouse.gov/news/releases/2003/12/20031217-5.html

ISO 17799, www.iso.org (International Organization for Standardization's INFOSEC recommendations)

National Strategy to Secure Cyberspace, www.whitehouse.gov/pcipb/

Sarbanes-Oxley (SOX), www.aicpa.org/sarbanes/index.asp

Most technical people are left wondering how any of this applies to what they do in respect to information security. *I just hack things.* But the truth is that the information derived during the assessment process is *very* important to the evaluation process and the final deliverables that we provide to the customer. The more I work in both of these areas, the assessment piece and the evaluation piece, the more relevance I find.

How many times have you watched helplessly as a so-called security expert ran one of those off-the-shelf vulnerability tools on a customer network, printed out the results, changed the logo on the report, and handed it to the customer as his or her own work? It isn't just infuriating, it's a ripoff. The customer needs to know not only what vulnerabilities exist in their environment but how those vulnerabilities affect them, their information, and their company's sensitive information.

That's where the IEM comes into the picture. The IEM lays out a baseline of activities to be conducted, ensuring a comprehensive evaluation of the customer's information technology. And although it's intended to be comprehensive, the value of the IEM doesn't end there. The final analysis compares the discovered technical vulnerabilities to the information the customer has given to us in the IAM—information such as the customer's defined mission, critical information types, impact definitions, and more. This information is used to customize the findings to the customer organization. That means that every customer receives a final deliverable that is actually valid for their environment and mission.

A Flexible Baseline

The IEM was a joint venture between the NSA, a few commercial security firms, and other interested parties. The processes you will read about in this book are the final product of years of hard work, research, and discussion. No individual party or entity is responsible for the entire methodology. It is a collective work intended to provide a baseline of repeatable and consistent processes for security evaluation.

As with any other project that contains the work of so many diverse individuals, you'll encounter some aspects of the methodology that apply to your organization or processes and others that don't. We hope that you read this book with no preconceived goals to tear it apart. Instead, as you read, look for those potential tidbits of information or new processes that might help improve and evolve your own assessment and evaluation processes.

The IEM and all its component pieces are intended to provide a foundation—a place to start from each and every time. Does that mean that you can't modify the processes to better fit your operating environment? No. In fact, we highly recommend that you consider how the IEM will fit into your business model and tweak it according to your own needs. Our goal is not to make everyone adhere to a strict methodology; rather, we'd like to know that when a customer calls you up and asks for a *security assessment, evaluation, penetration test,* or *red team activity,* they're going to get a similar answer from everyone involved.

As with most other industries, the manner in which you eventually implement this methodology will differentiate you from your competitors. When I speak about these methodologies in public forums, I prefer to use the analogy of building a body as we perform the assessments and evaluations. The NSA methodologies provide a "skeleton" on which to build the "body" of your security offerings. Several other things come into play along the way, including the regulations the customer is required to adhere to, any internal or corporate policies they have, their definitions of what is important to them, your own processes in actually performing the work, and your expertise in the field of information security. In the end, all these pieces come together to create a custom and valuable security solution for your customer.

Terms and Topics

Before we dive head first into the remainder of the book, let's cover a couple of information security concepts that we believe it's important you understand before moving forward. These concepts play a vital role in information security. So here's where we tip our hats to these titans of information security.

Defense in Depth

The concept of defense in depth (DiD) is utilized by the NSA as well as NIST. In short, the primary goal of DiD is to achieve information assurance through a balanced approach focusing on three primary areas: people, technology, and operations. These three focus areas are covered throughout the IAM and IEM processes and are documented within both NSA and NIST guidelines.

The *people* portion of this concept deals with senior level buy-in and understanding of the information assurance life cycle. This includes its value to the organization. NIST documentation refers to this area as *management*. This is not incorrect, and we often see the terms *people* and *management* used interchangeably. This buy-in is most often seen in the form of up-to-date security policies that are relevant to the organization, consistent security awareness training programs for employees, and defined procedures for physical and personnel security within the organization. These activities and many more are indicative of an organization whose management realizes and prioritizes information security.

Technology in relation to DiD needs to ensure that the information assurance architecture is in place and functioning. When we speak about technology related to information security, it's important to note that the technology must be useful and meaningful to the organization. Buying the Product A Intrusion Prevention solution might seem like a great idea after the amazing sales demonstration you sat through, but does the product actually address the organization's security goals? Implementing the wrong security products can be as detrimental as having no security products in place. A false sense of security often pervades organizations in which security products have been installed, but the truth of the matter is that those products are normally purchased without in-depth thought about how well they really meet organizational information assurance goals.

Security products should be considered in light of the manner in which they achieve security policy or regulation standards. For instance, what are the requirements for secure communication of critical information types across the network? Will a Public Key Infrastructure (PKI) implementation achieve the goal of securing those communications?

Finally, when we think about *operations* in the DiD context, we're talking about those active processes that are occurring and recurring to help ensure the security of the organization's information assets. Incident response and system certification activities are good examples of what should be taking place in these areas. Are there active tests to see how well the organization responds to potential incursions? Are all new networks or systems attached to the corporate network analyzed in detail so that there is a complete understanding about the potential security vulnerabilities being brought online with the new system?

Layered Security

The idea of layered security is certainly not a new one, nor does it break new ground. Regardless of its actual age, the idea of layered security adds value to any assessment and evaluation process by ensuring that multiple facets of a customer's information security profile are addressed.

There have been hundreds of interpretations of layered security, but everyone agrees on some core areas that need to be addressed:

- Network perimeter protection
- Internal network protection
- Intrusion monitoring and prevention
- Host and server configuration
- Malicious code protection
- Incident response capabilities
- Security policies and procedures
- Employee awareness and training
- Physical security and monitoring

These areas are key points of failure within the information security architecture at many organizations. Building information security mechanisms into each of these areas will help improve the security posture of the organization. If a flaw can be found at one of these points, hopefully the mechanisms at other levels will pick up the slack.

It's also worth mentioning that there is no such thing as 100-percent secure. No organization can be totally secure, without fear of compromise. Every security assessment or evaluation is no more than a snapshot in time. As soon as you walk away, the situation has already changed. New vulnerabilities have been released or a new server has been loaded and plugged into the network, just since you packed up your laptop. But by addressing the process-level security issues along with the technical findings, we can improve our chances to mitigate problems before they occur.

Chapter 1

Introducing the INFOSEC Evaluation Methodology

Solutions in this chapter:

- **What Is the IEM?**
- **What the IEM Is Not**
- **Standards and Regulations**

☑ **Summary**

☑ **Solutions Fast Track**

☑ **Frequently Asked Questions**

Introduction

Security providers around the world have been trying for years to engineer an effective means for conducting technical evaluations that is meaningful to the customer. For too long, we've seen fly-by-night consulting companies walk into a customer organization, run a security vulnerability scanner, print out the default application report (after replacing the logo), and present that to the customer as the final deliverable. Although the initial paper factor of this type of work might be impressive to the uneducated customer, once they start digging into the actual contents of the report and trying to understand how it applies to their organization, they normally discover that this level of service is lacking.

Until recently, the use of a repeatable, structured, and flexible methodology to provide these services was on a per-company basis. Customers could never really be sure what to expect when they asked for a security evaluation. Would it be a penetration test? A full Red Team? Would it even be comprehensive, or did the consultants see the work as a game? It all really came down to *who* was doing the work. The majority of final reports the customer dealt with lacked even enough basic similarity to allow the customer to compare results from year to year.

The INFOSEC Evaluation Methodology (IEM) presents a viable solution to this problem. It's offered by the National Security Agency (NSA) as a baseline set of criteria for conducting technical evaluations for any organization. The deliverables of this methodology are intended to have meaning for all customers. And although the format and core components of the final deliverables remain the same across evaluations, no two final reports will be the same. A number of variables at each customer organization directly impact the manner in which the evaluation, and the assessment, must be conducted. For instance, assuming we have two similar banking customers that require technical evaluations of their network infrastructure, they will still have differences. These include the network architecture and layout; the organization's management and vision; software and applications that are utilized; and the policies and procedures put into place by the organization's management. When each of these banks receives its final report, it should look familiar, be interpretable, and apply specifically to the organization. That means that even through the reports look similar, the results of one cannot be applied to the other.

Admitting we have a problem is the first step in the healing process, and there's no doubt that the majority of experienced INFOSEC professionals in the industry have found themselves looking for a solution. The NSA IEM is one of the solutions that is finding widespread acceptance in the community. In this chapter, we'll present the reader with the basic layout of the IEM. By the time you finish this chapter, you will understand what the IEM is intended to address, why this type of work is requested, where it could potentially be applied, and the phases into which the IEM is organized. We also include a discussion on how the NSA INFOSEC Assessment Methodology (IAM) and IEM relate to one another, helping to achieve a comprehensive and meaningful security assessment/evaluation solution for our customers.

What Is the IEM?

The IEM is a follow-on methodology to the NSA IAM. It provides the technical evaluation processes that were intentionally missing from the IAM. The IEM is a hands-on methodology, meaning you'll be actively interacting with the customer's technical environment. As such, the NSA intended for the IAM and IEM processes to work hand in hand. The IEM can be placed directly atop the IAM, much like two Lego blocks.

But in contrast to the origins of the IAM, which was originally developed for use within the federal and military arenas, the IEM was developed over a period of three years and included input from government and commercial entities. With the resounding success of the IAM in the commercial world, it was decided that the IEM should be applicable to a wide range of organizations and industries. Input and feedback were solicited from commercial firms, contracting companies, and a variety of government agencies. The IEM is the final result of all the hard work put in by all these organizations and individuals.

Whereas the IAM provides us with an understanding of organizational security as it relates to policies and procedures, the IEM offers a comprehensive look into the actual technical security at the organization. Together, these two processes allow us to more accurately determine the information security posture of our customers. The ratings of our findings are based on the customer's view of their information's criticality, industry-accepted ratings for each of the findings, and the expertise of the evaluation team.

Consider for a minute what we learned from the IAM. The core of the IAM was customer input. Our customer defined their organizational mission and told us what information types were critical for achieving their mission goals. With your guidance, they also went so far as to create impact definitions that help gauge the actual impact on their organization should they lose the confidentiality, integrity, or availability of those pieces of information. These customer-defined components are taken into account as we step through the 18 areas of the IAM and perform our analysis.

This concept is key because, as a security professional, you must admit that you understand security, not widgets. If the customer has been creating widgets for 45 years, they likely have a greater understanding concerning what is required to make quality widgets and retain a competitive advantage in the widget marketplace. *Your* role is to provide guidance and recommendations on information security. If we utilize both the customer expertise and your expertise, the final deliverables from any security assessment or evaluation will have greater value and impact.

Tying the Methodologies Together

As we begin engaging the customer and working to determine their objectives, we're simultaneously setting the scope of the security work. The IEM is no different. The process begins with the basic coordination processes, which can be conducted concurrently with the IAM pre-assessment phase. In the IEM we call this the *IEM pre-evaluation*. You'll notice as you look at the names of the phases in the IEM that they match almost exactly the names we use in the IAM. This is intentional and aids in coordinating the performance of both the IAM and IEM concurrently.

In Figure 1.1, you see a depiction of the IAM phases. Notice that we have three phases, beginning with the pre-assessment and ending with the post-assessment. As you'll find out in later chapters, the activities in the IAM pre-assessment are required before moving to the follow-on IAM activities or beginning the IEM.

Figure 1.1 The Phases of the IAM

Pre-Assessment Phase	On-Site Phase	Post Assessment Phase
* Identify Information Criticality * Identify System Configuration * Set Scope of the Assessment * Documentation Request * Documentation Review * Team Assignment * Pre-Analysis * Site Visit Coordination	* On-Site In-Brief * Interview Site Personnel * System Demonstrations * Documentation Review * On-Site Out Brief	* Additional Documentation Review * Finalize Analysis * Consult Additional Expertise * Generate Recommendations * Final Report Coordination

The IEM also contains three phases. Figure 1.2 provides a general overview of the activities in the three IEM phases. Notice how similar these are to the IAM. Although the IEM is much more technically focused, we'll use a lot of the same type of information that we used in the IAM. The distinction between the two is the organizational nature of the IAM versus the technical nature of the IEM. The devil is in the details, and we'll be moving from the higher-level activities we focused on in the IAM to a much more granular approach in the IEM.

If you compare Figures 1.1 and 1.2, you'll see that the on-site phase in each one is where the rubber meets the road. In the IAM, this is where we delve into the policies, procedures, and regulations to determine the customer's security posture from an organization viewpoint. In the IEM, however, it's where we actually check the technical proficiency of the target networks, servers, hosts, and high-assurance components, such as routers, firewalls, or switches.

Figure 1.2 The Phases of the IEM

Pre-Evaluation Phase	On-Site Evaluation Phase	Post Evaluation Phase
* Identify Systems and Boundaries * Determine System Architecture * Legal Coordination * Create Rules of Engagement * Determine Evaluation Scope * Develop Evaluation Plan * On-Site Visit Coordination	* On-Site In-Brief * Evaluation Testing - 10 Baseline Activities * On-Site Out Brief	* Conduct Final Analysis * Consult Additional Expertise * Generate Final Report * Create Security Road Map * Deliver Final Report * Follow Up with Customer

NOTE

The IEM is not just a network evaluation methodology. Although we do run scanning tools and look for network accessible services or applications, the IEM delves much deeper into the customer's technical presence. This includes testing the configuration on all servers, hosts, routers, firewalls, and other high-assurance components. We'll also be testing password strength and analyzing the architecture of the customer network from a security perspective. Don't make the assumption that this is just another book about running a vulnerability scanner. The IEM is a comprehensive evaluation methodology, and therefore, we must address the entirety of the customer's technical exposure.

Figure 1.3 shows these two methodologies together as a cohesive unit, allowing you to better visualize how the processes of each methodology can work together. The image tries to convey the fact that many of the activities we're already performing for the IAM require very little modification or addition to be useful to the IEM. For example, the final analysis and report-generation activities can all be performed at the same time without too many problems. We're already working on detailing the findings for the customer and laying out appropriate recommendations to improve their organizational security. It doesn't require a huge stretch of one's imagination to see that we can easily integrate the technical findings and recommendations into this phase as well.

Looking at Figure 1.3, you get an idea of how the entire security assessment and evaluation process is intended to operate. In the pre-analysis phase, we're performing all our up-front work. This entails finding out what the customer is expecting, laying out our acceptable rules of engagement, protecting the customer and ourselves by utilizing the appropriate legal documentation, and working with the customer to define the critical information within the organization.

Warning

Never underestimate the importance of the pre-analysis phase. This area is often neglected and can result in unsatisfied customers, poor results, findings that lack true value, or even legal liability on the part of you or your organization. As mentioned before, the customer understands widgets, but not necessarily the evaluation process. In many cases, the customer has had a different understanding of the evaluation process than the evaluation team intended. If this is the case, your deliverables may not meet customer expectations. Bear in mind that word of mouth spreads quickly when the news is negative.

The other negative side effect most often associated with poor performance of the pre-analysis phase is a lack of total understanding on the part of the evaluation team. The customer has requested *A* and your team provides *B*. By the time you realize the disconnect, you're already behind schedule and over your intended budget for the work. Now your team has to go back and fix the work to meet the actual customer expectations.

In the analysis phase, we've combined all the activities from the IAM and IEM. Because the methodologies differ so dramatically in this area, it can be difficult to visualize how a single team could accomplish all the critical points. But you do have options.

Using two teams that work simultaneously is not unheard of and often works quite well. I've seen many large consulting or contracting companies operate in this fashion, especially internally. For instance, a single team might have the primary responsibility to perform IAM-like functions on the organization. They might gauge organizational compliance with federal regulations, industry security guidelines, or regulations and policies based on the organization's mission. Another independent team might be responsible solely for the technical security within the organization. They're the ones that come in twice a year and run all the nifty tools on the network to ensure that the organization understands its actual security exposure.

Figure 1.3 Combined Assessment and Evaluation Activities

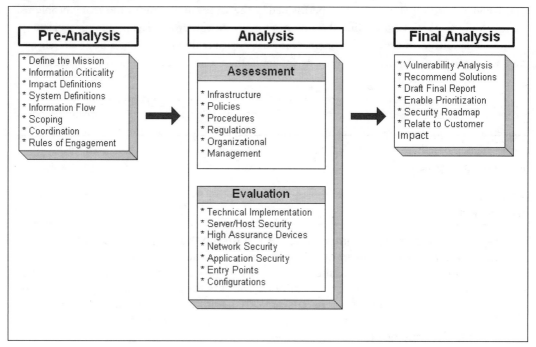

Another option that works quite well is one that we've used in the past: Members of a single team with both organizational and technical experience work together on both methodologies at the same time. So let's say we have a team of four individuals that goes into a large hospital to conduct the IAM and IEM. Many of the onsite activities for the IEM can be completed while the interviews or documentation review is being done for the IAM. Not all evaluation tools require active participation by the security professional. With that said, we try not to leave while the tools are running in case they cause some accidental downtime. Still, this process works very well. We prefer to have a larger office with multiple network connections, allowing us to maintain our technical work while we're conducting interviews of documentation review for the IAM.

One thing that every team lead should understand is that the qualifications and skills required for the IEM are vastly different, in most instances, from those required in the IAM. For instance, whereas the IAM is focused around the organizational layer of information security, the IEM is decidedly more technical in nature. For this reason, the individuals on an evaluation team will need to understand the details of how the network, operating systems, and applications operate. The members of an IAM team will need to understand information criticality; regulations, policies and procedures; and how to communicate with a cross-section of employees at most organizations, from management to the cleaning crew. These skill sets are not, however, mutually exclusive, and at times you'll be lucky enough to have an individual on your team who can operate fluently within both arenas.

In the final analysis phase, we combine our efforts to create a cohesive final product for the customer. This is where we ensure that all our findings are correct for the customer and that our recommendations are useful to the customer environment. We're not just dumping the report from a commercial product and changing the logo. In fact, the IEM is so intent on providing value and presenting our findings to the customer in an understandable way that we create a security road map, which you'll read more about in Chapters 13 and 14. If the customer doesn't understand or can't use the information we give them, their money and time went to waste. NSA addresses this issue in this final stage of the methodologies.

NOTE

Although we stress the importance of utilizing both the IAM and the IEM, they do not have to be conducted concurrently. At times it simply is not feasible for the customer organization to undertake both activities at the same time. These occasions could include financial, time, or resource restrictions. However, it's important to note that in instances where the IAM has been conducted six months or more prior to the evaluation activities, it might be beneficial to revisit the original IAM pre-assessment process to verify that the customer information is still relevant. As with all things in life, information ages as time progresses. But in contrast with some things in life, information does not always improve with age. Corporate vision and priorities often change as the organization's leadership and infrastructure change. The IEM depends on an accurate representation of these items to provide the customer with a final product of the highest relevance and quality.

What the IEM Is Not

The IEM is just one part of the overall picture of information security presented by the NSA. Three levels of security analysis must occur, according to the NSA (see Figure 1.4). The level 1 process is the INFOSEC assessment, on which the IAM is based. This is a cooperative methodology with heavy customer involvement. It's the start of the information security triad and measures organizational security at a policy and procedural level. The IAM is a hands-off process. This means that we're not actually going to sit at a customer computer or run security tools against their technology.

The level 2 process consists of the INFOSEC evaluations, on which the IEM is based. For this level, we actively test the technical security of the organization. This is a hands-on process. We use state-of-the-art software and methods to detail misconfiguration weaknesses, system exposures, and potential vulnerabilities.

Although the customer is still involved in the IEM, it's not as profound as we saw in the IAM. We want to gain a comprehensive look at all the potential problem areas we can in the amount of time we have available. The objective is not to "break in" or "get root." This is not a penetration test, nor is it adversarial. Activities are performed internally and externally, where appropriate.

Level 3 is where the process becomes adversarial. There is currently no NSA sponsored methodology for conducting Red Team activities, so there is no officially endorsed training course or process. But the NSA defines these Red Team activities as the Red Team Methodology, or RTM. Simulating the appropriate adversary, the Red Team tests every possible security scenario until it manages to break into the customer network. Red Team activities are *not* comprehensive. We're trying to find a way to the customer's information, through any path possible. In most real-world cases, this means that we sit outside the customer network and organization, trying to find a way in that hasn't been locked down.

To best understand the difference between the IEM and a Red Team, let's look at what happens in a Red Teaming situation. Most teams of this nature start out *in the dark*, meaning they are given very little information from which to start the testing. This information could be limited to as little as a domain name on the Internet. The testing team is then left to its own devices to discover information that would further its attempts to break into the customer network. This is often referred to as a *black box assessment*.

As the team members start out, they look specifically for the easiest potential targets on the customer network—those that could provide the easiest path into the network. As they progress, only vulnerabilities along that path are analyzed, leaving potential vulnerabilities on other paths untested, unaltered, and intact. At the end of the process, the customer receives a report detailing how the intrusion occurred and what vulnerabilities were taken advantage of, but all other potential vulnerabilities remain hidden away on the network.

The IEM is *not* a Red Team activity. The IEM is comprehensive in that we want to find every possible security finding we can so that the customer can lock it down. The Red Team simply tries to get to the information using any means possible. The IEM is cooperative with the customer; the Red Team is adversarial based on the industry in question. If we're looking at a military customer, maybe we're simulating a terror organization. If the customer is a research and development firm, maybe we're simulating a competitor and trying to get at the organization's "crown jewels." The IEM aims to find the vulnerabilities without exploiting or compromising the customer network. The primary goal of a Red Team *is* to compromise the network, especially by exploitation.

Figure 1.4 The NSA INFOSEC Triad

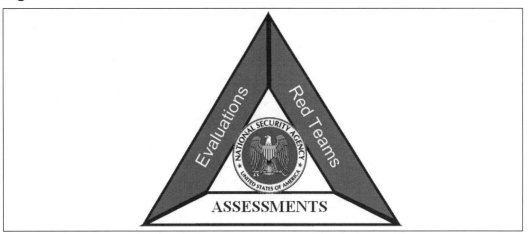

NOTE

All three phases of the NSA information security triad have their value, but we need to remain cognizant of the timing of each one. For example, if we conduct the IEM prior to performing the IAM, our findings cannot be related back to the customer organization. What value do the findings hold if we can't relate them back to the impact they have on the organization? In this same manner, it's considered unwise to conduct an *attack and penetration test,* or *pen test,* before the customer has had the luxury of a full evaluation. Breaking into a customer when they haven't had the opportunity to see the full representation of their security posture or the chance to lock down their information is a waste of time and money.

For the purposes of this book, we'll work from the premise that the information security life cycle will be conducted with the IAM occurring just before or concurrently with the IEM, followed sometime after by a Red Team activity. Conduct the IAM and IEM, give the customer a chance to put up their defenses, and then test those defenses through Red Team activities.

The IEM Is *Not* an Audit or Inspection

As with most things in life, people don't typically react favorably to being put under a microscope and analyzed. No one likes feeling as though someone is peering over his shoulder, trying to find mistakes he's made. These are connotations often associated with internal audits or inspections. When you discuss the evaluation methodology with the customer, ensure that you avoid these terms. We need their help if we want them to have a real understanding of their security posture. For example, say that an evaluation team comes in, conducts interviews, reviews documentation, tests processes, and associates shortfalls with particular areas or individuals. People in situations like this tend to withhold information, be less than helpful, and shy away from dangerous situations.

When we consider evaluations in the context of the NSA IEM, we want to ensure that every person we interact with understands the nonattribution characteristics of the NSA methodologies. We associate no blame to particular individuals; we're only interested in the truth. In many instances, it's useful to let the end users or administrators know that we're trying to find all the holes in the system so they can be fixed before the organization is audited or inspected. This view makes our job easier, makes the employee more comfortable, and allows the findings to better reflect reality.

What does this do for the security professional who is going to work in these potentially hostile environments? It means that you, as the consultant, will need to act as both a security professional *and* a human psychologist. You need to understand how your actions may be interpreted by the various human minds that exist and work within the target organization. This requires a certain finesse and ability to communicate. The evaluation team lead is normally responsible for mediating customer perception, but each team member should have training in how to communicate with the customer.

You'll also want to know how to *sell* the process to each person you run into. I'm not talking about being one of those over-the-top sales folks who push the product down the customer's throat, but you want to understand the aspects of the work you'll be performing that appeal to the person you're speaking with. Explain how your work will benefit them and they're more likely to help make the process successful.

Every good security consultant understands that even though he or she is there to help secure the customer, they'll also need to manage the individuals within the organization. You're never *just* a security professional. Forgetting these key aspects of human interaction could result in a painful evaluation experience.

The IEM Is Not a Risk Assessment

Let's get this straight right now: The IAM and IEM are *not* risk assessment or risk management methodologies. It's true that many of the activities associated with the NSA methodologies are similar to the requirements for a risk assessment, but no one is pretending that they meet *all* the requirements. The IAM and IEM are vulnerability assessment methodologies. The intent is to identify as many vulnerabilities as possible, allowing the customer to fix or mitigate those findings to improve their security posture. Although we do address threat and risk from a cursory level within the IAM and IEM, the NSA methodologies don't go into the detail needed for actual risk assessments or risk management.

If we look at modern definitions of risk, we see that risk is a combination of the value of the asset (or impact of the loss), the associated threats, and the existing potential vulnerabilities. Taking these three things into account, we notice that the vulnerabilities are the only area in which the customers can effect dramatic change.

> I've seen countless articles written by individuals who don't truly understand the goals of the IAM and IEM. These have resulted in some confusion for readers and practitioners of the NSA methodologies. The primary goal of the NSA processes is to identify vulnerabilities. It make no attempt to become a risk assessment methodology. We are aware that using the IAM and IEM will get you *closer* to a risk assessment, but readers should not mistakenly associate the two as one and the same.

Standards and Regulations

Nations around the world are implementing a number of information security-related regulations with the intention of protecting consumers and organizations. The United States has led the way in this arena by creating a massive number of regulations based on varying industries, from the federal government and military to healthcare, education, and utilities.

At first glance, it's almost intimidating. How is an organization supposed to understand all these differing pieces of legislation? Even companies in other countries that do work within the United States are starting to pay attention. For instance, companies around the world with a U.S. presence are starting to work on becoming Sarbanes-Oxley compliant. Fortunately, the inherent flexibility that NSA built into the IAM and IEM allow security firms to address necessary security regulations.

Take a real-world example: We utilize parts of the NSA processes to address the certification and accreditation (C&A) requirements of the federal government. The IEM lends itself nicely to performing the requisite security testing and evaluation (ST&E). We've used the entire process on organizations from high-level universities to healthcare offices.

Most security regulations are fairly general, preferring to give vague allusions to what is intended versus laying out the law directly. The term most used for meeting these general requirements is *best practices*. Best practices are simply what are commonly thought to be the best course of action regarding security. But an organization that makes widgets probably hasn't got a clue as to where to begin. This is where *your* expertise and experience come into play.

Lack of Expertise

The NSA methodologies have the ability to be used in nearly every industry in existence. The key component that the IAM and IEM cannot give you is experience. If I sat you down in the NSA courses and taught you, one on one, the methodologies and how they work, I still couldn't teach you what experience will show you. We could expand the course to two weeks and still not meet our goal.

Performing the IAM and IEM is simple. You follow some basic guidelines consistently to create a final product. We teach these methodologies to college students at the University of

Advancing Technology. They have a project requirement associated with each course to perform the methodologies on the university. But when they begin the courses, they have little to no experience in performing these types of activities. They have lots of questions and many things they need to learn.

We've had individuals like this in our courses, and it's important to note that simply understanding the methods and following the steps will not provide the customer with the required value in the final deliverables. The value is derived from your ability to interpret the results of the assessment and evaluation and associate those back to the customer. Ask yourself these questions:

- Does this vulnerability apply?

- How does this finding affect the information the customer told me was critical to their mission?

- How does the finding impact the customer from a regulatory or privacy perspective?

- How will the organization be changed by implementing the recommendations provided for each finding?

- Are there any limitations on the types of security controls that can be introduced into the organization's environment?

My point here is that understanding the methodologies is not enough, in and of itself, to provide value to the customer. There are steps in experience level that begin with being a team member in training and eventually lead to being the team leader. Failure to adhere to these basic facts concerning information security experience results in so many customers being dissatisfied with the results of their final reports. It's easiest to think of it along the lines of the blacksmith's apprentice: There are basic things you need to know before you go out and do this work on your own. Try to work under an experienced and reputable mentor before performing this work for your own customers.

Certification Does Not Give You Expertise

I've seen more and more requests for proposal (RFPs) and bid items requiring any number of certifications from the individuals who will be performing the work. These could include anything from the standard Certified Information Systems Security Professional (CISSP) certification that ISC(2) maintains to even the NSA IAM and IEM certifications. What customers don't understand is that these methodologies mean that certified individuals understand core concepts about information security. They don't indicate those individuals' ability to provide value on the customer's findings.

As with any other certification, the NSA IAM and IEM certifications only state that you understand what we taught you in class; you understand how to perform the methodologies based on what we've taught you. The piece we will not certify is that you can perform these tasks in such a way as to provide the necessary value to the customer. Learning these methodologies is only the first step.

Summary

This chapter is intended solely to act as your introduction to the IEM process. Although the IEM is extremely effective as a standalone methodology, it is intended to work in conjunction with the organizational focus provided by the IAM. Whereas the IAM focuses on the critical information, identifying critical systems, and looking for vulnerabilities related to processes, procedures, documentation, and operations, the IEM delves into much deeper detail, looking for vulnerabilities within the technical infrastructure and providing recommendations for customers on how to eliminate or mitigate those findings.

The IEM is a vulnerability evaluation methodology, nothing more. Although we must have a solid understanding of threat and risk, the IEM does not attempt, nor does it pretend, to become a full risk assessment or threat management methodology. It is also much more comprehensive than a penetration test or a Red Team activity. Instead of focusing our effort solely on finding a pathway into the network, we look at all possible avenues. By doing so, we can locate the greatest number of vulnerabilities and exposure, allowing the customer to better protect their informational assets.

Finally, you should also understand from this chapter that simply knowing how to work within the methodologies presented by the National Security Agency does not make you a security expert. The value derived from the methodologies depends heavily on your own expertise and knowledge, which only come with time, effort, and working within the field. The NSA methodologies for performing assessments and evaluations are simply tools to be added to your tools kit and used as appropriate to aid you in helping create positive change in your customer's information security posture.

Solutions Fast Track

What Is the IEM?

- ☑ The NSA IEM is a follow-on to the NSA IAM.

- ☑ It provides technical evaluation activities to locate technical findings within the customer network.

- ☑ It is designed to work in conjunction with the NSA IAM. The IEM is comprehensive in that it attempts to locate as many technical vulnerabilities as possible.

What the IEM Is Not

☑ The NSA IEM is not a Red Team or penetration activity. It is not a risk assessment methodology.

☑ It is not a threat management methodology.

☑ It is not useful *only* for the federal or military arenas and can provide value across industries.

Standards and Regulations

☑ The IEM is equally applicable to all information security standards, guidelines, and regulations.

☑ This is due to its inherently flexible nature.

Frequently Asked Questions

The following Frequently Asked Questions, answered by the authors of this book, are designed to both measure your understanding of the concepts presented in this chapter and to assist you with real-life implementation of these concepts. To have your questions about this chapter answered by the author, browse to **www.syngress.com/solutions** and click on the **"Ask the Author"** form. You will also gain access to thousands of other FAQs at ITFAQnet.com.

Q: I've noticed that the NSA methodologies were originally written specifically by the NSA for use within the federal government. Will it still provide value for me?

A: The NSA IAM and IEM are extremely useful to both the federal and private sectors. In fact, only the IAM was written with the federal world in mind. Over the past six years, the IAM has evolved into something more than that and has been successfully utilized in nearly every type of industry available. The NSA IEM, however, was written specifically to address the needs of the private sector as well as the public.

Q: Will the NSA IEM be useful for conducting penetration tests, even though it was not written with that in mind?

A: Yes and no. The tools and techniques covered within the IEM are good places to start for penetration testing, but the depth of the methodology makes it overly comprehensive for a penetration test. We're not looking for a way to compromise the customer's network when we perform IEM activities. In addition, the IEM attempts to find all potential vulnerabilities, giving the customer the best chance to protect themselves from a real-world compromise. Penetration testing does not provide these things and should be conducted only after a real assessment and evaluation have occurred and the customer has had the opportunity to remedy any findings from those processes.

Q: You say in your chapter that this is not a risk assessment methodology, yet it seems to me that risk *has* to play a part or there would be no value in this methodology.

A: You are correct. The NSA methodologies are not geared toward risk assessment. However, if we consider the primary parts that comprise risk (threat, impact, and vulnerabilities), we notice that the only real noticeable area that customers can control lies within vulnerabilities. By closing or mitigating as many potential vulnerabilities as possible, the customer can decrease their risk and improve their security posture.

Q: Where can I go to find out more information about the NSA Information Assurance program?

A: Visit the NSA Web site at www.iatrp.com.

Q: What does IATRP stand for?

A: Information Assurance Training and Rating Program.

Chapter 2

Before the Evaluation Starts

Solutions in this chapter:

- **The Evaluation Request**
- **Validating the Evaluation Request**
- **The Formal Engagement Agreement**
- **Customer and Evaluation Team Approval**

☑ **Summary**

☑ **Solutions Fast Track**

☑ **Frequently Asked Questions**

Introduction

Some actions are necessary precursors to the actual evaluation. To effectively conduct the evaluation, you must first obtain a subset of information about the customer and its network for you to determine that an evaluation is really desired. This chapter focuses on those activities that occur prior to the start of the evaluation. This chapter includes discussion on how and why the evaluation may be requested, the process of validating the evaluation request, and the formal evaluation agreement. These are all actions that occur primarily before the IEM pre-evaluation phase. These are also business process areas that NSA does not cover in the IEM.

The Evaluation Request

The evaluation request plays a critical role in understanding the scope of the evaluation effort. It provides an opportunity to understand the requesting organization's market position, industry, and internal desires. This process also provides an opportunity to educate the customer on the difference among assessments, evaluations, and penetration testing.

Why Are Evaluations Requested?

Evaluations are requested for many different purposes. They are related to the organization's needs, the industry in which it works, and its internal policies, procedures, and goals. Some of the primary reasons are related to legal and regulatory compliance requirements, response to suspicious activities, third-party reviews, and the knowledge that it is the right thing to do for the organization. For the evaluation to be effective, we do need to understand the answers to these questions so that we can effectively implement the evaluation process.

Compliance With Laws and Regulations

Laws and regulations are a driving force for determining the proper INFOEC posture for an organization. Without this knowledge, the security implementation will be flawed. The following sections discuss a few of the U.S. laws and regulations that can affect an organization's security posture requirements. Additional detail on many of these laws and regulations will be discussed in Chapter 5.

The Sarbanes-Oxley Act

The Sarbanes-Oxley Act, also called SarbOx or SOX, was established in 2002 to address public company financial accountability in the wake of the Enron and MCI accounting scandals. SOX holds public companies and their officers directly accountable for accurate reporting of their companies' fiscal condition. SOX also contains provisions to assure the protection of sensitive information and the accuracy of accounting statements.

Federal Information Security Management Act

The Federal Information Security Management Act (FISMA) is focused on a requirement for each federal agency to develop, document, and implement an agencywide program to provide information security for the information and information systems that support the operations and assets of the agency, including those provided or managed by another agency, contractor, or other source (FISMA Implementation Project, http://csrc.nist.gov/sec-cert/).

Health Insurance Portability and Accountability Act of 1996

Health Insurance Portability and Accountability Act of 1996 (HIPAA) legislation covers two primary considerations:

- **Health insurance reform** This provision covers protecting health insurance coverage for workers and their families. It does not have an information security-related provision.

- **Administrative simplification** This provision establishes standard code sets and identifiers for providers, health plans, and employers. It also has an information security and privacy area for protecting health information. HIPAA's goal is to establish standards that will improve the efficiency and effectiveness of the health care system by encouraging the use of electronic data interchange (EDI) in health care (see Centers for Medicare & Medicaid Services, www.cms.hhs.gov/hipaa/).

The Gramm-Leach-Bliley Act

The Gramm-Leach-Bliley Act (GLBA), also known as the Financial Services Modernization Act of 1999, provides limited privacy protections against the sale of your private financial information. GLBA also established protections against the practice of obtaining personal information through false pretenses.

The Family Educational Rights and Privacy Act

The Family Educational Rights and Privacy Act (FERPA) is focused on protecting the privacy of student educational records. This law applies to any school that receives funds from the U.S. Department of Education (see www.ed.gov/policy/gen/guid/fpco/ferpa/index.html).

The DoD Information Technology Security Certification and Accreditation Process

The DoD Information Technology Security Certification and Accreditation Process (DITSCAP) is applicable to Department of Defense (DoD) only. Also known as DoD Instruction 5200.40, DITSCAP provides the certification and accreditation (C&A) guidance on establishing whether systems/networks can operate in the DoD environment. Approval to operate is required for the organizational Designated Approval Authority (DAA). This process includes system documentation and formal security test and evaluation (ST&E).

The National Information Assurance Certification and Accreditation Process

Virtually identical to the DITSCAP, the National Information Assurance Certification and Accreditation Process (NIACAP) is focused on the U.S. federal civilian departments, agencies, contractors, and consultants.

Defense Information Assurance Certification and Accreditation Process

The Defense Information Assurance Certification and Accreditation Process (DIACAP) will eventually replace DITSCAP as a more robust process that will not only standardize the C&A process, C&A documentation, and the requirements traceability process but will also standardize the requirements definition process.

ISO 17799

An international standard that provides relatively comprehensive guidance on establishing a set of controls that comprise security best practices, ISO 17799 covers the following key security areas:

- Security policy
- Organizational security
- Asset classification and control
- Personnel security
- Physical and environmental security
- Communications and operations management
- Access control
- Systems development and maintenance
- Business continuity management
- Compliance

The North American Electric Reliability Council

The mission of the North American Electric Reliability Council (NERC) is to ensure that the bulk electric system in North America is reliable, adequate, and secure. At the time of writing, NERC has a set of draft cyber-security Critical Infrastructure Protection (CIP) standards that address the cross-section of security concerns. The current Web site for NERC is www.nerc.com. These standards are organized as follows:

- CIP-002-1 Critical Cyber Assets
- CIP-003-1 Security Management Controls
- CIP-004-1 Personnel & Training
- CIP-005-1 Electronic Security
- CIP-006-1 Physical Security
- CIP-007-1 System Security Management
- CIP-008-1 Incident Reporting and Response Planning
- CIP-009-1 Recovery Plans

Response to Suspicious Activities

One of the primary reasons an evaluation is requested is as a result of recent or ongoing suspicious activity. This suspicious activity is often a "wake-up call" to an organization that they need to further examine their INFOSEC posture. Why does it take this kind of action for an organization to start addressing INFOSEC? Primarily it's because of the fear of the security problems directly or indirectly affecting the customer, the fear of bad press, and/or the fear that the cost of implementing information security will damage the financial bottom line.

Recent Successful Penetration

Organizations often ask for a security evaluation because of a recent successful penetration. The purpose of this type of request has three objectives:

- Identify the method and source of the attack.
- Assure the penetration recovery is complete.
- Ensure that there are no other vulnerabilities that can be exploited to attack the systems/networks.

Suspected Possible Penetration

In other incidents, a customer may request an evaluation because they are concerned that they have been penetrated, but they do not know for sure. In this case, the evaluation is requested for four reasons:

- Identify whether a penetration has occurred.
- Ensure that if a penetration has occurred, steps are taken to recover from the penetration.
- Identify the method and source of the attack.
- Ensure that there are no other vulnerabilities that can be exploited to attack the systems/networks.

Unsuccessful Penetration Attempt

Why would an organization want to conduct an evaluation after an unsuccessful penetration attempt? Primarily it is part of the organization's due-diligence process. They have obviously been a target. Just because the attacker was unsuccessful the first time, that does not mean the attacker will not keep trying and may find exploitable vulnerabilities. For the unsuccessful penetration, we really want to accomplish the following in our evaluation:

- Identify the method and source of the attack.
- Review system/network security to ensure that the attack truly was not successful.
- Ensure that there are no other vulnerabilities that can be exploited to attack the systems/networks.

"I Don't Know If Our Organization Has Been Penetrated"

Unfortunately, many organizations do not know the current security posture of their systems/networks. Without this knowledge, they are not meeting basic due-diligence requirements and certainly are not meeting any legal or regulatory requirements. Organizations that claim not to know their security posture put themselves at risk of both being attacked and encountering legal issues. In this case, the evaluation does the following:

- Baselines the current security posture of the organization
- Establishes a road map to improve the overall security posture of the organization

Third-Party Independent Reviews of Security Posture

In many cases, independent reviews are required, perhaps because of an organization's customers, service-level agreements (SLAs), and/or insurance provider requirements. The independent review provides a powerful and valuable mechanism for verifying and improving security posture. One form of independent review you might have heard of is the *independent verification and validation* (IV&V). This activity was very prevalent in addressing the year 2000 software issues and was used to basically verify that software functioned appropriately. Such a review was handled by an independent third party to avoid a conflict of interest and help to address the problem of being so close to the programs that important issues were missed.

At times an organization may develop "blinders" and miss important security considerations. The independent security review should provide an unbiased review of the organization's security posture and should catch areas that may have been missed by the internal security reviews.

Customer-Required Reviews

In our security practice, we have seen a third-party review requested by an organization to satisfy one of their customers' contractual requirements. Customers want to have a sense of confidence that the organizations they deal with have addressed important areas such as data protection and sensitive customer information. In some cases, we have seen where the concerns of many customers have driven the need for an organization's security. This has been prevalent in the banking and credit card industries. Identity theft is a very high-profile issue, and individual customers would like some level of confidence that their information is protected.

Insurance-Required Reviews

Insurance companies have begun to require companies in some industries to conduct independent security reviews before they issue insurance or initiate reduced rates on insurance. The insurance industry has recognized the importance of information security from a business and liability perspective. The insured must prove a level of due diligence to reduce the threat of liability concerns.

Notes from the Underground...

Security for Insurance

Several insurance companies have resorted to a security questionnaire to be answered by the potential insured party to determine the level of security within an organization. For example, our team did some support for a company that was insured by AIG Insurance. A 14-page questionnaire had to be filled out, and if the company got an 80 or better on the questionnaire, they were eligible for up to $100,000 in insurance premium adjustments. Results may vary; check with your insurance provider first.

SLA-Required Reviews

SLAs often drive how people do business. When you think of the SLA, you generally think in terms of uptime, availability, response time, and the like. From an information security perspective, the SLA can require a minimum level of security on the provider's systems or some required duration between security reviews to include both internal reviews and third-party reviews. The SLA plays an important role in how much a provider is paid for the services provided. If they default on the SLA, the business is damaged as a result.

It's The Right Thing To Do

What motivates an organization to do the right thing? Sometimes it is truly a desire to protect its information for the sake of protecting its information. But in reality, an organization is most likely driven by one or more of the other factors we've discussed. Whether it is protect the organization's image, customers, or bottom line, when it comes to information security, it generally comes down to some business purpose being the motivator. Most organizations will only spend the minimum amount necessary on security. In reality, they need to determine the value of the information to determine the appropriate level of security implementation.

How Are Evaluations Requested?

The evaluation request can possibly come from any source available to a customer. In our practice, we have received requests via the typical e-mails and phone calls. But we have also received requests in uncommon locations, including on an airplane and while sitting in an audience at a technology event. The most common methods of receiving requests are:

- **Referrals** Probably the most important way we get ongoing business is by doing a quality job for our customers. Word-of-mouth advertising should never be slighted. Providing a quality service to a customer at a reasonable rate is a great way to spread the word about your services.

- **Statements of work (SOWs)/requests for proposals (RFPs)** These are very common mechanisms for receiving requests for an evaluation. The intent of these documents is to detail the customer's requirements for the evaluation. Depending on who develops the SOW/RFP, the packages can include a wide range of detail. These documents can be very short in length (one page) or very long and detailed with a great deal of legal jargon, or somewhere in between. At times, you could have the opportunity to assist in writing an SOW or RFP for a potential work effort. Doing so can help you gain a greater understanding of requirements for the work.

- **Conference/meeting presentations** Often, we receive requests for information about the evaluation process as a follow-up to presentations we make on the IEM throughout the country at various conferences or meetings.

- **Informal discussions** These are discussions that can occur at the airport, in an airplane, on a train, or in a hallway. These informal discussions often start with the "What do you do?" question. The answers can lead to IEM opportunities.

- **Warm contacts** These are people who might have heard of us through conferences or advertising and may call for information on having an IEM conducted on their organization.

- **Cold contacts** These are people who contact us by finding us in the phone book or through an Internet search.

Validating the Evaluation Request

Once the evaluation request is received, it is important to evaluate the request to ensure that there is a common understanding of the customer's desires. There also must be a common understanding of the definitions of the various types of requests that may be received.

NOTE

- **Assessment** A security review that is focused on the security of the organizational aspects within a customer's environment. This includes policies, procedures, information flow, and architecture.
- **Evaluation** A security review that is focused on the technical security aspects of systems, networks, and high-assurance components.
- **Penetration test** A security review that takes the perspective of the adversary to determine the avenues of attack that could be used to gain access to systems and networks.
- **Red team** A security review that takes the perspective of the adversary to determine the avenues of attack. This can include systems and networks and may also involve social engineering, dumpster diving, and other technical and physical security violations.

Sources of Information for Validation

You must approach the validation process from a logical perspective and determine what information is available to help with this process. The two primary areas where this information comes from are the customers themselves and publicly available information. Figure 2.1 gives a basic flow of how the engagement process may occur and who has responsibility or must take action within that process.

Figure 2.1 Engagement Process Flow

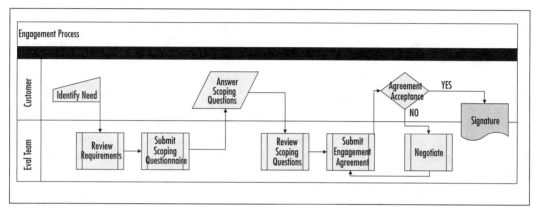

Validating with the Customer

The source of the greatest amount of information, and hopefully the most accurate, is customers themselves. The process of validation should be approached as a learning opportunity for the customer. Frequently used buzzwords, such as *penetration test* and *red team*, may throw the customer off from their true objective. The time you spend with the customer validating information is crucial to a successful effort. Without this time, the likelihood of a miscommunication of need will occur.

There are two primary recommended means of validation with the customer:

- The engagement scoping questionnaire
- Customer discussions and information confirmation

The Engagement Scoping Questionnaire

The scoping questionnaire is identified as part of the pre-evaluation phase of the IEM. The information, however, serves a key role in the contracting process. The scoping questionnaire is necessary to determine the level of effort for the evaluation, which ultimately drives the cost of the evaluation process. The scoping questionnaire is discussed in detail in Chapter 4. You will want to consider utilizing the scoping questionnaire or a subset of the scoping questionnaire in the process of putting the formal engagement documents in place.

Customer Discussions and Information Confirmation

Once information is collected from the customer about the actual work to be conducted, you'll need to confirm the validity of the information with the customer to ensure that the appropriate actions take place.

Publicly Available Information

Public sources of information can be used to validate some of the information the customer provides and can also be used to identify where the customer may have missed a critical area that should be evaluated. You can use multiple sources of public information to obtain this information:

- **Customer Web site** This source is generally useful to verify the customer's mission, industry, and business/product focus.

- **Customer marketing material** This information provides valuable information on the customer's business/product focus.

- **10K/10Q** These publicly available reports are required for publicly held companies on a quarterly basis. Key information such as number of employees and number of physical work locations can be useful in determining whether a key customer area was missed.

- **Blogging sites** You can use forums, such as Raging Bull, to gather some information about an organization.

- **Arin.net** Publicly available information can be found out about a URL or an IP address based on the registration through Arin.net. This information can be used to validate IP range ownership and/or point of contact within the organization being evaluated.

WARNING

Information collected from sites like Raging Bull should not be taken as absolute. In many cases, people post to such sites just to vent and might not have an appropriate or true view of the actual workings of the organization.

Understanding the Level of Effort

A good understanding of what the customer is asking for is essential. As we said before, to ultimately set the boundaries for the evaluation, you might have to spend some time educating the customer on the details of an IEM evaluation. Expectations will be different for each customer you work with. Here are some things to consider:

- Identify the level of detail the customer requires for recommendations. This assists in determining the level of effort required to develop and document the recommendations that are created as part of the evaluation. Level of detail includes the amount of technical detail put into each recommendation and determining whether saying something as simple as "Upgrade the server operating system to Windows 2000 or higher" is enough of a recommendation or whether step-by-step "how-to" will be required.

- Knowledge of any regulations or legislation with which the customer will have to be compliant at the end of the evaluation. This information is used to determine some of the organization's security objectives and directly affects the recommendations that are made to the customer.

- Knowledge of any evaluations that were conducted in the past is useful to show the level of detail in previous evaluations as well as to provide a good indicator of whether the customer will implement your recommendations.

The Formal Engagement Agreement

The formal engagement agreement will be in the form of a contract, a memorandum of understanding (MOU), or a memorandum of agreement (MOA). MOUs and MOAs are primarily used for evaluations of organizations by an internal entity. Contracts are more formal and contain more protective clauses for both the customer and the evaluation team. The purpose of this section is not to provide you with a cut-and-paste contract suitable for all occasions but to give you a reference guide to the items that should be included. Chapter 5 will give you additional understanding of the legal aspects related to the evaluation process.

> **WARNING**
>
> It is highly recommended that you address your evaluation contracts with your contracting specialists and your legal counsel. Each organization has varying levels of contracting requirements that should be addressed for the engagement.

Nondisclosure Agreements

Executing a nondisclosure agreement between the customer and the evaluation team is essential to maintain the customer's comfort level. Portions of the customer's most critical and sensitive assets will be exposed to the evaluation team. The nondisclosure agreement puts a legal requirement for protection of sensitive information in place to avoid any misunderstanding about the use of the customer's sensitive information.

Engagement Agreement Composition

Every organization has its own contracting format, proposal methodology, and bidding process. The information in the following sections is not intended to replace those elements but is included to assist you in ensuring that your review include a minimum set of information. In all cases, consult with your contracting department and/or legal counsel on appropriate and acceptable contents of the contract. In today's business market, contracting is a combination of multiple skills, including project management, negotiation, financial analysis, risk management, and intellectual property management.

Minimum Engagement Agreement Contents

The following items should be included in some form in all contracts for evaluations. Evaluation companies may want to consider these elements in proposals and SOWs. Many times, these documents are rolled directly into a contract or agreement:

- **Purpose** This section describes in simple terms the purpose of the evaluation, how it relates to the customer, and the benefits the organization will receive from the evaluation process. It is essential that you use common terminology relevant to the organization to ensure that this material is understood.

- **Methodology** This section describes the methodology that will be used to conduct the evaluation. This is a good place to emphasize the IEM as a standard methodology to conduct technical INFOSEC evaluations, developed and approved by the National Security Agency. This section includes the phases, processes, and steps to be used during the evaluation.

- **Scope** This section is a detailed demonstration of the level of effort, boundaries, and limitations of the evaluation. Appropriate assumptions are a critical part of the scoping process. The scope section provides a detailed listing of known assumptions affecting the evaluation. Assumptions are critical in demonstrating an understanding of the customer environment and detailing how that environment will affect the evaluation. The types of assumptions may include number of physical locations, number and type of systems, number and type of networks, relevant POC information, information about scheduling of the technical scans and conducting the 10 baseline IEM activities, and any associated constraints that can be listed as assumptions.

- **Roles and responsibilities of customer staff** This section identifies the expectations of the customer's staff to support the evaluation effort. Activities can include introductions, scheduling, coordination, and communications. Utilize this space to ensure that the customer has an understanding of what they need to do to support the evaluation effort.

- **Roles and responsibilities of the evaluation team** This section identifies the expectations and responsibilities of the evaluation team to support and communicate with the customer staff.

- **Deliverables** An accurate list of deliverables with a brief description of each will assist in managing expectations. Often the customer's expectations of a deliverable will be different than what was planned by the evaluation team. Ensuring that you have given an accurate description of the deliverables in the signed agreement is important to the process.

- **Change control** This section identifies the process for managing change within the terms of the contract to avoid "scope creep" and out-of-scope work. Change control should include a process whereby both the customer and the evaluation team will approve any changes to the scope of the effort as well as any related cost changes.

- **Letter of authorization requirement** Due to the nature of the evaluation effort, a formal approval to conduct the evaluation must be given in writing to avoid issues with law enforcement and other security-monitoring agencies. A copy of this letter of authorization should be in the evaluator's possession any time they are conducting the evaluation effort.

- **Period of performance** The necessary schedule for the evaluation can be extremely important. Gaining an understanding of customer availability and the consultant's availability is key to planning a successful evaluation. Depending on the schedule requirements, it might not be possible to list specific dates at this point. If this is the case, be sure to include the expectation of time for activities so the customer's staff can look at their calendars and begin planning when the evaluation makes sense.

- **Location of the work** Work location figures directly into the cost of the evaluation. In this section, be sure to list where the onsite work is to be conducted, where offsite work is to be conducted, whether multiple locations will need to be visited, and where the analysis and reporting will be conducted. Be sure to take into account whether the evaluation team will be dealing with classified information and the potential necessity for additional security controls while conducting evaluation activities.

- **Service fees with any relevant quotation notes** This is your pricing table for the effort. Be as detailed as possible to show the plan of action along with associated costs. The actual cost of your evaluation service depends entirely on your own organization's policy and will not be addressed.

- **Payment schedule** Generally, net 30 days or net 45 days are common payment schedules. However, with some customers, you might have to work out a special agreement for payment. This is a business process specific to your organization and is not covered in detail in this book.

- **Deliverable acceptance/rejection process** This section identifies the process for accepting or rejecting a deliverable and how to resolve issues. It is also important to establish timeframes for when draft deliverables become final deliverables, if the customer does not provide any comments on the deliverables.

- **Signatures** The signature section of the contract addresses your organization's approved statement of terms and conditions. The acceptance section may include information on the length of the agreement, scheduling coordination requirements, termination terms and costs, any other related penalties for cancellation, and acceptance of the terms of the proposal/agreement.

- **Organizational qualifications** This section describes and demonstrates how your organization is best qualified to execute the work the customer requires. This will likely be a detailed background of your organization, your organization's qualifications, qualifications of the proposed members of the team, and how those qualifications will assist the customer in meeting their goals.

Understanding the Pricing Options

Fixed price? Time and materials? When scoping, it is important to understand what the customer may consider reasonable in terms of evaluation costs. Can a customer endure three to four months of hourly billing at a standard hourly rate? You won't know how long the evaluation is going to take before you have completed the pre-evaluation process. These are all challenges that make the commercial contracting world different from the government contracting world.

Government Contracting

In federal government contracting, a great deal of the professional services work is accomplished using a time-and-materials (hourly) costing basis. There is a direct correlation between cost and the number of hours worked under the contract. Rates in government contracting are generally lower; however, there is generally more flexibility in terms of time to accomplish activities necessary to complete the evaluation. However, be cautious to ensure you are meeting the customer expectations from a scoping and time perspective.

The strategy with government contracting is to be involved as a prime contractor or as a subcontractor on various possible contract vehicles to include indefinite delivery, indefinite quantity (IDIQ) contracts, or Government Services Administration (GSA) schedule. Although these are common ways to gain government contracts for evaluations, they are not the only mechanism to get a government contract. Ultimately, it comes down to contacts, being at the right place at the right time. Keep in mind that, generally speaking, labor and other direct costs (travel, equipment, and so on) have to be billed under different "colors of money" with the government.

NOTE

A *prime contractor* is an organization that has a direct contract with the government to provide services or products. A *subcontractor* is an organization that has an agreement with a prime contractor to provide services in support of the prime's contract with the government.

Colors of money refers to how the funding is allocated in the budget. For example, there are different budgetary line items for labor, equipment, travel, and so on. Each of these is a type of "color of money."

Commercial Contracting

Commercial contracting often functions differently than government contracting. Corporations take multiple avenues to meet their contracting needs. These include basic purchase orders, signed proposals, and extensive contracts with page after page of stipulations and requirements. Be sure to include the minimum amount of specific project-related data that is needed to meet your needs; also have your contracting department and/or legal counsel review any information you might not be familiar with. It's always a good idea to include your legal counsel in the process, especially when something changes from standard templates. The actual contracting process is a specific business-related process for your organization and varies from company to company.

Fixed Price vs. Hourly Rate

So what's the best choice? Obviously we cannot tell you what is best for your organization, but Table 2.1 shows the pros and cons of each. There are other contract avenues not addressed here. Fixed price is popular with many of our customers, since they know what they are getting for the money. Open-ended and hourly rate contracts tend to be scary at a time when organizations are keeping a tight rein on their pocketbooks.

Table 2.1 Fixed Price vs. Hourly Rate

	Advantages	Disadvantages
Fixed price	Flexibility with staffing Flexibility with charge rates Incentive to keep down costs	All major and minor scope changes require a change order Difficult to bill until the evaluation is complete, unless specific interim payments are authorized in the contract Generally a higher risk and therefore higher cost for same level of effort compared with hourly rate

Continued

Table 2.1 continued Fixed Price vs. Hourly Rate

	Advantages	Disadvantages
Hourly rate	Typically lower cost for same level of effort compared with fixed price Flexibility with scope changes since any increase in effort will simply result in more hours burned (until the maximum hours run out)	More closely monitored in both labor hours and other direct costs Loss of staffing flexibility since rates are based on labor categories and skill sets

WARNING

The technical evaluation plan, which is developed in the pre-evaluation phase of the IEM, may change the level of effort thought to be needed for the evaluation. You should consider having a clause in the contract allowing for rescoping for significant changes once the pre-evaluation phase of the IEM is completed and accepted. Another approach would be to contract the pre-evaluation as a separate agreement from the remaining phases of the IEM evaluation. This allows the technical evaluation plan to be used as the scoping input for an onsite evaluation contract.

Additional Engagement Agreement Contents

As we discussed earlier, organizations will have to follow their own contracting processes when bidding and contracting work with customers. There are many more possible inclusions in a contract; the following is only a sampling of items you might find. Consult the appropriate legal and contractual expertise for purposes of creating contracts that will meet your organization's needs. Some of the additional items you might find in your contracts or required by the customer are as follows:

- **Insurance information** Many organizations require specific levels of insurance, both general liability and professional liability, before they'll work with an organization. This information needs to be included in any final agreement.

- **Personnel qualifications** Proof of qualifications for personnel proposed to work a contract may be required by the contracting organization. This proof can include certifications, year of experience, educational levels, and specific types of insurance.

- **Warranties** Include any associated warranty information for products or services provided.

- **Representations** Generally identifies that there are no other representations other than the written contract or agreement.

- **Independent contractor statement** To avoid tax issues, many contracts include independent contractor statements and associated responsibilities for wages and benefits for each organization.

- **Assignment of rights** This section normally does not allow for the contract rights to be assigned to another entity without the express written approval of the contracting organization.

- **Confidentiality statements** This section focuses on protecting the confidential information of both the contracting and the contracted parties.

- **Document ownership statements** For our purposes, this section specifically identifies that all documents belong to the customer.

- **Indemnification** An indemnification statement might look like the following: "The Contractor and contractee agree that they shall indemnify and hold harmless the other and its respective officers and employees from any loss, cost, damage, expense, or liability of every kind and nature which they may incur, arising out of, or in connection with performance under this Agreement, occasioned in whole or in part, by the negligent actions or willful misconduct of other, or by its lower tier subcontractors." This is a legal protection mechanism to avoid huge lawsuits for normally acceptable problems that arise due to anything other than neglect or misconduct.

- **Survival of obligations** This section focuses on the length of time that obligations within the contract will persist. This section also specifies that if one section of the contract is deemed unusable, the other sections still remain intact.

- **Waiver and severability** This section states that any provision or portion thereof of the contract is held to be invalid under any applicable statute or rule of law, it shall be, to that extent, deemed omitted without invalidating the remaining portions of the contract.

- **Governing law** This section addresses what federal and state laws shall government the legal aspects of the contract.

- **Force majeure** This section addresses failure of a contract due to circumstances beyond the control of the contractor. Wording may look like the following: "Neither party to the Subcontract shall be considered to be in default of its obligations under this Subcontract to the extent that failure to perform any such obligation arises out of causes beyond the control and without the fault or negligence of the affected party. Examples of these causes are (1) acts of God or of the public enemy, (2) acts of the Government in either its sovereign or contractual capacity, (3) fires, (4) floods, (5) epidemics, (6) quarantine restrictions, (7) strikes, (8) freight embargoes, and (9) unusually severe weather. In each instance, the failure to perform must be beyond the control and without the fault or negligence of the affected party. *Default* includes failure to make progress in the work so as to endanger performance. However,

Subcontractor shall not be excused for failure to perform any obligation under this Subcontract if such failure is caused by a subcontractor of the Subcontractor's at any tier and the cause of such failure was not beyond the control of both the Subcontractor and its lower-tiered subcontractor, and without the fault or negligence of either."

Dealing with Contract Pitfalls

An awareness of contracting pitfalls and how to deal with them is essential to the effective handling of the contracting process. Failure in the contracting process could result in lost time, lost money, and a great amount of frustration for both the customer and the evaluation team. Our goal is to make the customer happy, so avoiding the contract pitfalls is key to continuous management of customer expectations.

"Scope Creep" and Timelines

Unplanned and unbid scope changes in projects, often called "scope creep," occur when a project deviates from the written scope to a higher level of effort. Controlling scope creep effectively can assist in effectively managing the overall project. Scope creep not only has an impact on the financial aspects of the project—it also has an impact on project timelines and the ability for the evaluation team to complete the job on time.

Scope creep can be caused by poor planning, unknown areas of the organization that need to evaluated, or a customer's desire to further investigate a certain security area that is being analyzed by the evaluation team. Scope creep can also occur when a customer wants to get more out of the effort than they are paying for. The project manager, team lead, and customer representative should work closely together to avoid scope creep. Any agreed-on changes need to appropriately documented and, if necessary, recosted into the project. This doesn't mean that all scope changes have to be considered in a negative light or even that they require a cost increase. But it does recommend an evaluation of the change on a case-by-case basis to ensure that expectations are being met.

Notes from the Underground...

Common Scope Creep

The most common example of scope creep occurs when more systems or more locations need evaluating than the customer originally identified. This is generally due to the lack of full communication by the customer with their technical staff or a communications disconnect between the evaluation team and the customer. For this reason, it is extremely important to be detailed in the assumptions section of

Continued

your contract. Another example of scope creep occurs with the discovery of additional systems that need to be reviewed as part of the evaluation that were not originally identified as part of the effort.

Uneducated Salespeople

Educate your security sales staff on the evaluation process before they are sent out to the field to sell an evaluation. They do not have to be experts on the entire process, but they need to understand what an evaluation is composed of, reasonable expectations from the process, the role of the customer in the process, and the impact of customer complexity on the process. Then, working in conjunction with the evaluation "experts," they can put together a quality sales presentation and proposal. Ensure that they understand not to make promises that they are not sure your organization can keep. This includes factors such as level of effort, cost, and unreasonable expectations regarding timeframes.

Evaluations 101

The purpose of an INFOSEC evaluation is to:

- Provide a technical security review of systems and networks
- Examine the customer's technical security from an internal and external perspective
- Analyze the network architecture
- Examine the security configuration of servers, workstations, and network devices for vulnerabilities and exposures
- Examine the security configuration of critical applications
- Identify vulnerabilities and exposures
- Recommend solutions to mitigate or eliminate those vulnerabilities

Notes from the Underground...

Sold Up the River

The following comment is not intended as a general slam on salespeople; however, we have experienced several incidents where an uneducated salesperson sold a service without knowledge of what the effort entailed or how it could be accomplished. Package-pricing a security evaluation without knowledge of who the evaluation is for or how the evaluation will be conducted can result in serious mission and financial failure for your organization. Success is not only measured by how well you do your job but also whether the customer is satisfied with the service they were provided at the price they paid.

Bad Assumptions

Making poor assumptions can kill your contract. A great deal of effort needs to be put into developing and reviewing the assumptions that are made for each contract. Assumptions list the understood environment in which the evaluation will be conducted. They will also identify the expected involvement of the customer in the process—staff availability, scheduling requirements, and timeframes.

Assumption Topic Areas

The following are examples of information that need to be included in the assumptions section and that must be as accurate as possible to avoid confusion and poor scoping:

- Location in which the evaluation will be conducted
- Number of sites at which the evaluation will conducted
- Availability of customer personnel for the evaluation
- Scheduling of evaluation scanning
- Travel requirements
- Documentation availability
- Necessary support from the customer in managing the evaluation
- Technical and organizational points of contact for the evaluation
- The process for determining the systems, network devices, and applications to be evaluated
- Availability and currency of the network architecture diagrams
- Operating system types for servers and workstations
- Technical expertise of the customer

Poorly Written Contracts

Poorly written contracts are the basis for poor evaluations. Generally, poor contracts are based on bad information, bad assumptions, and lack of attention to detail. A boilerplate evaluation contract can be dangerous if not properly tailored to the current customer. Every organization has different expectations and requirements to meet. The worst kind of evaluation contract will not have any specific detail related to the customer being assessed.

Poor Scope Definition

Poor scope definition generally results from a poor understanding of the requirements and expectations associated with the project. From a provider perspective, poor scope definition could mean a loss in revenue and profits for an effort. Poor scoping can result in your consultants having to spend unplanned hours on the job and eventual cost overruns. Another major mistake in the scoping effort is not having the customer approve the scope with a signature. By having the customer sign for approval of the scope, you'll help avoid future issues such as the customer denying that they agreed to the scope or possibly forcing additional work for no additional money. Be sure to protect your company. Don't assume anything. Document the terms of the agreement in detail.

NOTE

Contracts are one area in which large companies generally have an advantage over smaller companies. Large companies normally have years of experience, a dedicated contracting staff, and strong legal counsel that support their needs in the contracting process.

Underbid or Overbid: The Art of Poor Cost Estimating

Pricing a proposal can be as critical as the quality of the information put into the proposal. Understanding the customer environment and limitations from a financial perspective will help you properly price the effort. This closely ties into the assumptions section of the project. The assumptions help determine the level of effort. It's always dangerous to price a project low to win the work. Bidding low cuts into the flexibility and profit margin the project may carry. Bidding high can price you out of contention for the project. True pricing has to come from actual expected effort and your experience as to what it will take to complete the effort.

Many outside influences can impact the costing efforts. As mentioned previously, a poor understanding of the requirements and expectations associated with the project are one influence. Another is salesperson influence on the process. If a salesperson tries to pressure the pricing process in an attempt to win a bid, the end result may be an improperly priced effort. Another pressure from the sales staff is along the lines of, "I said we could do this for $25,000, so we have to do the evaluation for $25,000." (See Chapter 4 for more on over/underbidding.)

Notes from the Underground...

Contracting Differences

Don't assume that your experience with either government contracting or commercial contracting fully prepares you for all aspects of contracting for the other. Government contracts and commercial contracts are as unique in nature as the differences between government agencies or commercial industries. Be prepared to learn something new with the different entities you will be working with, and don't get frustrated when one entity does contracting differently than another.

Customer and Evaluation Team Approval

The final step before starting the actual evaluation is to finalize the formal approval of the engagement agreement. Both the customer and the evaluation team must be prepared for the time and possible negotiations required to reach a formal and mutual agreement. The goal is to develop an engagement agreement that meets the needs of both the customer and the evaluation team. This includes critical scoping information, legal statements, timelines, and pricing.

The Customer Approval Process

The customer is likely to have the more rigid approval process for the engagement agreement. Most customers will pass the agreement to their contracts and legal department for review and comment. Many times, the customer will request an additional provision or a wording change to clarify things. if the evaluation team has been writing evaluation engagement agreements for awhile, the changes will usually be minor. However, every organization is unique, and you could find that significant changes are needed. The end result may be a signed agreement or a purchase order (PO) that directly references the final agreement. This signed agreement or PO is the formal approval to proceed with the evaluation.

The Evaluation Team Approval Process

The evaluation team will likely be the entity that is writing up the agreement due to their experience with the process. The evaluation team will have to review any customer requests for changes to the agreement and determine the appropriateness of the request. If significant changes are requested, the evaluation team's legal counsel will likely have to be involved before final approval.

Summary

Before the actual formal evaluation begins, a series of activities must take place. Since NSA does not address business processes that occur prior to the start of the pre-evaluation process within their methodologies, we have attempted to address those needs in this chapter.

Evaluations are requested for many reasons to help organizations meet their security goals. This includes consideration for laws and regulations within the industry or industries in which the organization functions, concerns about being attacked, concerns about market position from a security perspective, or insurance requirements. The reason the evaluation is requested will drive some of the considerations and content of the engagement agreement and, ultimately, the final evaluation report. This understanding is essential to meeting the customer's expectations.

The engagement request validation process is critical to ensuring that you reach a common understanding with the customer and avoid missing some of the fine detail needed to properly scope the level of effort for the evaluation. The primary source of validation is through the customer, but you can also use publicly available information to further validate the information.

The formal engagement agreement is the contract between the evaluation team and the customer. It outlines the activities that will occur and identifies the estimated cost to conduct the evaluation. Since this activity is likely taking place before the technical evaluation plan is developed and as part of the pre-evaluation phase of the IEM, the engagement agreement must be flexible enough to address scope changes identified in the IEM pre-evaluation.

The final step before starting the actual evaluation is to finalize the approval of the engagement agreement through the processes of both the customer and evaluation team organizations. This will address the final contracting and legal means necessary to meet each organization's needs from both the engagement and a liability protections point of view.

Solutions Fast Track

Evaluation Requests

- ☑ The purpose of the evaluation will vary by industry needs and organizational mind sets.
- ☑ Requests are received from multiple sources for many different purposes.

Validate the Evaluation Request

- ☑ Validation is critical to ensure that customer expectations are defined.
- ☑ Improper validation can result in higher costs and greater workload.
- ☑ Improper validation can result in embarrassment to the customer and the evaluation team.
- ☑ Utilize the customer and public information to validate the evaluation request.

Understand the Level of Effort

- ☑ Gain an understanding of customer needs.
- ☑ Level of effort drives number of resources needed.
- ☑ Level of effort drives evaluation cost.

Develop the Engagement Agreement

- ☑ Ensure that nondisclosure agreements are in place to protect customer and evaluation team interests.
- ☑ Address all critical areas of the engagement agreement to obtain a common, acceptable understanding of the work that will be performed.
- ☑ Gain approval by the appropriate personnel in both the customer and evaluation team organization.

Frequently Asked Questions

The following Frequently Asked Questions, answered by the authors of this book, are designed to both measure your understanding of the concepts presented in this chapter and to assist you with real-life implementation of these concepts. To have your questions about this chapter answered by the author, browse to **www.syngress.com/solutions** and click on the **"Ask the Author"** form. You will also gain access to thousands of other FAQs at ITFAQnet.com.

Q: Can I develop a single engagement agreement for a combined assessment (IAM) and evaluation (IEM)?

A: Absolutely, yes. You gain some synergy when conducting an IAM and IEM together. Doing so can reduce the level of effort needed on the front portion of the evaluation because the same types of information are needed to start both an IAM and IEM process. This will ultimately result in cost savings for the customer as well.

Q: How much should I charge for an evaluation?

A: This is the unanswerable question. Too many factors play into the level of effort to conduct the evaluation. Complexity of the customer's security technology, number of physical locations, number of servers, number of workstations, number of network devices—all play into this decision. We have priced comprehensive evaluations between $25,000 to $75,000, depending on the factors mentioned. Your cost depends on your organization's hourly rates, required margins, and expertise of resources provided.

Q: How can a potential customer check our IEM credentials as part of their vendor selection process?

A: The NSA's IATRP Web site (www.iatrp.com/) contains a listing of individuals certified in the IAM and IEM. This is a public site available to anyone who wants to view it. Another option is to include a copy of the individual certificate of completion from NSA as part of the proposal process.

Q: I have completed the validation process, but I am still not confident that we have all the information needed to effectively scope the effort. What should I do?

A: You really have three options: seek additional confirmation through the customer, further strengthen your assumptions and limitations section of the engagement agreement, or do not bid on the evaluation.

Q: My customer wants me to start work next week, but I don't have a signed engagement agreement yet. Should I start work?

A: This is a tough question. The answer should be a resounding *No*. With out the signed engagement agreement, you have no means of getting compensation for the work conducted, but you also will be liable for any and all damage that could come as a result of the evaluation.

Q: How much cost savings is there in conducting an IAM and an IEM together?

A: This will vary depending on your organization, but on average we suggest a 25 percent to 35 percent cost savings over the combined price based on the complexity of the customer and their ultimate goal.

Q: How are the IEM certification and using the IEM methodology a selling point to the customer?

A: The IEM is a value-added credential showing prospective customers that an individual is recognized for understanding a methodology that was developed and supported by one of the most prominent security organizations in the world, the National Security Agency (NSA). The 10 Baseline IEM Activities provide a comprehensive technical view of the security posture of an organization, taking into account customer policy, industry laws and regulations, and security best practices.

Part I
Pre-Evaluation

49

Chapter 3

Setting Expectations

Solutions in this chapter:

- **Objectives of the Pre-Evaluation Phase**
- **Understanding Concerns and Constraints**
- **Obtaining Management Buy-In**
- **Obtaining Technical Staff Buy-In**
- **Establishing Points of Contact**

☑ **Summary**
☑ **Solutions Fast Track**
☑ **Frequently Asked Questions**

Introduction

In this chapter we delve into one of the most crucial preparation aspects of doing any evaluation: assessing customer expectations, the tangible and intangible factors, that will affect the outcome of the evaluation. If you fail to adequately address your customer's expectations, you can expect to waste your time and the customer's money. A good example is to show up for a technical evaluation and find out at the in-briefing that the customer is expecting a full risk assessment. Your team will be unprepared and probably missing some skill sets needed to accomplish the customer goals. From that point on everything that can go wrong will, and you will fail to achieve the prime goal of any provider of services to any customer: customer satisfaction. Setting expectations is more than just asking what the customer is concerned with or what they want. You and your customer need to come to an understanding of what is going to be done and what is *not* going to be done.

This is the reason for this chapter. The focus of this book is the accomplishment of the technical evaluation of a customer's computing environment, but it is essential that you understand how this fits together with an overall security posture review.

Objectives of the Pre-Evaluation Phase

As already covered in the previous chapters, you need to define the timeline for performing the evaluation. As you already know, the timeline is essential from the evaluator's perspective to define the resource requirements. It is also essential from the customer's perspective for resource scheduling. Will the evaluation be performed as a follow-on to the organizational assessment or will it be performed concurrently with the IAM? Both approaches are good and will work. But each provides only a picture of the security posture at any given point in time; it's a snapshot. As such, it is most effective to have the evaluation accomplished at the same time as the organizational assessment. From the customer's perspective doing the evaluation does provide an output of findings that need to be mitigated. But have you provided enough information to tie the findings back to what is critical to the mission of the organization? With out the organizational assessment your team will not have enough information to tie the findings to what is really important to the customer. If no organizational assessment has been accomplished within the last six months the odds are that your team will either not have any Organizational, or System, Information Criticality Matrix. These are essential to providing a quality output for the customer as you have to have both the matrixes and the impact definitions that accompany them. You can see in Figure 3.1 that conducting the organizational assessment and evaluation at the same time is easily accomplished. Most all customers, that understand the process, will want to have them done concurrently. This allows for that defined point in time definition of the security posture to be easily related to each other. This also prevents their internal arguments about what is/was/will be fixed from the organizational assessment to the organizational evaluation.

Figure 3.1 The NSA View of IAM and IEM Utilization

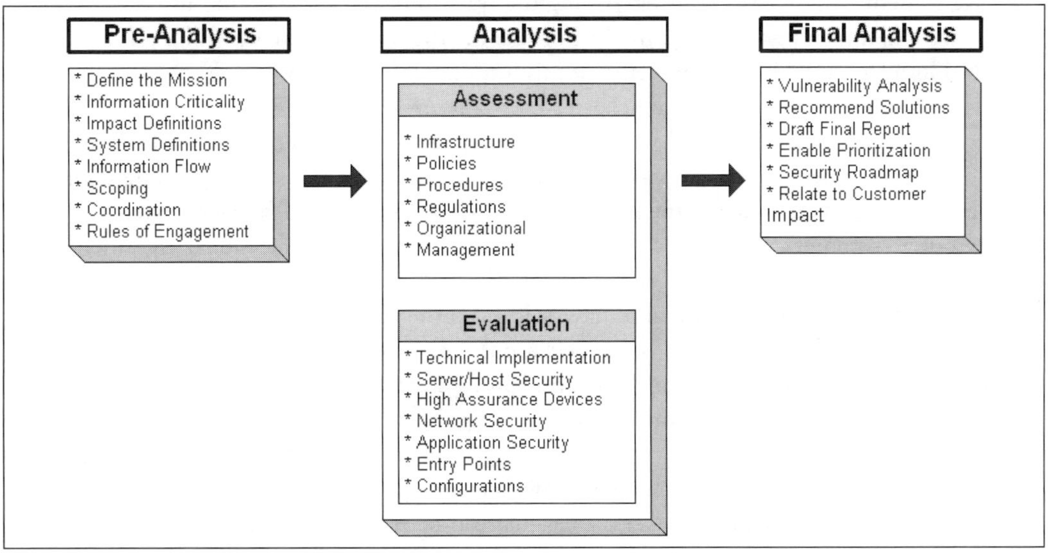

Pre-Analysis	Analysis	Final Analysis
* Define the Mission * Information Criticality * Impact Definitions * System Definitions * Information Flow * Scoping * Coordination * Rules of Engagement	**Assessment** * Infrastructure * Policies * Procedures * Regulations * Organizational * Management **Evaluation** * Technical Implementation * Server/Host Security * High Assurance Devices * Network Security * Application Security * Entry Points * Configurations	* Vulnerability Analysis * Recommend Solutions * Draft Final Report * Enable Prioritization * Security Roadmap * Relate to Customer Impact

Conducting the organizational assessment and evaluation concurrently provides for a complete analysis of your customer's security posture. One of the objectives when you have finished the work and delivered the final report is that the report tie the proposed security road map back to the defined impact definitions and, ultimately, to the mission impact. This is how you will provide the customer with sufficient information to do good risk management without you there holding their hand. This is a project-oriented approach in that both the assessment and evaluation have a starting point, which is the pre-analysis phase; an analysis phase; and a final analysis phase. The pre-analysis phase is designed to define the customer needs and expectations and is the focus of this chapter. This includes setting the evaluation's goals and objectives. The analysis phase is the validation of the actual security posture and will be covered in depth in future chapters. This is where your team will provide proof by showing the customer's actual exposures. The final analysis phase is the data-crunching and reporting phase and will also be covered in depth in future chapters. Remember, if you cannot tie the findings to the impact definitions, the customer will have insufficient information for good risk management after you are gone.

Understanding the customer requirements is both complicated and easy. It is complicated because each customer and its social/political environment are unique and require you and your team to understand the environment. It is easy because you and your team have the knowledge and experience to understand the currently implemented technical and operational controls. The first part involves simply gaining an understanding of the customer mission. When all is said and done and you have delivered the final report, how has what you've done affected the customer mission? Providing technological recommendations without understanding the reason for the way the current technology is used does a disservice to the customer. Improving an organization's security posture does not involve stopping business or providing solutions that do not fit the organization's goals. If you don't have the organizational assessment report, you will have to define these parts yourself. Asking the question "Why are you in business?" is one way to find out a firm's goals, but it might not provide the answers you are looking for. Every organization in the world has an underlying mission of making money. It does not matter what the organizations is. You could get the charter from a nonprofit or not-for-profit organization to see why they are in business and you'd still find that money is the bottom line. Even the U.S. federal government needs to make money. They get a bigger budget by spending their entire budget every year to allow them to ask for more money in their budget next year. Finding out a customer's mission is something we covered in the organizational assessment and discussed in the book *Security Assessment: Case Studies for Implementing the NSA IAM*. We need to know the organization's mission and draw it in from the organizational assessment.

Understanding customers' needs or expectations is as simple as understanding why you were brought in to do the evaluation. You can identify these needs from your discussions with the customer about their expectations and by defining their concerns or constraints. Sometimes the customer will not tell you more that what is based on an RFP or an SOW. Sometimes their needs are based on unspoken issues such as a merger or acquisition where the customer is looking to identify unnecessary or excess areas that can be trimmed, making the organization more efficient and effective. But in today's world of legislative requirements, the real reason for doing most evaluations tends to be compliance. Don't get us wrong—there is nothing the matter with having compliance be the reason for the evaluation, but we have seen occasional customers who feel they are being forced to do an evaluation to meet a higher-authority requirement. When the only reason is to "get the check mark," there is usually little or no management support to implement mitigation or improve the security posture.

In Chapter 4 we discuss in depth how to adequately scope the evaluation. In Chapter 5 we cover how to coordinate with the customer the rules of engagement (ROE) and the legal activities that need to be accomplished. Chapter 6 will pull all of this information together into the technical evaluation plan (TEP). All these activities are needed in this order, but they present a foundation in understanding the customer, their environment, and the limitations that will directly affect the evaluation.

Customer expectations will be defined as part of the scoping of the evaluation. It is not unusual for the customer to refine their expectations as they become familiar with the evaluation process or better understand their compliance requirements in more detail. This process often results in the customer adding pieces to the evaluation. That can result in "scope creep," or the addition of work that your team is not prepared for, if the customer's input is not controlled or expectations are not readdressed during the onsite evaluation process instead of during the pre-evaluation phase.

Understanding Concerns and Constraints

Customers will always have specific reasons for asking for an evaluation. It is crucial that you and your team understand what the customer is concerned about and address those concerns throughout the evaluation. Understanding the concerns and addressing them are significant steps in creating positive customer satisfaction. In the organizational assessment, we addressed the concerns from the executive level, some of which could be:

- Legislative or regulatory requirements
- FISMA, Sarbanes-Oxley, Gramm-Leach-Bliley, and so on

What Are the Requirements?

Responding to public issues of identity theft and fraud, the U.S. government has passed legislation to enhance and strengthen previously existing legislation dealing with infrastructure security through bills that include Sarbanes-Oxley (SOX), the Health Insurance Portability and Accountability Act (HIPAA), the U.S. Government Federal Information Security Management Act (FISMA), the Gramm-Leach-Bliley Act (GLBA), and the Children's Internet Protection Act (CIPA). What are these pieces of legislation, and why does management care? A more detailed description of these regulations and standards can be found in Chapter 2 of this book.

Other Significant Regulations

California has passed a law, known variously as Senate Bill (SB) 1386 or the California Database Protection Act, requiring companies doing business with customers in California to notify them if they suspect that any of their customers' personal information has been accessed by an unauthorized party. This law applies to any company that has California customers, even if the company has no physical presence in California.

And this is only the start. You can expect that more states will start adopting similar regulations to try to provide some measure of protection for their constituents. Personal privacy is always a hot topic, and with the rise in publicity that occurs when a company loses customers' personally identifiable information, more legislation will be forthcoming. Another example is the new law signed by the governor of Colorado. Consumers in Colorado will have the right to put a security freeze on their credit files, effective July 1, 2006. This is to prevent identity thieves from opening new credit accounts in their names. Colorado is the sixth state to provide some form of security freeze directly to consumers. Many other states around the country are considering such laws in the wake of a string of data security breach and identity theft scandals in 2004–2005.

Finally, the private sector has joined in, with Visa and MasterCard regulating both their merchants and service providers. Visa's initiative is called the Cardholder Information Security Program (CISP); MasterCard's is called the Site Data Protection (SDP) program. Both programs require that all merchants and service providers be assessed for key information security best practices and, depending on the size of the merchant, evaluate systems involved in the handling or processing of cardholder information for security vulnerabilities.

Visa USA has instituted the CISP, first mandated in June 2001. The program is intended to protect Visa cardholder data, no matter where it resides. The idea is to ensure that cardholders, merchants, and service providers maintain the highest information security standards. CISP compliance is required of all merchants and service providers that store, process, or transmit Visa cardholder data. The program applies to all payment channels, including retail (brick-and-mortar), mail/telephone order, and e-commerce.

The MasterCard SDP Program is a proactive, global solution offered by MasterCard through its acquiring members. The program provides acquiring members with the ability to deploy security compliance programs, assisting online merchants and Member Service Providers to better protect against hacker intrusions and account data compromises. The program takes a proactive approach to security by identifying common possible vulnerabilities in a merchant Web site and makes recommendations for short- and long-term security improvements. The solution addresses the security issues that online merchants and their acquiring banks face in the virtual world and concerns arising from these issues, such as Internet fraud, chargebacks, brand image damage, consumer information safety and privacy, and the cost of replacing stolen account numbers.

To achieve compliance, merchants and service providers must adhere to the Payment Card Industry (PCI) Data Security Standard (see Table 3.1), which offers a single approach to safeguarding sensitive data for all card brands. This standard is a result of the collaboration between Visa and MasterCard and is designed to create common industry security requirements. Using the PCI Data Security Standard as the framework, the Visa and MasterCard security programs provide the tools and measurements needed to protect against cardholder data exposure and compromise. The PCI Data Security Standard, downloadable at http://usa.visa.com/download/business/accepting_visa/ops_risk_management/cisp_PCI_Data_Security_Standard.pdf?it=i 1|/business/accepting_visa/ops_risk_management/cisp.html|PCI%20Data%20Security%20Standard, consists of 12 basic requirements supported by more detailed subrequirements:

Table 3.1 PCI Data Security Standard

Goal	Execution
Build and maintain a secure network.	1. Install and maintain a firewall configuration to protect data. 2. Do not use vendor-supplied defaults for system passwords or other security parameters.
Protect cardholder data.	3. Protect stored data. 4. Encrypt transmission of cardholder data and sensitive information across public networks.
Maintain a vulnerability management program.	5. Use and regularly update antivirus software. 6. Develop and maintain secure systems and applications.
Implement strong access control measures.	7. Restrict access to data by business "need to know." 8. Assign a unique ID to each person with computer access. 9. Restrict physical access to cardholder data.
Regularly monitor and test networks.	10. Track and monitor all access to network resources and cardholder data. 11. Regularly test security systems and processes.
Maintain an information security policy.	12. Maintain a policy that addresses information security.

Budgetary Concerns

Security has been and will continue to be an overhead expense for all organizations, much like payroll and other administrative tasks that are required to keep an organization running. The question that seems to pop up every few months in the security industry is, what is the value of all the security work that takes place within an organization? Organizations want to see the current *and* expected return on investment (ROI) for the security budget.

When talking about IT security, ROI has historically focused on returning actual organizational payback where implementing tools, devices, or training, should be reducing operating costs. This is almost never the case. Since security acts as a version of insurance for your data or information, any return from required security should focus on this aspect.

There have been many endeavors over the years to find the ROI for security. All the studies have yet to be able to define the ROI calculation. There is by no means only one way to determine ROI for security; currently, several projects are under way that are still working to determine this calculation. You can find more information on this topic by doing a simple search on the Internet for *security ROI*.

For our purposes, we use a simplified formula that is based on annual loss expectancy. Simply put, how much do you expect to lose from a single security incident each year? So the annual loss expectancy of a single security breach that costs $1 million and that has a 35 percent probability of occurring can be reflected as:

Incident Cost × Probability = Annual Loss Expectancy

$1,000,000 × 0.35 = $350,000

Although this is good, it does not include the factor of mitigation into the equation, so we add this factor by multiplying the probability by the mitigation factor. Consider the impact that computer worms have had over the past few years, or even the various Sober virus variants. If you have installed up-to-date antivirus software, you can expect to have mitigated about 50 percent of the probability of loss. Or if you implemented strong user awareness training, you could mitigate about 80 percent of the probability of occurrence. (Can anybody say customer choices?) This makes the formula slightly different, as follows:

Incident Cost × (Probability × Mitigation) = Annual Loss Expectancy

$1,000,000 × (0.35 X 0.5) = $1,000,000 × 0.175 = $175,000 (Antivirus Software Mitigation)

$1,000,000 × (0.35 X 0.2) = $1,000,000 × 0.07 = $70,000 (User Awareness Training Mitigation)

So if the cost of implementation is known—antivirus $75,000, user awareness program $10,000—you can show a simple ROI by showing that the cost of mitigation is less than the cost of loss. Please note that this does not take all factors into account and is not meant as an introduction or tutorial on determining ROI.

Cyber-Insurance

Traditional insurance companies cover physical types of risks and exposures. They do not cover nonphysical types of risks and exposures that come from the Internet—such issues as cyber-terrorism, hacking, and electronic fraud and theft. That's where cyber-insurance comes in. Cyber-insurance can cover denial-of-service (DoS) attacks that bring down e-commerce sites, electronic theft of sensitive information, virus-related damage, losses associated with internal networks crippled by hackers or rogue employees, privacy-related suits, and legal issues associated with Web sites, such as copyright and trademark violations.

Like its real-world equivalents in a brick-and-mortar environment, a cyber-insurance company provides insurance and risk management services against various types of Internet risk. From a process point of view, the first thing that an insurance company does before quoting a policy to a customer is try to assess the customer by asking them to complete a short questionnaire. This self-assessment questionnaire is sent to the risk analysis department. After reviewing the questionnaire, the risk analysis department comes up with a solution that the insurance agent can then use for quoting a policy price based on the customer's existing security model. The simpler the solution that has to be implemented, the lower the cost of insurance premiums.

Cyber-insurance policies are already being issued by companies such as Lloyd's e-comprehensive, Chubb's cyber security, and AIG's Net Advantage Security. These policies can provide coverage for business interruption, electronic data damage, extortion, network security liability, (downstream) network liability, media liability, professional errors and omissions, coverage for financial loss resulting from data damage, destruction, corruption, and loss of income from network security apart from the coverage. Some insurers also offer risk management services, including online and onsite security assessment.

Brick-and-mortar insurance policies have evolved over several decades. Insurance and risk mitigation are backed by decades' worth of valuable data, speculations, statistical analysis, and projections. In contrast, Internet and cyber-policies such as insurance are relatively new concepts. Due to lack of quantifiable data on cyber-risk, cyber-insurance policies require high premiums and deductibles. Depending on the size of the company and the coverage, the required premiums can run into the hundreds of thousands of dollars. If an insurer's assessment does not find appropriate levels of computer network security, the policy may even be denied unless the applicant meets or exceeds the insurer's recommended security specifications. In the absence of decades' worth of information, some of the biggest challenges for an insurance firm in providing a cyber-insurance package are calculating the cost of investment for a particular policy and determining the cost of loss.

System Accreditation

System Accreditation is the official management authorization to operate a system or network and is based on the formal certification of the how a defined system or network meets a prescribed set of security requirements. The accreditation statement affixes security responsibility with the accrediting authority. System Accreditation addresses the system's internal controls, perimeter and interconnections to other systems or networks. The internal controls and perimeter surrounds a specific set of equipment and peripherals under the control of the Designated Approval Authority (DAA). The interconnections or boundary covers what may be a much larger environment that includes, for example, remote, dial-in users or other network users, who are not controlled by a single DAA.

FISMA

The Federal Information Security Management Act (FISMA) utilizes NIST Special Publication (SP) 800-37, *Guide for the Security Certification and Accreditation of Federal Information Systems,* as its compliance standard. NIST SP 800-37 provides guidelines for certifying and accrediting information systems supporting the executive agencies of the federal government. NIST SP 800-37 applies to all federal information systems other than those systems designated as national security systems, as defined in FISMA.

The certification and accreditation package consists of the following documents:

- System security plan (SSP)
- Security assessment report
- Plan of action and milestones (POAM)

The key document for the certification and accreditation process is the system security plan (SSP), detailed in NIST Special Publication 800-18, *Guide for Developing Security Plans for Information Technology Systems.* The purpose of the SSP is to:

- Provide an overview of the system's security requirements and describe the controls in place or planned for meeting those requirements
- Delineate responsibilities and expected behavior of all individuals who access the system

DoD Information Technology Security Certification and Accreditation Process

DoDI 5200.40 (DITSCAP) establishes a standard DoD-wide process, set of activities, general tasks, and a management structure to certify and accredit information systems (IS). Certification and accreditation (C&A) uses a single-document approach for all classified and unclassified systems in the DoD. All the information relevant to the C&A is collected into one document, the systems security authorization agreement (SSAA), which is then submitted to the Designated Approval Authority for approval.

National Information Assurance Certification and Accreditation Process

The National Security Telecommunications and Information System Security Instruction (NSTISSI) 1000 defines the National Information Assurance Certification and Accreditation Process (NIACAP). The NIACAP establishes a standard national process, set of activities, general tasks, and a management structure to certify and accredit systems that will maintain the information assurance (IA) and security posture of a system or site. NSTISSI 1000 provides an overview of the NIACAP process, roles of the people involved, and the documentation produced during the process. More detailed procedures will be included in the NIACAP implementation manual when it is released.

Defense Information Assurance Certification and Accreditation Process

The Defense Information Assurance Certification and Accreditation Process (DIACAP) (now in draft form) will supercede the DITSCAP (DoDI 5200.40). The DIACAP will establish the standard DoD process for identifying, implementing, and validating IA controls, for authorizing the operation of DoD information systems, and for managing IA posture across DoD information systems consistent with Title III of the E-Government Act, FISMA, and DoD Directive 8500.1. All DoD systems will be required to transition to DIACAP in the future.

The DIACAP is independent of the system life cycle, and its activities may be initiated at any system life-cycle stage—during acquisition, during operation, or at the inception of a major system modification. Generally, the earlier in the system life cycle the DIACAP is initiated, the less expensive and problematic is the implementation of IA capabilities and services.

Response to Suspected Threats or Intrusions

All of these concerns and possibly many others could be drawn from the organizational assessment. This is far from an extensive list of possible management concerns. You will have to understand customers and their motivations to identify the real management concerns. These could be the same reasons for requesting the evaluation, but there are usually more. Technical concerns should be addressed equally with the organizational concerns. Technical concerns usually come from senior technicians and are not normally expressed by management. Some of these could be:

- Blame for findings
- Impact to normal operations
- System downtime
- Loss of data

As you can see, these are concerns that will not normally come from the executive or senior management level of an organization. Middle management or senior technicians are usually the source of technical concerns. Technical concerns during an evaluation will be identified as the team begins working with the technical POCs and can be added as you proceed and discover the previously unknown quirks of the network operations.

Constraints are the factors that will limit or hinder the team in doing the evaluation. Every customer has constraints. The constraints can range from financial considerations, timeframes, resource limitations, and politics to third-party connectivity, legacy applications, and proposed environmental changes. If you fail to address and fully understand the customer constraints in the pre-evaluation, as you proceed with the evaluation you will fail to meet customer expectations. Some of the constraints will be drawn from the organizational assessment and can also be identified by asking common questions such as:

- What are the available times for evaluation activities?
- Are there any financial restrictions on mitigation?

- What personnel staffing issues will limit mitigation or evaluation activities?

- Are there any organizational politics to deal with?

- What third-party connections are there?

If you merge these questions with the technically focused questions to identify any, and hopefully all, of the technical constraints, your team should be able to address all the customer issues. Technical issues have to do with the daily operations and limitations to the evaluation caused by these issues. Some of the technical constraints that you should address include but are not limited to:

- Level of invasiveness

    - Will DOS testing be allowed?

    - How will password-compliance testing be handled?

- Level of detail for recommendations

- Periods of time that the evaluation cannot interfere with normal operations

    - Batch processing periods or expected surge activities

- Are there components that should be considered out of scope of the assessment?

- Are legacy applications or hardware running?

The sources of concerns and constraints can vary from formal discussions held during the scoping of the evaluation or even from informal discussions held during tours of the facility. Just sitting down in the break room with the system administrators will yield information that should be addressed in terms of how it will affect the evaluation. One of the best ways to identify constraints after the initial executive interviews is to do a tour of the facility to see exactly where the systems are maintained and operated. As you are doing the tour, your expertise and experience will lead you to ask questions that will usually bring to light any constraints that were not previously identified. Identifying and continuously managing your customer's concerns and constraints will greatly assist you in obtaining and maintaining management buy-in.

Obtaining Management Buy-In

Why do you need management buy-in to the evaluation process? Without management buy-in, the process will have a significantly lower probability of success and usefulness to the customer. Furthermore, if management agrees with the purpose, goals, and concepts behind an evaluation, finding money for security becomes easier. The "worker bees" will quickly realize that this is important to management and will be more willing to open up and assist in completing the evaluation.

What is buy-in? Buy-in is the visible and tangible support given from the executive level down to ensure that the evaluation is completed fully and in a timely manner. This can be seen by something as simple as the sponsor saying a few words during the opening kick-off meeting or as complicated as having a daily reporting of accomplishments and status.

Figure 3.2 Management and Security

Alright, Russ. Tell me everything I need to know
to have good INFOSEC. You've got 10 minutes

Understand that in terms of evaluations, management usually comes in two flavors. First is the most common management knuckling under to "forced compliance"; the second less likely to be seen as the "Make us better" type. Both will have hired your team to do the evaluation, but their reasons and motivations are different.

The forced compliance group is likely to want the least impact needed to meet regulatory compliance. They usually do not want to do any more than is strictly required to meet the regulatory compliance guidelines. If possible, they would like you to show that the evaluation isn't really necessary because they've already met all the requirements. These evaluations tend to be lowball ones in terms of pricing and to want everything done as quickly as possible so they can get back to business. The final report is viewed as the "check mark in the box" needed for compliance. Motivating this type of management involves more education and perseverance than anything else. Educating without making it seem like you are teaching will, hopefully, cause a leap of logic in their minds and convert them to the second type of management.

The "Make us better" management group is one that we all wish we had all the time. This is the management team that is truly concerned with improvement in organizational security posture. Due to constraints, they may not have had the opportunity to do an evaluation prior to your team being hired. Sometimes the management that is new and really wants to have a fresh set of eyes tell them the truth about their organization's security posture. Either way, positive management will need little if any motivation. "Make us better" management is already motivated to complete a through evaluation. The only help that they will need is usually in understanding new technical issues and the options for mitigation. Again, this will involve covert education of the management team.

Having ready access to the sponsor or senior management during the evaluation allows for timely response to issues or obstacles that cannot be addressed at lower levels. If management is willing and able to show their public support for the evaluation, workers will realize that the evaluation is important and be willing to cooperate. Workers who respect their management will see the value of the evaluation and in turn be advocates for the process.

Notes from the Underground...

Overzealous Management

On occasion we have seen a case where the management has taken what could be construed as too great an interest in what is being accomplished during an assessment. This is the prime cause of what we call the 4-14 syndrome, since it usually is federal service GS-14s or DoD officer grade 04 or above that level who are "afflicted." This syndrome occurs when management wants to ensure that they get a positive report output from the evaluation. Senior management then ensures that the primary POC understands that their promotion or evaluation will be directly tied to the outcome of the evaluation report.

This "promise" causes the primary POC to try to become overly involved and try to steer the evaluation report. The primary POC spends an excessive amount of time trying to "over-the-shoulder watch" everything that occurs and take immediate action to mitigate any finding. Although this is a noble effort, the result involves continually asking the team to revalidate the findings as closed or mitigated, which will significantly increase the evaluation team resources need to complete the evaluation in a timely manner.

Figure 3.3 IT Staff and Security

The boss says that security is extremely important and top priority.
That is, unless it makes something inconvenient.

Obtaining Technical Staff Buy-In

Technical staff buy-in is different from management buy-in. We have seen three types of technical staff buy-in from our experience in doing evaluations. First there is the *IT zealot*. Second is the *IT status quo* personality. Third is the *Keep-it-running* personality. One thing to note here is that all three personality types usually exist within any IT staff.

The zealot is the one that we most prefer to work with. They are hungry to learn anything they can and see the evaluation as a way to learn. The zealot is anxious to find everything that could possibly be wrong because they see it as a significant method to improve the operations and security, which in turn makes them look good to management. These people are easily identified by management as the go-getters. They are ready to start the evaluation before your team is. They will usually come to the initial meeting with network diagrams in hand and try to anticipate anything your team will need. When doing console reviews or scans, they will normally be at your side asking questions and taking notes. They are most likely to try to fix any finding as soon as it is identified. Zealots don't take much motivation to get them involved or get their buy-in. Most of the work is in controlling them or slowing them down. They do not like having any findings on their systems. For a zealot, your team will have to explain that it is not possible to rescan or review every machine every time they fix something. They should understand that it is in their best interest to show how much they have already fixed when the final report is delivered.

The status quo person is the most common one that we find and work with. They are the balancers of requirements and user requests. They see their job as not to improve but to maintain operations, to keep users happy. These workers can be identified as the "always busy" IT staff. They will show up to the initial meeting with a notepad and wait to see what they have to do. These are the people who will be most involved with identifying when network scans or console reviews should *not* be done. They will be at your side to observe console reviews but usually disappear during scans. They want to evaluate any finding and the recommended mitigations. Status quo people are ready to fix any critical findings but are hesitant to fix any other finding until they evaluate the impact to operations. Status quo people need motivation to get their buy-in. Usually it can be done by showing them how implementing mitigations will improve the overall system operations.

The keep-it-running folks are the worst that we have to work with. They usually don't have any emphasis from management or drive to improve security. They usually take the stance, "If it's not broken, why fix it?" They are usually reluctant to give access and question everything that is done. They will argue that identified findings are not really as important as the team makes them out to be and will not want to implement changes that will make them spend time doing what is not already in their schedule. Keep-it-running people are not easy to work with and fortunately are not a very common type to find in an IT shop.

The easiest way to get these people to buy into the evaluation and be willing to assist in the evaluation is to show how this evaluation will benefit them. Part of this effort is ensuring that they understand that you are not part of an audit or inspection, unless of course you are. Set the technical staff at ease as much as possible right at the start by showing how the results are intended not to carry retribution. We normally ensure that all levels of participants understand that we will, as much as possible, assist them with real-time fixes. One point we like to make is that we would love to be able to have a final report with only positive findings.

Figure 3.4 IT Project Assignments

Greg, this is the perfect way to pick who is going to work this project.

Establishing Points of Contact

In learning how to implement the INFOSEC Assessment Methodology (IAM), you learned that there has to be a single senior management point of contact. This person has the responsibility to coordinate the administrative issues such as workspace and access for the evaluation team. This administrative POC is critical to completing the evaluation and will have all the same responsibilities. Your team may even choose to utilize the administrative POC during interviews and system demonstrations. That's your call, but don't underestimate the importance of the administrative POC in crossing the political boundaries that exist in every organization. You need to identify the senior system administrator for each and every system that is included in this evaluation. Use the administrative POC to coordinate the assignment of the technical POCs.

In a perfect world, we would work with all the administrators of each system. Reality check: They have other work that they'll be required to finish even while you are doing the evaluation. Hopefully you will get to work with the most experienced administrators for each system, but don't be surprised if that is not always the case.

So how many is too many technical POCs? The answer is really up to you. From our perspective, we look to have the senior system administrator assigned to each system. This is an issue in many organizations because they may have organized the administrators by host or network operating systems. In this case, you should try to organize the evaluation time periods to consolidate the time requirements of the technical POCs assigned. This means that you might want to look at grouping particular operating system components such as Windows into one evaluation time period. This will allow for the customer to schedule any extra hours required without detriment to the technical POC. Remember, if you are the cause of an administrator being forced to work extra hours, that administrator is not likely to be very cooperative with you.

What is the job or role of these technical POCs? They are both your safety net and operational expertise for the organization. They are the people who will provide you with the root or administrator access for console reviews. Technical POCs will be able to show you how applications interface with the network and what the normal operating conditions are. When you are doing network vulnerability scans, technical POCs represent the body of knowledge for what is normal and what is abnormal. When you are doing network scans, it is entirely possible that some machines will freeze and require restarting. One single job or responsibility of the technical POCs is to validate that when you are complete with each evaluation scenario, the system is functioning normally. To do this, the technical POC checks each of the components to validate normal operation. You and your team want this to occur after each session to ensure that you did not introduce operational errors or unnecessary downtime.

Summary

In this chapter we covered the most significant aspect of doing an evaluation: the pre-assessment. The pre-assessment is crucial to the successful completion of the evaluation. In the pre-assessment, you will identify and obtain the required information that was gathered during the organizational assessment. This information is normally available in the INFOSEC assessment plan or in the final report, if the organizational assessment was accomplished prior to the evaluation. From experience we have found that it is easier and more comfortable for the customer to accomplish the assessment and evaluation at the same time, but there is no requirement to do so. As long as the information from the assessment is available, you can accomplish the evaluation. But without the information from the assessment, you cannot complete the evaluation. Some of the things that you will need include the mission statement, the organizational information criticality matrix and system information criticality matrix(es), customer concerns and constraints, and background requirements that have been identified. These are the absolute minimum pieces of information you'll need, and it is strongly recommended that you get the entire plan or report. If the assessment plan was not done or is not available, you and your team will have to create them to proceed with the evaluation. Without this information you will not be able to adequately map findings back to what the customer has determined is important or to the impact on the organizational mission.

Understanding the customer concerns and constraints is the next area covered in this chapter. This is where you as the evaluator need to understand why you were brought in to do the evaluation. This requires that you completely understand what the customer is concerned about. Most of the time the concerns are focused on compliance issues, and we did cover many of the common requirements, with brief descriptions, that drive executive management. We also include a brief and simplistic way to look at the ROI for security. Management is very concerned with the value of the work being accomplished, and though there is no industry standard for determining the ROI, you can provide some input to the customer on the value of the mitigation versus the probability of expected annual loss.

Next we covered an almost intangible topic: obtaining management buy-in. This is an area in which every evaluator must be knowledgeable. Without management buy-in, the evaluation will have a significantly lower probability of success. When there is management buy-in, the layers of the hierarchy below senior management will quickly realize that the evaluation is important, and this leads to significant improvement in cooperation. We discussed the two most common types of management support: forced compliance and "Make us better." In the forced compliance situation, the management is supporting this evaluation based on pressure from external sources, which tends to lead to minimal support to accomplish the evaluation and not much else. The second type is the preferred one—when management is sincere about improving the security posture, they tend to be more open and flexible to accomplishing the evaluation. When senior management is proactive, they will be accessible and interested in the project's progress. This normally leads to positive evaluations because everybody involved has a positive attitude toward the goal.

Obtaining technical staff buy-in is different. In our experience, you will normally have to deal with three different personalities: the *IT zealot, IT status quo,* and *keep-it-running.* You need to be aware that all three of these types of personality usually exist within any given organization. It has always been out preference to work with the zealot's as they are the most proactive and anxious to learn. Zealots tend to show up to meetings well prepared and ready to hit the ground running. Zealots ask a lot of questions and are almost always taking notes to improve their work habits. Although the zealots are our favorites, the most common type of worker is the status quo type. They are the ones that seem to be always busy. Status quo people are the IT staff personnel who try to maintain a constant balance between management requirements and user requests. They tend to be very observant during console reviews but tend to disappear during scanning activities. The worst to work with are the keep-it-running people. These are the folks who do not want to make changes. They tend to question every request and do not want to implement any changes or fixes without doing research first.

In the last section of the chapter, we talked about the establishing the POCs. As you know, you will always need the administrative or organizational POC. This POC is critical to completing the evaluation because they have the functions of coordinating interviews, demonstrations, technical POC accessibility, and reporting to management how the evaluation is going. The administrative POC is very important to your evaluation team because they are knowledgeable about your customer's political landscape and usually have the authority to be able to cross political boundaries. But how many technical POCs do you want? It is our desire to work with the senior administrator for each system. The role of the technical POC is to be your source of knowledge on how and why components are configured the way they are. Technical POCs should be used to validate that all components are functioning correctly when you are done with each evaluation step. They are also the individuals who will be responsible for implementing any recommendation that your team makes, and their understanding of the operational requirements will make your evaluation go more smoothly.

Solutions Fast Track

The Objectives of the Pre-Evaluation Phase

☑ Obtain the INFOSEC assessment plan or generate that information if it's not available.

☑ An INFOSEC evaluation cannot be accomplished with information from the INFOSEC assessment.

☑ Conducting the evaluation at the same time that you conduct the assessment is beneficial to both the customer and your team.

Understanding Concerns and Constraints

☑ The evaluation team must clearly understand customer concerns and constraints.

☑ Customer concerns are based on requirements, either external or internal.

☑ Customer constraints are based on operational limitations.

☑ A simplistic start to providing ROI can be produced to assist in addressing customer concerns.

Obtaining Management Buy-In

☑ Management buy-in is critical to gaining organizational buy-in and cooperation.

☑ Management buy-in filters down the organizational hierarchy and defines worker cooperation.

Obtaining Technical Staff Buy-In

☑ There are three types of personalities that you will work with: the IT zealot, the IT status quo, and "keep-it-running."

☑ IT zealots are the most proactive and best to work with.

☑ IT status quo is the most common to work with; these are the balancers between requirements and user requests.

Establishing Points of Contact

☑ There are two types of POC, administrative and technical.

☑ The administrative POC handles political issues and scheduling of resources from the customer side.

☑ The administrative POC is your coordination point with management.

☑ The technical POC is usually the senior system administrator for each system being evaluated and is responsible for ensuring that no harm comes to the system from your evaluation activities.

☑ The technical POC should be used to validate that the system is functional when you are done with the evaluation.

Frequently Asked Questions

The following Frequently Asked Questions, answered by the authors of this book, are designed to both measure your understanding of the concepts presented in this chapter and to assist you with real-life implementation of these concepts. To have your questions about this chapter answered by the author, browse to **www.syngress.com/solutions** and click on the **"Ask the Author"** form. You will also gain access to thousands of other FAQs at ITFAQnet.com.

Q: What do you do if you don't have executive-level sponsorship for the evaluation?

A: You have three choices: Scope the evaluation for the portion of the organization that you *do* have sponsorship for (this can be a division or shop), try to do a pre-evaluation meeting with the executives involved to educate and gain sponsorship, or be prepared for noncooperation and a painful evaluation.

Q: What if there has never been an assessment accomplished and they only want the evaluation?

A: The answer is really in two parts. First, you cannot accomplish an INFOSEC evaluation without the INFOSEC assessment being done concurrently or previously. Second, the results provided by your team will not map to what is important to the customer and will not be as useful.

Q: How long does it take to actually do a pre-assessment/evaluation?

A: NSA says it takes three days, but we normally schedule a week onsite to do it.

Q: What do you do when the POC does not respond or do anything?

A: First we try talking to the POC and then we elevate the issue to the sponsor. If that does not work, we work around the POC. That will definitely make for more work for the team lead.

Q: What happens when the system administrator disappears during the evaluation and cannot be found?

A: We normally continue the evaluation and when we are done we contact the administrative POC to have them contact the technical POC to validate that the system is functioning correctly.

Chapter 4

Scoping the Evaluation

Solutions in this chapter:

- Focusing the Evaluation
- Identifying the Rules of Engagement
- Finding the Sources of Scoping Information
- Staffing Your Project

☑ Summary

☑ Solutions Fast Track

☑ Frequently Asked Questions

Introduction

Scoping a project to meet the customer's needs and the evaluation team's capabilities is probably the most challenging activity of the evaluation process. The quality of the evaluation scope is directly correlated to the quality of the evaluation itself. The adage "Measure twice, cut once" applies here. Just as in systems engineering, if you do a good job in the requirements and design phase, the rest of the project will go much more smoothly.

The scoping process identifies the agreed-on steps that will occur during the evaluation process. The scope will ultimately be documented and approved in the technical evaluation plan (TEP). Doing a poor job in the scoping process will result in wasted resources for both the customer and the evaluation team. This will cause extra hours on the job and over-expenditure of financial resources. Poor scope results from a poor understanding of the requirements and expectations of the customer, which may ultimately result in failure to meet customer expectations.

In this chapter, we discuss the components and activities of the scoping process that will give us the majority of the information needed to do an effective and efficient job during the evaluation process. We will look at the process of focusing the evaluation to meet customer expectations. We will talk about what can happen when, and if, the scoping process fails. We also address the areas that will be required to complete the TEP (discussed in Chapter 6) to include reporting level of detail, identifying the rules of engagement, ascertaining system boundaries, and staffing the project. We also look at sources of scoping information and the importance of the scoping questionnaire.

The bottom line is that without a quality scoping process, you will not have a quality evaluation. Doing a good job on the scoping process will give you the greatest opportunity for project success.

Focusing the Evaluation

The purpose of the evaluation scoping process is to ensure that the proper focus is placed on the customer's critical security interests. This focus must take into account customer expectations, deliverables, customer requirements beyond their expectations, and a critical understanding of what happens when scoping fails.

The true success of any project is driven by whether the customer is happy with the process and the end result of the project. This is especially true where the NSA IEM is concerned. The management of expectations starts from the initial customer contact and runs to the end of the project life cycle, during which the evaluation team will answer any remaining questions about the results. If at any point the customer appears not to be satisfied with the process, the evaluation team should make extra efforts to understand the dissatisfaction and come to some resolution.

The Power of Expectations

Expectations drive the customer's sense of satisfaction from the evaluation process and the resulting final deliverables. Well-managed expectations will result in a satisfied customer who feels they have gotten the greatest value for their money. Poorly managed expectations may result in a dissatisfied customer who feels their money and time have been wasted. The really damaging thing about poorly managed expectations, beyond the obvious, is that the customer is less likely to spend the funds necessary for security evaluations in the future, which could reduce their overall security posture. Managing customer expectations and ultimate satisfaction is critical to the success of the evaluation. Chapter 3 goes into additional detail about setting the expectations with the customer.

What Does the Customer Expect for Delivery?

Many evaluations start with the customer not understanding what they are truly looking for as a result of the evaluation process. Providing customer satisfaction can be difficult if you don't exert the appropriate effort during the scoping process to understand the customer needs. This requires an understanding of the level of detail for the recommendations, the boundaries desired for the evaluation, and a strong understanding of the desired use of the results.

Understanding the desired use of the evaluation results will assist the evaluation team lead in determining how the final report can be focused to meet the customer needs. For example, if a department within a company requested the evaluation for the purpose of enlightening senior company management on issues they are not currently addressing, the evaluation results must address those areas of concern. Or the evaluation may be done as proof of due diligence for the organization's insurance company in the current liability insurance renewal process. Understanding what the customer expects for delivery will assist the evaluation team in properly focusing the evaluation effort.

Tools & Traps…

Common Definitions

Approximately 50 percent of the evaluation, assessment, and/or penetration-testing engagements for which we are invited to submit a proposal do not use consistent terminology and definitions and therefore result in an initial misunderstanding of what the customer is looking for. Buzzwords are prevalent throughout the technology industry, including the information security arena. Many customers approach us with a request for a "penetration test." After discussing the project with the customer and understanding what results and deliverables they want out of the process, we find they are commonly looking for an evaluation or a combination assessment/evaluation.

Adjusting Customer Expectations

Expectations will change throughout the evaluation process. Over time, the customer will gain a greater understanding of the evaluation process and the added value of the evaluation to the organization. This normally results in "extras" added to the evaluation and a slightly expanded scope. This could include adding systems to the list of systems to be evaluated and increasing the number of sites or divisions to be included in the process. Changing expectations may also change some of the details of the final deliverable. The business process for changes will determine whether pricing or time lines will need to change as well. Ultimately, the deliverable will be a combination of the original expectations plus the customer's changing expectations or desires as the evaluation process moves forward.

When Scoping Fails

Common mistakes during the scoping process can derail the evaluation effort. Although we can't address every possible scenario, taking into consideration the concerns discussed here will help you avoid the common pitfalls associated with scoping the evaluation. A poorly implemented scoping process will result in an unhappy customer, poor word-of-mouth advertising about your firm, and a frustrating experience for all individuals involved. Changes in the scope of the effort are expected, but they need to be controlled. Otherwise we end up with "scope creep," lost revenue, and busted time lines.

"Scope Creep" and Time Lines

Unplanned and unbid scope changes in projects are often called *scope creep*. This occurs when a project deviates from the written scope at a higher scale. Controlling scope creep can help you effectively manage the overall project. Scope creep not only has an impact on the financial aspects of the project, it also has an impact on the project time lines and the evaluation team's ability to complete the job on time.

Scope creep can be caused by poor planning, unknown areas of the organization that need to be assessed, or a customer desire to further investigate a certain security area that is being analyzed by the evaluation team. Scope creep can also occur when a customer wants to get more out of the effort than they are paying for.

Tools & Traps...

Scope Creep

The most common example of scope creep occurs when more systems or more locations need to be evaluated than were originally identified by the customer. This is generally due to the lack of full communication by the customer with their technical staff or a communications disconnect between the evaluation team and the customer. This is why it is extremely important to be detailed in the assumptions section of the evaluation agreement (the contract). Another example of scope creep occurs with the discovery of additional systems that need to be reviewed as part of the evaluation that were not originally part of the effort.

Restricting Scope Slippage in the Contract

The project manager, team lead, and customer representative should work closely together to avoid scope creep. Any agreed-on changes need to be appropriately documented and, if necessary, those costs should be added into the project. This doesn't mean that all scope changes have to be considered negative or even require a cost increase. However, we do recommend an evaluation of the changes on a case-by-case basis to ensure that expectations are being met.

There are legal ramifications within government contracts for things like scope slippage. To better understand government contracting, you need to go deeper into contracting than is possible this book. Entirely different sets of terminology are related to government contracting. Obtain the necessary expertise to create an appropriate contract for the situation.

Contracting Differences

Don't assume that your experience with either government contracting or commercial contracting fully prepares you for all aspects of contracting. Government contracts and commercial contracts are unique in nature, as are the differences between the government agencies or commercial industries. Be prepared to learn something new with the various entities you work with, and don't get frustrated when one entity does contracting differently than another.

You'll find many sources out there on government contracting. Try a Web search for the most current links, but some possibilities include:

- Business.Gov (www.business.gov/)
- The Small Business Administration (www.sba.gov/GC/)
- Federal Business Opportunities (www.fedbizopps.gov/)

Uneducated Salespeople

Educate your security sales staff on the evaluation process before they are sent into the field to sell an evaluation based on the IEM. They do not have to be experts on the entire process, but they do need to understand what an evaluation is composed of, reasonable expectations of the process, involvement of the customer in the process, and the impact of a complex customer environment on the process.

If you are using the IEM process for evaluations, consider sending the sales staff to an IEM training course. It is an excellent method of obtaining a better understanding of the process and will hopefully result in a better understanding of security overall for the sales staff. Working in conjunction with the evaluation "experts," sales staff can put together a quality sales presentation and proposal. Ensure that they understand not to make promises that they are not sure your organization can keep. This includes level of effort (which impacts cost) and unreasonable expectations on time frames.

Evaluations 101

Here is a simple, high-level overview of the various purposes of an INFOSEC evaluation:

- Reduce the likelihood of external and internal attacks on the network or system
- Identify exposed information through the identification and verification of customer information system assets
- Identify vulnerabilities to systems that process, store, or transmit critical information
- Identify network vulnerabilities
- Identify unintended network presence or services
- Link customer needs, regulatory requirements, and industry best practices to identify the proper INFOSEC posture for the customer
- Validate the technical INFOSEC posture for these systems
- Recommend solutions to mitigate or eliminate those vulnerabilities
- Implement security measures to assist with cost avoidance

Tools & Traps...

Sold up the River

This is not intended as a general slam on salespeople, but we have experienced several incidents where an uneducated salesperson sold a service without knowledge of what the effort entailed or how it could be accomplished. Package pricing a security evaluation without knowledge of who the evaluation is for or how an evaluation is conducted can result in serious mission and financial failure for the evaluation team. Success is measured not only by how well you do your job but also by whether the customer is satisfied with the service they were provided at the price they paid.

Bad Assumptions

Making poor or inappropriate assumptions can have a serious negative impact on your evaluation. A great deal of effort needs to be put into developing and reviewing the assumptions that are made for each evaluation agreement. Assumptions detail the understood environment in which the evaluation will be conducted. They will also identify the expected involvement of the customer in the process in terms of staff availability, scheduling requirements, and time frames.

Why do we have assumptions to begin with? Assumptions are the anticipated conditions or actions that will occur in preparing for or conducting the evaluation process. The assumptions are listed in agreements to ensure that the customer understands what is anticipated of them to support the evaluation team or what they can expect from the evaluation team.

Assumption Topic Areas

The following are examples of information that needs to be included in the assumptions section and that must be as accurate as possible to avoid confusion and poor scoping:

- Location(s) at which the evaluation will be conducted
- Availability of customer personnel for the evaluation
- Scheduling of the evaluation activities to avoid customer impact
- Travel requirements (if any)
- Documentation availability
- Necessary support from the customer in managing the evaluation
- Availability and currency of the network diagrams
- Operating system types for servers and workstations
- Technical expertise of the customer for the detail of recommendations

Poorly Written Contracts

Poorly written contracts are the basis for poor evaluations. Generally speaking, poor contracts are based on bad information, bad assumptions, and lack of attention to detail. A boilerplate evaluation contract can be dangerous if not properly tailored to the current customer. Every organization has different expectations and requirements to meet; the worst kind of evaluation contract has no specific detail related to the customer being evaluated. Several factors can contribute to poorly written contracts: poor scope definition, underbidding, or overbidding of a contract.

Poor Scope Definition

Poor scope definition generally results from a poor understanding of the requirements and expectations associated with a project. From a provider perspective, poor scope definition could mean a loss in revenue and profits for an effort. Poor scoping can result in your consultants having to spend unplanned hours on the job as well as eventual cost overruns. Another major mistake in the scoping effort is *not* having the customer approve the agreed-on scope with a signature. By having the customer sign off on their approval of the scope, you help avoid future issues of the customer denying that they agreed with the scope or possibly forcing additional work for no additional money. Be sure to protect your company. Don't assume anything. Document the agreement in detail.

> **NOTE**
>
> Contracts are one area in which large companies generally have an advantage over smaller companies. They normally have years of experience, a dedicated contracting staff, and strong legal counsel that support their needs in the contracting process.

Underbid or Overbid: The Art of Poor Cost Estimating

Pricing of a bid can be as critical as the quality of the information put into the bid. Understanding the customer environment and limitations from a financial perspective will help you properly price the effort. This closely ties into the assumptions section of the project agreement and the TEP's rules of engagement. The assumptions help determine the level of effort you'll need to put into a project. It is always dangerous to bid a project low to win the bid. Bidding low cuts into your flexibility and profit margin. Bidding high can price you out of contention for the project. True pricing has to come from actual expected effort and your experience as to what it will take to complete it.

Many outside influences can impact the costing efforts. As mentioned, a poor understanding of the requirements and expectations associated with the project is one. Another is salesperson influence on the process—trying to force undue pressure on the process in an attempt to win the bid. This pressure may result in mistakes being made in the costing of the effort. Another pressure from the sales staff runs along the lines of "I said we could do the evaluation for $25,000, so we have to do it for $25,000."

Identifying the Rules of Engagement

The rules of engagement are the boundaries and limits that currently exist or are established to help control the execution of the evaluation. Rules of engagement will basically become a list of "do's" and "don'ts" for the evaluation. The primary concern of the rules of engagement is to ensure the understanding of the customer's and the evaluation team's expectations and limits while the evaluation is under way.

Customer Concerns

Generally a customer will have specific reasons for asking for an evaluation. It will be important to understand the specific concerns the customer wants to address as part of this process. This information contributes directly to the scoping process and helps meet customer expectations. (Customer concerns are further discussed in Chapter 3.) Some of the reasons customers ask for an evaluation are:

- Legislative/regulatory requirements
- Insurance requirements
- Protection of critical infrastructure
- To provide the system owners a certain level of confidence that their information is protected
- As part of a good security engineering and management practice
- In response to suspected threats, security incidents, and Red Team activities
- For an independent review to validate internal reviews
- Because it's the right thing to do

Stating the Evaluation Purpose

Customer concerns have a direct tie to the purpose for the evaluation. We need to understand this purpose as part of the scoping process to better define and document the customer needs. This information will then be included in the TEP, as discussed in Chapter 6.

Customer Constraints

All customers have constraints of some kind, whether time, financial, human, political, or third-party involvement. Failure to discuss, recognize, and clarify constraints with the customer up front and throughout the evaluation process can result in failure of the evaluation project. Some common constraints that may be missed or ignored include:

- Ascertaining available time frames to execute the evaluation
- Financial constraints on the organization to conduct the evaluation
- Personnel resources to support the effort
- Organizational politics
- Third-party control of resources (boundaries)

Impact Resistance and Acceptable Levels of Invasiveness

The evaluation process is not meant to damage or change the customer's business operations or business practices. The intent of the evaluation is to *help* the customer. However, by their nature hands-on evaluations can be intrusive. Therefore, a good understanding of the customer's business processes will help you define factors such as scanning times, node exclusions, and tool limitations. Evaluations that include activities such as DoS testing, war dialing, and password-compliance testing add complexity and intrusiveness to the process. Be sure to address this up front with the customer because this issue will drive the level of effort the evaluation team needs to put into the project, which is a key part of the scoping process. Ultimately you are trying to limit the impact to the customer by not being overly intrusive.

Identifying Scanning Times

To avoid impact to the customer during peak operational and processing times, you need to reach an agreement on when the technical scans and technical testing will be conducted. Often our customers ask us to do scanning between 8:00 P.M. and 6:00 A.M. to avoid operational impact.

When considering this area, you may have four different possible allowable time frames for testing based on the type of testing that is occurring. Discuss with the customer the acceptable testing time frames for the following:

- Administrative network components and systems (noncritical)
- Sensitive information segments
- Mission-critical information segments
- Host evaluations (must be physically present at the system)

Off-Limit Nodes

There may be some systems the customer does not want you scan for vulnerabilities. Work with the customer to define these systems and gain an understanding about the purpose of the exclusion. Be sure to document this understanding in the TEP. The reasons for these off-limit systems will vary, but they could include:

- The system is owned by someone other than the customer.

- The system is so critical that they cannot afford even a remote chance that the system's operations might be impacted.

- The customer knows the system will crash and might not be brought back to operation.

- The customer knows the system will be replaced in the next few days or weeks.

Are You 0wned?

Systems Too Critical to Evaluate

Some customers identify systems they do not want touched because they are too critical to operations to even risk a remote chance that the system might crash. This, of course, is the proverbial "Catch-22." If you don't test a system to know whether it's vulnerable, you cannot have some level of assurance that a malicious hacker or even an accidental hacker won't be able crash the system for you. It is better to crash a system in a controlled environment than to leave the system hanging out there with unknown vulnerabilities. This type of situation may also indicate issues with a customer's business continuity planning or disaster recovery planning processes and procedures, which could need to be identified and addressed on the organizational security side (the IAM).

Evaluation Tool Limitations

Some customers may have had previous negative experiences with some evaluation tools and will not want them run on their network. This should be documented in the TEP and understood by the evaluation team. There may also be an opportunity to further educate the customer on evaluation tools and be able to explain to the customer why they had issues with the tools. The customer could appreciate your candor and change their mind about that specific tool. Some customers also have policies against the use of freeware or shareware tools, which might need to be taken into account when planning the toolkit for the evaluation. This is especially true in some federal government and military locations.

Notification Procedures

Just as every company should have a tested disaster recovery plan, every evaluation should have established procedures in case something goes wrong during the evaluation process. The intent of the evaluation is to *not* break anything, but accidents do happen due to testing tool misconfiguration, misconfigured customer systems, and sometimes just plain old bad luck. Establish who you are going to call in case something seems to quit responding. Normally you'd call the technical POC for the department or group you are evaluating or their designate. Also identify who will be contacted in the event a critical security finding is identified and the evaluation team feels that the customer needs to address it immediately.

Evaluation Addressing

When you're conducting an evaluation, it is best for the evaluation team to utilize static IP addresses for both internal and external evaluation testing so there is no question of whether a potential security incident is a result of the evaluation or a real, malicious hacker. In doing external scanning, be sure to provide the customer with the IPs that the testing is coming from. Don't forget to have the evaluation team members keep a copy of the LOA with them at *all* times while the evaluation is under way, to avoid problems with the customer's internal incident response team or law enforcement. It's also helpful for the evaluators to maintain a constant log of their activities so that if problems or issues do crop up, you'll be better equipped to backtrack and locate the reason for the outage.

   Some customers may prefer that you perform the external scanning from just outside the router or firewall instead of over the Internet. Discuss this with the customer to clarify their expectations from an external testing perspective.

Reporting Level of Detail

Working with the customer on identifying the level of detail required for the findings, discussion, and recommendations in the final report is an important process during scoping. The NSA identifies three specific levels of technical detail for the purposes of completing the final report. These are:

- **Low detail** This level of detail is reserved for the executive summary. Low detail is not overly technical and serves the purpose of providing executives with a view of the security posture without bogging them down in the technical detail.

- **Moderate detail** This is the standard level of detail for the main body of the final report. It is a level of detail that is very technical in nature but not a step-by-step "how-to." This level of detail generally addresses the needs of the supervisors or system/security administrators.

- **High detail** This level of detail is reserved for customers that do not have the technical depth to understand the detail at the moderate level. Developing the recommendations for findings with this level of detail will generally require a great deal more time. High detail will be very technical and will include step-by-step implementation procedures for the customer to follow.

When conducting the scoping process, it is important to address the level-of-detail expectations with the customer. This will drive the level of effort that needs to be estimated in the delivery of the final report. This level of effort clearly affects the resources and amount of time needed to prepare the final report. In other words, time is money.

Clear and Concise Writing

All writing, whether for the TEP or the final report, needs to be clear and concise to ensure proper understanding by the customer and to increase the chance that the customer will actually implement your recommendations. Your writing does not need to be verbose, but it should be easy to understand at the appropriate level to which it is written. Avoid slang and jargon that will potentially confuse the reader. Try to write around the industry you are addressing, using the appropriate terminology for the customer you are working with. We all have a tendency to speak in slang, but this should be avoided in the formal documentation.

Establishing the Evaluation Boundaries

One of the biggest challenges that any evaluation team will confront while trying to define the evaluation process will be locating known or perceived boundaries for the system. Boundaries provide a delineation of the system and limit the scope of each system. A system in the context of the evaluation activities is something that transmits, stores, or processes the critical information types within the customer organization as defined by our IAM pre-assessment process. A system can be a single server or include the workstations that communicate with the server and all media between the two. When we define boundaries, we define them based on the physical aspect of the boundary or the logical transfer of the information from one responsible hand to another.

Physical Boundaries

Physical boundaries are often the easiest for the customer and the evaluation team to understand. The physical boundary of a system may be as simple as the network jack on a wall, a port on a switch, or an interface on a perimeter firewall. In a more metropolitan-based system, the system could be delineated by the particular building within a city in which the system is used exclusively. On a more global basis, perhaps the system is defined by a particular set of replicated servers and workstations at each of 12 global sites that all share the same information database. Again, physical boundaries tend to be more tangible than logical boundaries because they can be "touched" in some physical manner. The following list gives common examples of some physical boundaries you'll see during evaluations:

- Switch port
- Firewall interface
- Perimeter router
- Subnet router interface
- Building entrances and exits

NOTE

> Physical boundaries are defined by the locations (for instance, a room, a building, or a complex) of the system equipment and local procedures regarding the handling and processing of particular types of information.

Logical Boundaries

Logical boundaries are less tangible than physical boundaries and often more difficult for the customer to understand and define. These types of boundaries refer to where the critical information changes hands to another entity that then becomes the responsible party for controlling access to the data. A good example is where a bank transfers information on customer transactions to a partner bank. Once the information leaves the hands of the local bank and moves into the customer's own bank, the information then becomes the responsibility of the partner bank. Thus the security of that information passes to the partner bank as well.

These types of relationships are the best way to view logical boundaries. From an internal customer perspective, maybe we're dealing with multiple entities or branches within the organization that control the same information in different phases of its life cycle. Information may arrive in the system via a Web environment that is strictly controlled by the Web or IT teams and then passes from this network to the procurement department. When the information changes hands and the originating party loses control of and responsibility for the information, we've located a logical boundary for the system at hand. The easiest method for locating these logical boundaries is to create a data flow diagram with the customer. Data flow diagrams emulate the flow of critical information types within the network. This includes flows from primary servers to workstations or hosts that use the information. Network components, such as routers, switches, hubs, and cabling, are also considered during this process.

Logical boundaries are something that might not be easy for upper management and most middle management to understand and recognize. A logical boundary is the point at which the customer has lost their logical control over the information. Usually management does not recognize that this is an issue. The problem is that senior management often does not understand that they really don't have any control over all their information components. This is where you, as the evaluator, must educate them. The customer must understand how the logical boundaries will affect the evaluation scoping. Consider the issues of having the logical boundary set at the perimeter router. Who owns the router? In many organizations, the ISP or a parent organization owns the perimeter router. If the ISP is one of the major providers such as Sprint, MCI, or AT&T, they might not agree to allow any evaluation of the router. The service-level agreement could even forbid review of the rule sets used.

> **NOTE**
>
> Logical boundaries are defined by understanding where responsibility for or authority over the critical information changes hands.

Critical Path and Critical Components

The concepts of critical path and critical components play a key role in how information is handled across the network and how much protection is put into place on the customer's network. *Critical path* is the logical path of communications across the network in which critical information flows. If the path breaks at any point along the critical path, it hampers the organization's ability to perform its mission or serve its customers.

Critical components are those devices that process, transmit, and/or store the critical information. The compromise of critical components, or high-assurance devices, can also hamper the organization's ability to perform its mission or serve its customers.

As part of the scoping effort, the evaluation team needs to work with the customer to ensure that there is a mutual understanding of these key concepts. This is directly related to the processes of identifying critical information and critical systems within the customer's environment as defined by IAM pre-assessment process.

> **NOTE**
>
> Third-party connectivity also plays a key role in the definition of physical and logical boundaries. Typically a third-party connection ends up being both a physical and a logical boundary at the same time. This is due to the fact that control of the information is generally handed off at this point (logical) and there is normally some device or location (firewall, perimeter router, or the like). These are physical boundaries.

Finding the Sources of Scoping Information

Scoping information can come from multiple sources. One of the obvious sources for scoping information is the SOW or RFP that the customer issues to obtain the evaluation services. Generally this information is truncated and requires additional details to properly determine the scope. Additional sources of scoping information can include the customer representative assigned to the project. They will generally provide additional nonproprietary information that is specifically requested of them. If it is a competitive bid, they will generally be required to provide this information to all potential bidders.

Additionally, customer documentation is an excellent source of information about the organization and any related security programs, if the information is available. Useful documentation can include acceptable-use policies, security policies, network architecture diagrams, and results of previous evaluations or audits. Another excellent source of scoping information comes through asking the right questions on a scoping questionnaire.

Customer

The customer is the most critical source of information for the evaluation scope. The customer has some idea what they are looking for and a (normally) general idea of how the results will be used. The customer will provide technical information through the scoping questionnaire, the administrative staff, and the technical POCs.

The Scoping Questionnaire

Obtaining the information you need to properly scope an effort can be a challenge for the proposal team or evaluation team. More often than not, we find that customer SOWs or RFPs are poorly scoped when they are developed. They do not contain enough information or are boilerplate RFPs that contain erroneous information. Many times we have to go back to the customer to collect additional information to finalize any bidding or scoping process we are working on.

This is one instance in which a scoping questionnaire can be useful in obtaining the information needed. A scoping questionnaire provides customers with an easy-to-complete form that asks the relevant questions relating to information needed to properly scope the level of effort for a project. The questionnaire gives a good baseline of information and may lead to additional necessary questions to finalize the details. The scoping questionnaire answers many of the normal questions up front to provide the clarification needed on the project.

NOTE

You should create your own scoping questionnaire using your INFOSEC experience as the basis. This gives you the information you need to develop your contractual scope and make estimates of level of effort and pricing for the contract. Here we provide examples to help get you started.

Information Gained from the Questionnaire

The evaluation scoping questionnaire is the most valuable source of information for collecting the initial information about the customer and the type of work to be conducted. This questionnaire, combined with clarification from the customer, will result in a well understood, documented, and accomplishable evaluation. The critical types of information you are looking for include the following:

- Name of the customer (don't laugh, many forget to tell you)
- POC information for business activities (address, phone, e-mail)
- Administrative POC for the evaluation (address, phone, e-mail)
- Technical POC(s) for the evaluation (address, phone, e-mail)
- Customer mission/industry information
- Emergency situation POC(s) (address, phone, e-mail)
- Physical access coordination information for internal evaluation (site visit requirements and internal scanning information)
- Primary customer concerns for themselves and for their industry
- Applicable legislative, regulatory, or other industry security drivers
- Number of sites they have (including location)
- Number of sites involved with the evaluation (including location and reasons for exclusions)
- Number of internal IP addresses to be evaluated
- Number of external IP addresses to be evaluated
- Network protocols in use by the customer
- Number of workstations to be evaluated
- Number of servers to be evaluated
- Operating systems in use
- How many and type of web servers
- Primary services running on the servers
- Firewall information
- Intrusion detection/prevention information
- Remote access information
- Virtual private network (VPN) information
- Wireless network information
- Converged network information
- Identifiable physical and logical boundary information
- Security architecture that is currently implemented (layered security?)
- Implemented access controls (key cards, biometrics, passwords, single sign-on, and so on)
- Previous evaluation, assessment, audit information
- Security policy and procedure information

- Risk management information, including an understanding of what is being protected and why (IAM information and system criticality information)

- Security review policy (how often are internal and third-party reviews conducted?)

- Physical security policy and procedures

- Incident response policy and procedures

- Disaster recovery policy and procedures

- Personnel security policy and procedures

- Type of evaluation the customer is looking for (how comprehensive)

- IEM baseline activities inclusion and exclusion information

- Date the customer expects/must have the evaluation completed by

- Any limitations/restrictions on the evaluation team

Tools & Traps…

Assumptions Will Hurt You Again and Again and Again

Do not assume anything about your customer. Verify even the most basic anticipated actions to be sure that the customer is on the same page in relation to the rules of engagement and expectations from the evaluation process. Ask questions even when you think you already know the answers. It is better to confirm an answer than be surprised. For example, when dealing with the network protocol used by the customer, you know that 95 percent of the world uses TCP/IP, but through our own painful experiences; we have found that some customers still use IPX as their primary networking protocol. Not many commercial tools will do scanning on IPX networks. This is a bit of critical information that would be helpful to understand prior to starting the evaluation effort.

Value of the Questionnaire

The scoping questionnaire clearly provides a tremendous amount of information for the evaluation team and the customer. The benefit of the scoping questionnaire is twofold:

- It provides critical information for the evaluation team to determine the scope of the effort to make a reasonable estimate of level of effort and, ultimately, the cost of the evaluation.

- It forces the customer to think in detail about what they are trying to accomplish and what they really want to be asking for and can expect from the evaluation process.

Example Responses on a Scoping Questionnaire

The following information shows an example of responses you could see on a scoping questionnaire.

Q: ORGANIZATION NAME

A: Organization for Critical Healthcare

Q: How many physical sites do you have?

A: 3

Q: What is the address of the location(s)?

A: OUCH Headquarters

> 123 Main St.
>
> Mt. Anywhere, US 11111

OUCH Pediatrics

> 125 Main St.
>
> Mt. Anywhere, US 11111

OUCH Rehab

> 121 Main St.
>
> Mt. Anywhere, US 11111

Q: Mission or Business Description

A: The Organized Union for Critical Healthcare (OUCH) has been contracted by Our Lady of Perpetual Pain, Memorial Hospital to handle their information processing. The facility can house up to 5000 patients at a time. The day-to-day operations require automated information systems support for tracking and controlling information that includes admitting/releasing patients, administering medications, scheduling surgeries, feeding patients, tracking traffic to and from the hospital morgue, and various other information for doctors, nurses, and staff. OUCH has developed a single networked system that allows all the functions to be performed from terminals throughout the facility. The connectivity includes all databases and applications, so the information is readily available no matter where in the facility it is needed.

Q: Are there any regulations or legislation that governs your business operations from a security or privacy perspective? (Please list.)

A: Health Insurance Portability and Accountability Act (HIPAA), Joint Commission on Accreditation of Healthcare Organizations (JACHO)

Q: How many total active users are there?

A: 568

Q: How many internal server IP addresses are to be evaluated (by locations)?

A: HQ–5, Pediatrics–0, Rehab–0

Q: How many internal workstation IP addresses at each site to be evaluated?

A: HQ–427, Pediatrics–11, Rehab–5

Q: How many external server IP addresses are to be evaluated?

A: 5

Q: How many external workstation IP addresses are to be evaluated?

A: None

Q: What networking protocols are you running? (TCP/IP, IPX, etc.)

A: TCP/IP

Q: What operating systems are on the workstations?

A: 4 on 98, 4 on Windows XP, remainder on 2000

Q: What operating systems are on the servers?

A: Windows NT and Windows 2000

Q: What services are running on the servers? (Web, DNS, etc.)

A: WINS, DNS, Web

Q: Do you have a firewall(s)?

A: Yes, 2—Checkpoint NG running on Nokia

Q: Do you have an active network and/or host-based IDS?

A: No

Q: Will you require war dialing at any/all sites to detect rogue modems?

A: Yes, all sites, 65 numbers

Q: Do you require any tests on denial of service (DOS) vulnerabilities?

A: Yes, during nonpeak hours

Q: How many Web servers are active and accessible by the public?

A: Web servers hosted by external third party

Q: What type of Web servers (Apache, IIS)?

A: Apache over Slackware

Q: How many Web servers are active and for internal use only?

A: 1

Q: What type of Web servers (Apache, IIS)?

A: IIS on Windows 2000

Q: Do you currently utilize a RAS server for external access?

A: Yes, Cisco

Q: Do you currently utilize a remote VPN product for external access (i.e., Altiga VPN concentrator)?

A: Yes, Checkpoint VPN

Q: Who will be the primary point of contact (POC) at your organization?

A: Name: Bob Smith

Phone: 555-111-1111

Cell: 555-222-3333

E-mail: bsmith@ouch.me

Job title: IT Director

Q: Are you utilizing a domain architecture?

A: Yes

Q: Are you utilizing a Windows Active Directory-based architecture?

A: No

Q: Are you utilizing a Novell NDS-based architecture?

A: No

Q: Do you have wireless networking?

A: Yes

Q: Do you have mainframe environments?

A: Yes, RS6000

Q: Is there third-party connectivity?

A: Yes

Q: Are you using voice-over-IP (VOIP) or IP telephony?

A: No

Q: Are you using a converged network architecture?

A: No

Q: Do you have documented security policies?

A: Yes, but outdated

Q: Are there any known limitations we need to be aware of?

A: No

Q: Do you have a date on which the assessment/evaluation must be completed?

A: Yesterday

Evaluation Requestor

The individual or group requesting the evaluation will provide key evaluation information. The requestor may not be the primary person or even in the group inside the organization for which you will be doing the evaluation. Normally this occurs in some kind of formal services request such as SOW or RFP. These formal requests normally don't contain the level of detail necessary to fully scope out an effort. This identifies the importance of the scoping question-naire and the interaction with other individuals.

Customer Senior Leadership

The customers' senior leadership will have a general idea of what they want to accomplish with the IEM process. They generally possess information about their customers, mission, and suppliers and what they need to accomplish from the evaluation process.

Administrative Customer Contact

The administrative customer contact will play multiple roles in the scoping process. One role is to be a central location for the collection of information as it is requested and provided. They will also be able to recommend people to talk to for collecting additional detailed information. They also arrange for evaluation team office space, phone access, and facility access. The administrative customer contact will likely be the person coordinating answers for the scoping questionnaire.

Technical Customer Contacts

The technical customer contacts (remember, there is likely to be more than one) will provide critical technical information in the scoping process. They will identify the appropriate IPs and subnets that will be scanned, along with the appropriate and acceptable time frames for each of the subnets being dealt with. The technical customer contacts will also know the critical nodes and the off-limit nodes within their environments. These individuals may be the emergency contacts for their area or department during the evaluation. You will want to have this information well documented.

Evaluation Team

The evaluation team is also a reasonable source of information for scoping information. They will spend time researching the customer and collecting information on their operations before you begin the evaluation effort. They will be able to speak to the validity of some of the information provided. The evaluation team is composed of the team lead and team members, each of whom may be able to provide good scoping information.

Evaluation Team Lead

The evaluation team lead plays a crucial role in the scoping process. The team lead will likely have spent time talking to the customer and gaining valuable information on evaluation objectives and goals. The team lead may have also been involved in previous engagements with the customer, such as assessments, evaluations, Red Teams, or other activities that would add value to the scoping process.

Evaluation Team Members

The evaluation team members also play a key role in the scoping process. They will likely have spoken with the technical members of the customer's staff and gained additional understanding of the customer's technical security needs. This can help bring forward scoping issues that might otherwise be overlooked by the customer's management.

Validating Scoping Information

After you complete the process of gathering scoping information, it is helpful to validate the information through multiple sources, as available. Chapter 2 covers some possible options for scope information validation. Always keep in mind that the customer will have likely missed something that should have been included. Once an error is discovered, discuss with the customer the options and implement the necessary changes with as little impact as possible.

Staffing Your Project

Deciding on the correct composition of the evaluation team is important in making the project a success. Having the wrong mix for the team can result in an unsatisfied customer and potentially the failure of the project. In this section, we look at how the team composition for each evaluation is important and some of the assurances needed when naming the evaluation lead and the evaluation team.

Job Requirements

The actual scope of the project determines the team composition for the evaluation. It is important for the team lead and the team members to be knowledgeable of the industry the customer is working in, the related regulations and guidance that govern the customer, and any legislative requirements that drive the customer's business. For example, if your team has been contracted to perform an evaluation on a medical institution, it would be most beneficial to have team members familiar with HIPAA. A close examination of the customer's environment will also determine the technical composition of the evaluation team.

> **TIP**
>
> The critical thing to remember is that the success of the evaluation process depends on the technical expertise and critical thinking of the evaluation team members. Almost anyone can run a scanning tool, but it takes specific expertise to understand and accurately interpret the results.

Networking and Operating Systems

Gaining an understanding of the technical operating environment is critical for selecting the best team members. A major failure in many evaluations is having the wrong technical expertise on the team. Having an individual with primarily strong UNIX skills evaluate Microsoft Windows systems would probably prove to be a bad decision, as would having a Cisco Networking expert evaluate UNIX systems. The technologies are not the same, and to garner respect and cooperation in the evaluation efforts, the evaluation team needs to speak the same language as the person or team being evaluated. This is not to say that you cannot have an individual on your team with strong skills in multiple technical areas. In fact, your evaluation team will most likely be more successful if you have technical team members with multiple applicable skills that can be utilized during the evaluation process.

Some of the most critical expertise to have involved on your team could include Windows Server and WorkStation Operating Systems (Win NT, Win 2000, Win 2003, Win XP), UNIX expertise (Sun Solaris, HPUX), Linux expertise (Red Hat, Slackware, Mandrake), Cisco IOS expertise, and possibly mainframe expertise (AS400, VAX, or VMS). Each customer has a different combination of technical networking and computer operating systems. Good sources of this information are the network architecture descriptions and current network diagrams.

Hardware Knowledge

Understanding the various types of hardware the customer uses is also helpful. These can include various types of firewalls, intrusion detection systems, server platforms, routers and switches, and phone systems. This information will also be useful in conducting the evaluation. If you have a customer that is purely a Cisco shop, you will want an individual who is versed in Cisco on the team. If they have a combination of hardware and software, consider having a very knowledgeable generalist on the team.

Picking the Right People

Final selection of the evaluation team is a process of matching the understood needs of the customer with the expertise of available team members. Finding the right match for the IEM pre-evaluation phase and ultimately the onsite phase is critical to team success.

Matching Consultants to Customers

Consultants are matched to each customer based on the industry the customer is working in and the specific technologies the customer utilizes in their operational environment.

- **Team lead characteristics** The team lead is the single most critical member of the evaluation team and should be the team leader for both the pre-evaluation and onsite evaluation phases. This individual is responsible for constant communication and coordination with both the evaluation team and the customer. The team lead should have a minimum of three security evaluations supporting other team leaders to ensure that he or she understands the dynamics involved and has adequate experiences to fall back on and share with the customer. This individual must be an extremely dynamic person capable of facilitating discussion in multiple types of environments and multiple political situations. The team lead should be knowledgeable in the industry in which the customer is primarily working. The team leader does not necessarily have to be a technical expert, but understanding the terminology of the organization and industry is important. It is wise to assign a dynamic technical team member to back up the team lead in case of emergency or some other situation.

- **Technical team members** Technical team members need to be experienced in a variety of technologies specifically related to the technical environment of the customer. Industry expertise would be a value-add, but technical expertise is more essential in this case. Technical team members need to be dynamic enough to communicate well with the customer team to obtain the information needed to fully evaluate the customer security environment.

Personality Issues

In any effort, there is the possibility of personality conflicts between team members or with members of the customer organization. The team lead needs to understand this possibility and attempt to avoid these situations or implement buffers to prevent the situation from being an issue. This is more of a political issue than anything. Customers will sense tension between team members, which can detract from the overall success of the evaluation. When a conflict does arise and the issues cannot be resolved in a less restrictive manner, team member reassignment may be necessary. Since the effort is about customer satisfaction, the team members need to attempt to adjust to the customer first before trying to force a change in the customer.

Summary

Effectively scoping your evaluation will save a great deal of time and headaches as the evaluation moves forward. This basic foundation sets the tone for the entire evaluation process, gives the evaluation team its first opportunity to gain detailed information about the customer, and gives the customer its first opportunity to communicate with the evaluation team. Creating a good environment throughout the scoping and contracting process generally leads to positive results throughout the entire evaluation process.

Once the customer is convinced that an evaluation is needed, they may begin working with you directly or may be required to go out for competitive bid through an RFP or some other proposal solicitation process. The RFP will contain important information necessary to write a proposal or a contract. The most critical challenge is establishing the scope of the effort and related assumptions to determine the level of effort and costing required for executing the project.

Another challenge is avoiding the normal pitfalls that can occur with any scoping process. The pitfalls come from lessons learned over years in the contracting process. Be sure to use recommendations from your legal staff and experienced team members in putting together your final scope and contract. Unfortunately, the pitfall information is made up of primarily "thou shall not" statements:

- Thou shall not miss addressing specific customer concerns in your scoping process.
- Thou shall not make bad scope assumptions.
- Thou shall not allow outside influences to affect the accuracy of the scoping process.
- Thou shall not let "scope creep" go unmanaged.
- Thou shall not write bad contracts that either underbid or overbid a project.

You must establish, early in the process, the customer's expectations as related to the level of detail of recommendations that must be included in the final reporting process. *High* level of detail will require additional resources during the reporting process and are not considered standard, whereas the standard *medium* level of detail will be easier to estimate. *Low* level of detail is reserved for the executive summary.

The rules of engagement encompass several activities that will determine certain actions and help you manage customer expectations. These activities help establish ground rules for executing the task. The areas that will be addressed in this process include:

- Determine acceptable levels of invasiveness for the evaluation.
- Determine time frames for the actual technical testing.
- Establish notification procedures during the evaluation process (emergency and none-mergency).
- Establish and report the IPs that will be used for the evaluation.
- Carry out legal reviews and a letter of authorization (Chapter 5).

Critical to the success of the evaluation is understanding the physical and logical boundaries for the evaluation process. This can also include third-party relationships and network architecture limitations. The evaluation team and the customer want to avoid crossing these boundaries and creating problems within the customer organization.

There are several sources of scoping information to include regarding both the customer and the evaluation team. The most valuable source of initial detailed customer information is via the scoping questionnaire. The scoping questionnaire plays a vital role in information collection and will help to get the customer focused on thinking about the critical technical resources within their environment.

Selecting your project staff depends on the size of the customer organization being evaluated, the industry in which the customer works, and the technologies the customer employs. The number of people necessary to conduct the evaluation depends on similar factors and also must take into consideration the customer's desired time line and the geographic separation of the customer's organizational components. Technical drivers to consider include the types of hardware and software the customer is using as well as the operating systems in use on the servers, workstations, and network components. Experience will drive the process of matching the consultants to the customers. No technology or cookie-cutter template can replace the experience and critical thinking of the evaluation team.

Throughout the entire process of scoping and preparing for the evaluation, never lose sight of your number-one goal: meeting customer expectations. How do you do this? Through effective communication with the customer, communication with the evaluation team, customer education, working with customer time lines, and gaining a common understanding of the level of commitment required to complete the evaluation process.

Solutions Fast Track

Focusing the Evaluation

- ☑ Be sure to address and understand the expectations of the customer.

- ☑ Common definitions of evaluation activities are critical to meeting expectations.

- ☑ The evaluation team is a facilitator and may have to attempt to adjust customer expectations to be able to accomplish the evaluation.

- ☑ Failures with scoping will make it difficult to have a successful evaluation.

Identifying the Rules of Engagement

- ☑ Identify customer concerns and constraints.

- ☑ Determine scanning time frames.

- ☑ Identify notification procedures while the evaluation is ongoing (emergency and general).

☑ Provide evaluation addressing (IP) information to the customer.

☑ Determine necessary level of technical detail for the final report.

☑ Get appropriate legal reviews.

☑ Physical boundaries are ones you can touch.

☑ Logical boundaries are where information control changes.

☑ Some boundaries can be both logical and physical.

Finding the Sources of Scoping Information

☑ Get information from the customer.

☑ Get information from the evaluation team.

☑ Effectively utilize the scoping questionnaire to gain information.

Staffing Your Project

☑ Select the team leader based on facilitator and leadership skills as well as knowledge of the customer's industry area being evaluated.

☑ Select evaluation team members based on technical expertise and their ability to communicate with the customer.

☑ Have a backup plan for team member augmentation in case a situation arises (emergency, termination, conflict, or the like).

Frequently Asked Questions

The following Frequently Asked Questions, answered by the authors of this book, are designed to both measure your understanding of the concepts presented in this chapter and to assist you with real-life implementation of these concepts. To have your questions about this chapter answered by the author, browse to **www.syngress.com/solutions** and click on the **"Ask the Author"** form. You will also gain access to thousands of other FAQs at ITFAQnet.com.

Q: Can I always meet customer expectations?

A: Unfortunately, no. You can be the greatest evaluation company to ever exist and you could still run into a customer that just cannot be satisfied. Hopefully you will be able to identify this early in the scoping process so that you can get out of it early. In most case (but not all), you can identify a problem like this early in the evaluation process.

Q: Why are rules of engagement so important?

A: Rules of engagement establish the "do's" and "don'ts" of conducting the evaluation. They are important to ensure that you have established rules for executing the evaluation process and help maintain customer expectations.

Q: Am I limited to only the customer and the evaluation team for information related to scoping?

A: No. Scoping information can come from additional places. Two possible additional sources that have been mentioned are: publicly available information (Internet and public reports) and third parties associated with the customer (contractors and the customer's customers). The publicly available information is important to see what types of information are shared and available with the public. You can look for consistencies and discrepancies with the information you have collected. Third-party information should only be collected if the customer is aware you are doing this activity.

Q: I thought scoping was mostly a paperwork drill. Can't the salespeople put this together?

A: The scoping process requires a combination of technical and managerial input to provide the greatest value. It's more than a paperwork drill—it is an information collection and validation process that is critical to the success of the project. Do you want to trust that a salesperson has the necessary background and current technical experience to do this correctly and completely? No!

Q: Shouldn't the RFP or SOW tell me everything I need to know about the scope of the evaluation?

A: In an idea world, yes. However, in over 16 years of doing information security for government and commercial sectors, I have never found an RFP or SOW that had all the information needed to scope the evaluation. There are always additional questions that need to be answered.

Q: Once the initial scope has been finalized, should I allow the scope to change?

A: It's likely that the scope will change through the conducting of the evaluation. How you manage that change is an internal decision. Not every scope change will require a modification of costing to the customer, but many will. Be sure to address the handling of scope changes early in the evaluation scoping process.

Chapter 5

Legal Principles for Information Security Evaluations[1]

Solutions in this chapter:

- **Uncle Sam Wants You: How Your Company's Information Security Can Affect U.S. National Security (and Vice Versa)**

- **Legal Standards Relevant to Information Security**

- **Selected Laws and Regulations**

- **Do It Right or Bet the Company: Tools to Mitigate Legal Liability**

- **What to Cover in IEM Contracts[2]**

- **The First Thing We Do…? Why You Want Your Lawyers Involved From Start to Finish**

☑ Solutions Fast Track

☑ Frequently Asked Questions

WARNING: THIS CHAPTER IS NOT LEGAL ADVICE

This chapter provides an overview of a number of legal issues faced by information security evaluation professionals and their customers. Hopefully, it will alert readers to the issues on which they should consult qualified legal counsel experienced in information security law. This chapter, however, does not, and cannot, provide any legal advice or counsel to its readers. Readers should not, under any circumstances, purport to rely on anything in this chapter as legal advice. Likewise, following any of the suggestions in this chapter does not create an "advice-of-counsel" defense to regulatory or law enforcement action or to civil legal claims. Readers involved in information security are strongly urged to retain qualified, experienced legal counsel.

Introduction

You have watched the scene hundreds of times. The buttoned-down, by-the-book police lieutenant and the tough-as-nails, throw-out-the-rules-to-save-lives detective debate in front of the police chief. A child is kidnapped and the clock is ticking; a murder is about to be committed and the judge will not issue a warrant. The world-weary police chief has to make a split-second decision. Is there a way to live within the law but save the child? How does the police chief balance the duty to protect the people of the city with fealty to the rulebook? Is there a creative way to do both? On television, this scene usually happens in an aging, shabby, police headquarters office furnished with Styrofoam cups of stale coffee, full ashtrays, fading green walls, and rickety metal desks. Now, imagine this same drama being performed on an entirely different stage.

Uncle Sam Wants You: How Your Company's Information Security Can Affect U.S. National Security (and Vice Versa)

It is September 2011. As the tenth anniversary of al-Qa'ida's devastating attacks on our nation approaches, the president is faced with increasingly clear intelligence that what's left of the infamous terrorist group has fulfilled its longstanding ambition to be able to launch a devastating attack on the U.S. through cyberspace. Perhaps they will disable our air traffic control or financial exchange network. Perhaps they will penetrate Supervisory Control and Data Acquisition (SCADA) systems to attack dams or other energy facilities. Perhaps they will shut down power to hundreds of hospitals where surgery is underway. Or maybe they will directly target our heavily information systems-dependent military forces. The targets and magnitude are far from clear.

As September 11, 2011 dawns though, it becomes obvious that cyber-attacks are underway, even though the perpetrators are undetermined. What becomes increasingly clear is that the attacks are striking us directly, not from overseas; from dozens, perhaps hundreds, of university and corporate servers right here in the U.S. The scene that follows plays out in the stately, wood-paneled, electronically sophisticated confines of the Situation Room in the West Wing of the White House. Our protagonists here are The Secretary of Defense, the Director of National Intelligence, the National and Homeland Security Advisors to the president, and the Attorney General. And, of course, in this scene, the decision maker carrying the weight of the world is not a big city police chief, but the President of the United States.

In all likelihood, the president will receive conflicting advice from his senior advisors. Some will insist that U.S. law prohibits the government from disabling the servers within the U.S. from which the attacks are coming, or even trying to learn who is behind the attacks. These advisors urge caution, despite intelligence indicating that the attacks are actually coming from terrorists overseas, using the servers in the U.S. as "zombies" to carry out their plot. These advisors will further argue that the president has no option but to use the cumbersome and time-consuming criminal law process to combat these attacks. The attorney general's law enforcement officers must collect information, go to a federal judge, and get a warrant or, in this case, dozens or hundreds of warrants, to try to determine who is behind the attacks (unless emergency access without a warrant is authorized by law). Even in such emergencies, organizing and directing law enforcement control over hundreds or thousands of zombies is an overwhelming effort.

Other officials will advise the president that by the time any progress will be made going the law enforcement route, devastating damage to the critical infrastructure may already have occurred, and the overseas perpetrators disappeared, covering their tracks. These advisors will argue strenuously that the president has ample constitutional and legal authority to use any element of U.S. power (military, intelligence, or law enforcement) to defeat the attacks and defend the nation. They will argue that using the normal law enforcement route would not only be futile, but would amount to an abdication of the president's primary constitutional responsibility to protect our nation and its people from attack. Finally, they will respectfully remind the president of the sage advice of Vietnam War era U.S. Supreme Court Justice Arthur Goldberg that "While the constitution protects against invasions of individual rights, it is not a suicide pact."[3]

As a purely legal and constitutional matter, the president's more hawkish advisors will likely be correct.[4] However, that in no way will lessen the terrible moral, ethical, and political burden that will fall on the president: whether or not, in the absence of perfect information, to order counterattacks on information infrastructures inside the U.S.

While reasonable experts still disagree on the probability that such a scenario will arise in the next decade (and there are differences of opinion even among the authors of this chapter), most agree that the scenario is technically possible.[5] The U.S. National Strategy to Secure Cyberspace describes the following necessary conditions (which exist today) for "relative measures of damage to occur [to the United States] on a national level, affecting the networks and systems on which the Nation depends:

- Potential adversaries have the intent.
- Tools that support malicious activities are broadly available.
- Vulnerabilities of the Nation's systems are many and well known.[6]

Thus, even in an unclassified publication, the U.S. government has confirmed that our adversaries, whether terrorists, rogue states, or more traditional nation-state enemies, possess a classic combination for the existence of threat: intent + capability + opportunity. If September 11, 2001 taught us anything as a nation, it is that when these three are present, we had better be prepared.

More concretely, senior Federal Bureau of Investigation (FBI) officials and others have testified before Congress that terrorist groups have demonstrated a clear interest in hackers and hacking skills; the FBI predicts that, "terrorist groups will either develop or hire hackers."[7] Material found in former al-Qa'ida strongholds in Afghanistan showed al-Qa'ida's interest in developing cyber-terror skills.[8] Former U.S. government "cyberczar" Richard Clarke pointed out that a University of Idaho student, arrested by FBI agents on allegations of terror links, was seeking a PhD in cyber security. Clarke warns that, "similarly to the fact that some of the Sept. 11 hijackers had training in flight training, some of the people that we're seeing now related to [al-Qa'ida] had training in computer security."[9] Several experts, including cyber experts at Sandia National Laboratories and the U.S. Naval Postgraduate school, have bluntly asserted that adversaries could disrupt significant portions of the U.S. power grid, for time periods ranging from minutes, to days, and even longer.[10]

Cyber attacks have already been used to disrupt online elections in Canada, and attacks by terrorist groups have been launched to "crash" government computers during elections in Indonesia, Sri Lanka, and Mexico.[11] Finally, apart from terrorist groups and rogue states, a number of nations potentially adversarial to the U.S. now openly include cyber warfare as part of their existing military doctrine, including China and Russia.[12]

This scene, then, is plausible,[13] except that we will be lucky if it takes until 2011 to play out.

Many international legal experts assert that, under internationally recognized laws of armed conflict, attacks by foreign nations or international terrorists using bits and bytes through cyberspace can be acts of war just as can the use of guns or bombs or fuel-laden airliners.[14] If a nation determines that a cyber attack is an act of war against it, that determination, in turn, triggers a number of rights on the part of those attacked to take defensive or responsive action against their attackers.[15] Recognizing the threat of a cyber attack and the potential need for more than a law enforcement response, President Bush in 2003 announced a new U.S. policy with regard to such attacks:

> "When a nation, terrorist group, or other adversary attacks the United States through cyberspace, the United States response need not be limited to criminal prosecution. The United States reserves the right to respond in an appropriate manner. The United States will be prepared for such contingencies."[16]

In a cyber attack (unlike in a conventional military attack), it may be difficult for decision makers to know against whom to take action to stop the attack and/or respond. Unlike a terrorist bombing, though, or even the heinous September 11, 2001 attacks, a cyber attack may continue for a long enough period of time that rapid defensive action may dramatically reduce the damage done to the critical infrastructure and economy, even where the perpetrator is still unknown.

Thus, a cyber attack in progress using "zombied" servers inside the U.S. will present decision makers with a uniquely vexing dilemma. If they do nothing in the initial minutes and hours after the attack is underway, they may allow far greater damage than if they take decisive action to stop the attack and disable the attacking machines. Taking such action, however, risks damage or destruction to the zombied servers themselves, perhaps without identifying the guilty parties. Further, doing so can destroy information that may be needed later to identify and apprehend the perpetrator(s).

Making the situation even more dangerous and complex is the fact that, "distinguishing between malicious activity originating from criminals, nation state actors, and terrorists in real time is difficult."[17] In many cases, affirmative attribution will be nearly impossible with today's technology. Thus, decision makers facing the agonizing choice of taking action to disable or destroy zombied servers inside the U.S. or risking greater damage to our nation if they wait, may not know in time to make a sound decision on whether a true attack is underway or whether what looks like the initial stages of an attack is instead other malicious activity.

What does this mean to information security evaluation professionals and their customers? First and foremost, it means that *you do not want the "zombied" servers used in a cyber attack to be yours.* When the U.S. (or another nation)[18] decides to mount an official response against the hijacked servers being used to launch an attack, it will be a very bad day for the entity whose servers are being used. Additionally, though prudent information security consultants will remain current on all potential threat vectors for purposes of protecting your customers' networks, the identity of any particular threat will be largely irrelevant, even if the origin could be determined. Custodians of sensitive information of any kind have myriad reasons to develop and maintain a reasonable information security posture: business operational needs; preventing economic loss and industrial espionage; mitigating potential litigation, regulatory, and prosecution risks; and maintaining a reputation for responsible security vis-à-vis others in the same business.

The risk of involuntarily becoming part of a cyber attack, or defending against such an attack, adds another important incentive to do what most businesses and educational institutions already recognize as the right thing to do. Unlike other motivations for information security, however, avoiding involvement in a cyber attack is important even if an organization does not maintain any "sensitive" information. Unlike "traditional" hackers, criminals, and others who might exploit information security vulnerabilities, terrorists do not ignore companies simply because they are unable to find sensitive information. Instead, terrorists care about what damage can be done using your servers as proxies. And governments (ours or others) also will not care what information you have or do not have, if it is determined that your servers are involved in an attack and must be neutralized (or worse).

Second, understanding the way governments see information security provides a context for understanding how policy statements contribute to the development of a legal "duty" for individuals and organizations to secure their portions of cyberspace (discussed in greater detail below). In a nutshell, the actual knowledge or constructive knowledge (i.e., information in the public domain) of public policy mandating private "owners" of cyberspace to secure their components, may create a legal "duty" to do so, which could be the subject of future litigation. Likewise, emerging federal policy on potential cyber attacks could well contribute to the movement, already gathering steam, to further regulate private information security at the federal level.

Legal Standards Relevant to Information Security

Laws are made by politicians and politicians are driven by public and media reaction to specific incidents. Laws, therefore, are made piecemeal, at least until a critical mass is reached, which then leads lawmakers to conclude that an emerging patchwork of related, but often inconsistent, laws and regulations require an omnibus law to create consistency and greater predictability. In the absence of such a unifying federal law, particular industries or sectors are targeted for regulation as perceived problems in those industries become public. Laws and regulations covering targeted industries are gradually expanded through civil litigation and regulatory action that is limited only by the patience of judges and the imagination of plaintiffs' lawyers, prosecutors, and regulators.

This is the current situation in the law of information security. As discussed in "Selected Federal Laws" below, federal law regulates information security for, among other things, personally identifiable health care information, financial information of individuals, and, to an increasing degree, financial information in the hands of publicly traded companies. Though there is no "omnibus" federal statute governing all information security, the standards of care being created for these specific economic sectors are being "exported" to other business areas through civil litigation, including by regulators and state attorneys general.[19]

For information security practitioners, this is a good news/bad news story. Often, attempts at "comprehensive" regulation turn out to be a jumbled mess, particularly when multiple economic sectors with differing operational environments and needs are being regulated. Such regulation can be particularly ineffective (or worse) when promulgated before the private sector, which has developed solid, time-tested best practices, implements a workable solution. On the other hand, a patchwork of different federal, state, and international laws and regulations (as is the current state of information security law), can be confusing and puts a premium on careful, case-specific legal analysis and advice from qualified and experienced counsel

Selected Federal Laws

To illustrate the array of laws that impact information security, the following provides a general survey of statutes, regulations, and other laws that may govern information security consultants and their customers. This list is not exhaustive, but may help identify issues in working with customers and in understanding which "best practices" have actually been adopted in law.

Gramm–Leach–Bliley Act

One of the earliest U.S. government forays into mandating information security standards was the Gramm-Leach-Bliley Act (GLBA).[20] Section 501(b) requires each covered financial institution to establish "appropriate safeguards" to: (1) ensure the security and confidentiality of customer records and information; (2) protect against anticipated threats or hazards to the security or integrity of those records; and (3) protect against unauthorized access to, or use of, such records or information which could result in substantial harm or inconvenience to any customer.[21] GLBA required standards to be set by regulation for safeguarding customer information.[22] This task was accomplished with the promulgation of the Interagency Guidelines Establishing Standards for Safeguarding Customer Information (the "Guidelines").[23]

The Guidelines apply to Customer Information maintained by covered "financial institutions," both of which terms are broadly defined under applicable law and regulations. The Guidelines require a written security program specifically tailored to the size and complexity of each individual covered financial institution, and to the nature and scope of its activities.[24]

Under the Guidelines, covered institutions must conduct risk assessments to customer information and implement policies, procedures, training, and testing appropriate to manage reasonably foreseeable internal and external threats.[25] Institutions must also ensure that their board of directors (or a committee thereof) oversees the institution's information security measures.[26] Further, institutions must exercise due diligence in selecting and overseeing, on an ongoing basis, "service providers" (entities that maintain, process, or otherwise are permitted access to customer information through providing services to a covered institution).[27] Institutions also must ensure, by written agreement, that service providers maintain appropriate security measures.[28]

Health Insurance Portability and Accountability Act

The Health Insurance Portability and Accountability Act of 1996 (HIPAA) became law in August 1996. Section 1173(d) of HIPAA required the secretary of Health and Human Services (HHS) to adopt security standards for protection of all Electronic Protected Health Information (EPHI).[29] Development of these security standards was left to the HHS secretary, who promulgated the HIPAA Security Final Rule (the "Security Rule") in February 2003.[30] All covered entities, with the exception of small health plans, must now comply with the Security Rule.[31]

Because HIPAA has, in some ways, the most elaborate and detailed guidance available in the realm of federal law and regulation with regard to information security, we focus more on the HIPAA Security Rule than any other single federal legal provision. In addition, many of the general principles articulated in the Security Rule are common to other legal regimes dealing with information security. As a general framework, the HIPAA Security Rule: (a) mandates specific outcomes; and (b) specifies process and procedural requirements, rather than specifically mandated technical standards. The mandated outcomes for covered entities are:

- Ensuring the confidentiality, integrity, and availability of EPHI created, received, maintained, or transmitted by a covered entity[32]

- Protecting against reasonably anticipated threats or hazards to the security or integrity of such information[33]

- Protecting against reasonably anticipated uses or disclosures of EPHI not permitted by the HIPAA Privacy Rule[34] and

- Ensuring compliance with the Security Rule by its employees.[35]

Beyond these general, mandated outcomes, the Security Rule contains process and procedural requirements broken into several general categories[36]:

- **Administrative Safeguards**[37] Key required processes in this area include: conducting a comprehensive analysis of reasonably anticipated risks; matrixing identified risks against a covered entity's unique mix of information requiring safeguarding; employee training, awareness, testing and sanctions; individual accountability for information security; access authorization, management, and monitoring controls; contingency and disaster recovery planning; and ongoing technical and non-technical evaluation of Security Rule compliance.

- **Physical Safeguards**[38] Physical security safeguard measures include: mandated facilities access controls; workstation use and workstation security requirements; device and media controls; restricting access to sensitive information; and maintaining offsite computer backups.

- **Technical Safeguards**[39] Without specifying technological mechanisms, the HIPAA Security Rule mandates automated technical processes intended to protect information and control and record access to such information. Mandated processes include authentication controls for persons accessing EPHI, encryption/decryption requirements, audit controls, and mechanisms for ensuring data integrity.

The Security Rule contains other requirements beyond these general categories, including: ensuring, by written agreement, that entities with whom a covered entity exchanges EPHI, maintain reasonable and appropriate security measures, and holding those entities to the agreed-upon standards; developing written procedures and policies to implement the Security Rule's requirements, disseminating such procedures, and reviewing and updating them periodically in response to changing threats, vulnerabilities, and operational circumstances.

Sarbanes-Oxley

The Sarbanes-Oxley Act of 2002 (SOX) creates legal liability for senior executives of publicly traded companies, potentially including stiff prison sentences and fines of up to $5,000,000 per violation, for willfully certifying financial statements that do not meet the requirements of the statute.[40] Section 404 of SOX requires senior management, pursuant to rules promulgated by the Securities and Exchange Commission (SEC), to attest to: "(1) the responsibility of management for establishing and maintaining an adequate internal control structure and procedures for financial reporting; and (2) ...the effectiveness of the internal control structure and procedures of the issuer for financial reporting." [41] Section 302, also requires that pursuant to SEC regulations, officers signing company financial reports certify that they are "responsible for establishing and maintaining internal controls," and "have evaluated the effectiveness" of those controls and reported their conclusions as to the same.[42]

Federal Information Security and Management Act

The Federal Information Security and Management Act of 2002, as amended, (FISMA) does not directly create liability for private sector information security professionals or their customers.[43] Information security professionals should be aware of this law, however, because the law:

- Legally mandates the process by which information security requirements for federal government departments and agencies must be developed and implemented

- Directs the federal government to look to the private sector for applicable "best practices" and to provide assistance to the private sector (if requested) with regard to information security

- Contributes to the developing "standard of care" for information security by mandating a number of specific procedures and policies

FERPA and the TEACH Act

The Family Educational Right to Privacy Act (FERPA) prohibits educational agencies and programs, at risk of losing federal funds, from having a policy or practice of "permitting the release of" specified educational records.[44] FERPA does not state whether or not the prohibition places affirmative requirements on educational institutions to protect against unauthorized access to these records through the use of information security measures. It is certainly possible that a court could conclude in the future that an educational institution, which fails to take reasonable information security measures to prevent unauthorized access to protected information, is liable under FERPA for "permitting the release" of such information. The 2002 Technology, Education and Copyright Harmonization Act (the "TEACH Act") explicitly requires educational institutions to take "technologically feasible" measures to prevent unauthorized sharing of copyrighted information beyond the students specifically requiring the information for their studies, and, thus, may create newly enforceable legal duties on educational institutions with regard to information security.[45]

Electronic Communications Privacy Act and Computer Fraud and Abuse Act

These two federal statutes, while not mandating information security procedures, create serious criminal penalties for any persons who gain unauthorized access to electronic records. Unlike laws such as HIPAA and GLB, these two statues broadly apply, regardless of the type of electronic records that are involved. The Electronic Communications Privacy Act (ECPA) makes it a federal felony to, without authorization, use or intercept the contents of electronic communications.[46] Likewise, the Computer Fraud and Abuse Act of 1984 (CFAA) makes the unauthorized access to a very wide range of computer systems (including financial institutions, the federal government, and any protected computer system used in interstate commerce) a federal felony.[47] As a result, information security professionals must take great care—and rely on qualified and experienced legal professionals—to ensure that the authorizations they receive from their customers are broad and specific enough to mitigate potential criminal liability under ECPA and CFAA.[48]

State Laws

In addition to federal statutes and regulations implicating information security, there are numerous state laws that, depending on an entity's location and the places in which it does business, can also create legal requirements related to the work of information security professionals.

Unauthorized Access

In Colorado (and in other states), it is a crime to access, use, or exceed authorized access to, or use of, a computer, computer network, or any part of a computer system.[49] It is a crime to take action against a computer system to cause damage, to commit a theft, or for other nefarious purposes. However, it is particularly important for information security professionals to be aware that it is also a crime to knowingly access a computer system without authorization or to exceed authorized access. This is one reason it is critical for information security professionals, with the advice of qualified and experienced counsel, to negotiate a comprehensive, carefully worded, Letter of Authorization (LOA) with each and every customer (discussed in detail below).

Deceptive Trade Practices

Deceptive trade practices are unlawful and may potentially subject anyone committing them to civil penalties and damages.[50] In Colorado (as in many other states), "deceptive trade practices" include:

- "Knowingly mak[ing] a false representation as to the characteristics . . . [or] benefits of goods, . . . services, or property"[51]

- "Fail[ing] to disclose material information concerning goods, services, or property which information was known at the time of an advertisement or sale if such failure to disclose such information was intended to induce the consumer to enter into a transaction"[52]

Deceptive trade practices laws have been used by regulators to impose (through lawsuits) information security requirements on entities in industries not otherwise subject to statutory or regulatory standards.

These are only two of the many types of state laws potentially applicable to information security professionals and their customers. In addition, common law negligence doctrines in every state can create civil legal liability for information security professionals and their customers (discussed below in "Do it Right or Bet the Company: Tools to Mitigate Legal Liability").

Understanding the myriad state laws that apply to information security, and to any particular entity, and how such laws overlap and interact with federal laws, is complex and constantly evolving. Information security professionals and their customers should consult qualified and experienced legal counsel to navigate this challenging legal environment.

Enforcement Actions

What constitutes the "reasonable standard of care" in information security, as in all areas of the law, will continue to evolve, and not only through new statutes and regulations. Prosecutors and regulators will not be content to wait for such formal, legal developments. In lawsuits, and enforcement actions against entities not directly covered by any specific federal or state law or regulation, prosecutors and regulators have demonstrated the clear intent to extend "reasonable" information security measures even to those entities not clearly covered by specific existing laws. This is being done through legal actions leading to settlements, often including consent decrees (agreements entered into to end litigation or regulatory action) wherein a company agrees to "voluntarily" allow regulators to monitor (e.g., for 20 years) the company's information security program.[53]

Since these agreements are publicly available, they are adding to the "standard of care" to which entities will be held, in addition to providing added impetus for similar enforcement actions in the future. Thus, customers of information security professionals should take scant comfort in the fact that there are not yet specific laws explicitly targeted at their economic sectors or industries.

Three Fatal Fallacies

Conventional wisdom is a powerful and dangerous thing, as is a little knowledge. Unfortunately, many entities realizing they have legal and other requirements for information security have come to believe some specific fallacies that sometimes govern their information security decisions. More disturbingly, a significant number of information security providers, who should know better, also are falling victim to these fallacies. Herewith, then, let the debunking begin.

The "Single Law" Fallacy

Many information security professionals, both within commercial and educational entities, and among the burgeoning world of consultants, subscribe to the "single law" fallacy. That is, they identify a statute or set of regulations that clearly apply to a particular institution and assume that, by complying with that single standard, they have ended all legal risk. This assumption may be true, but in many cases is not. Making such an assumption could be a very expensive error, absent the advice of qualified and experienced legal counsel.

Take, for example, a mid-sized college or university. Information security professionals may conclude that, since FERPA clearly applies to educational records, following guidance tailored to colleges and universities based on what they conclude are the appropriate Department of Education standards, is sufficient to mitigate any potential legal liability. Worse yet, they may decide to gamble that, given current ambiguity about whether FERPA requires affirmative action to prevent unauthorized access to such records, they need not take any affirmative steps to try and prevent such access. This could be an expensive gamble, particularly if the educational institution does not ask itself the following questions:

- Does the school grant financial aid or extend other forms of credit? If so, it could be subject to GLBA.

- Does it operate hospitals, provide psychiatric counseling services, or run a student health service? If so, it could be subject to HIPAA.

- Does the school's Web site contain any representations about the security of the site and/or university-held information? If so, it could be subject to lawsuits under one or more (depending on whether it has campuses in multiple states) state deceptive trade practices laws.

The Private Entity Fallacy

Focusing on SOX and the resulting preoccupation with publicly traded companies, some institutions take solace in being private and in the fact that, so the argument goes, they are not subject to SOX and/or that they can somehow "fly under the radar" of federal regulators and civil litigants. Again, a dangerous bet. First, the likelihood of comprehensive federal information security regulation reaching well beyond publicly traded companies grows daily. Second, anyone who believes that lawyers for future plaintiffs (students, faculty, victims of attack or identity theft) will be deterred by the literal terms of SOX is misguided. The argument (potentially a winning one) will be that the appropriate "standard of care" for information security was publicly available and well known. The fact that one particular statute may not apply, by its plain terms, does not relieve entities of awareness of the standard of care and duty not to be negligent. Third, and most importantly, a myopic focus on SOX (or any other single law or regulation) to the exclusion of the numerous other potential sources of liability, will not relieve entities of the responsibility to learn about, and follow, the dictates of all other sources of law, including, but not limited to, HIPAA, GLBA, state statutes, and common law theories and, depending on where an entity does business, international and foreign law, such as the complex and burdensome European Union Privacy Directive.[54]

The "Pen Test Only" Fallacy

Every information security professional has dealt with the "pen test only" customer, probably more than once. This customer is either certain that their information security posture is so good that they just need an outside party to try and "break in" (do a penetration test) to prove how good they are, or feels an internal bureaucratic need to prove to others in the company how insecure their systems are. Generally, the customer has a limited budget or simply does not want to spend much money and wants a "quick hit" by the information security professional to prove a bureaucratic point. One variation on this theme is the customer who wants the penetration test as a first step, before deciding how far down the Information Security Assessment/Evaluation road to walk.

There is no way to say this too strongly: ***starting with a penetration test is a disaster***, particularly if there is no way to protect the results from disclosure (see "Attorney–client Privilege" below). The NSA methodology itself, as outlined herein and in *Security Assessment: Case Studies in Implementing the NSA IAM*, demonstrates this, with its sound reliance on a holistic and evolving set of assessments, rather than a one-shot test and report. At least as important are the horrendous legal consequences that can flow from starting with a penetration test without establishing a more comprehensive, longer-term relationship with qualified and experienced lawyers and, through them, information security technical consultants. Not only will the customer almost certainly "fail" the penetration test, particularly if done as the first step without proper assessment, evaluation, and mid-stream remediation, but this failure will *be documented in a report not subject to any type of attorney-client privilege or other protection from disclosure.*

   In short, testing done at the worst possible time in the process in terms of exposing vulnerabilities will be wide open to discovery and disclosure by your customers' future adversaries. From the standpoint of the information security technical professional, this also could lead to your being required later to testify, publicly and under oath, as to the minutest of details of your work for the customer, your methodology and "trade secrets," and your work product.[55]

Do It Right or Bet the Company: Tools to Mitigate Legal Liability

In recent years, numerous articles have been written on how to protect your network from a technical perspective,[56] but, at least throughout mid-2005, the headlines swelled with examples of companies that have lost critical information due to inadequate security. Choice Point, DSW Shoes, several universities, financial institutions including Bank of America and Wachovia, MasterCard and other credit providers, and even the FBI have been named in recent news articles for having lost critical information. As one example, ChoicePoint was sued in 2005 in actions brought in states ranging from California to New York and in its home state of Georgia. Allegations in the lawsuits included that ChoicePoint failed to "secure and maintain confidential the personal, financial and other information entrusted to ChoicePoint by consumers"[57]; failed to maintain adequate procedures to avoid disclosing some private credit and financial information to unauthorized third parties; and acted "willfully, recklessly, and/or in conscious disregard" of its customers rights to privacy.[58] Legal theories used in future information security-related lawsuits will be limited only by the imagination of the attorneys filing the suits.

   It is hardly a distant possibility that every major player in information security will be sued sooner or later, whether a particular suit is frivolous or not. It is a fact of business life. So, how can information security consultants help their customers reduce their litigation "target profile?"

We Did our Best; What's the Problem?

Many companies feel that their internal information technology and security staffs are putting forth their best efforts to maintain and secure their networks. They may even be getting periodic penetration tests and trying to make sense out of the hundreds of single-spaced pages of "vulnerabilities" identified in the resulting reports. So why isn't that good enough? The answer is that "doing one's best" to secure and maintain a network system will not be enough unless it is grounded in complying with external legal standards (discussed above). Penetration tests alone are likely not enough to demonstrate reasonable efforts at meeting the standard of care for information security. In ChoicePoint's case, at least based on what has been made public as of mid-2005, penetration tests would not have helped. ChoicePoint appears to have fallen victim to individuals who fraudulently posed as businessmen and conned people into giving them what may have been otherwise secure information.

Ameliorating any one particular potential point of failure will almost never be enough. Companies today must understand the potential sources of liability that apply to all commercial entities, as well as those specific to their industry. Only through understanding the legal environment and adopting and implementing policies to assure a high level of compliance with prevailing legal requirements can a company minimize the risk of liability. Of course, this system approach cannot be not static. It requires ongoing review and implementation to assure compliance in an ever-changing legal environment.

The Basis for Liability

A company's legal liability can arise as a result of: (a) standards and penalties imposed by federal, state, or local governments; (b) breach of contractual agreements; or (c) other non-contractual civil wrongs (torts) ranging from fraud, invasion of privacy, and conversion to deceptive trade practices and negligence. Avoiding liability for criminal misconduct also involves an understanding of the statutes and regulations applicable to your business and adhering to those requirements. Federal and state statutes may impose both criminal penalties as well as form the basis for private lawsuits.

Negligence and the "Standard of Care"

The combination of facts and events that can give rise to civil claims when information security is breached and the specific impact on business operations, are too numerous to discuss in detail. Understanding the basis for liability and conducting business in a manner designed to avoid liability is the best defense. In many cases, the claim of liability is based in a charge that the company and its officers and directors acted "negligently." In law, "negligence" arises when a party owes a legal duty to another, that duty is breached, and the breach causes damages to the injured party. Generally speaking, acting "reasonably" under the circumstances will prevent information security consultants or their customers from being found "negligent."[59] The rub is that what is "reasonable" both: (1) depends on the particular circumstances of individual situations; and (2) is constantly evolving as new laws and regulations are promulgated and new vulnerabilities, attack vectors, and available countermeasures become known.

Certainly, when a company maintains personal or confidential customer information, or has agreed to maintain as confidential the trade secret information of another business, its minimum duty is to use reasonable care in securing its computer systems to avoid theft or inadvertent disclosure of the information entrusted to it. Reasonable care may range from an extremely high standard when trust and confidence are reposed in a company to secure sensitive information, to a standard of care no more than that generally employed by others in the industry.

A reasonable "standard of care" is what the law defines as the minimum efforts a company must take not to have acted negligently (or, put another way, to have acted reasonably). A strong foundation to avoid liability for most civil claims begins with conducting the company's affairs up to the known standard of care that will avoid liability for negligence.

The appropriate, reasonable standard of care in any given industry and situation can arise from several sources, including statutes, regulations, common law duties, organizational policies, and contractual obligations. Courts look to the foreseeability of particular types of harm to help determine an industry standard of care. In other words, a business must exercise reasonable care to prevent an economic loss that should have been anticipated. As a result of ongoing public disclosure of new types of harm from breaches in information security, it is increasingly "foreseeable" that critical information may be lost through unauthorized access, and the policies and practices used to protect that information will take center stage in any negligence action.

What Can Be Done?

Fully understanding the risks, as assessed by qualified and experienced counsel, is an essential first step. Taking action that either avoids liability or minimizes the consequences when things go wrong is the next stride. The following are some suggestions that will help in the journey.

Understand your Legal Environment

Mitigating legal liability begins with understanding the laws applicable to a company's business. (A variety of potentially applicable legal requirements are outlined in the "Legal Standards Relevant to Information Security" section above.) Ignorance of the law is no excuse, and failure to keep pace with statutory requirements is a first source of liability. Working with professionals, whether inside or outside of the company, to track changes in legislation and tailor your information security policies is the first line of defense. Careful compliance with laws not only helps reduce the potential for criminal liability or administrative fines, but also evidences a standard of care that may mitigate civil liability.

Comprehensive and Ongoing Security Assessments, Evaluations, and Implementation

Working with qualified and experienced legal counsel and technical consultants, a company must identify and prioritize the information it controls that may require protection, and catalogue the specific legal requirements applicable to such information and to the type of business the company is in. Next, policies must be developed to assure that the information is properly maintained and administered and that the company's personnel conduct themselves in accordance with those policies. Policy evaluations must include the applicable legal requirements, as well as reasonable procedures for testing and maintaining the security of information systems.

Critically, the cycle of using outside, neutral, third-party assessments/evaluations, implementation and improvement, and further assessment, must be ongoing. A static assessment/evaluation sitting on your shelf is worse than none at all. Almost equally bad is actually implementing the results of assessments/evaluations, but never reassessing or modifying them or insufficiently training employees on them, or evaluating those employees on their understanding and implementation of such results.

Use Contracts to Define Rights and Protect Information

Most businesses understand the process of entering into contracts and following the terms of those contracts to avoid claims of breach. What is not so easily identified is how contractual obligations impact the potential of civil liability based on how information is secured and managed within a particular business? Many areas within a company's business require contracts to be developed and tailored to avoid liability and preserve the integrity of the business. One example is the Uniform Trade Secrets Act (UTSA), adopted in nearly all states and intended to protect confidential information of value to a company's business. Under the UTSA, confidential information may include formulas, patterns, compilations, programs, devices, methods, techniques, or processes that derive independent economic value from not being generally known to the public and for which the company has made reasonable efforts to maintain confidentiality. Almost every company has trade secrets—from its customer lists to its business methodologies afford a competitive advantage. Any protection for these valuable assets will be lost if a company fails to make reasonable efforts to maintain the information as confidential.

At a minimum, contracts must be developed that commit employees not to disclose the trade secrets of the company, or any information legally mandated to be protected (e.g., individual health care or financial information). These agreements are often most effective if entered into at the time of, and as a condition to, employment. This is because most contracts require value to support enforceability and because a delay in requiring a non-disclosure agreement may allow sensitive information to be disclosed before the contract is in place.

Employment policies should reinforce the employee's obligation to maintain confidentiality. These policies should also provide clear guidance on procedures to use and maintain passwords and to responsibly use the information secured on the network. Regular interviews and employee training should be implemented to reinforce the notion that these requirements are mandatory and taken seriously by management. Vendors and service providers that may need to review confidential information should only be permitted access to such information under an agreement limiting the use of that information and agreeing to maintain its confidentiality. Hiring a consultant to perform a network security evaluation without a proper confidentiality agreement could later be found to be sufficient evidence that a company failed to take reasonable efforts to maintain information as confidential, with the result that the information is not longer a trade secret entitled to protection.

Use Qualified Third-party Professionals

Working with qualified information security professionals to implement proper hardware and software solutions to minimize a security breach is critical, but never enough. These functions need to be performed in conjunction with a system of evaluation testing and retesting that integrates legal considerations, and under the supervision and guidance of qualified and experienced legal counsel.

In addition, working with qualified and experienced outside counsel can substantially improve success in the event that claims of negligence are asserted (using attorneys and technical professionals trained to conduct comprehensive and ongoing systems assessments and eval-uations is evidence of the reasonableness of the efforts to prevent the loss). Companies' internal staff may be equally competent to develop and implement the strategies of information secu-rity, but regulators, courts, and juries will look to whether or not a company retained qualified and experienced outside counsel and technical consultants before a problem arose. Working with these experts increases the probability that best practices are being followed and indepen-dent review is the best way to mitigate against foreseeable loss of sensitive information.

As discussed in more detail below, retaining outside professionals in a way that creates an attorney-client privilege may offer protection (in the event of civil litigation, regulatory, or even criminal, action) from disclosure of system vulnerabilities discovered in the information security assessment and evaluation processes. The privilege is not absolute, however, and may have dif-ferent practical applications in the civil and criminal contexts and, in particular, when a cus-tomer elects to assert an "advice-of-counsel" defense.

A key requirement emerging as a critical part of the evolving information security stan-dards of care is the requirement to get an external review by qualified, neutral parties.[60] These requirements are based on the sound theory that, no matter how qualified, expert, and well intentioned an entity's information technology and information security staff is, it is impossible for them to be truly objective. Moreover, the "fox in the hen house" problem arises, leaving senior management to wonder whether those charged with creating and maintaining informa-tion security can and will fairly and impartially assess the effectiveness of such security. Finally, qualified and experienced outside legal counsel and technical consultants bring perspective, breadth of experience, and currency with the latest technical and legal developments that in-house staff normally cannot provide cost-effectively.

Making Sure Your Standards-of-Care Assessments Keep Up with Evolving Law

As suggested above, the legal definition of a "reasonable" standard of care is constantly evolving. Policymakers take seriously the threats and the substantial economic loss caused by cyber-attacks. New laws are continually being enacted to punish attackers and to shift liability to companies that have failed to take reasonable information security measures. Contractual obli-gations can now be formed instantly and automatically simply by new customers accessing your customer's Web sites and using their services, all over the Internet and, thus, all over the world. As new vulnerabilities, attacks, and countermeasures come to public attention, new duties emerge. In short, what was "reasonable" last month may not be reasonable this month.

Information security assessments and evaluations provide a tool to evaluate, and enhance compliance with, best practices in protecting critical information; however, they are, at best, only snapshots unless they are made regular, ongoing events. Best practices begin with under-standing and complying with applicable laws, but can only be maintained through tracking and implementing evolving statutory requirements. Working with qualified and experienced counsel to follow new legal developments in this fast-moving area of the law and advise on the proper interpretation and implementation of legislative requirements is becoming essential to navigate through this ever-changing landscape.

Plan for the Worst

Despite all best efforts, nothing can completely immunize a company from liability. Failing to plan a crisis management and communications strategy in the event of lost or compromised information can invite lawsuits and create liability despite a track record showing your company exercised a reasonable standard of care in trying to protect information. Avoiding liability involves planning for problems. For example, one class action filed against ChoicePoint alleges that shareholders were misled when the company failed to disclose (for several months) the existence of its security breach and the true extent of the information that was compromised. Having had policies in place to provide guidance to executives in communicating with customers and prospective shareholders may well have avoided these allegations. California currently has a Notice of Security Breach law that was enacted in 2002.[61] As of May 2005, Arkansas, Georgia, Indiana, Montana, North Dakota, and Washington have followed suit by enacting some form of legislation requiring disclosure relating to breaches of security, and bills have been introduced in not less than 34 other states to regulate in this area.[62] As of mid-2005, there was no similar federal regulation, although, several disclosure bills have been introduced in Congress.

A strategic policy to deal with crisis management must take into account disclosure laws in all states in which a company operates. Making disclosures that comply with multiple laws and that minimize the adverse impact of information security breaches and disclosures of them must be planned far in advance of a crisis. Again, this is a constantly changing landscape, and these policies need to be reviewed and updated on a regular basis. It is critical that these policies and plans are developed and carried out with the assistance of qualified and experienced counsel.

Insurance

As more information security breaches occur and are disclosed, the cost to businesses and individuals will continue to rise. In 2002, the Federal Trade Commission (FTC) estimated that 10 million people were victims of identity theft. According to Gartner, Inc., 9.4 million online users in the U.S. were victimized between April 2003 and April 2004 with losses amounting to $11.7 billion.[63] Costs to business from these losses will likely grow to staggering levels in the coming years, and this trend is capturing the attention of some of the more sophisticated insurance companies. Some companies are developing products to provide coverage for losses resulting from breaches of information security. Companies should contact their carriers and do their own independent research to determine what coverage, if any, is or will become, available.

Customers of information security consultants, with the advice of qualified and experienced counsel, must take into account all of these issues in determining how best to mitigate their legal risk. A key component of mitigating that risk is the relationships established with information security consultants, including qualified and experienced counsel and skilled and respected technical consultants. Those relationships, of course, must be established and governed by written contracts (discussed in the next section).

What to Cover in IEM Contracts[64]

The contract is the single most important tool used to define and regulate the legal relationship between the information security consultant and the customer. It protects both parties from misunderstandings and should clearly allocate liability in case of unforeseen or unintended consequences, such as a system crash, access to protected, proprietary, or otherwise sensitive information thought secure, and damage to the network or information residing on the network. The contract also serves as a roadmap through the security evaluation cycle for both parties. A LOA (described in the next section) serves a different purpose from a contract and often augments the subject matter covered in a contract or deals with relationships with third parties not part of the original service contract. In most evaluations, both will be required.

The contract should spell out each and every action the customer wants the provider to perform. Information security consultants should have a standard contract for a packages of services, but should be flexible enough for negotiation in order to meet the specific needs of the customer. What is, or is not, covered in the contract, and how the provisions should be worded, are decisions both parties must make only with the advice of qualified and experienced counsel familiar with this field. As with any other legal agreement between parties, both signatories should fully understand all the terms in the contract, or ask for clarification or re-drafting of ambiguous, vague, or overly technical language. Contract disputes often arise in situations where two parties can read the same language in different ways. Understand what you are signing.

What, Who, When, Where, How, and How Much

The following paragraphs provide an overview of what should be included in IEM contracts, though these principles are equally applicable to contracts for the Information Security Assurance Methodology (IAM) and many other types of information security service contracts. They include checklists of questions that the contract should answer for both parties; however, remember that each assessment is different because customer's needs and the facts of each evaluation process will differ. Make sure the contract you sign clearly covers each of the topics suggested here, but keep in mind that this is not an exhaustive list and cannot replace the specific advice of your own legal counsel for your specific circumstances.

What

The first general requirement for a contract for information security evaluation services is to address the basic services the consultant will perform. What are the expectations of both parties in performing the non-technical aspects of the business relationship, such as payment, reporting, and documentation? What services does the contract cover? What does the customer want? What can the information security consultant provide? A number of categories of information should appear in this first section.

Description of the Security Evaluation and Business Model

In the initial part of the contract, the information security consultant should describe the services to be provided and, generally, how its business is conducted. This information provides background on the type of contract that is to be used by the parties (e.g., a contract for services or a contract for services followed by the purchase and installation of software to remediate any identified vulnerabilities). This initial section should also identify the customer and describe its business model. For example, is the customer a financial organization, a healthcare organization, an organization with multiple geographic locations under evaluation, or subject to specific legal requirements and/or industry regulations?

Definitions Used in the Contract

Each contract uses terms that will need further explanation so that the meaning is clear to both parties. Technical terms such as "vulnerability" and "penetration" should be spelled out. Executives sign contracts. Attorneys advise executives whether or not to sign the contracts. Both must understand what the contract means.

Description of the Project

The contract should provide a general statement of the scope of the project. If the project is a long-term endeavor or a continuing relationship between the two parties, this section should also include a description of how each part of the project or phase in the relationship should progress and what additional documents will cover each phase or part of the project. This section also clearly defines what the information security consultant will and will not do throughout the evaluation. Also, in the description of the project, the customer should clearly define the objectives it wants the information security consultant to accomplish. Are all the entity's networks included? What types of testing are required? This section should also include the types of vulnerabilities that the information security consultant is not likely to discover based on the types of testing, the networks tested, and the scope of the overall evaluation, as permitted by the customer.

Assumptions, Representations, and Warranties

In every assessment, the parties must provide or assume some basic information. These assumptions should appear in the contract. Assumptions are factual statements, not a description of conversations the parties have had (e.g., "The schedule in this contract is based on the assumption that all members of the evaluation team will work from 8:30 A.M. to 5:30 P.M. for five days per week for the full contract period."). With regard to the network assumptions, the customer should provide basic information on network topology upon which the assessment team can base assumptions for the types of vulnerabilities they will look for and testing methodologies that will successfully achieve the customer's objectives (e.g., "The evaluation methodology applied to the customer network under this contract relies on the assumption that the customer maintains servers in a single geographic location, physically secured, and logically segregated from other networks and from the Internet.")[65] The language in this section should also address responsive actions should the assumptions prove false: Under what circumstances is the contract voided? What can make the price go up or down? In the event of unexpected security or integrity problems being created during an evaluation, when should the testing be stopped? Who decides? When should the customers' management be informed? At what levels?

IEM contracts should include "representations and warranties" by the customer spelling out certain critical information that the customer "warrants" to be true such as: descriptions of the customer's business operations and information they hold within their systems; what agreements the customer has with third-party vendors and/or holders of their information; what information systems external to those controlled by the customer, if any, could be impacted by the evaluation and testing to be done, and what measures the customer has taken to eliminate the possibilities of such impact; and the degree to which the customer exclusively owns and controls information and systems to be evaluated and/or tested or has secured written agreements explicitly authorizing evaluation and testing by others that do own or control such information and systems.[66]

Boundaries and Limitations

In addition to stating what the evaluation will cover, this initial section should also address what the assessment will not cover in terms of timing, location, data, and other variables. The general goal of the evaluation cycle is to provide a level of safety and security to the customer in the confidence, integrity, and availability of its networks. However, some areas of the network are more sensitive than others. Additionally, each customer will have varying levels of trust in the evaluation methodology and personnel. Not all evaluation and testing methodologies are appropriate for all areas of a network. The customer should give careful consideration to what is tested, when and how, as well as what the evaluators should do in the event of data contamination or disclosure.

If a customer runs a particular type of report on a specific date to meet payroll, accounting, regulatory, or other obligations, that date is not a very good time to engage in network testing. Even if the testing methodology is sound and the personnel perform at peak efficiency and responsibility levels, human nature will attribute any network glitch on that date to the testing team. Sensitive data requires an increased level of scrutiny for any measure taken that could damage or disclose the information, or make the use of the information impossible for some period of time. Such actions could result in administrative or regulatory penalties and expensive remediation efforts.

Data privacy standards vary by industry, state, country, and category of information. A single network infrastructure may encompass personnel records, internal audits or investigations, proprietary or trade secret information, financial information, and individual and corporate information records and databases. The network could also store data subject to attorney-client or other legal privilege. Additionally, customers should consider where and how their employees store data. Does the customer representative negotiating the scope of the project know where all the sensitive data in his/her enterprise are stored, and with what degree of certainty? Again, much of this information should have been developed during the IAM phase of a comprehensive information security assessment/evaluation. Does the customer have a contingency plan for data contamination or unauthorized access? How does the security evaluation account for the possibility that testing personnel will come into contact with sensitive data (see Non-Disclosure and Secrecy Agreements section below)? In this portion of the contract, the customer should specify any areas of the network where testing personnel may not conduct evaluations, either for a period of time or during specific phases.

Both parties should be sensitive to the fact that the customer may not own and control all areas of the network. A customer can only consent to testing those portions of the network it owns and controls.

NOTE

Evaluation of other portions of a larger corporate network or where the evaluation proceeds through the Internet, requires additional levels of authorization from third parties outside the contractual relationship, and should never be carried out without explicit agreements negotiated and reviewed by qualified and experienced counsel.

In some cases, the evaluation can continue through these larger networks, but will require additional documentation, such as a LOA (see " Where the Rubber Meets the Road: the Letter of Authorization as Liability Protection" below).

Identification of Deliverables

Without feedback to the customer presented in a usable format, evaluating and testing the network is a waste of resources. The contract should state with a high degree of specificity what deliverables the customer requires and for what level of audience. For example, a 300-page technical report presented to a board of directors is of little use. A ten-slide presentation for the officers of a customer company that focuses on prioritizing the vulnerabilities in terms of levels of risk is far more valuable. Conversely, showing those same ten slides to the network engineering team will not help them. The key in this section of the contract is to manage expectations for the various levels of review within the customer's structure.

Who

The second general requirement for a contract for security evaluation services is to spell out the parties to the agreement and specify the roles and responsibilities of each (including specific names and titles of responsible individuals) for successfully completing the evaluation. This identity and role information is critical for reducing the likelihood of contract disputes due to unmet expectations.

Statement of Parties to the Contractual Agreement

Each party should be clearly identified in the contract by name, location, and principal point of contact for subsequent communications. Often, the official of record for signature is not the same person who will be managing the contract or engaged in day-to-day liaison activities with the evaluation personnel. Additionally, this section should spell out the procedures for changing the personnel of record for each type of contact.

Authority of Signatories to the Contractual Agreement

Ideally, the level of signatory to the contract should be equal, and, in any event, the signing official must be high enough to bind the entities to all obligations arising out of the contractual relationship. It is often also helpful for the customer signatory to be a person empowered to make changes based on recommendations resulting from the evaluation.

Roles and Responsibilities of Each Party to the Contractual Agreement

Spelling out the levels of staffing, location of resources, who will provide those resources, and the precise nature of other logistical, personnel, and financial obligations is critical. It allows both sides to proceed through the evaluation cycle with a focus on the objectives, rather than a daily complication of negotiating who is responsible for additional, unforeseen administrative issues. Some common areas of inclusion in this section are:

- Who provides facilities and administrative support?
- Who is responsible for backing up critical data before the evaluation begins?
- Who is responsible for initiating communication for project status reports. Does the customer call for an update, or does the evaluation team provide regular reporting? Must status reports be written or can they be oral and memorialized only in the information security consultants' records?
- Who is responsible for approving deviations from the contract or evaluation plan and how will decisions about these be recorded?
- Who will perform each aspect of each phase of the evaluation (will the customer provide any technical personnel)?
- Who is responsible for mapping the network before evaluation begins (and will those maps be provided to the evaluation team, or kept in reserve for comparison after the evaluation ends)?
- Who is responsible for briefing senior officers in the customer organization?
- Who is responsible for reporting discrepancies from the agreed project plan to evaluation POCs and executives?
- Who is responsible for reporting violations of policies, regulations, or laws discovered during the evaluation?
- Who has the authority to terminate the evaluation should network irregularities arise?
- Who bears the risk for unforeseen consequences or circumstances that arise during the evaluation period?

Non-disclosure and Secrecy Agreements

Many documents and other information pertaining to information security evaluations contain critical information that could damage one or both parties if improperly disclosed. Both parties bear responsibility to protect tools, techniques, vulnerabilities, and information from disclosure beyond the terms specified by a written agreement. Non-disclosure agreements should be narrowly drawn to protect sensitive information, yet allow both parties to function effectively. Specific areas to consider including are: ownership and use of the evaluation reports and results; use of the testing methodology in customer documentation; disclosures required under law; and the time period of disclosure restrictions. It is often preferable to have non-disclosure/secrecy agreements be separate, stand-alone documents so that, if they must be litigated later in public, as few details as possible of the larger agreement must be publicly exposed.

Assessment Personnel

A security evaluation team is composed of a variety of expert personnel, whether from the customer organization or supplied by the contractor. The contract should spell out the personnel requirements to complete each phase of the assessment successfully and efficiently. Both parties should have a solid understanding of each team member's skills and background. Where possible, the contract should include information on the personnel conducting the assessment. Both parties should also consider who would fund and who would perform any background investigations necessary for personnel assigned to evaluate sensitive networks.

Crisis Management and Public Communications

Network security evaluations can be messy. No network is 100 percent secure. The assessment team will inevitably find flaws. The assessment team will usually stumble across unexpected dangers, or take actions that result in unanticipated results that could impact the network or the data residing on the network. Do not make the mistake of compounding a bad situation with a poor response to the crisis. Implementing notification procedures at the contract phase often saves the integrity of an evaluation should something go wrong. The parties also should clearly articulate who has the lead role in determining the timing, content, and delivery mechanism for providing information to the customer's employees, customers, shareholders, and so forth. This section should also spell out what role, if any, the customer wants the assessment team or leader to play in the public relations efforts. A procedure for managing crisis situations is also prudent. Qualified and experienced legal counsel must be involved in these processes.

Indemnification, Hold Harmless, and Duty to Defend

Even more so than in many other types of contracts for services, the security evaluation contract should include detailed provisions explicitly protecting the information security consultants from various types of contract dispute claims. In addition to standard contract language, these sections should specifically spell out the responsibilities (and their limits) of both the customer and the information security consultants to defend claims of damage to external systems or information and intellectual property or licensing infringement for software, if any, developed by the information security consultant for purposes of the evaluation.

Ownership and Control of Information

The information contained in the final report and executive level briefings can be extremely sensitive. Both parties must understand who owns and controls the disclosure and dissemination of the information, as well as what both parties may do with the information following the review process. Any proprietary information or processes, including trade secrets, should be marked as such, and covered by a separate section of the contract. Key topics to cover include: use of evaluation results in either party's marketing or sales brochures; release of results to management or regulatory bodies; and disclosure of statistics in industry surveys, among other uses. The customer should spell out any internal corporate controls for the information in this section. If the customer requires encryption of the evaluation data, this section should clearly spell out those requirements and who is responsible for creating or providing keys.

One important ownership area that must be specifically covered in information security evaluation contracts is how reports and other resulting documentation from the evaluation are to be handled. May the information security consultants keep copies of the documents, at least for a reasonable period of time following the conclusion of the evaluation (e.g., in case the customer takes legal action against the consultant)? Who is responsible for destroying any excess copies of such information? May the information security consultant use properly sanitized versions of the reports as samples of work product?

Intellectual Property Concerns

Ownership and use of intellectual property is a complicated area of the law. However, clear guidance in the prior section on the ownership and use of evaluation information will help the parties avoid intellectual property disputes. The key to a smooth legal relationship between the parties is to clearly define expectations.

Licenses

The evaluation team must ensure that they have valid licenses for each piece of software used in the evaluation. The customer should verify valid licensing.

When

The third general requirement for a security evaluation services contract is to create a schedule for conducting the evaluation that includes all of the phases and contingency clauses to cover changes to that schedule. At a minimum, the contract should state a timeline for the overall evaluation and for each phase, including:

- A timeline for completing deliverables in draft and final formats
- Estimated dates of executive briefings, if requested
- A timeline for any follow-up work anticipated

Actions or Events that Affect Schedule

Inevitably, something will happen to affect the schedule. Personnel move, network topography changes a variety of unforeseen factors can arise. While the contract team cannot control those factors, it can draft language in the contract to allow rapid adaptation of the schedule, depending on various factors. Brief interruptions in assessments can mean long-term impacts if the team is at a sensitive point in the assessment. At the contracting phase, both sides should consult with other elements in their companies to determine what events could affect the schedule. Failure to plan adequately for scheduling conflicts or disruptions could result in one party breaching the contract. Both parties should agree on a contingency plan if the evaluation must terminate prematurely. Contingency plans could include resuming the evaluation at a later time or adjusting the total amount of the contract cost based on the phases completed.

Where

The fourth general requirement for a contract for security evaluation services is to define the location(s), both geographic and logical, subject to the evaluation. Where, precisely, are you testing? To create boundaries for the evaluation and prevent significant misunderstandings on the scope of the assessment or evaluation, list each facility, the physical address and/or logical location, including the Internet Protocol (IP) address range. Make sure that each machine attached to that IP space is within the legal and physical control of the customer. If any of the locations are outside the U.S., seek the immediate advice of counsel on this specific point. While covering the rapid developments in overseas law of this field is beyond the scope of this section, understand that many countries are implementing computer crime laws and standing up both civil and criminal response mechanisms to combat computer crime. Various elements of a network security evaluation can look like unauthorized access to a protected computer. Both the evaluation provider and the customer need to take additional cautionary measures and implement greater notification procedures when considering an evaluation of a system located even partially abroad. Additionally, this section should cover the location the evaluation team will use as their base of operations. If the two locations are separate geographically, the parties must address the electronic access needed for the evaluation.

Exercise an extra level of caution if the evaluation traverses the Internet. Use of the Internet to conduct evaluations carries an additional level of risk and legal liability because neither party owns or controls all of the intermediate network structures.

WARNING

Do not act where your evaluation and testing must traverse the Internet without the advice of qualified and experienced counsel.

How

The fifth general requirement for a contract for security evaluation services is to map out a methodology for completing the evaluation. This section should identify and describe each phase of the evaluation and/or the overall testing cycle if the contract will cover a business relationship that will span multiple assessments (e.g., IAM and IEM). The key is to prevent surprises for either party. Breaking complex assessments and/or evaluations up into phases in the contract allows the reviewing officials to understand what they are paying for and when they can expect results. State with precise language what the evaluator will be doing at each phase, the goals and objectives of each phase, each activity the evaluation team will complete during that phase, and the deliverables expected. Do not use technical slang. A separate background document on evaluation and testing methodology (i.e., NSA/IAM, IEM, ISO 17799, and so on) is often more useful than cluttering the contract with unnecessary technical detail. This section should also state and describe the standards the evaluation team will use for measuring the evaluation results. Testing should bear results on a measurement scale that allows for comparisons over time and between locations.

How Much

The sixth, and final, general requirement for a contract for security evaluation services is to spell out the costs of the evaluation and other associated payment terms. This section is similar to any other business service contract. At a minimum, it should include the following five elements.

Fees and Cost

The parties should discuss and agree to a fee structure that meets the needs of both parties, which in most cases will call for multiple payments based on phase completion. A helpful analogy is the construction of a house. At what phases will the homeowner pay the general contractor: excavation and clearing the lot; completion of the foundation; framing; walls and fixtures; or final walkthrough? Also, consider the level of customer management that must approve phase completion and payment. In most cases, the final payment on the contract will be tied in some way to the delivery of a final report. Both parties should also carefully discuss the costs for which the customer is responsible. If evaluation teams must travel to the customer's location, who pays for the travel, food, lodging, and other non-salary costs for those personnel, and what level of documentation will be needed to process payment? Do the costs include airfare, lodging, mileage, subsistence (meals and incidentals), and other expenses? Does the customer require that the expenses be "reasonable" or must a customer representative authorize the expenses in advance? To avoid disputes that detract the team's attention from the assessment, spell out the parties' expectations in the contract. The parties should also cover who pays for extraordinary unanticipated expenses such as equipment failure. In some circumstances, the best method for dealing with truly unexpected expenses is to state affirmatively in the contract that the parties will negotiate such costs as they arise.

Billing Methodology

In order for the customer's accounting mechanisms to adequately prepare for the obligations in the contract, the billing or invoicing requirements should be spelled out. If the customer requires a specific type of information to appear on the invoice, that information should be provided to the contractor in writing, preferably in the contract. The types of fees and costs that will appear on the invoice should also be discussed, and the customer should provide guidance on the level of detail they need, while the contractor should explain the nature of their billing capabilities.

Payment Expectations and Schedule

The contract should clearly represent both parties' expectations for prompt payment. Will the contractor provide invoices at each phase or on a monthly cycle? Are invoices due upon receipt or on a specific day of the month? Where does the contractor send the invoice and to whom within the customer's structure? Does the contractor require electronic payment of invoices, and if so, to what account? What penalties will the contractor assess for late payments or returned checks? Again, the key factor is to address both parties' expectations to prevent surprises.

Rights and Procedures to Collect Payment

In the event of problems in the contractual relationship or changes in management that affect the contract, what are the parties' rights? As with other commercial contracts, articulating the rights and remedies is essential to minimize or avoid altogether the expense of disputes.

Insurance for Potential Damage During Evaluation

Which party, if either, will carry insurance against damage to the customer's systems and information as well as to those of third parties?

Murphy's Law (When Something Goes Wrong)

The final standard set of clauses for the contract deals with the potential for conflict between the parties or modifications to the contract.

Governing Law

Where both parties are in the same state, and the evaluation is limited to those facilities, this clause may not be necessary. However, in most cases, the activities will cross state borders. The parties should agree on which state's law applies to the contract and under which court's jurisdiction parties can file lawsuits. Determining venue for disputes before they arise can reduce legal costs.

Acts of God, Terror Attacks, and other Unforeseeable Even

Attorneys and network engineers share at least one common trait; neither can predict with any certainty when things will go wrong, but all agree that something will eventually happen that you did not expect. Natural disasters, system glitches, power interruptions, military coups, and a thousand other events can affect a project. Where the disruption is the fault of neither party, both sides should decide in advance on the appropriate course of action.

When Agreement is Breached and Remedies

When one party decides not to fulfill or becomes incapable in some way of performing, the terms of the contract, or believes the other party has not met its contractual obligations, a party can claim a breach (breaking) of the agreement and demand a remedy from the opposing party. Many types of remedies exist for breach of a contract. Either party can also take the matter to court, which can be very messy and extremely expensive. Anticipating situations such as these and inserting language in the contract to deal with potential breaches could save thousands of dollars in attorney fees and court costs. Both parties should discuss the following options with counsel before negotiating a contract for security evaluation services. First, are arbitration or mediation options appropriate or desirable? Second, should the matter proceed to court, one party will inevitably claim attorney's fees as part of the damages. Anticipate this claim and include language that specifies what fees are part of the remedy and whether the party who loses the dispute will reimburse attorney's fees, or whether each side will be responsible for its own attorney's fees.

Liquidated Damages

Liquidated damages are an agreed, or "liquidated," amount that one party is required to pay the other in the event of a breach or early termination of a contract. Liquidated damages are valuable to bring certainty to a failed relationship but are not appropriate if used to create a windfall or punish a party for not completing their contractual obligations. Instead, to be legally enforceable, a liquidated damages clause must estimate the parties' reasonably anticipated damages in the event of a breach or early termination of the contract. Liquidated damages cannot be a penalty and are not appropriate if actual damages can be readily determined.[67] Courts in Colorado, for example, generally will enforce a liquidated damages clause in a contract if: (1) at the time contract was entered into, anticipated damages in case of breach were difficult to ascertain; (2) parties mutually intended to liquidate them in advance; and (3) the amount of liquidated damages, when viewed as of the time the contract was made, was a reasonable estimate of potential actual damages a breach would cause.[68] If these factors apply to your transaction, liquidated damages should be considered to avoid protracted debates regarding the parties' harm when a breach occurs.

Limitations on Liability

Limitations on liability should always be considered and, if possible, incorporated in any contract for evaluation services. Typical clauses might state that liability is limited to an amount equal to the total amount paid by the customer under the contract. Other limitations on damages may require the customer to waive incidental or consequential damages or preclude recovery arising from certain conduct by the information security consultant. Like liquidated damages, however, the ability to limit or waive damages may be restricted by both statute and court decisions. For example, in some states, contractual provisions that purport to limit liability for gross negligence or for willful or wanton conduct are not enforceable.[69] In most states, limitations of liability are acceptable and will be enforced if the agreement was properly executed and the parties dealt at arms length.[70] Accordingly, you should try to limit the customer's right to recover consequential damages, punitive damages, and lost profits. Working with qualified counsel will assist in determining what limitations are enforceable in each specific transaction.

Survival of Obligations

This section makes clear what happens to specific contractual obligations, such as duties of non-disclosure and payment of funds owed, following the expiration of the contract.

Waiver and Severability

This section of the contract describes what happens if either party wants to waive the application of a portion of the contract, and allows for each section of the contract to be severable from the contract as a whole should a court rule that one clause or section is not enforceable. This section is also standard contract language and should be supplied by the attorney for the party drafting the contract.

Amendments to the Contract

For contracts that span significant periods of time, it is likely that one or both parties may require modifications to the contract. To avoid disputes, the original contract should spell out the format for any amendments. Amendments should be in writing and signed by authorized representatives of both parties. The parties should also discuss the financial arrangements surrounding a change to the contract. Proposed amendments to the contract must be accepted by the receiving party.

Where the Rubber Meets the Road: The LOA as Liability Protection

The contract functions as the overall agreement between the organization performing the security assessment and the company or network that will be tested or assessed. A LOA should be used between any two parties, whether party to the same original evaluation contract or not, to document consent to specific activities and protect against different types of adverse liability. For example, Widgets-R-Us contracts with Secure-Test to test the security of a new online shipping management network linked to Widgets' warehouses. ISP-anywhere provides the bandwidth for Widgets' east coast warehouses. Widgets should provide a LOA to Secure-Test consenting to specific network traffic that could trigger ISP-anywhere guards or intrusion detection systems. A copy of the letter should be provided to ISP-anywhere, in advance of the testing, as notice of the activity and a record of Widgets' consent. Additionally, depending on the language of the service agreement between Widgets and ISP-anywhere, Widgets may need to ask ISP-anywhere to provide a LOA for any of Secure-Test's activities that could impact their network infrastructure or otherwise void the bandwidth service agreement. ISP-anywhere was not a party to the original information security evaluation contract and, therefore, Secure-Test needs this additional form of agreement for the activities.

It is an unusual case in which a customer is the sole user of a third-party network system. Accordingly, the network hosts information for businesses and individuals that may maintain confidential information or information not owned by the customer. Merely accessing this information without proper authorization can result in both criminal and civil penalties. In addition, agreements between the customer and the network host may prohibit such access to the system altogether. You, along with your counsel, must always review these relationships with your customer, comply with contractual limitations, and obtain appropriate authorizations.

In many cases, the LOA will turn out to be the single most important document you sign. In addition to the potential civil liability for any damage to your customer's or third parties' systems that occur during periods when you arguably exceed your authorized access, failing to obtain adequate authorization may result in the commission of a crime. As discussed in "Legal Standards Relevant to Information Security" above, the federal Computer Fraud and Abuse Act imposes criminal liability for unauthorized access to computer systems and for exceeding the scope of authorization for accessing certain computers. Every state has passed some form of law that prohibits access to computer systems without proper authority.[71] Working with qualified and experienced legal counsel is vital to assure that your work avoids violation of law and the potential for criminal liability.

Another typical use of a LOA is augmentation of a part of the evaluation or correction of unforeseen technical challenges during the course of the contract (e.g., Widgets-R-Us acquires a warehouse on the west coast after the security evaluation begins, and wants to add this warehouse to the list of facilities Secure-Test will review). Widgets-R-Us does not need a new contract, and most likely does not need to amend the current contract, so long as both parties will accept a LOA to expand the scope of the security assessment. Whether or not to allow LOA amendments to a standing contract should be a term written into the original contract itself.

An important section of a LOA (similar to the overall contract itself) is a comprehensive and detailed statement of what a customer is not authorizing (i.e., certain systems or databases that are off limits, specific times that testing is not to be done, the tools the information security consultant will, and will not use, security measures that the customer will not permit the consultant to take, and so forth). This is equally important for the customer and the information security consultant.

LOAs should be signed by officials for each party with sufficient authority to agree to all specified terms. Importantly, LOAs between a customer and information security consultant should identify any and all types of information or specific systems for which the customer does not have the authority to authorize access. While LOA provisions can be part of the basic contract itself, as with non-disclosure agreements, it is often preferable to have the LOA be a separate, stand-alone agreement so that, if the LOA must be litigated later in public, as few details as possible of the larger agreement must be publicly exposed.

Beyond You and Your Customer

Simply obtaining your customer's consent to access their computer systems is necessary, but it is not always enough. Your customer has obligations to its customers, licensors, and other third parties. Honoring these commitments will avoid potential liability for both you and your customer.

Software License Agreements

Typically, software used by the customer will be subject to a license agreement that governs the relationship between the customer and the software provider. It is not uncommon for software license agreements to prohibit decompilation, disassembly, or reverse engineering of the software code, and to limit access to the software.

The use of tools to penetrate computer systems can constitute the use, access, and running of executable software using the computer's operating system and other programs in a manner that may violate the license agreement. To avoid civil liability, the consultant should have qualified and experienced legal counsel review applicable license agreements and, where appropriate, obtain authorization from the licensor prior to conducting tests of the customer's system.

Your Customer's Customer

To avoid creating liability for your customer, you need to understand your customer's customers and their expectations. Your customer should be able to identify their customer's confidential information and any specific contractual requirements. Understanding the source of third-party information (how it is stored and where appropriate or required), and obtaining consent to access their information is essential. To maintain the integrity of your work, you must respect the confidentiality of your customer and third party-information available to your customer. This is true even if no formal demand is made or no written agreement is entered into. You will be perceived as an agent of your customer; professionalism requires discretion and maintaining privacy.

Similarly, you need to recognize and honor intellectual property rights of your customer and its customers. In general, to protect your customer, you must also protect its customers with the high standards of respect for information privacy and security you provide to your customer.

The First Thing We Do...?
Why You Want Your Lawyers
Involved From Start to Finish

Few of Shakespeare's words have been more often quoted (and misquoted) than the immortal words of "Dick the Butcher": "The first thing we do, let's kill all the lawyers."[72] What generally is left out by modern lawyer bashers cheering Dick on in his quest is that Dick, and the band of rogues to which he belonged, were planning to overthrow the English government when this battle plan was suggested. The group followed up the lawyer killing idea shortly thereafter by hanging the town clerk of court.

The most reasonable reading of this passage is that Shakespeare intended to demonstrate that those who helped people interpret and litigate the law were, in fact, necessary to the orderly functioning of society. This interpretation is not without fierce challenge, however. In fact, a cottage industry emerges from time-to-time on the Internet debating whether Shakespeare was pro- or anti-lawyer. One prolific Internet lawyer-basher even suggests that the fact that lawyers use Shakespeare to justify our existence is conclusive evidence both of our ignorance and, to put it more charitably than the author, willingness to twist the facts to our own ends.[73]

Two things are certain. First, lots of people hate lawyers, some with very good reason. Second, the only thing worse than your own lawyer is the other guy's lawyer.

Having litigated numerous cases, and advised information security professionals inside and outside the federal government, we can assure information security professionals and their customers that, if and when you are sued by victims of attack or identify theft, or find yourselves in the sights of regulators or prosecutors, you will look to your lawyer as, if not a friend, at least a most necessary evil. And you will wish you had consulted that lawyer much, much sooner. Here's why.

It would seem obvious that, when the task is to determine how an entity may most effectively come into compliance with the numerous and complex legal requirements for information security, a qualified and experienced attorney should be involved. Surprisingly, this often does not appear to be the case today with information security evaluations. Most assessments and evaluations are conducted by computer engineers, accounting, and consulting firms. To be sure, that each of these professional competencies plays a necessary role in information security evaluations. However, since a key question is how to best comply with the current standards of care and, thus, mitigate potential legal liability, experienced and qualified counsel should be quarterbacking this team, much as a surgeon runs an operating room, even though nurses, anesthesiologists, and other competent professionals are crucial parts of the operating team.

WARNING: DO NOT PRACTICE LAW WITHOUT A LICENSE

In virtually every U.S. state, individuals are legally prohibited from practicing law without a license. For example, in Colorado, "practicing law" is defined, by law, to include, "counseling, advising and assisting [another] in connection with" legal rights and duties.[74] Penalties for the unauthorized practice of law in Colorado can include fines or imprisonment.[75] Information security consultants should not, under any circumstances, purport to advise customers as to the legal implications of statutes such as the HIPAA, Gramm-Leach-Bliley financial information privacy provisions, or other federal, state, or local laws or regulations. First, the consultants risk legal action against them by doing so. Second, they do their customers a grave disservice by leading them to believe that the customers can take any legal comfort from advice given them by non-lawyers.

Beyond this seemingly obvious reason for including the services and expertise of experienced and qualified legal counsel in conducting information security evaluations, a number of other factors also support doing so.

Attorney-Client Privilege

The so-called attorney-client privilege is one of the oldest protections for confidential information known to the law, and it is quite powerful. In every state, though with varying degrees of ease in establishing the privilege and differing degrees of exception to it, communications of legal advice from legal counsel to a client are "privileged," that is, protected, from compelled disclosure, including in civil lawsuits.[76] Information given by the client to the lawyer for the purpose of seeking legal advice is similarly protected.[77] In many, but not all jurisdictions, at least in civil litigation, once a court finds that the privilege applies, no amount of need for the privileged information claimed by a legal adversary cannot outweigh the protection created by the privilege.[78] This near-absolute protection is less certain, however, in at least some jurisdictions, in the criminal context.[79]

Further, courts in many states appear to apply a heightened level of scrutiny to corporate counsel and other "in-house" attorneys than they do to outside law firms retained by a corporation to perform particular legal services.[80] That is, courts force corporations to jump through more evidentiary "hoops" before allowing the attorney-client privilege for communications with in-house counsel than they do to communications with outside law firms.[81]

Importantly for information security consultants, courts have held (albeit in contexts analogous, but not identical, to information security, such as work with environmental consultants and accountants) that technical work performed by expert consultants can also enjoy attorney-client privilege protection.[82] Critically, though, this protection can attach to the consultant's work if, and only if, the client hires the attorney to perform a legal service (i.e., advising the client on how best to comply with HIPAA and/or other laws, and then the attorney hires the consultant to provide the attorney with technical information needed to provide accurate legal advice).[83] And this chain of employment cannot be a sham or mere pass-through used by the client to get the technical information but improperly cloak that data improperly with the privilege protection.[84]

The potential for the technical aspects of information security evaluations to enjoy enhanced protection from disclosure has obvious implications for information security evaluation results. If done honestly and correctly, the "chain of employment" (the hiring of a lawyer to provide legal advice which, in turn, requires assessment/evaluation work by technical experts) can protect all of the work. The legal advice, as well as, for example, technical reports showing identified potential vulnerabilities in the client's information security, may be protected under the attorney-client privilege.

It is important to recognize that, like information security measures, the attorney-client privilege is never "bullet proof." It is not absolute and there are, in every jurisdiction, well-recognized exceptions and ways to waive the protection (e.g., information provided to an attorney for the purpose of perpetrating a crime or fraud is not protected).[85] The protected nature of appropriately privileged information may disappear if the client or the attorney reveals that information to third parties outside the communication between the attorney (and consultants hired by the attorney) and certain company personnel (or in the presence of such third parties, even if the attorney is also present).[86] There are also times when it is appropriate to waive the privilege (e.g., a business or educational institution may choose to waive the privilege in order to assert an "advice-of-counsel" defense.) Also, the so-called Thompson Memorandum, issued by U.S Deputy Attorney General Larry Thompson in January 2003,[87] encourages companies to cooperate with the government in investigations by setting forth factors that are used to determine whether the government will pursue criminal prosecution. One important factor is whether the company is willing to waive the attorney–client and other privileges. Still, it is better to have these privileges to waive in an effort to encourage the government not to prosecute than not to have the privileges at all.

Courts have concluded that the societal benefit of not discouraging entities from conducting their own assessments of their compliance with applicable law outweighs any potential downside of the privilege, such as preventing all relevant information from coming out at trial.[88] This also makes good common sense. Entities will be far more likely to initiate their own compliance assessments/evaluations in information security, as in numerous other areas, if they are confident the results will be protected.[89]

Advice of Counsel Defense

Unfortunately, many information security consultants, auditors, and others attempt to advise customers about how to comply with laws and regulations they believe are applicable. This is problematic for several important reasons. First, generally speaking, experienced and qualified attorneys will be better able than others to accurately interpret and advise concerning the law. Second, as noted several times already, non-attorneys may run afoul of state law by purporting to provide legal advice.

In addition to these reasons, following the advice of non-lawyers as to how to comply with the law does not provide the same level of legal defense in future lawsuits, regulatory proceedings, or prosecutions as following an attorney's advice. In general, a client who provides full and accurate information to an attorney in the course of seeking advice on how to comply with information security law, and makes a good faith effort to follow that advice, can enjoy what is known as the "advice of counsel" defense.[90] This defense is a significant protection against legal liability. Following an attorney's advice on information security legal compliance can protect the client, even if that advice turns out to have been in error.[91]

Establishment and Enforcement of Rigorous Assessment, Interview, and Report-Writing Standards

Important components of information security evaluations and assessments are the interviews of key customer personnel and reviews of their documents. While this work can be, and often is, performed exclusively by engineers or other consultants, interviewing and document review are skills in which lawyers tend to be particularly proficient. These two tasks form major portions of the daily work of many lawyers. As important as actually conducting interviews and reviewing documents is making certain that the right people are interviewed and that all relevant documents are located and carefully reviewed. These tasks, in turn, require the evaluation team to be flexible and alert to new avenues of inquiry that arise during the course of an evaluation (as well as during preparation for, and follow up to, the evaluation). Again, these skills are ones that lawyers exercise virtually every day in their ordinary practices.

Regardless of how much information is collected, it is useless to the customer until it is put into a form that is clear, understandable, and placed in its appropriate context. Extraneous information must be removed. Simple, declarative language must be used. The implications of each piece of information included in the report must be clearly identified. Here again, clear, understandable writing is the stock-in-trade of good lawyers. Attorney involvement in the drafting, or at least reviewing and editing, of information security evaluation reports can add significantly to the benefit of the process, and the final product, to the customer.

Creating a Good Record for Future Litigation

Many qualified and experienced lawyers also know how to write for judges and juries. There is a flip side of the coin of attorney-client privilege to help protect confidential results of information security evaluations from compelled disclosure in court. That is, the benefit of managing the process so that the resulting reports will work well in court in the event that the privilege fails for some reason (inadvertent waiver of it by the client, for example) and a report must be disclosed, *or* a report ends up being helpful in litigation and you *want* to disclose it. In such circumstances, two things will be important. First, the evaluation process and resulting report(s) must stand up under the evidentiary standards imposed by the civil litigation rules. For example, good records of interviews and document reviews should be kept in such a way as to prove a defensible "paper trail" that will convince the court that the information is reliable enough to be allowed into evidence in a trial. Second, reports should be written in a way to clearly describe threats and vulnerabilities, but not overstate them or speak of them in catastrophic terms when such verbiage is not warranted.

Lawyers, and especially experienced trial lawyers, tend to be skilled at both tasks.

Maximizing Ability to Defend Litigation

In a real sense, all of the benefits of involving qualified and experienced counsel previously discussed will help information security professionals and their customers defend against future litigation and, as important, deter would-be litigants from suing in the first place. There is an additional benefit for defense of potential litigation, often phrased as "in on the takeoff, in on the landing." Particularly in business areas with a significant inherent risk of litigation or enforcement action, having qualified and experienced trial lawyers involved early in the business process and throughout that process, will help maximize the ability of the work of information security consultants and their customers stand up to future litigation.

Dealing with Regulators, Law Enforcement, Intelligence, and Homeland Security Officials

Your meeting with Uncle Sam could happen in at least two ways: you may call him, or he may call you. The first is preferable.

The first scenario may unfold in several ways. Your customer may believe it is a victim of an attack on its information systems, terrorism-related or otherwise, and either not be able to stop the attack as it unfolds, not be able to ascertain its origin after it is over, or not be able to determine whether the attackers left behind surprises for further attack at a later time. Or your customer may simply believe contacting the authorities is the right thing to do. In any event, those authorities may want to talk with you—and potentially subpoena you to testify in court—as part of their investigation. Alternatively, an attack may take place while you are working on the customer's systems, making you, in effect, the "first responder."

The second scenario, Uncle Sam reaching out affirmatively to you and/or your customers, also may unfold in multiple ways, but two things are fairly constant. One, the government will be looking at your customer's systems well before they contact your customer. Two, when they come, they generally will get the information they need, even if a subpoena or warrant is necessary. As demonstrated by the National Strategy to Secure Cyberspace, and, particularly since 9/11, the existence of some type of "cyber unit" at many national law enforcement, intelligence, and homeland security organizations, Uncle Sam is keenly interested in any breaches of cyber security that could threaten our national security. This interest, and the government's aggressiveness in pursuing it, is likely only to increase.

In either scenario (voluntary or involuntary contact with the government, including state law enforcement agencies), what you and/or your customers do in the first few hours may be critical to how intact their information systems and sensitive information are when the process is complete. Who has the authority to speak to government authorities? What can and cannot be said to them? How much legal authority (request vs. search warrant vs. subpoena) will be required before allowing them in? Is there any information that they should not be allowed to review? What is the potential legal liability for sharing too much information? Too little? Obviously, your customers (and you, if you are involved) will want to cooperate with legitimate requests and, in fact, may have requested the government's help, but all businesses, educational institutions, and information security consultants must take care not to create civil or criminal liability for themselves by how they conduct their contacts with governmental authorities.

Here again, the keys are: (1) immediately gain the assistance of qualified legal counsel experienced both in information security law and in dealing with law enforcement, intelligence, and homeland security officers; and (2) have a plan in place beforehand for how such authorities will be dealt with, including having legal counsel retained and ready to go.

Notes from the Underground...

What to Look For in Your Attorneys

There are a number of obvious characteristics one should seek in any attorney retained for any purpose. These include integrity, a good reputation in the legal community, and general competence. You also want to consider an attorney with a strong background in corporate and business transactions who is familiar with the contracting process. One useful tool for evaluating these qualities as you attempt to narrow your list of potential attorneys to interview is a company called Martindale Hubbell (*www.martindale.com*). Look for lawyers with an "AV" rating (Martindale's highest).

(Note: Never hire any attorney without at least one face-to-face meeting to learn what your gut tells you about whether you could work with him or her.)

In the area of information security evaluation, you will want to look for attorneys with deep and broad expertise in the field. The best way to do so is to look for external, independently verifiable criteria demonstrating an attorney or law firm's tested credentials (e.g., is the lawyer you seek to retain listed on the National Security Agency Web site as including individuals certified as having been trained in NSA's Information Security Assurance Methodology (IAM)? If so, on the appropriate NSA Web page (e.g., www.iatrp.com/indivu2.cfm#C), you will find a listing similar to this: Cunningham, Bryan, 03/15/05, (303) 743-0003, bc@morgancunningham.net)

Has an attorney you are considering authored any published works in the area of information security law? Has he or she held positions, in the government or elsewhere, related to information security? Finally, there's the gut check. How does your potential lawyer make you feel? Are you comfortable working with him or her? Does he or she communicate clearly and concisely? Does he or she seem more interested in covering their own backside than in providing you with legal counsel to protect your interests?

The Ethics of Information Security Evaluation[92]

The eighteenth century philosopher, Immanuel Kant, observed, "[i]*n law a man is guilty when he violates the rights of others. In ethics he is guilty if he only thinks of doing so.*"[93] To think and act ethically requires more than just strict compliance with the law. It requires an understanding of your customer, their business environment, and the duties your customer owes to others, under statutory requirements as well as private contracts. The reward is an increased likelihood of compliance with laws and establishing credibility in the community that will reduce the likelihood of disputes with customers and increase your marketability. Ethics relate to your conduct and not to the conduct of those with whom you are transacting business. However, it is not unethical to be alert to the possibility that others with whom you are dealing are themselves unethical. Do not be naive. Pursuit of an ethical practice does not replace the need to protect yourself through reliable processes, consistent methodologies, and properly drafted contracts that include defined work, limitations on liability, and indemnifications.

Do not think of violating the rights of others. Do not take short cuts. Do not assume that you can conduct your work without understanding the needs and rights of others and acting to protect them. Failing to understand the rights of customers you have been retained to help, or of those involved with your customers is tantamount to thinking of violating their rights. Ethical business, therefore, requires you understand the players and whose rights are at stake.

Finally, though it sounds obvious, do your job well. Martin Van Buren counseled that "[i]t is easier to do a job right than to explain why you didn't." Customers often insist on short cuts and reject proposals that require time delays to document the relationship and obtain the appropriate consents before the work begins. Customers soon forget their front-end demands for cost savings and expedience in completing the project. Hold firm. Do the job right and avoid having to explain to an angry customer, a prosecutor, a judge, or a jury why you did not.

Solutions Fast Track

Uncle Sam Wants You: How Your Company's Information Security Can Affect U.S. National Security (and Vice Versa)

☑ The U.S. Government has announced both the possibility of a significant information security attack on our U.S. critical infrastructure, and its intent to respond forcefully to such an attack if necessary, and the duty of the private sector to better secure its portion of cyberspace.

☑ Although no one can predict when and how severe such an attack may be, prudent commercial and educational entities, after the attacks of September 11, 2001, also should assume it will happen and act accordingly.

☑ This is an additional reason, beyond business operational needs, legal and regulatory requirements, and customer confidence, why commercial and educational entities should engage qualified and experienced legal counsel and technical information security providers sooner rather than later.

Legal Standards Relevant to Information Security

☑ A complex web of federal, state, and international statutes, regulations, and common law is evolving to create legal duties for commercial and educational entities in the area of information security.

☑ Non-lawyer consultants, even knowledgeable ones, cannot lawfully give advice on compliance with these laws, and commercial and educational entities should not rely on them to do so.

☑ This chapter cannot provide commercial and educational entities (or anyone else) with legal advice. Only qualified, licensed, and experienced legal counsel in a direct relationship with individual corporate and educational clients can do so.

Selected Laws

☑ At the U.S. federal level, HIPAA, GLBA, SOX, the Computer Fraud and Abuse Act, and other statutes and the regulations under them, as well as new ones yet to emerge, are constantly creating new information security legal obligations.

☑ State laws and "common law" theories such as negligence also may result in liability for failing to follow emerging "standards of care."

☑ Civil damages, regulatory action and, in some cases, even criminal liability, may result from failure, on the part of commercial and educational entities and the information security consultants who provide services to them, to seek (and follow) the advice of qualified and experienced legal counsel concerning these many emerging legal obligations.

Do It Right of Bet the Company: Tools to Mitigate Legal Liability

☑ Hire qualified, outside, legal and technical professionals.

☑ Effectively manage your contractual relationships to minimize liability.

What to Cover in IEM Contracts[94]

☑ Information security consultants must ensure that their legal obligations and rights, and those of their customers, are clearly spelled out in detailed written agreements.

☑ At a minimum, these should cover the topics discussed in the body of the chapter.

☑ In most cases LOAs, which are separate documents appended to an overall contract, should be used to clearly establish the authority, and any limitations on it, of information security consultants, to access and conduct testing on all types of information, systems, and portions of the Internet necessary to carry out the requested work.

The First Thing We Do…? Why You Want Your Lawyers Involved From Start to Finish

- ☑ Lawyers are a necessary evil to all information security consultants and their customers.

- ☑ Lawyers add value by, among other things: (1) helping to establish protection from disclosure, both for discovered customer information security vulnerabilities and the trade secrets and working methodology of information security consultants; (2) creating additional legal defenses against future liability.

- ☑ Lawyers (and only lawyers) may lawfully advise clients as to how best to comply with HIPAA, GLBA, SOX, and other federal and state statutory, regulatory, and common law legal requirements.

Frequently Asked Questions

The following Frequently Asked Questions, answered by the authors of this book, are designed to both measure your understanding of the concepts presented in this chapter and to assist you with real-life implementation of these concepts. To have your questions about this chapter answered by the author, browse to **www.syngress.com/solutions** and click on the **"Ask the Author"** form. You will also gain access to thousands of other FAQs at ITFAQnet.com.

Q: Why can't I advise customers about compliance with HIPAA or SOX information security requirements if I'm a knowledgeable information security consultant?

A: Doing so would not only put you at risk for violating state law prohibitions against the unauthorized practice of law, but also fail to provide your customers either with attorney-client privilege protection against disclosure of vulnerabilities information or an "advice of counsel" defense.

Q: Why doesn't my in-house lawyer's involvement give me sufficient attorney-client privilege protection?

A: Contracting information security evaluations through in-house counsel is better than not having that involvement. However, as discussed, courts in multiple jurisdictions impose a higher standard for allowing attorney-client privilege for in-house counsel than for outside, retained lawyers.

Q: How often do I need to have information security evaluations?

A: Courts and regulators will apply a "reasonability" determination on this question, and it will be fact-specific, depending on the industry you are in, the types and amount of sensitive information you hold, and the then-current status of legal and regulatory requirements applicable to your business. In general, however, they should probably be no less frequently than once a year and, in many cases, more often.

Q: If I have a limited budget, why wouldn't I just buy a penetration test?

A: First, you likely will fail the first penetration test unless you have engaged in a more thorough NSA IAM/IEM process. Second, unless the test is part of a larger evaluation program under the guidance and supervision of retained outside counsel, the results of this test (i.e., your failure) will not enjoy protection from disclosure. Third, penetration tests, by definition, cannot identify a myriad of information security vulnerabilities that are not strictly technical in nature, and patching whatever holes are identified by the test may not only give you a false sense of security, but also demonstrate your awareness of security issues, creating potential future legal problems if you do not take more comprehensive measures.

Q: How much does having a lawyer involved add to the cost of information security evaluations?

A: Assuming you locate qualified and experienced counsel working with equally qualified technical consultants, and those two groups, in partnership, provide an integrated product that is priced in a reasonable and packaged way, your costs may well be less than using large, expensive, hourly rate-based consulting companies alone.

Q: How likely is a catastrophic information attack on our country?

A: There is a great deal of disagreement on this question, including among the authors of this chapter. However, the U.S. government has based a publicly stated policy on the possibility of such an attack and, post-9/11, it is prudent to assume such an attack could take place. Perhaps most importantly, assuming such an attack could occur only supports the myriad other business reasons to take reasonable information security measures, including one that lawyers rarely talk about: it is the right thing to do.

Q: Why are scientists now using lawyers more than rats for experiments?

A: (1) There are now more lawyers available than there are rats;(2) it is possible for scientists to get emotionally attached to the rats; and (3) there are some things you just can't get a rat to do.

References

[1] This chapter was written jointly by: Bryan Cunningham, Principal at Morgan & Cunningham LLC, a Denver-based homeland security consulting and law firm, and formerly Deputy Legal Adviser to the U.S. National Security Council and Assistant General Counsel, Central Intelligence Agency; C. Forrest Morgan, Principal at Morgan & Cunningham LLC, and Amanda Hubbard, Trial Attorney, U.S. Department of Justice with extensive experience in the U.S. Intelligence Community. The authors also gratefully acknowledge the research and analysis assistance of Nir D. Yarden. The views expressed herein are solely those of the authors and do not necessarily represent the views of the publisher or the U.S. government.

[2] This section drew, in part, from portions of pages 7–11 of *Security Assessment: Case Studies for*

Implementing the NSA IAM, used by permission of Syngress Publishing, Inc.

[3] *Kennedy v. Mendoza-Martinez, 372 U.S. 144, 160 (1963).*

[4] *See, e.g.,* the 1993 opinion of the U.S. Department of Justice Office of Legal Counsel: "The concept of 'enforcement' is a broad one, and a given statute may be 'enforced' by means other than criminal prosecutions brought directly under it." *Admissibility of Alien Amnesty Application Information in Prosecutions of Third Parties*, 17 Op. O.L.C. (1993); *see also* the 1898 opinion of Acting Attorney General John K. Richards:

> *The preservation of our territorial integrity and the protection of our foreign interests is intrusted, in the first instance, to the President. . . . In the protection of these fundamental rights, which are based upon the Constitution and grow out of the jurisdiction of this nation over its own territory and its international rights and obligations as a distinct sovereignty, the President is not limited to the enforcement of specific acts of Congress. [The President] must preserve, protect, and defend those fundamental rights which flow from the Constitution itself and belong to the sovereignty it created.*

> *Foreign Cables,* 22 Op. Att'y Gen. 13, 25-26 (1898); *see also Cunningham v. Neagle,* 135 U.S. 1, 64 (1890).

[5] As Discussed in FN 13.

[6] United States National Strategy to Secure Cyberspace, February 14, 2003 (hereinafter "National Strategy") at 10. The National Strategy is available at: *http://www.whitehouse.gov/pcipb/*.

[7] See Testimony of Keith Lourdeau, Deputy Assistant Director, Cyber Division, FBI Before the Senate Judiciary Subcommittee on Terrorism, Technology, and Homeland Security, February 24, 2004 ("The FBI assesses the cyberterrorism threat to the U.S. to be rapidly expanding, as the number of actors with the ability to utilize computers for illegal, harmful, and possibly devastating purposes is on the rise. Terrorist groups have shown a clear interest in developing basic hacking tools and the FBI predicts that terrorist groups will either develop or hire hackers, particularly for the purpose of complimenting large physical attacks with cyber attacks."); Robert Lenzner and Nathan Vardi, Cyber-nightmare, http://protectia.co.uk/html/cybernightmare.html.

[8] *Id.*

[9] *Frontline* interview conducted March 18, 2003, at *http://www.pbs.org/wgbh/pages/frontline/shows/cyberwar/interviews/clarke.html*.

[10] *http://www.pbs.org/wgbh/pages/frontline/shows/cyberwar/interviews/clarke.html*.

[11] *http://www.pbs.org/wgbh/pages/frontline/shows/cyberwar/interviews/clarke.html*; Hildreth, CRS Report for Congress, *Cyberwarfare*, Updated June 19, 2001, at 18, at http://www.fas.org/irp/crs/RL30735.pdf

[12] *Cyberwarfare.* at 2.

[13] The idea of a catastrophic cyber attack against the U.S. by terrorist groups is far from universally accepted. *See, e.g.,* James A. Lewis, *Assessing the Risks of Cyber Terrorism, Cyber War and Other Cyber Threats,* Center for Strategic and International Studies, December 2002, at *http://www.csis.org/tech/0211_lewis.pdf.* Indeed, as noted above, one of the three authors of this chapter believes that, while technically possible, this threat is often overstated, at least as a near-term possibility. For information security professionals and their customers, however, the prudent course—given our adversaries' capability, intent, and opportunity and the stated U.S. Government policy of being prepared to respond to cyber attack—is to assume the possibility of such an attack. In addition, the plethora of known active threats to information security, including extortionists, identity thieves, gangs attempting to amass and sell financial and other valuable personal informa- tion, malicious hackers, and others, provide precisely the same incentive to secure information sys- tems' as do would-be cyber-terrorists.

[14] *See, e.g., Law of Armed Conflict and Information Warfare—How Does the Rule Regarding Reprisals Apply to an Information Warfare, Attack?,* Major Daniel M. Vadnais, March 1997, at 25 ("To the extent that information warfare is manifested by traditionally understood damage to sovereign integrity, the law of armed conflict should apply, and proportional reprisals may be justified. On the other hand, to the extent that damage to a sovereign's integrity is not physical, there is a gap in the law."). *http://www.fas.org/irp/threat/cyber/97-0116.pdf.*

[15] *Id.*

[16] National Strategy at p. 59 (A/R 5-4).

[17] National Strategy at p. 49 (Priority V: National Security and International Cyberspace Security Cooperation).

[18] Nearly as dangerous for our Nation as attacks from within the U.S. directed *at us,* would be if zombied servers here were being used to launch an attack *against another nation.* Imagine the reaction of China or Iran if servers inside the U.S. were being used to damage their infrastructure or harm their people. First, they likely would not believe denials by our government that these acts of war were being carried out deliberately by our government. Second, even if they did believe such denials, they still might feel compelled to respond with force to disable or destroy the systems of, and/or punish, those they perceived to be their attackers.

[19] Particularly in the wake of the 2005 publicity surrounding security breaches at ChoicePoint, LexisNexis, MasterCard, major banks, other commercial entities, and universities, a number of pieces of legislation requiring disclosure of information security breaches and/or enhanced information security measures were working their way through the U.S. Congress, or were threatened in the near future. *See* Roy Mark, *Data Brokers Step Into Senate Panel's Fire,* e–Security Planet.com, http://66.102.7.104/search?q=cache:REXdffBCvEYJ:www.esecurityplanet.com/trends/article.php/ 3497591+specter+and+information+security+and+disclosure&hl=en.

[20] 15 U.S.C. §§ 6801, et. seq.

[21] 15 U.S.C. § 6801(b).

[22] 15 U.S.C. §§ 6804 – 6805.

[23] Available at *http://www.ffiec.gov/ffiecinfobase/resources/elect_bank/frb-12_cfr_225_appx_f_bank_holding_non-bank_affiliates.pdf*.

[24] *Guidelines.*

[25] *Id.*

[26] *Id.*

[27] *Id.*

[28] *Id.*

[29] EPHI is defined in the law as individually identifiable health information that is transmitted by, or maintained in, electronic media, except several narrow categories of educational, employment, and other records. 45 C.F.R. part 106.103. Note, however, that the separate HIPAA Privacy Rule also requires "appropriate security" for all PHI, even if it is not in electronic form.

[30] 45 C.F.R. part 164.

[31] Compliance with the Security Rule became mandatory for all but small health care plans in April 2005. "Small" health care plans have until April 2006 to comply.

[32] 45 C.F.R. part 164.

[33] *Id.* One reason it is crucial for information security professionals to retain, on an ongoing basis, qualified, experienced counsel is that "reasonably anticipated" is essentially a legal standard best understood and explained by legal counsel and because what is "reasonably anticipated" is constantly evolving as new threats are discovered and publicized, and information security programs must evolve with it in order to mitigate legal liability,

[34] *Id.*

[35] *Id.*

[36] It is worth remembering that a significant majority of the process and procedural requirements are *not* technical. This, among other considerations, counsels the use of multidisciplinary teams, of which technical experts are only one part, to conduct and document information security evaluations.

[37] 45 C.F.R. Part 164.308.

[38] 45 C.F.R. Part 164.310.

[39] 45 C.F.R. Part 164.312.

[40] 18 U.S.C. § 1350.

[41] SOX § 404.

[42] SOX § 302.

[43] FISMA, Title III of the E-Government Act of 2002, Public Law No. 107-347.

[44] FN: 20 U.S.C § 1232g

[45] As enacted, the TEACH Act amended Section 110 of the Copyright Act. 17 U.S.C. §110.

[46] 18 U.S.C. § 2510, *et. seq.*

[47] 18 U.S.C. § 1030, *et. seq.*

[48] Other federal laws and regulations potentially relevant to the work of information security professionals and their customers include, but are not limited to, the Children's Online Privacy Protection Act of 1998, information security standards promulgated by the National Institute of Standards, Presidential Decision Directive 63 (May 22, 1998), and Homeland Security Presidential Directive 7 (December 17, 2003). In addition, numerous state laws, including provisions of the Uniform Commercial Code and Uniform Financial Transactions Act, as enacted in the various states, implicate information security requirements for specific economic sectors and/or types of transactions.

[49] Colorado Revised Statutes § 18-5.5-102.

[50] Colorado Revised Statutes § 6-1-105.

[51] Colorado Revised Statutes § 6-1-105(e).

[52] Colorado Revised Statutes § 6-1-105(u).

[53] Between 2001 and 2005 such actions included those against: Microsoft Corporation, Victoria's Secret, Eli Lilly, and Ziff Davis Media, Inc., among others. *See, e.g.,* http://www.ftc.gov/os/2002/08/microsoftagree.pdf; http://www.oag.state.ny.us/press/2002/aug/aug28a_02_attach.pdf.

[54] *Directive 95/46/EC of the European Parliament and of the Council of 24 October 1995 on the protection of individuals with regard to the processing of personal data and on the free movement of such data, Official Journal of the European Communities of 23 November 1995 No L. 281, 31, available at* http://www.cdt.org/privacy/eudirective/EU_Directive_.html.

[55] *See, e.g.,* Transcript of Hearing Before U.S. District Judge Royce Lamberth, in which an information security consultant is examined and cross-examined under oath, in public, for multiple days, concerning penetration test work done for the U.S. Bureau of Indian Affairs. http://66.102.7.104/search?q=cache:d30x73ieDSwJ:www.indiantrust.com/_pdfs/3am.pdf+lamberth+and+cobell+and+transcript+and+miles&hl=en

[56] For example, B. Grimes *The Right Ways to Protect Your Net* PC World Magazine, September 2001, offers tips for tightening your security and protecting your enterprise from backdoor hackers and thieves.

[57] *http://wsbradio.com/news/0223choicepointsuit.html.*

[58] *Harrington v. ChoicePoint Inc.,* C.D. Cal., No. CV 05-1294 (SJO) (JWJx), 2/22/05).

[59] Generally, a post-hoc calculation of "reasonability" will be based on balancing such factors as: (1) the probability of reasonably anticipated damage occurring; (2) the expected severity of the damage if it does occur; (3) reasonably available risk mitigation measures; and (4) the cost of implementing such measures.

[60] *See, e.g., Assurance of Discontinuance, In the Matter of Ziff Davis Media Inc.*, at 7, available at *http://www.oag.state.ny.us/press/2002/aug/aug28a_02_attach.pdf.;*
Agreement Containing Consent Order, In the Matter of Microsoft Corporation, at 5, available at *http://www.ftc.gov/os/2002/08/microsoftagree.pdf.*

[61] California Civil Code Sections 1798.29 and 1798.82 accessible at *http://www.leginfo.ca.gov/calaw.html.*

[62] 2005 Breach of Information Legislation. http://www.ncsl.org/programs/lis/CIP/priv/breach.htm.

[63] P. Britt, *Protecting Private Information* Information Today (Vo. 22 No. 5 May, 2005) *http://www.info-today.com/it/may05/britt.shtml.*

[64] This section drew, in part, from portions of pages 7-11 of *Security Assessment: Case Studies for Implementing the NSA IAM*, used by permission of Syngress Publishing, Inc.

[65] Assuming the NSA IAM is used, of course, much of this critical work will already have been documented prior to initiation of the IEM.

[66] The issue of securing complete authorization for all types of information and systems (internal and external) that may be impacted by evaluation and testing, is intentionally covered in multiple parts of this section. It is absolutely critical to the legal well being of both the consultant and the customer to ensure clarity of responsibility for these, which is why this section provides multiple different avenues for addressing this problem. Equally critical is a clear understanding of the "division of liability" for any damage that, notwithstanding best efforts of both sides, may result to external systems. This should be taken care of through a combination of indemnification (described below), clear statements of responsibility in the contract, written agreements with third parties, and insurance.

[67] *See, e.g., Management Recruiters, Inc. v. Miller, 762 P.2d 763, 766 (Colo.App.1988).*

[68] *Board of County Commissioners of Adams County v. City and County of Denver, 40 P.3d 25 (Colo.App.,2001).*

[69] *See, e.g., Butler Manufacturing Co. v. Americold Corp., 835 F.Supp. 1274 (D.Kan. 1993).*

[70] *See, e.g., Elsken v. Network Multi-Family Sec. Corp., 838 P.2d 1007 (Okla.1992)*

[71] National Conference of State Legislatures information page accessible at *http://www.ncsl.org/programs/lis/cip/hacklaw.htm.*

[72] *Henry VI*, Part 2, act iv, scene ii.

[73] *See, e.g.,* Seth Finkelstein, "The first thing we do, let's kill all the lawyers" – It's a Lawyer Joke, *The Ethical Spectator,* July 1997., available at: *http://www.sethf.com/essays/major/killlawyers.php.*

[74] *Koscove v. Bolte, 30 P.3d 784* (Colo.App. 2001*).*

[75] *See, e.g.* Rule 238(c), Colorado Court Rules (2004).

[76] *See, e.g., Pacamor Bearings, Inc. v. Minebea Co., Ltd.*, 918 F.Supp. 491, 509-510 (D. N.H. 1996).

[77] *Id.*

[78] *See, e.g., Diversified Indus., Inc. v. Meredith, 572 F.2d 596, 602 (8th Cir. 1978).*

[79] *See, e.g., People v. Benney, 757 P.2d 1078 (Colo.App. 1987).*

[80] *See, e.g., Southern Bell Telephone & Telegraph Co. v. Deason, 632 So. 2d 1377 (Fla. 1994); McCaugherty v. Sifferman, 132 F.R.D. 234 (N.D. Cal. 1990). United States v. Davis 132 F.R.D. 12 (S.D.N.Y. 1990).*

[81] *See, e.g., United States v. Chevron,* No. C-94-1885 SBA, 1996 WL 264769 (N.D. Cal. Mar. 13, 1996).

[82] *See, e.g., Gerrits v. Brannen Banks of Florida 138 F.R.D. 574, 577 (D. Colo. 1991).*

[83] *See, e.g., id.*

[84] *See, e.g., Sneider v. Kimberly-Clark Corp.,* 91 F.R.D. 1, 5 (N.D. Ill. 1980)

[85] *See, e.g., In re Grand Jury Proceedings,* 857 F.2d 710, 712 (10th Cir. 1988).

[86] *See, e.g., Winchester Capital Management Co. vs. Manufacturers Hanover Trust Co.,* 144 F.R.D.170, 174 (D. Mass. 1992).

[87] U.S. Department of Justice, *Federal Prosecution of Business Organizations* in *Criminal Resource Manual* No. 162 (2003) available at *http://www.usdoj.gov/usao/eousa/foia_reading_room/usam/title9/crm00162.html* and amended and available at *http://www.usdoj.gov/dag/cftf/corporate_guidelines.html.*

[88] *See, e.g., Union Carbide Corp. v. Dow Chem. Co.,* 619 F. Supp. 1036, 1046 (D. Del. 1985)

[89] A related protection to that of the attorney-client privilege is the so-called "work product" doctrine. This protection for materials that might tend to show the strategies or other "mental impressions" of attorneys when such materials are prepared "in anticipation of litigation" would cover the work of information security consultants assisting attorneys in preparing materials for use at a trial or to deal with regulators or law enforcement officials. Work-product protection is significantly more susceptible to being held inapplicable by the court, upon a sufficiently high showing of need by your adversary, than is the attorney-client privilege.

[90] *See, e.g., United States v. Gonzales,* 58 F.3d 506, 512 (10th Cir. 1995).

[91] *Id.*

[92] Entire books could be written on this topic, and some have, at least on the broader topic of IT ethics. *See, e.g., IT Ethics Handbook: Right and Wrong for IT Professionals,* Syngress Publishing, Inc. A comprehensive discussion of Information Security Evaluation ethics is beyond the scope of this book. This discussion is simply to remind us all of some things we learned from our parents that translate into our business relationships.

[93] Available at *http://en.thinkexist.com/quotation/in_law_a_man_is_guilty_when_he_violates_the/7854.html.*

[94] This section drew, in part,, from portions of pages 7-11 of Security Assessment: Case Studies for Implementing the NSA IAM, used by permission of Syngress Publishing, Inc.

Chapter 6

Building the Technical Evaluation Plan

Solutions in this chapter:

- Purpose of the Technical Evaluation Plan
- Building the Technical Evaluation Plan
- Customizing and Modifying the Technical Evaluation Plan
- Getting the Signatures

☑ Summary

☑ Solutions Fast Track

☑ Frequently Asked Questions

Introduction

The *technical evaluation plan* (TEP) plays a critical role in setting and meeting customer expectations. The TEP also establishes how the entire evaluation will be accomplished. In the previous chapters we went into great detail about the TEP's sections and the fact that the TEP should be considered the core product of the pre-evaluation process. The TEP combines any and all created or discovered the information into an easily understood summary of the organization about to be evaluated.

The purpose or goal of the TEP is to be an integral part of the IEM. In fact, the TEP *becomes* the IEM road map after the pre-evaluation is complete. Not only is the TEP a summary of the *understood* status of the target organization, it also discusses the major action items to be covered during the evaluation process as well as any fundamental concerns, constraints, or focal points the customer would like addressed. In this chapter we discuss the various aspects of the TEP and some of the things we want it to accomplish.

We also lay out the TEP in a detailed format for discussion. Each portion of the plan covers different topics in different levels of detail. Some of the topics share concerns, such as ease of use and level of detail. Both of these are factors to be determined between the customer and the evaluating teams, as we'll see later. And of course we review the topic-specific items and how they support the IEM process and the overall goal of improving the customer's total INFOSEC posture.

Lastly, we cover some of the options you can use to customize the TEP. As we detail the requirements, keep in mind that some pieces may be added or modified to fit the needs of individual scenarios. We don't cover all possible changes, but we do look at some of today's more common ones. Don't worry—the major components of the TEP that are considered vital by NSA standards are explained throughout the chapter. The goal is to create the most customer-centric management tool possible, without losing the key concepts that promote information security best practices.

Purpose of the Technical Evaluation Plan

The TEP is designed to tie together all aspects of an IEM between the customer and the evaluation team. It is the primary agreement used to maintain customer expectations, which is crucial to successful security evaluations. The TEP is meant to be the guide for the evaluation process as well as a tool the customer organization and the independent evaluation team use to maintain focus during the project. Expect the TEP to be a heavily used and discussed document. The TEP focuses on some of the most important, and often dynamic, aspects of a security evaluation:

- Dates and scheduling
- Personnel involvement
- Understood boundaries
- Deliverables
- Priority concerns

- Priority constraints
- Evaluation tools and tool limitations

This is only a brief list of items addressed in this chapter, but as you can see, they would be considered major management topics for just about any project or engagement. In simplified terms, the IEM TEP lays out those concerns with a focus on security practices and makes them clear and easily understood topics for all involved parties.

In both commercial and government environments, you can see that this tool is an excellent method for maintaining scope between the customer and the evaluation team. It can help prevent the misunderstandings that often occur in very large organizations such as government agencies or multinational corporations. From a consulting perspective, the TEP also manages to help protect payments, since it gives you approved documentation clearly stating the objectives, deliverables, and timeline of the project as agreed on by both parties. It also helps eliminate scope drift, which can be a real killer in any fixed-price engagement agreements.

The IEM TEP, like all other documentation you create or send the customer, should be considered a controlled document that would have security implications if released publicly. The information disclosed in the TEP alone should not be enough to cause a security incident, but it will discuss architectures, security measures, current concerns, and other issues that the organization most likely would not like to become public knowledge. There is no reason to make available *any* extra information to possible criminal threat sources. Here are some specifically dangerous topics that a TEP will include (but you're not limited to these):

- Detailed network diagrams
- Software brands and version levels
- Internal addressing schemes
- Descriptions of high-assurance components

The IEM TEP plays two roles in the IEM process. It serves as an agreement between the customer and the evaluation team. It also serves as a road map for the execution of the evaluation.

The IEM TEP as an Agreement

As an agreement, the TEP's focus is to assure that all the customer and evaluation team concerns and constraints are addressed to a mutual satisfaction. Just like any agreement or contract, it will contain legal terminology addressing the legal concerns of the evaluation, but it will also give a great deal of detail about what the customer expects before, during, and following the evaluation. After completing and reviewing the IEM TAP, both the customer and the evaluation organization should approve the document via signature. This helps ensure the understanding of both parties and works to keep everyone fully informed. It also provides direct evidence to the original agreement in regard to the deliverables expected and their timeframes.

The TEP is often compared to a statement of work (SOW) because it outlines and details actions and deliverables as well as the level of effort and objectives intended. It would not be unheard of to define this in any contracts or SOWs as the proper method for handling change control issues. Depending on your legal counsel's advice, it may be acceptable to simply create addendums to the TEP, approved by mutual signature, as the process for documenting and accepting any changes in scope within the original project. For independent firms, this is an excellent method for ensuring proper adherence to accepted responsibilities.

The TEP is a living document that can and probably will be modified during the execution of the evaluation process. Often, these changes occur following a meeting with the customer leadership, when the progress of the evaluation is being discussed and the customer realizes they desire additional activities to occur. In such a situation, a simple change-order process can be utilized. It doesn't always require a change in cost, but it certainly does require documenting the change and having both parties sign off on it. Since the TEP is a road map to conducting the evaluation, changes may impact the customer and require additional resources or time to accomplish the evaluation. Ultimately, the final TEP will become part of the final report.

WARNING

Don't make the mistake of using the same TEP content for every customer. This TEP is a customized document that helps define the IEM process for that specific customer only. The outline for the TEP is good, but the content is customized on a customer-by-customer basis.

The TEP as Road Map

As a road map, the TEP functions as the guide for conducting the evaluation for the customer. The TEP should be detailed enough to address items such as scheduling, scan time, customer preparation, customer and evaluation team contacts, and a great deal of other items. The TEP identifies the expectations and the tempo for the evaluation process. It should cover all the pieces that go into an IEM-derived evaluation—from the work completed during the pre-evaluation all the way to the expectations for final report delivery. The TEP also incorporates information from the IAM that is directly relevant to the IEM process.

The TEP should be used to help document the overall evaluation and organize activities for the remaining phases. The TEP is really a map that has been approved by both sides of the evaluation in terms of actions that will be taken to evaluate the customer's INFOSEC status and the timing of each action, such as site visits, opening meetings, periodic updates, exit briefings, scanning windows, rules of engagement, and so on. If an action or task is planned for inclusion in the process, it should be included and detailed in the TEP for reference.

The document also acts as a record of the events to occur during the process. As the evaluation begins, the document is used for assisting coordination, managing customer expectations, and providing guidance. Then, as objectives are met and functions or information are documented, the TEP also begins functioning much like a checklist and validation tool. By the end of the evaluation, the TEP should show the process in a summarized format from beginning to end, including any changes in objectives, methods, plans, and so forth. In essence, you could consider the TEP a life-cycle report, documenting where the project began and with whom and leading all the way up to the completed findings. Figure 6.1 illustrates the road map to a successful IEM.

Figure 6.1 The TEP Road Map

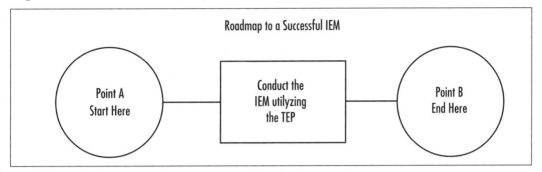

Building the Technical Evaluation Plan

By now, you should have most of the information you need to put together the TEP, since the TEP is completed at the end of the pre-evaluation phase of the IEM. Appendix B of this book gives an example TEP to assist you in seeing the format and content of a TEP. The TEP is composed of 10 specific areas. They are:

- Points of contact
- Methodology overview
- Criticality information
- Detailed network information
- Customer concerns
- Customer constraints
- Rules of engagement
- Coordination agreements
- Letter of authorization
- Timeline of events

Source of the Technical Evaluation Plan Information

Throughout the pre-evaluation phase, we identified multiple activities that start to build the evaluation process for our specific customer. To effectively manage customer expectations, we must incorporate this knowledge into an easy-to-use plan of action for conducting the evaluation. This is our TEP. The information for the TEP comes from four primary sources: the IEM pre-evaluation process, the IAM pre-assessment process, the evaluation team, and the customer. Working in concert, these various sources of information can be combined to effectively address customer needs and manage customer expectations, which is the key to a successful implementation of the IEM. Figure 6.2 shows how multiple information sources feed into the TEP.

Figure 6.2 TEP Sources

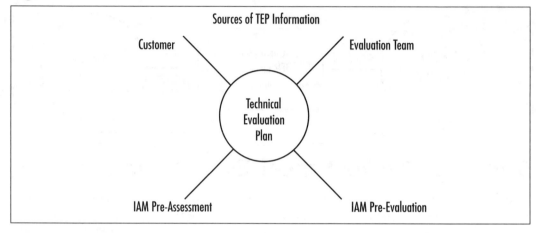

TEP Section I: Points of Contact

The first section of the TEP contains contact information for key players in both the customer and the evaluation team organizations. All means of communication should be documented here—phone numbers, e-mail addresses, site addresses, and so on. The requirements for number of contacts, roles of contacts, and so on are up to your team. At a minimum, the primary point of contact (POC) for both the customer and the evaluation team should be listed. Hopefully, most of the POC information was already gathered during the pre-evaluation and is located either in the IEM planning survey or the IEM checklist.

Contact information should come first in the TEP, since it often is the most needed type of information for customer staff who might not be working directly with the evaluation team. It will help the customer organization's executives understand a project they might be getting requests about, as well as giving them a starting point as to who can answer their questions. These types of questions are perfectly valid, especially coming from the involved parties who might not have been included in the beginning stages of planning for the IEM. You may also tend to get questions from people requesting a refresher on definitions relevant to any of the specific areas.

Evaluation Team Contacts

List all contacts for the planned evaluation team. Be sure to include roles and multiple ways to reach evaluation team personnel. The most important contact is obviously the team leader. In this section, it might be helpful to include a listing of individuals' expertise or a technology contact.

Customer Contacts

Remember, the organizational POC should be designated as someone who has the proper authority to make decisions in regard to this security evaluation. That person is likely being contacted by people within his or her own organization, whether to ask questions, voice concerns, or possibly to announce conflicts with scheduling. Keep in mind that in the IEM process, we are likely to have more than one customer representative. Probably we will have a single person handling the management side of things, but we will also have technical contacts to assist us in getting our technical needs addressed. List all contacts that have been identified so far in the IEM process.

TEP Section II: Methodology Overview

Section II of the TEP is specifically focused on describing how the IEM process will be conducted and the overall benefit to the organization. Since the TEP is a record of the agreed-on scope, having a detailed description of the IEM methodology and how it will be specifically applied to your customer will help with the overall understanding of the organization. Remember that some individuals who read the TEP will not have participated in any fashion with the IEM process to date. Therefore, it is important to clearly describe the entire IEM process.

Purpose of the IEM

This section should include discussion on why the IEM is being conducted for this specific customer. Remember that in Chapter 2 we talked about the many reasons an IEM is conducted; include that information here.

Description of the IEM

The IEM description is key to continued understanding of the IEM process. It would be prudent to have the description entail key elements of the IEM training to include, at a minimum:

- Overall IEM description
- IEM as part of the NSA toolkit for conducting security reviews
- Ten IEM baseline activities (with descriptions)
- Benefits of doing the IEM activity
- IEM results

Here is a sample introduction to the IEM methodology. This is only a beginning. Check out the sample TEP provided in Appendix B for a more detailed example. Based on your knowledge of the customer and the industry they function within, you can customize the description to meet your needs:

> The INFOSEC Evaluation Methodology (IEM) is a hands-on methodology for conducting evaluations of customer networks utilizing common technical evaluation tools. The IEM covers the steps involved in a comprehensive

evaluation of a customer's technical components, beginning with customer coordination and the definition of applicable scope for each project. Students will learn how the information defined during the IAM process will be used to create customized road maps for increased security posture.

Evaluation Tools to Be Used

The IEM uses the 10 baseline activities. Each of these activities requires some form of technical tool or manual technical process to address conducting these activities. In this section, list the tools that you plan to use to complete each of the baseline activities that you will conduct for the customer. Once again, remember that NSA *does not* recommend or endorse any specific technical tools for the IEM. This is where your technical expertise comes into play in defining your toolkit for the IEM process.

For purposes of the TEP and as a complete record of the scope agreed on by the customer and the evaluation team, it is helpful to include a listing of how the tools will be configured. Based on discussions with the customer to this point, the level of possible intrusiveness the customer is willing to accept should be clear. Some considerations that need to be included are:

- Settings of the tools for how extensive the scans will be. Include such factors as number of concurrent scans, how many threads in the scans, any automatic denial-of-service testing, or any automatic password checking by the tools.

- Handling of certain tools for host-based testing and password cracking. Will the customer install and operate, or will the evaluation team install and operate?

Any other configuration information related to the specific tools that are planned to be used will assist in greater understanding of is to occur during the testing process.

Tools & Traps...

Tool Misconfiguration

Correct configuration of the evaluation tools is important to avoid negative impact on the customer. If you run some evaluation tools in default mode—for example, denial-of-service tests and password cracking—you may be running scans on the customer that they have specifically requested not be run. If a customer is using account lockout after three unsuccessful logon attempts, an evaluation tool that runs a password cracker against all user accounts with a default of three attempts will lock out all user accounts and create issues for the customer. It's always good to have a custom configuration of the tools based on your expertise and what you feel provides the best value to the customer.

TEP Section III: Criticality Information

The majority of the information for this section comes from work done in the IAM pre-assessment process. This translates directly to the IEM process and the IEM TEP. The organizational criticality matrices and the system criticality matrices will map directly into the final report, creating a deliverable that is a trending and tracking mechanism the customer can use to help improve its INFOSEC posture.

Organizational Criticality Matrices

We looked at the organizational information criticality in the IAM process. Here we simply need to gather the already generated data and present it in a readily understood format. As we have tied the mission to INFOSEC goals and objectives, here we tie the goals and objectives to the actual information types present in the organization. As the evaluation progresses, documenting information and findings will map directly back to the TEP and information you have listed.

As discussed in Chapter 4, if you haven't completed an IAM for the organization you are planning an evaluation for, you need to complete the IAM pre-assessment process to create the organizational and system criticality matrices and associated impact definitions. Based on the IAM process, information types are cataloged and their impacts based on the organization's mission, as follows:

- The first things that should be documented are the already categorized information types the customer defined. List each and every category the team defined, and give a brief description of each. If you rolled up subcategories into larger categories, go ahead and list them here as well. This will help further the definition of information types as well as give greater detail to people looking for information regarding a specific category.

- The next thing we need to define are the impact attributes (confidentiality, integrity, and availability). Because these terms can have different meanings to different people, it's a wise choice to explain them as they pertain to this assessment, to avoid any confusion.

- Next, list the impact definitions. Again, these are the High, Medium, and Low attributes that were discussed in prior chapters. Make sure they are clearly explained here as defined during the visit meetings. These descriptions can vary greatly in size and detail based on the customer organization and the number of impact attributes used in the process, but generally they should not exceed a page per definition.

- Last is the actual criticality matrix that was created involving the High, Medium, and Low impact attributes and all the organizational information types (as demonstrated in Table 6.1). A simple table here will do the trick. You can format or display the matrix and define and list information types any way you like. Just be sure that that information ends up here.

Table 6.1 Organizational Criticality Matrices Example for Company *X*

	Confidentiality	Integrity	Availability
Customer information	Medium	High	Low
Account information	High	High	Low
Employee information	High	Medium	Medium
Corporate finances	High	High	Medium
Research and development	Medium	Medium	Low

System Criticality Information

The System Information Criticality section of the TEP is very much like the Organizational Information Criticality section, though less detailed. The information attributes of High, Medium, and Low have already been defined and documented in the IAM pre-assessment process and should now be in the TEP; since the definitions must be the same at the organizational and system levels, they do not need to be listed again here. Information type definitions and rollups also need not be restated here, but the defined information types *do* need to be listed in regard to the system of which each may be a part.

For this section, document the system information criticality of each separately defined system. Although the system will be detailed in a later section of the TEP, a brief description of each system here will help readers understand what the criticality matrix of each system means in relation to their environment. All systems falling into the scope of the evaluation must be recognized here. Table 6.2 shows two system criticality matrices based on the Table 6.1 organizational criticality matrices.

Table 6.2 System Criticality Matrices Examples

System 1	Confidentiality	Integrity	Availability
Customer information	Medium	High	Low
Account information	High	High	Low
Employee information	High	Medium	Medium

System 2	Confidentiality	Integrity	Availability
Corporate finances	High	High	Medium
Research and development	Medium	Medium	Low

TEP Section IV: Detailed Network Information

The Detailed Network Information section is, obviously, expected to be very detailed. This section should be a technical and environmental description of all systems to be included in the IEM evaluation activities. If a system is not listed here, the final report should not include it in any capacity beyond an unreviewed or nonevaluated system—for example, an out-of-scope system connected to an in-scope system.

At a minimum, each system must be mapped to specific hardware, software, and connection configurations. It is understood that much of this information might not truly be available or known until after the evaluation is performed. That is acceptable, but every effort must be made to define each system in detail to eliminate any confusion in terms of system and scope boundaries. Just as you listed and detailed the information types comprising the organization's makeup, you should include in each system's description the relevant information types it contains. This is a very important characterization of the system, since this will be one of the main deciding factors when the time comes to determine which findings require priority in regard to mitigating resources.

Any available customer diagrams should be included here as well—the more detailed, the better. If none is available, it is highly recommended that you create one based on the verbal descriptions listed in this section. Many people are more adept at visual learning, and this process may be new to many of your customer contacts. Nontechnical individuals can more readily understand diagrams than text, so they will help minimize misunderstandings.

Include in this section any logical and physical boundaries that will impact the execution of the IEM process. We are still scooping the effort, and this information is critical to accomplishing this task.

TIP

Be sure that the customer and the evaluation team share a common definition of the terms *system* and *network*. Add those definitions in this section. A misunderstanding of these definitions can lead to serious issues in the IEM process. The National Center for Education Statistics (NCES) (nces.ed.gov/pubs98/tech/glossary.asp) defines a system as "a group of elements, components, or devices that are assembled to serve a common purpose. In a technological system, this refers to all hardware, software, networks, cables, peripheral equipment, information, data, personnel, and procedures (i.e., all technology resources) that comprise a computer environment." NCES (nces.ed.gov/pubs2003/secureweb/glossary.asp) defines a network as a "group of computers connected to each other to share computer software, data, communications, and peripheral devices. Commonly, the definition of a network includes the hardware and software needed to connect the computers together." So basically, a system does a specific task, and a network provides communications and interconnectivity.

TEP Section V: Customer Concerns

This section of the TEP addresses customer concerns—anything the customer mentions is an area of particular concern for them and they would specifically like more information about. For example, if a customer says they are concerned about their wireless networking implementation, then wireless networking should be listed as a customer concern. They haven't specifically limited the engagement to *only* the areas they are concerned about, but this section does identify areas of greater concentration for the IEM, or at least areas where more specific focus is required in the final report. Examples of customer concerns include (but obviously are not limited to):

- Is my wireless network secure?

- I'm not sure my staff is handling the antivirus tools correctly.

- My security manager says the network is 100 percent guaranteed secure. Is this correct?

- Is my configuration management process effective?

- I'm not sure I am meeting the regulatory requirements that are levied on me. Am I?

- Are there new regulations and legislation I need to be concerned about?

- I hear testing of system backups is important, and I want to assure we are doing it correctly.

- Are there new technologies that can cut my security management time?

- We seem to be getting hit a lot from the Internet. Is this normal?

Many of the concerns that were expressed during the IAM process can be carried over into the IEM process, since many concerns cross both the organizational security and technical security arenas. Addressing the customer concerns is an important part of managing customer expectations.

TEP Section VI: Customer Constraints

This section specifically addresses any identified customer constraints—any limitations placed on the customer or evaluation team that will affect the evaluation process. This is also a good place to identify necessary actions in emergency or crisis situations that could arise later in the evaluation process. Examples of customer constraints in the evaluation process include these:

- You are allowed to scan only during nonpeak processing hours.

- The evaluation cannot take place during a major system upgrade.

- The evaluation cannot occur during the last three business days of the month nor the first two business days of the month because of end-of-month processing.

- The customer does not have control of nor does it own the entire network IP range they are sitting on.

- Actual servers are located across the country, making it difficult to do a cost-effective host evaluation.

This list is just a few of the constraints you might see from the customer side. Transfer to this section any concerns that are applicable from the IAM process as well. Managing the IEM effort with an eye to the constraints goes a long way toward meeting the customer's expectations.

TEP Section VII: Rules of Engagement

The Rules of Engagement section addresses specific rules while the IEM is under way to ensure communication and minimize the impact on the customer's operations. You may have some crossover from the concerns and constraints sections here, but it is better to have the same information repeated more than once than to have it missed entirely.

Evaluation Team Requirements

The evaluation team members will need to understand their rules from both the internal and external side. Use this section to identify "do's and don'ts" for the evaluation process.

External Requirements

During the external portion of the IEM, the evaluation team needs to know, at a minimum, the following information:

- IP ranges (external) that are permitted to be scanned
- Timeframes during which scans can occur
- Immediate contact information within the customer organization for people who can be contacted in the event that servers, systems, or networks seem to react negatively to the IEM process
- Copy of the LOA in each evaluation team member's possession

Internal Requirements

During the internal portion of the IEM, the evaluation team needs to know, at a minimum, the following information:

- IP ranges (internal) that are permitted to be scanned
- Timeframes during which scans can occur
- Immediate contact information within the customer organization for people who can be contacted in the event that servers, systems, or networks seem to react negatively to the IEM process
- Physical access to the facility where the scanning will occur
- Copy of the LOA in each evaluation team member's possession

Customer Requirements

The customer must participate with the evaluation team in the overall rules of engagement. Certain information and actions are necessary to ensure a smooth evaluation:

- The evaluation team's scanning IP addresses (both internal and external addresses)
- Immediate contact information for the evaluation team
- Notification to any internal group, such as a Computer Incident Response Team (CIRT), that needs to know scans are occurring
- Information on the evaluation tools that will be used and any known exclusions to the toolset

TEP Section VIII: Coordination Agreements

Coordination agreements refer to items that need to be documented related to the understanding between the customer and the evaluation team. This section specifically addresses the level of detail of recommendations, deliverables, and any other agreements not otherwise documented in the TEP. Remember, the purpose the TEP is to *fully* document the scope of the effort.

Level of Detail of Recommendations

During the IEM pre-evaluation, you should have directly discussed with the customer the required level of detail of the final report's recommendations. This addresses the technical depth of the customer staff and identifies the level of effort necessary for the final report. According to NSA and our discussion in Chapter 4, we can break out the level of detail into three categories:

- Low level of detail or executive level (low detail)
- Moderate level of detail (normal)
- High level of detail (step by step)

For the main body of the final report, the normal acceptable level of detail for recommendations is the moderate level. This provides technical management and technical personnel enough detail to address the problem, without requiring a step-by-step procedure to accomplish the fix.

List of Agreed-On Deliverables

Including in the TEP a list of the agreed-on deliverables for the IEM process will assist you in meeting the customer needs and expectations. We have encountered situations where the customer needed an additional summary report for a client, vendor, bank, or insurance company, identifying the results of the evaluation in more detail than an executive summary but less detail than the full final report. Possible deliverables include:

- Weekly update reports (verbal presentation or written)
- Weekly financial expenditure reports
- Initial findings report
- Draft final report
- Final report
- Security road map/first-order prioritization of findings

The Coordination Agreements Section: A Catchall

The Coordination Agreements section of the TEP is the location in which you can put anything else that needs to be addressed to meet specific customer needs. As a "catchall," this section gives the TEP tremendous flexibility in meeting customer and evaluation team needs.

TEP Section IX: Letter of Authorization

Include the letter of authorization (LOA) in your TEP. Remember, the TEP is a *complete* record of the scope of your IEM effort. See Chapter 5 for details on the LOA.

TEP Section X: Timeline of Events

Here, in the last NSA IEM TEP required section, dates and events are recorded to ensure that both the customer and the evaluation team are in concert with regard to scheduling. The amount of detail you include regarding any activity or milestone is up to you and the customer, but make sure that each item can be readily understood without multiple phone calls for explanation. Minimum milestones to include are:

- Date of initial request
- Date of pre-evaluation site visit
- Date of onsite evaluation
- Date of final report delivery
- Dates of any major modifications

For some smaller evaluation engagements, this section can be an efficient tool for project management where the cost of a separate management effort may be unwarranted. On the other hand, large scenarios could require more detailed reporting and management effort, especially when multiple sites are involved. Here you might also want to define the method of delivery for products or the method of information gathering, whether you use online collaboration tools, conference calls, or even site visits.

TIP

Build a logical timeline that can the evaluation team can accomplish. Be sure the timeline includes time for the approval process on documents like the TEP and the final report.

Customizing and Modifying the Technical Evaluation Plan

Now we've outlined the main components of the IEM TEP, but to make the best use of this tool, it should be morphed into a document that's central to the way the customer and the evaluation team will operate together. NSA realizes that every situation is different and that some concessions may be required to perform an effective evaluation. It's understood that an independent firm may require particular aspects in their business practice or that some customer policies may require specific assurances or inclusions. In this regard the IEM is meant to be fluid, allowing for change; so too the TEP.

Modifying the Ten NSA-Defined Areas

One way to customize the TEP is through changes in the TEP's composition. By default, you may not remove sections and still be within the IEM guidelines. NSA considers the components discussed to be minimum requirements for any plan to be used in an evaluation. If a conflict arises and a section cannot be completed, the reasons or events leading to these issues need to be clearly documented. The section will remain, but the information detailed will relate to the lack of completion, not the actual topic itself. Adding sections is entirely up to the customer. Several items may be added as requested or as part of an overall independent business practice. Just a few items that can be used to add value to the document are these:

- **Executive summaries** Summaries can go a long way toward providing descriptions and instructions on how to read and understand the plan. They can also be used to summarize the methodology or provide background into the purpose or goal of this particular assessment.

- **Version history information** This can be very useful for dealing with very fluid engagements where change is the standard. In the example in the appendices, you'll notice that a version control page was combined with approval authority to demonstrate acceptance and understanding of each change on one simple page.

Level of Detail

The level of detail is a very important aspect of the IEM TEP. Detail level can depend on many things, such as the level of involvement the customer organization wants to have with the evaluation process. A hands-on approach may dictate requirements for a very detailed plan as well as increase the chances for multiple revisions down the road. What exactly you include as detail should be based on your interactions with the customer. This should be worked out early in the pre-evaluation phase, and an introduction to a sample TEP during initial meetings would not be overboard. The amount of information recorded in each section is flexible, as long as all required aspects are included.

Format

The format of this document is almost entirely up to you. Certain basic rules should apply, such as the inclusion of a cover sheet and the original order of topics, but most of this is fair game for adjustment based on what is more effective in a given scenario. Some evaluations can be so large, with multiple evaluation teams in action, that an overall TEP is created as the main repository, with several detailed plans attached as appendices. Some systems may be in such revolving states and of sufficient size to warrant breaking out diagrams and detailed technical descriptions or inventories into subdocuments for ease of management.

Keep in mind that the TEP is a tool. Whatever helps improve the efficiency or usability of the tool should be considered appropriate, as long as you account for all required components and it can be used effectively by the customer and the evaluation team.

Getting the Signatures

No agreement is complete without signatures. The TEP is no different. Don't underestimate the importance of the signatures. The TEP is a document both parties will be held accountable for in the execution of the IEM process. It must be signed at the right time and at the right level within each organization. Spend time in the early stages of the pre-evaluation phase determining what the customer approval process will be for the TEP and any subsequent changes. As mentioned before, the TEP is a living document; therefore, the current approval process for the primary TEP must be understood, but expect that there will be changes to the TEP as the IEM moves forward. Address the engagement change process early.

Customer Approval

Sounds pretty simple, but the process of getting the customer to sign off on the TEP can be quite time consuming and tedious. Small to medium-sized organizations may only have one or two people who need to concur to get the signature on the TEP. Larger organizations may have a bureaucracy that will require multiple levels of approval before signature. You need to keep this in mind when determining a timeline for TEP approval. The other avenue most customer organizations will need to run the TEP through is the legal department. This is wise, especially considering the LOA that needs to be signed, as addressed in Chapter 5.

Evaluation Team Approval

With any luck, the evaluation team will be very familiar with the TEP format and content. Most likely the TEP will be written by the evaluation team, with the customer doing the approval process. Unless there are major additions or concerns about the scope or legality of some of the added items in the TEP, the signature would occur fairly easily by the evaluation team signature authority. If there are major changes or additions, the TEP may need to go through the evaluation team's approval process again. This includes team leader, senior management, and evaluation team legal counsel.

Summary

The TEP is a document that that is critical to the successful completion of the evaluation. The TEP is your IEM scope document. It lays out the critical details needed to successfully complete the evaluation process. It serves as your agreement between the evaluation team and your customer. Spend the necessary time putting together a good TEP and it will payoff in the end. The TEP is also your road map for completion of the IEM process for a specific customer.

To put together the TEP, you will use information from multiple sources: the customer, the evaluation team, the IAM pre-assessment process, and the IEM pre-evaluation process. If you haven't completed an IAM pre-assessment on the customer, you need to create the organizational and system criticality matrices to be able to complete the IEM process.

Understanding the background of the TEP or the goals behind it will aid you in putting together a plan that will efficiently manage IEM activities. Viewing the TEP is a working document should allow you to create a document that can be used and updated smoothly as the project rolls on. With the evaluation beginning under the added assurance of an approved and signed IEM TEP, both parties should have a better understanding of the level of effort and final products required to successfully complete the evaluation.

The 10 sections of the IEM TEP should encompass most of the information required to keep a good handle on the IEM activities. With the POC information, you know where to direct questions, and the remaining sections should supply everyone with information ranging from evaluation objectives to system configurations and diagrams. Detailed definitions and explanations further describe the story of this engagement. Boundaries have been set, and the likelihood of scope drift has been minimized with a signed agreement demonstrating the included systems.

With the amount of flexibility granted by the IEM, we can modify the TEP in many ways to fit the needs of our business practices as well as the customer's requirements. Understanding that the core 10 topics may not be removed, we can then add any pieces we deem necessary.

After this discussion centered around the IEM TEP, your understanding of NSA's expectations in terms of planning and assessment guidelines should be solid. If you like, feel free to use the example plan provided in Appendix B to create your own IEM TEP template. It is a great exercise and can assist both you and your organization in preparing to perform an IEM assessment.

Solutions Fast Track

Understanding the Purpose of the Technical Evaluation Plan

☑ Be sure the TEP and its importance are introduced to the customer early in the IEM process.

☑ Verify and agree on document security controls before starting.

☑ The TEP is an important document intended to improve the execution of the IEM evaluation; implementation of the TEP is critical to the evaluation success.

Understanding the Format of the TEP

☑ Start with an understanding of the critical plan items you are looking for through a well-organized outline (format).

☑ Document all identified customer constraints and concerns in the TEP. If something is important enough to be mentioned by the customer, it's important enough to be included in the TEP.

☑ Use network diagrams where possible. A picture is still worth a 1000 words.

☑ Build a logical timeline into the TEP and try to stick with it.

☑ Include all sections of the TEP, even if only to identify that there is no information available for a specific section.

Customizing the TEP

☑ Work closely with your customer to make desired adjustments to the TEP.

☑ Determine the level of detail required by the environment and the customer organization's needs.

Getting the Signatures

☑ Be sure you understand the approval process for the TEP and plan that into the schedule.

☑ Expect that both the customer and the evaluation team legal department will be reviewing and commenting, and plan accordingly.

☑ Have the signature in place before you start evaluation work.

Frequently Asked Questions

The following Frequently Asked Questions, answered by the authors of this book, are designed to both measure your understanding of the concepts presented in this chapter and to assist you with real-life implementation of these concepts. To have your questions about this chapter answered by the author, browse to **www.syngress.com/solutions** and click on the **"Ask the Author"** form. You will also gain access to thousands of other FAQs at ITFAQnet.com.

Q: Who should be involved in signing the TEP?

A: A representative from both sides must approve the TEP before actual work begins. Most often, a senior decision maker, information owners, and the primary customer POC are involved as well. In any event, just be sure that the highest required level of executive is on board to confirm management buy-in. Many organizations have quite a strenuous process to gaining formal signatures before the primary signatory will sign the TEP. Build in time for this process.

Q: If multiple people are involved with approval, how do you address addendums or revisions to the TEP, especially if multiple sites are involved as well?

A: If multiple people have approved the original from the customer point of view, you might consider naming an official "approver" for modifications. Usually this is the customer management POC who, with the approval of management, has been granted the ability to approve project-related changes. It also would not hurt to document this understanding in the section that discusses points of contact.

Q: Normally, how many pages should comprise the plan?

A: That really depends on the scenario and your customer involvement, but on average, for a small to medium-sized company, the plan should be around 15–20 pages. Keep in mind that this number will vary depending on things such as the number of systems, number of sites, custom additions, and complexity of the organization.

Q: Does NSA provide any templates for the IEM TEP?

A: At this time NSA does not provide any templates. The agency's goal is to provide the framework for an INFOSEC evaluation, and it relies on your industry experience and understanding of best practices. Some templates based on a combination of business practices and the NSA requirements are included with this book, but feel free to come up with your own or to alter these to suit your purposes. Appendix B has a sample TEP for your consideration.

Q: Can the IEM TEP and the IAM assessment plan be combined into one document when they are being conducted together?

A: Absolutely. As discussed in this chapter, the TEP can be adjusted to meet the needs of the customer. When you are adding the execution of the IAM into the TEP, you will be adding a few additional items not currently in the TEP to include the interviews to be conducted, documents reviewed, and how the assessment findings are going to be handled. Remember, the TEP is a living document and should be a *complete* agreement between the customer and the assessment/evaluation team.

Q: What title should I give a combined assessment plan and TEP?

A: You have some flexibility here. Just make sure that you and your customer can agree on the meanings of key terms. We often call it a *security review plan* when we execute a combined document.

Q: Can the terms *assessment* and *evaluation* be used interchangeably?

A: No. By NSA definition, *assessment* refers to the organizational portion of a security review. *Evaluation* refers to the technical portion of the security review.

Part II
On-site
Evaluation Phase

Chapter 7

Starting Your On-site Efforts

Solutions in this chapter:

- **Preparing for the On-site Evaluation Phase**
- **IAM vs. IEM**
- **IEM Baseline Activities**
- **The Role of CVE and CAN**
- **The In-Brief**
- **Solutions Fast Track**

☑ **Summary**

☑ **Solutions Fast Track**

☑ **Frequently Asked Questions**

Introduction

This chapter discusses the framework of the on-site evaluation phase, where the meat of the technical evaluation occurs. This also means that the majority of surprises are likely to occur during this phase, so flexibility is paramount. One of the objectives of the INFOSEC Evaluation Methodology (IEM) is to verify information regarding systems and controls documented during the INFOSEC Assessment Methodology (IAM). All technical controls are meant to support policy defined by the organization or any industry regulation or legislation.

The IEM has a set of 10 baseline activities that must be addressed to perform a comprehensive technical evaluation. These activities are designed to meet the need for evaluating the most common standard points of attack to a system and test the effectiveness of the security controls in place. Like the IAM, flexibility and the actual detailed execution of these activities is left up to the expertise of the evaluating team.

Part of the flexibility of the IEM also carries over into the requirement for the use of common vulnerabilities and exposures (CVE) identifiers in deliverable reports. CVE identifiers are one industry standard for identifying security weaknesses and are discussed in greater detail later in this chapter. Using these identifiers, we are able to maintain usefulness throughout the IEM process as well as into mitigation aspects, follow-up review, and research for the customer. Since the evaluation team is normally an outside entity, it is important for the customer to have the ability to interpret the deliverables, which may be needed a year or more down the road, after the evaluation team has finished its work.

To achieve a well-executed project, managing customer expectations is important. Through the use of the in-brief and TEP, we'll see how to set the tone for the evaluation by laying everything on the table before starting and achieving technical staff buy-in. The IAM and IEM methodologies present a "no surprises" attitude in that no critical security concerns should be a surprise to the customer in the final report. If issues are critical in nature, they should be brought to the organization's attention immediately. With the on-site evaluation phase, we take that same concept to heart: No activities or findings should come as a surprise.

With an appropriately built and agreed upon schedule, we can keep to a minimum many of the potential surprises during the evaluation efforts. At this point, the only surprises that should arise (and they usually do) will be for the evaluation team, requiring not just the IEM but also the team and its schedule to be able to adapt on the fly.

Preparing for the On-site Evaluation Phase

Preparations prior to beginning the IEM on-site evaluation phase are similar to those for the IAM Pre-Assessment Site Visit. Due to the often unexpected developments during on-site visits, a well developed plan of attack will facilitate a smooth process and ensure effective evaluation activities. On-site activities generally occur over a period of a few days to two weeks, depending on the scope and boundaries in place. A lot of work is covered in this timeframe, and a structured, organized approach is key to managing time constraints.

If the target system is of sufficient size and diversity or spread across multiple locations, consider what options you have for using multiple teams, but try to keep the timeline short. The sooner you can present findings, the sooner problems can be mitigated and the organization's security gap narrowed.

Scheduling

There is no predefined schedule or required plan of events to allow for IEM compliance during the on-site evaluation phase. The goal for creating a plan is simply to ensure that all 10 areas of the IEM baseline activities are addressed appropriately. This can be a fluid process, changing day by day, as long as all criteria are evaluated. The process for creating your schedule should be specific to your organization and is considered a business process by the National Security Agency (NSA).

A sample timeline with broad activities is outlined in the following sections. This sample obviously won't fit every environment, but it has been used successfully as a baseline schedule for multiple engagements. This schedule will need to be "fleshed out" with more specific and detailed events, but it serves well as a starting point in most situations. This timeline also hinges on the common practice of performing vulnerability testing during off-peak hours (such as evenings).

Day One Accomplishments

The first day is usually the least productive in terms of technical testing results, because you'll deal with the more routine tasks of getting set up in a working location, handling introductions, verifying the test windows and processes, and performing the in-brief. The main objectives are to complete the in-brief, begin ongoing automated testing, and initiate system mapping (discussed later in the chapter). Here are the typical accomplishments for Day 1:

- Conduct in-briefing
- Verify customer agreement with scope and schedule
- Site tour and working location setup
- Enumeration activities (system mapping)
- Off-hours vulnerability scanning configuration scheduling
- Begin password compliance testing procedures
- Begin network-sniffing procedures

Day Two Accomplishments

Day 2 is normally spent performing staff interviews, carrying out manual configuration checks, and reviewing the results of the previous evening's testing. Based on information gathered during the day, more detailed or system-specific scanning tools can be configured and scheduled for this evening's window. Day 2 accomplishments are typically:

- Testing results review
- Staff interviews
- Manual configuration checks
- Continued off-hours vulnerability scanning configuration scheduling
- Continued password compliance testing procedures
- Continued network-sniffing procedures

Day Three Accomplishments

On Day 3, we continue reviewing the results of previous testing and staff interviews. We add the validation and analysis process for eliminating false positives. Normally, any scanning schedule for this evening is based on the need for secondary verification of findings between tools. Typical Day 3 accomplishments are:

- Continued testing results review
- Continued staff interviews
- Manual configuration checks
- Validation and analysis
- Continued off-hours vulnerability scanning configuration scheduling
- Continued password compliance testing procedures
- Continued network-sniffing procedures

Day Four Accomplishments

The fourth day of the on-site evaluation is typically spent performing validation exercises and follow-up interviews as the validation process requires. At the same time, organization of the documented test results is started for reporting processes, as well as preparation of the out-brief materials. Typical Day 4 accomplishments are:

- Validation and analysis
- Follow-up interviews
- Documentation

Day Five Accomplishments

The last day is primarily dedicated to the out-brief. Depending on the size of the engagement and the number of findings, it can sometimes take most of the day to answer questions and detail specific recommended solutions, or debate the pros and cons of multiple solutions for a single finding. Often, the evaluation team provides hands-on assistance or guidance to help quickly mitigate more serious concerns. Typical Day 5 accomplishments:

- Out-briefing
- Mitigation assistance

In determining the schedule for more detailed technical testing of critical components (for example, Microsoft, Cisco, Solaris, and so on), the emphasis for time-intensive activities should be placed on priority systems as defined during the IAM process. Mapping this schedule into a basic timeline such as the one outlined here should give the plan a greater chance of success. On average, the technical evaluation team will usually consist of two or three members per customer site. This number will, of course, vary depending on the specifics of each location, such as a data center vs. a remote user installation.

Flexibility and Adaptation

As a starting point, a completed IAM planning survey from previous efforts will help build our original schedule. Combined with configuration documentation, such as system inventories and network diagrams, there should be plenty of information to build a detailed picture of what to expect when you arrive on-site. Flexibility, however, is critical in many instances.

Depending on the amount of time that has elapsed between the IAM and the on-site evaluation of the IEM, changes are likely to have occurred. If the time period exceeds a month, it's a good idea to verify your understanding of the target system with the POC to try to avoid any surprises such as the installation of a new system or device your team has no experience with.

When you have a complete understanding of the *organization's* perception of the system, you can begin to evaluate whether that view really matches the actual implementation. Be prepared for surprises, such as systems being taken down for maintenance during your testing window or an IDS blocking your IP address. Even with properly planned schedules and communication, unplanned hindrances often occur. Be prepared to adjust the schedule as needed, and be careful not to set too aggressive a schedule.

Administrative Planning

Administrative planning sets the tone for project organization that allows your on-site efforts to focus on the technical evaluation and hopefully minimize any hiccups that may arise. Primarily, administrative planning is focused on the business needs of both the organization and the evaluating team:

- **Customer coordination** We've said this before, but it needs to be emphasized: Communication between the team and the organization is integral to success. This includes scheduling of dates and times for meeting, testing windows, interviews, and the like. Similar to the IAM, data collection may occur throughout the process as new documents are created or updated by the organization.

- **Travel arrangements** Often it's the mundane things that lead to problems with an evaluation, such as incorrectly booked travel arrangements (say, your plane landing an hour after the scheduled in-brief). Also consider making hotel accommodations. With technical testing, late hours and midnight trips to the organization's offices sometimes can occur. Because research is frequently an evening side product of the day's events, high-speed Internet access from a hotel room is often a "must have." In all planning, consider how a travel arrangement can help improve or hinder an evaluation team's efforts.

■ **Checklists** It's not a bad idea to create and use checklists based on each evaluation. This will help ensure the effectiveness of the evaluation team once it's on-site. Things you might include are security clearances (if needed), background checks, physical access to the organization (temporary badges), timeline of events, test plans, tool licensing, and organizational documentation (including IAM documents).

Technical Planning

Technical planning deals directly with the expected components for discovering vulnerabilities. The goal is to ensure that the evaluators don't have to do a last-minute scurry to put these together on-site:

■ **Roles and responsibilities** As part of building your evaluation team, you will want to base the functions on each evaluator's expertise. This process will, of course, be evaluation-specific based on the technologies in place at the organization. By splitting out the specific tasks and technologies, you can ensure that a networking specialist is reviewing scan results and configurations of Cisco routers and switches or conducting interviews with network operations.

■ **Pre-visit technical review** As part of the technical planning, documentation gathered during the IAM phases must be reviewed to assist in setting up timelines, schedules, experience required, and so on. More documentation may need to be requested depending on the length of time that has elapsed since the IAM. As well as planning and scheduling benefits, architecture and documentation reviews allow an evaluator to prioritize a focus area where, in his or her experience, vulnerabilities are more likely to occur.

■ **Tool configuration** Once you've reviewed available documentation and designated personnel with the required expertise, you can choose tools to perform the evaluation that map to the environment and experience of those involved. As discussed in Chapter 4, these tools and configurations should be tied directly back to the rules of engagement (ROE). Make sure that all tools to be used are approved by the customer for use on their systems. Many organizations have an approved security list for tools.

■ **Support requirements** Planning some of the basics up front will support your technical efforts. Make sure that you've made arrangements that assist rather than hinder your testing. For example, make sure you have required VLAN configurations or access to a data center, depending on what controls are in place between the location set aside for your use and the target system. If you'll be performing any dialup testing, ensure that analog lines are available for your use. In short, make sure all the supporting resources, such as enough network drops for your team, are taken care of in advance.

IAM vs. IEM

As mentioned previously, the IAM and the IEM are meant to be complementing endeavors. During the IAM, an organizational-level review of information systems and their respective security controls is conducted. Data types are evaluated and given impact priority rankings within the organization based on the three common security goals: confidentiality, integrity, and availability (CIA). Policies and procedures (P&P) are reviewed for effectiveness and appropriateness. Definitions for the impact of the failure of CIA are created on a High, Medium, and Low scale. Essentially, the planned and implemented security controls are assessed in conjunction with the value of the information as defined by the customer.

The IEM then steps in and takes the review deeper. The specific technical controls that have been mapped out are tested to ensure they are functioning as planned and expected. This task is performed with data gathered during the IAM process and incorporates both hands-on manual reviews and automated testing techniques. At minimum, the IAM pre-assessment site visit must be completed to perform an IEM. All the collected data and results tie directly back to the information created in the IAM pre-assessment site visit.

It is normal to have to perform additional documentation review during the on-site evaluation phase, especially if the IAM was performed months prior to the IEM. Documentation may have been updated or created in that timeframe, especially in regard to any IAM findings that were presented.

Vulnerability Definitions

The concept of vulnerabilities can sometimes be confusing because it has two similar yet separate meanings between the IAM and IEM. To understand the differences, we need to understand that there are two distinct sets of vulnerabilities—one for the IAM and one for the IEM. In essence, they are both weaknesses, yet they are categorized separately to show their impacts on each other.

IAM vulnerabilities are weaknesses within a process. They are usually discovered during documentation review or interviews during the IAM engagement. They relate directly to failures within an organization's P&P that can lead to the compromise of data security. One possible example is the lack of efficient contingency plan testing discovered when the organization admits that formal plans and test result documents are not created. In the event that a disaster occurs, confidence in the mitigating controls to continue or restore operations is at a low, which results in an IAM finding regarding contingency planning P&P.

IEM findings on the other hand, are weaknesses discovered during IEM testing of the system. These findings can be discovered through both manual and automated testing, but they deal specifically with the technical configuration and operation of the system or services. An example is the testing of DoS weaknesses in a router's operating system or configuration. Perhaps during that testing the device goes down, but the expected failover device does not step in and continue the routing service. At this point, two IEM findings have been discovered: a weakness to DoS attacks and a failure in a technically based availability mitigation control.

We can easily see how the routing failover vulnerability the IEM discovered ties directly back to the IAM vulnerability discovered earlier in reference to contingency plan testing. For any security processes to be effective, the technical controls implemented must support the P&P enacted. We can likely tie the IEM DoS vulnerability back to an IAM patch management finding as well.

For now, we need to understand that the IAM and IEM vulnerabilities have distinct differences but are dependent on each other in much the same way a security manager may be dependent on a system administrator to implement appropriate controls that follow security guidelines. In the chapter discussing reporting, the methods used to correlate findings will be discussed in detail.

On-site Evaluation Phase Objectives

The objectives for the on-site evaluation phase are rather simple: Verify that the technical implementation supports the organizational security model and hunt for weaknesses and information exposure. Of course, breaking it down into just these two elements may be oversimplifying things a bit, since the amount of work tends to be much more varied and diverse; however, all testing results lead directly back to these two concepts.

The easy portion is to identify technical weaknesses. These days, tools abound that can automate most of the technical testing you will need to perform a search for vulnerabilities. Even with detailed manual testing or the creation of specific security control test criteria, there is really only one focus: Find as many weaknesses as possible, and create solution recommendations to mitigate those weaknesses. Here it is easy to see a direct correlation between the security evaluation being performed and the overall goal of closing the security gap.

A difficulty often comes into play during the validation—that the technical controls support the organization's P&P. An evaluator needs to be able to focus directly on the technical vulnerabilities and their ramifications while keeping an eye on the bigger picture that may have led to the vulnerability. In this phase, a large group of activities are performed, but all with the same intentions.

Verification of "Known" and "Rogue" Components

Part of the process for ensuring that the technical implementation supports organizational P&P is to verify "known" components and discover any possible "rogue" components on the network. The system in question should be fully documented as part of any comprehensive security program. But remember, that documentation is only as helpful as it is accurate. To validate that the organizational processes for security are operating effectively, the devices and services available within the system need to match what is documented as being part of the functionality requirement for the system.

Undocumented devices, services, or rogue components constitute a threat to the system because they are not likely included in typical security testing boundaries nor taken into consideration in evaluating possible risks to a system. By identifying these components, the organization is given the opportunity to review, approve, and document any needed components while removing or disabling any unnecessary technology. Simply put, an unknown access point (either device or service) to the system is an unknown risk.

By the same token, components that have been removed from the system and not documented constitute a lack of consistency between the organization's understanding of the system and the actual technical implementation. This can lead to serious concerns that may need to be investigated, such as the theft of assets, loss of functionality, or diminishing effectiveness of controls. Of course, the seriousness will depend on the devices or services that are missing. It is not unheard of to discover that a failover router was removed and used elsewhere in an emergency situation while system owners continue to believe they have redundancy supporting their system.

Tip

> Any findings of rogue or missing components also constitute a flaw in the organization's processes regarding configuration management and inventory management. In this case, we have used a technical evaluation activity to discover a process weakness in an organization security baseline area from the IAM.

Discovery of Technical Vulnerabilities

The discovery of technical vulnerabilities is performed by conducting the 10 IEM baseline activities. These are the areas that will be addressed in the process for finding technical weaknesses. One of the main objectives in the IAM is to bring to light weaknesses in an organization's security controls at an operational and management level. The IEM looks deeper into the technical level for ineffective security controls. Whereas all three types of control support each other directly, they require different skill sets and experience to manage.

The IEM baseline activities give a basic checklist of areas to test, based on common networking concerns and technologies, typical technical weaknesses, and the usual focus of malicious attackers. The IEM is not meant to simulate an attack or perform "red team" activities but to evaluate the current state of security controls and assist the organization in narrowing the security gap. The 10 baseline activities are discussed in greater detail later in this and subsequent chapters.

One item that may help in this endeavor is the concept of *system mapping*. This begins with collecting the information about a system or its devices and building a map of known services, products, and configurations. System mapping is discussed in more detail in the next chapter. This is not an IEM process but a simple tool that has been used over the years to make sure that a detailed review of a system occurs.

Validation != Value Add?

No matter how a project is scoped or billed out, validation and analysis of technical data *must* be performed. This is not an option or a "value add," as might be seen in some instances, but mandatory. The organization must be given a specific set of vulnerabilities and recommendations that will improve their security posture. A list of "possible" vulnerabilities in a deliverable will, at best, slow the process for mitigating the actual nuggets of real weaknesses. At worst, it will lead to the dismissal of the findings as irrelevant, leaving possibly serious vulnerabilities unmitigated and open for exploitation.

Automated security-testing tools are great for increasing the efficiency of an evaluator, but they cannot replace that expertise. No tool will give 100-percent accurate results 100 percent of the time. An automated vulnerability scan of a 500-device network may produce thousands of possible vulnerabilities. Once these vulnerabilities are analyzed and validated by an experienced INFOSEC professional, that list of vulnerabilities may be slimmed down by 80 percent or more. Experienced evaluators are brought in for a reason. Their technical knowledge and understanding are required components of any successful evaluation.

Validation of findings can be performed in a myriad ways. Manual system reviews, staff interviews, secondary tool testing, and, in some cases, exploitation can all be used to validate whether a vulnerability recognized by an automated tool is actually present. Exploitation may be out of scope in most instances, but a simple example is a Web-based directory-traversal vulnerability. The exploitation of this weakness by testing through a Web browser the ability to walk across unauthorized directories is not likely to cause any damage, whereas it will validate the finding and allow a screen capture for evidence.

Again, we must emphasize that to perform an IEM-compliant evaluation that provides an organization with quality deliverables, findings must be validated.

IEM Baseline Activities

The IEM sets forth a minimum baseline of 10 required activities, similar to the 18 required areas of review within the IAM baseline categories. Like the IAM baseline, these are the main categories of technical security controls where the required testing of control effectiveness must be completed.

Obviously, some specific tools are dedicated to performing evaluations within each of these areas, and some cover multiple areas. The only current NSA requirement is that at least one automated tool (or method) be used in evaluating the controls covered by each baseline activity. This does not mean a separate tool is required for each activity, but simply that each activity must be performed. For example, many vulnerability scanners in the market have incorporated additional functionality within the INFOSEC climate, such as password auditing, enumeration, or application-specific (normally Web related) auditing.

Nor does this mean that only one tool can be used per area when multiple tools may give a deeper technical review. In some instances, tools might overlap in areas, or different tools may be used against a separate resource in the system.

The evaluator is expected to bring knowledge of these automated tools into the process, with the capability to determine from the multiple tools available which ones fit the environment best. Each product has its own set of strengths and weaknesses within the baseline activity it represents that may need to be addressed for each engagement. Here the IEM framework relies on evaluator expertise and experience to ensure the effective review process conducted by each activity.

WARNING

Many automated tools are discussed in this book; however, the NSA does *not* officially support or endorse *any* specific products. Discussions and examples using several different mainstream INFOSEC tools are used to help explain in greater detail the actions and expectations for the 10 IEM baseline activities.

The following IEM baseline activities are discussed in greater detail in the following chapters; we introduce them briefly here to tie together the expectations of on-site activities and give a broad overview of how they work together. They are as follows:

I.   Port scanning
II.   SNMP scanning
III. Enumeration and banner grabbing
IV.   Wireless enumeration
V.   Vulnerability scanning
VI.   Host evaluation
VII. Network device analysis
VIII. Password compliance testing
IX.   Application-specific scanning
X.   Network sniffing

I. Port Scanning

Port scanning is a low-level review of the open ports on the target systems being tested. The main goal is to determine what TCP or UDP ports are operating or "listening" on the systems being evaluated. After any organizational assessments and documentation review, this is normally the first activity performed. After the completion of this activity, a system mapping that lists all the open ports per host should be documented and available for further use in the remaining activities. This mapping can then be used to help streamline the remaining functions as well as assist in the first-step validation techniques, which are discussed later in this chapter.

The information gathered during this process can be used to investigate unauthorized or unknown services that have not been documented or do not provide a function of the organization. An example is to discover the multiple management services that tend to be installed by default on many operating systems but are either not used or have been replaced in functionality by other services, but not disabled. These undocumented services can often lead to providing system configuration information to anonymous remote attackers that can assist them in planning more detailed system attacks.

TIP

Within IP networking, various remote communication services are separated from interfering with each other by operating over a specific port. Combining an IP address with a specific port number creates what is commonly referred to as a *socket address* to define, separate, and manage network connections based on the service in use. HTTP, for example, normally connects over port 80, which allows us to define a target for communications with an IP address and port number.

Common services tend to run over generally accepted standard ports. These, referred to as the *well-known* ports, range between 0 and 1023. Although services may be assigned to a well-known port, it has become common practice to deviate from these standards for varying reasons. A system administrator might have multiple instances of the same service running on different ports or may have moved a sensitive service to a less common private port in an attempt to hide the service.

For more detailed information regarding port descriptions, please refer to the IANA port assignments at www.iana.org/assignments/port-numbers.

II. SNMP Scanning

Simple Network Management Protocol (SNMP) scanning is the search for a specific management service, supported by most operating systems and network devices. SNMP is a basic protocol used to support the management of network resources. Most SNMP implementations use UDP and TCP over port 161 and 162 for communications. This ties into port scanning as being an investigation into one of the most commonly used management services for gaining more information about the system target. The amount of information freely given away by a system with a default read community string can be staggering in many cases, reaching thousands of lines of data. Obviously, this is not a service that should be easily available to those with less than honorable intentions.

In many cases, systems with SNMP enabled also support actual change capabilities through this service for remote users who know the actual write community string. This can include the functionality to change interface configurations, account settings, trust relationships, permissions, or other operational variables based on the system implementation. Some question whether this functionality within the SNMP implementation should be used at all due to some of the security concerns inherent to the service.

Some of the information garnered through the evaluation of SNMP services can be added to the system mapping to help further delineate the process for discovering weaknesses as we move forward through the baseline activities.

TIP

There is a lot of information on the Web regarding SNMP and its uses and security capabilities. Due in large part to SNMP's history of insecurities, you can find a multitude of articles on vulnerabilities and exploits. If any SNMP is located on a system, it's recommended that you research the vendor-specific implementations to better understand its functionalities. Because all SNMP products support differing functionality, understanding what that functionality is will help you determine the actual impact a vulnerability may have on the system.

III. Enumeration and Banner Grabbing

Enumeration and banner grabbing are the processes involved in gathering more information about the services running on the system. After completing a port scan, identified services should have been mapped for further review. With that information, the next step in discovering weaknesses is to discover what actual application or vendor product is providing that service.

Many vendors provide the same service capabilities with differing operations. Although they support the same functionality and often will be vulnerable to the same security risks, functionality implementation differences lead to vendor-specific weaknesses. With this in mind, we can perform testing on specific systems for known vulnerabilities that would actually affect that system. A common example is to prune the list of vulnerabilities you would test against a Microsoft Windows 2000 Server to exclude vulnerabilities that affect only devices running the Cisco IOS.

This activity or task is often referred to as *fingerprinting* the system. By identifying the vendors that have provided the service functionality, the underlying operating system can be determined, or at least narrowed down. For example, if you find Internet Information Server 6.0 through banner enumeration, you can combine that with other information in your system mapping, such as the Microsoft DS running on TCP port 445 for the same system to provide a fingerprint. At this point, the specific system will most likely be a Microsoft Windows product. With this information, you can begin tailoring your next level of testing as well as validate configuration documents and diagrams that have already been received.

IV. Wireless Enumeration

Wireless enumeration is a little bit different from the other enumeration activities due to the fact that you are trying to discover weakly controlled access points to the network and data exposure points. The most common weaknesses in wireless networking are based within the protocol or due to configuration issues. Using automated tools, you can identify wireless devices and then investigate them for inappropriate configurations. Commonly, unknown wireless devices can lead to unprotected or unauthorized entry points within a network.

The goal with wireless enumeration is to identify the weaknesses that have become incredibly prolific in today's technology environments. Wireless technology provides such flexible data delivery possibilities at such a low price that it has widely infiltrated home, government, and corporate environments without full attention being paid to the security concerns it represents.

News reports on *WarDriving*, the hobby of searching and cataloging wireless networks while driving through a neighborhood or region, has helped raise the concerns about wireless network security. It has also introduced litigation regarding the act of recording wirelessly transmitted data and the unauthorized use of systems. Currently, many people see this act in a bad light, even when it is performed as a security evaluation function. For these reasons, the IEM determines that this activity is optional although highly recommended. As with all baseline activities, make sure the customer understands the activity. When you perform this function, be sure to take all proper care with any captured data, and be wary of wireless devices outside the scope of the evaluation.

NOTE

Generally, the information just presented refers to any network wireless network based in the IEEE 802.11 family, commonly referred to as WiFi. Though the standards have been around a while and have been adhered to pretty regularly, the base insecurities in the 802.11 family to date have led many vendors to incorporate their own proprietary security controls. Most of these have been shown to be just as insecure as WiFi, but research on the platforms in place will need to be conducted to determine if there are any weaknesses outside the standard WEP or configuration aspects.

V. Vulnerability Scanning

Vulnerability scanning is the next baseline activity, using, when appropriate, a system mapping from previous activities or at least incorporating the information already learned. Through vulnerability scanning, targets are tested for possible known vulnerabilities.

Each evaluation scenario is likely to have a separate defining requirement for specific tool configurations. There could be availability requirements that limit the amount of DoS testing that can be performed on the system, for instance. Perhaps a specific vulnerability test is known to restart services that require manual intervention. The specific aspects of how this baseline activity is performed are left up to the evaluators, who bring the technical background and expertise in using these tools.

WARNING

Remember that all security scanning tools can only look for "known" vulnerabilities. Not all weaknesses in every product have been identified; therefore, you can never guarantee that any system is 100-percent secure. No security scanning tool can test for 100 percent of all known vulnerabilities, either, so you cannot even guarantee a system is 100-percent secure from all known vulnerabilities.

Since most vulnerability-scanning tools use a different database, it has become common practice to use at least two different tools during this effort. With the availability of open source tools, this should not incur any additional licensing fees and will also help validate the findings process.

VI. Host Evaluation

Host evaluation is the process of evaluating a specific host for weaknesses in configuration or patch level. Configuration mistakes are a very common source of attacks and unauthorized accesses and must be reviewed carefully. This process can be done using custom automated scripts, commercial and open source products, or a good, old-fashioned manual review.

Whether this activity is performed using a common configuration standard such as NIST or NSA guidelines or using the organization's custom in-house requirements, it is a must for all evaluations due to the wide-ranging effects of configuration errors. Hopefully, the organization has in-house guidance that has already been reviewed against industry standards or best practices, allowing the evaluator to tie technical results directly back to an operational control. The IEM stipulates that all critical components must be tested, whereas other systems may only be a sampling. A typical stance is to evaluate all servers and sample a base of workstations.

VII. Network Device Analysis

Network device analysis uses many of the other IEM baseline activities to focus on the high-assurance security components of a system. These devices are normally perimeter units that make up that hard exterior in the description of many IT systems—a hard candy shell with a soft, chewy center. Since more is expected of these devices, it is only appropriate to focus on them when performing a security evaluation.

Along with performing a system mapping, vulnerability scan, and other compliance tests on these devices, you'll want to take a step back and review the overall architecture. Verify that clear-text protocols are not enabled for managing the devices, or that DMZ connections really provide a staging area to separate public access from internal access. The lack of an IDS system may not be a technical finding, but if warranted, it can be a technical recommendation. For this activity, we want to review with a top-down approach to make sure that expectations of the perimeter are being met.

Performing host evaluations on high-assurance devices is a must. Manual reviews of configurations are normally not intensive, time-consuming efforts, as they might be with operating systems, so it is recommended that you validate the configurations by hand, even if an auto-mated tool is used to verify that these devices are properly configured to only pass or allow accepted traffic.

VIII. Password Compliance Testing

Password compliance testing is the validation of the organization's password policy. Most systems include the ability to define password requirements for users based on this policy. This testing is to ensure that technical controls support the policy and that they are not bypassed by system or individual accounts.

Remember that many organizational policies require (or at least they should require) that no passwords be transmitted or stored in clear text, so any Telnet or similarly unencrypted protocols, if used, should be considered a violation of this policy. Also, remember to appropriately schedule the timing of this activity because it normally will take longer than any other testing performed.

IX. Application-Specific Scanning

Application-specific scanning takes vulnerability scanning from a generalized system review to a more detailed, service-specific testing level. This activity is based on the organization's prioritization of the applications. Applications may include custom in-house systems, commercial databases, or clusters of single functioning resources such as Web sites and e-mail. This activity is very flexible based on environmental needs. Application-specific scanning can include limited testing as may be performed by general vulnerability scanners, custom application-specific vulnerability scanners, automated or manual configuration reviews, or any combination of these.

Code review may be an acceptable option as well, but considering the timeframe of an IEM, this would likely have to be done in a limited capacity or separated into another project. There are many ways to perform this activity, but employing an evaluator experienced in the application is important for obtaining a deeply detailed review.

X. Network Sniffing

Network sniffing is a way to see what is really traveling across the organization's infrastructure. Like password compliance testing, this activity can be time consuming and should be scheduled early in the on-site evaluation phase. It will also require a good bit of involvement from the local technical staff to mitigate the issues switched and routed networks place on sniffing in general. You need to remember to document your procedures for this activity in the ROE, to alleviate the concerns about data removal and privacy impact.

Due to the complex nature of this activity, the actual requirements are very flexible. The amount of data review required based on the environment may require it to be only a minimal activity to verify that routers or firewalls are only redirecting traffic as intended. One solution could be to place a sniffer behind a firewall being tested, to see what gets through. Another might be to validate the concerns of Telnet being used to manage a system by capturing a login session. These types of activities can be performed without the overhead of forwarding all traffic to a specific device, causing a large overhead on network devices and systems. Perform this activity as is appropriate for the environment.

Other Activities

The 10 IEM baseline activities set a standard minimum of activities and specific security controls for evaluating. Many other methods and concerns need to be evaluated on a case-by-case basis for the organization. Some of these methods or activities are not included as a part of the baseline due to their invasive nature. For example, DoS and war dialing are not standard requirements due to the amount of load they may place on a system as well as the opportunity for downtime they could represent. A detailed code review of an application will likely incur many more man hours than an IEM has scheduled and thus might be best served as a follow-on or additional project.

Penetration testing requires a very detailed level of expertise and often leaves the target system more vulnerable to exploit during and after the activity. Many exploits on a system include uploading root kits, backdoors, and loggers. One example is uploading the script *cmdasp.asp* to a vulnerable Microsoft Windows Internet Information Server (IIS). Although this exploit grants the attacker access to a shell prompt on the target, it also leaves that shell prompt available to anyone else with a Web browser.

These activities are not specific requirements, but an organization or environment may have an appropriate need for them. You can include these types of activities as needed to provide a valuable deliverable. An example is to perform war dialing on a dialup system or a separated range of phone numbers that the organization confirms will not interfere with daily operations.

The Role of CVE and CAN

The CVE project is meant to be a method for providing a standardized naming and information convention for discovered security vulnerabilities. Such a convention allows for cross-referencing a vulnerability across multiple vendor products and security tools. One need only look at the number of buffer overflow vulnerabilities that have been found for Sendmail over the years to realize that a method was needed to categorize and differentiate between distinct vulnerabilities that have similar exploits or impacts. For this reason, the CVE list is meant to be a dictionary of weaknesses, not a vulnerability database. Each weakness is treated like a word in a dictionary and details a specific criterion for information.

CVE identifiers (similar to serial numbers) are easy to recognize and understand. The identifier CVE-2001-0072 notes that this weakness is an approved CVE finding and was marked for review in 2001 with a unique number of 0072. On the CVE Web site, you can search on that name and discover its history, issue, and references. A weakness with CAN as the opening identifier—for example, CAN-2001-0073—is considered to be a candidate for inclusion into the list. All the same information is available for candidates; they have simply not been officially approved and may be modified in the future.

The CVE list also takes into consideration that not all weaknesses are vulnerabilities and has set aside a classification for exposures. These are not inherent vulnerabilities but rather weaknesses that may have little to no impact on an organization's environment. An example is having null sessions anonymously available on a Microsoft Windows environment. Although this is not a true vulnerability, it can assist a user in gathering more information that can help discover vulnerabilities on a system. The IEM, as you'll discover later in the book, ties each weakness back to an information criticality, to give the organization a true understanding of the way it could impact the system.

For greater usability and reference, the IEM requires all available findings to be labeled with a CVE compliant identifier. Obviously not all findings will have a relevant CVE identifier, but label the ones that do. Doing so assists the organization with mitigation and priority concerns as well as incorporating a reusability feature so that the organization can review past evaluations and more easily research and understand findings and recommendations.

The CVE list is free, maintained by the MITRE Corporation and funded by the U.S. Department of Homeland Security. MITRE has granted the IEM course materials CVE-compatible compliance. Many security tools have also been granted compatibility and can assist in maintaining a CVE-compliant deliverable product for the customer organization. Although the methodology does not promote any tools at all, those that are CVE compatible make the evaluating team's job easier.

> **NOTE**
>
> The CVE list can be downloaded or accessed with a search feature via a Web interface, using either the CVE identifier or a description keyword. For more detailed information regarding CVE and compatible products, please see the homepage at http://cve.mitre.org/.

The In-Brief

The in-brief meeting occurs on the first day of the on-site evaluation phase and continues the process of customer communication and management buy-in begun during the IAM. All members of the evaluation team are present, as usually are the system owners, management staff, and the organization's technical staff. The IEM process requires no specific format other than the review of the TEP. At this point, the TEP has been completed and can help serve as a road map for much of the meeting.

As a business process, you might want to ensure that the TEP is signed and dated during the in-briefing, especially if any changes have occurred. Even if the TEP has already been signed, this provides another step of due diligence in that it is presented and approved on-site, where the scope of work should be stable, since you are now dealing with actual accountable time and resources. The focus of the meeting should be to review the evaluation plan that has been agreed to as well as several overall project aspects. The in-brief should:

- Reintroduce the goals and objectives for the evaluation

- Act as an introduction to the evaluation team

- Confirm schedules and plans

- Provide an overview of accomplishments to date (including IAM activities)

- Reiterate management buy-in

- Focus on technical staff buy-in

- Describe the evaluation methodology

- Review the tools and processes for evaluation

The culture within the organization will help to determine the formality of the briefing. This includes the actual process of the meeting, such as PowerPoint presentations, open discussions, Q&A sessions, or any other methods of conducting the meeting. Appropriate attire should match the organization's expectations for formality along with the other aspects of the meeting. After presenting the TEP, the evaluation team may also discover new political issues that may present a cultural concern for the evaluation, which should then be addressed before the close of the in-brief.

Presenting the TEP

Presenting the TEP is a must for the in-brief, and it is a great tool for providing a basic agenda. The TEP review will help to ensure that there are no misunderstandings or miscommunications regarding the process and the goals of the on-site evaluation phase. Make sure to cover each portion of the TEP, and to ensure agreement, it is sometimes easier to make this more of a discussion than a presentation.

- **Points of contact** Make sure that all appropriate parties have the correct contact information for both the evaluation team members and the organization. Technical testing often leads to a schedule that is "off-peak" rather than normal business hours. If a system is inadvertently brought down, the organization should be notified immediately to rectify the situation, or the organization may need to contact an evaluator to stop a scheduled and unattended scan. Physical access to segments or after-hours access to facilities may be required on an ad hoc basis.

- **Methodology overview** Here the process of the IEM needs to be described in an "executive summary" type of format. Explain the goals and the reasons for performing this evaluation. A discussion of the expectations and planned accomplishments will help solidify the process in the minds of those who may not have been involved with either the previously conducted IAM or the IEM to date. For the technical administrators present, a discussion of the tools that will be used and some of the basic configurations is appropriate. This helps involve the technical staff as well as offering a "last chance" opportunity for someone to speak up about known issues. For example, previous audits might have pointed out that a Nessus scan will disable the organization's 3COM routers. Rather than bring down the network, a finding can be documented at this point regarding those devices and minimize downtime for both the organization and the evaluation team as they await full network operations capabilities to continue testing.

- **Organization and system criticality** Review the criticality matrices of the systems and the organization. Many times, the technical staff that is responsible for maintaining security controls on the systems might not have been involved with the part of the IAM process that maps out the business concerns and priorities. This will help them understand the value of the data and systems that are being evaluated. Combined with the definitions created by the organization for impact (high, medium, low), the technical staff that will be responsible for mitigating any findings will be able to understand and follow a prioritization list of technical findings that are tied directly to the value of the data or the system. At this point, review of the system description will help verify components for technical testing, especially if the plans call for deconstructed testing based on operating system, application, system, or the like.

- **Detailed network information** This is the comprehensive description of the networks or systems to be evaluated. A review with the technical staff to confirm the evaluating team's understanding of the technical configurations of the system to be tested needs to occur. This review should include IP ranges, or subnets, specific target host IP addresses, and correct contact information for technical administrators for these networks or devices in case of an outage or error.

- **Customer concerns** Reiterate the logic or reason that an IEM is being conducted. Why did the organization request an IEM? Make sure to cover all concerns that carry over from the IAM as well as any new technical concerns that have arisen for the IEM. Also include any concerns of the evaluation team regarding the technical testing based on the current understanding of the system.

- **Customer constraints** Verify that everyone is in agreement in terms of any constraints being placed on the evaluation team. These constraints should include any applicable constraints identified in the IAM process and any specific technical constraints identified for the IEM. Include any constraints that the evaluating team may be placing on the testing as well, such as refusal to perform exploitation testing based on legal liability concerns.

- **Rules of engagement** The ROE is a lengthy product, but there is a lot of information here. The TEP acts as a high-level overview of the process and objectives, whereas the ROE gets down and dirty with the details of exactly what you will be doing on the organization's systems. If technical staff members are getting involved for the first time, expect a lot of questions. This is your chance to really get buy-in from the technical members of the organization, who are likely feeling apprehensive about your visit and the actions you will be taking. Depending on how detailed your ROE is, you might also need to discuss several procedural items regarding what is expected not only of the evaluation team but the administrators as well. Exact procedures for password compliance testing and any other testing that may require the evaluators be granted elevated privileges should be documented and agreed on by the organization. When the organization's technical staff is comfortable with the process, or at least understands it, things will go much more smoothly when it's time to actually perform those tests.

- **Coordination agreements** Any other concerns or details need to be reviewed with the on-site staff—even the basics of discussing the level of detail in which to describe findings and solutions. It's not unheard of to have an organization request greater detail on how a finding may affect a priority system, or to have a new administrator request more information about solutions than others. Some organizations are required to respond to all security evaluations and have the evaluation teams validate their planned approach for mitigation. Reviewing this type of arrangement will remind technical staff that they will be expected to respond in a timely manner.

- **Letter of authorization** The LOA is the definitive document detailing the work to be completed. It should be reviewed with the technical staff, if for no other reason than to demonstrate the management level buy-in of the project.

- **Timeline of events** No matter how well communicated and planned the evaluation, changes in the timeline of on-site activities are common. The more granular a schedule becomes with a large number of parties involved, the more likely times or dates are to slip. As discussed earlier, flexibility is a necessity for the on-site evaluation phase. Review the timeline carefully to ensure that all parties who are responsible for assisting with the efforts are going to be available as planned or have backups ready. Events may cause the timeline to be affected, but they can be addressed as they arise as long as everyone is in agreement with the latest schedule.

Remember that the TEP is a living document throughout the course of the engagement. The on-site evaluation phase is normally fast and furious, so expect changes that could require you to update the TEP. Be sure to get the appropriate sign-offs when this occurs and continue moving forward.

By following the TEP as an agenda of topics for the in-brief, you can review and discuss the major points of the engagement with the facilitators for the on-site evaluation phase. Encourage questions throughout the meeting to ensure that everyone is on the same page before you begin. During the IEM, there is a constant need to set and maintain expectations; the in-brief is a great tool for taking care of this issue.

Notes from the Underground…

Operational Security Teams

Don't forget to address operational security (OpSec) concerns when you're getting detailed technical contact information. Not only does the system administrator need to be aware of time windows and the source address of the system performing the testing, but so does the organization's OpSec team. Whatever name the organization's OpSec team goes by (CERT, IT Security Operations, Security Operations Center, or something else), whoever in the organization performs the duty of monitoring and responding to security threats and incidents needs to be made aware of the evaluation efforts.

If security monitoring and response are outsourced to a third party, be very careful and very specific to make sure that your activities will not result in a third-party response, such as dispatch of armed guards or police officers. This would be a perfect time to verify that you have a copy of your LOA as well!

If part of your evaluation involves testing the response capabilities, plan to put this early in your schedule so that you can get your introductions out of the way quickly! After that, you need to involve the OpSec teams so that they don't initiate response procedures based on your activities.

Cultural Sensitivity

One of the concerns to remember for the on-site evaluation phase is the cultural sensitivity required of the evaluation team. Systems administrators could take offense that outsiders are being brought in to perform a security evaluation, even if they perform their jobs admirably. Some may take it as an affront that management or their superiors don't trust them, or they could simply see it as a waste of time in their already overloaded schedules of maintaining systems. Others may worry about what the findings could mean for them.

In the in-brief, take the opportunity to help them understand the need for and logic behind unbiased security reviews. Reiterate the fact that the evaluation is intended to help the organization improve its security by using experienced INFOSEC professionals to review current configurations of the system, with a goal of providing mitigation recommendations before someone more unsavory exploits them.

Assure them that the IEM does not report *who* did what, why, or when. The IEM reports weaknesses based on what is currently present and does not make an effort to attribute those findings to any administrators. The concept of nonattribution is practiced in the IEM to help staff feel more comfortable with the activities that are taking place. The IEM's goal is to help reduce the security gap, not point out incompetent staff.

Another staff concern will be the elevated privileges that may be required for the "outsiders" to perform the evaluation. Any administrators should be concerned about this, because they have the same goal as you: to protect their system. Depending on the level of trust between the teams, such as an internal organization reviewing department versus a third-party consultant, this concern can fluctuate widely. If there is deep concern, try to alleviate those fears through a set of procedures that don't compromise the results but may require additional time or input from the organization's technical staff. A good example is to decide who exports a copy of the SAM database off a Microsoft Windows server for password compliance testing and how that file is handled. It takes little effort on the part of the evaluation team to monitor the technical staff exporting this file to a disk and then be escorted to a physically controlled point where the testing occurs on an evaluator's system specifically set aside for this task. This prevents the evaluator from accessing the data without escort and ensures that the function occurs on an evaluator-controlled system.

If you make the technical staff a part of the process, their comfort level will increase, allowing them to be more open and helpful with the evaluation. We want to include the people who are responsible for maintaining these systems, and they in turn will hopefully want to include the tenets of security in their daily activities. The evaluation team is not just performing security work. They are acting in a "sales and marketing" capacity to constantly manage and maintain customer expectations. By realizing the issues the customer deals with, being sympathetic to those issues, and working around them without causing a major headache, the evaluator can perform his or her duties while helping the staff understand the value of the work being performed.

Summary

After reading this chapter, a basic understanding of the background behind the IEM baseline activities should be achieved, as well as the nontechnical factors for ensuring that those activities are a success. This chapter focused on many of those nontechnical factors, such as buy-in and expectations. Few things can ruin an evaluation more quickly than customer misunderstanding or dissatisfaction, and although these can easily be avoided through communication, it takes constant attention to maintain everyone's focus.

Detailed preparation and planning will help make an evaluation successful as well. You already laid much of the groundwork for this in the IAM process with the customer. By taking what was created in the IAM and successfully using the TEP and ROE, you can create a very detailed plan of attack to ensure the most effective use of time while on-site. Since this time is packed with activities, often leaving little time to breathe, that schedule will be paramount to creating a quality deliverable in the final report.

In keeping with the concept of getting the most possible use out of the product, compatibility with the CVE list is mandatory. This will make the final report usable to the customer long after the evaluation team has left the building. This works to your benefit as well in that if you're a consultant, you'll want your work to stand on its own so that customer follow-up calls are for assistance in mitigation or follow-on work, not for interpreting your documentation because details were not included or were difficult to research.

Remember that attention to detail also means attention to the customer. This includes acknowledging their concerns, constraints, and any sensitivity issues. The more your actions are perceived as helping, the more relevant and detailed your findings will be. Adapting to the environment and "working within the system" are attributes that will make this evaluation successful. The key best practices for accomplishing this goal that you should take away from this chapter are:

- Get technical staff buy-in.
- Pay attention to schedule and plan details.
- Be flexible in all aspects of the on-site evaluation phase.
- Incorporate CVE identifiers.
- Maintain a detailed technical focus through the 10 IEM baseline activities.
- Keep a big-picture focus to incorporate IAM criticalities and priorities.
- Validate all findings.
- Adhere to the TEP.
- Be aware of cultural sensitivities.
- Don't forget the little things.

Solutions Fast Track

Preparing for the On-site Evaluation Phase

☑ On-site scheduling should be done with as much flexibility as possible. Surprises are standard when performing a technical evaluation.

☑ Administrative planning may be dull, but it helps ensure a smooth evaluation while you're on-site.

☑ Technical planning is based on the specific customer environments, customer concerns and constraints, and the evaluating team's expertise.

IAM vs. IEM

☑ The IAM and IEM are complementary processes. The IEM cannot be performed without certain output from the IAM, such as criticality matrices.

☑ The IAM reviews organizational P&P weaknesses; the IEM reviews technical weaknesses. The IEM verifies the technical implementation of an organization's P&P.

☑ The IEM uses hands-on testing of the technical environment, whereas the IAM is based on interviews and system demonstrations.

☑ The IEM is a validation-based methodology. Automated tools are used to increase the speed and efficiency of testing, but they do not remove the need for an experienced security professional.

IEM Baseline Activities

☑ The 10 IEM baseline activities cover the main required technical security areas to be evaluated.

☑ A wide assortment of tools is available to perform multiple tasks, and the decision as to what tool to use depends on the evaluators' experience.

☑ The NSA and the IEM do not support or recommend any tools.

The Role of CVE and CAN

☑ CVE identifiers are meant to enable cross-system referencing of weaknesses and support simpler customer research efforts.

☑ CVE or CAN identifiers are required for all weaknesses that have been documented by the CVE project.

☑ Although not specifically recommended by the NSA, CVE-compliant tools do improve the ease of this finding labeling.

The In-Brief

☑ The in-brief ensures and demonstrates management buy-in and assists with earning that same level of buy-in from the technical staff.

☑ The TEP must be presented as part of the in-briefing as a last-step approval of the process details prior to beginning the technical evaluation.

☑ Be aware of any issues that may be introduced to the evaluation by cultural sensitivities in the organization.

Frequently Asked Questions

The following Frequently Asked Questions, answered by the authors of this book, are designed to both measure your understanding of the concepts presented in this chapter and to assist you with real-life implementation of these concepts. To have your questions about this chapter answered by the author, browse to **www.syngress.com/solutions** and click on the **"Ask the Author"** form. You will also gain access to thousands of other FAQs at ITFAQnet.com.

Q: If I'm using tools like Nessus that include port scanning, do I need to include a seperate port scanner in my toolkit?

A: No. The requirement is that a minimum of one tool be used to cover each activity. If one tool can be used for multiple activities and the evaluation team and customer approve, then this is acceptable.

Q: I often see different results with different technical scanning tools, which one is right and how do I know which is right?

A: This is why it is recommended that for some activities, like vulnerability scanning, it is recommended that two tools be used to assist in validation. If different results are obtained, it means a closer look is required to validate the findings.

Q: Is there value in doing validation onsite or can it be done remotely?

A: Validation is MUCH easier to do onsite. With direct access to speak to administrative staff, perform manual checks, and perform addition tool testing, validation efforts can be completed in a shorter period of time. Performing validation remotely, while not impossible, can be very time consuming and difficult.

Q: Application testing software is incredibly expensive, is there something that will accomplish this that falls into the category of freeware or shareware?

A: Some current utilities include very minimal test sets for specific applications. For example most vulnerability scanners have a common set of detection probes for common Oracle weaknesses. If a small Oracle database does not happen to be very high on the list of critical components, that testing combined with manual checks or a configuration test script may be appropriate.

Q: How in-depth should validation exercises be in Day Four?

A: Validation efforts should strive to validate every technical weakness discovered, otherwise it is simply a technical weakness assumed. Often times this can be achieved easily enough by simply verifying the version and patch level of a specific application. Some times more in-depth testing may be required. Anything that cannot be validated due to a lack of available time and resources, should be noted in the report.

Q: Customer's often ask "What can I do to prevent rogue devices from attaching to the network?", what is a good recommendation?

A: This will depend entirely on the organization's resources to manage an issue like this, and you experience as an INFOSEC Professional. Many of the common recommendations would be for a strict Change Management process within data centers. Some of this could be done with a segregation of duties policy, splitting network and server operations into two groups that have to work together, with technical controls on network devices that do not allow the installation of hosts without a configuration change on the switch or router. Again, the appropriate resolution will be different based on the customer environment.

Chapter 8

Network
Discovery Activities

Solutions in this chapter:

- **Goals and Objectives**

- **Tool Basics**

- **Port Scanning**

- **SNMP Scanning**

- **Enumeration and Banner Grabbing**

- **Wireless Enumeration**

☑ **Summary**

☑ **Solutions Fast Track**

☑ **Frequently Asked Questions**

Introduction

In this chapter, we'll discuss the network discovery portion of the onsite evaluation phase. We'll also see some brief introductions to multiple tools available for use in each of the IEM baseline activities covered by the network discovery stage and some of their expected or common uses. Network discovery activities include the first four baseline activities: port scanning, SNMP scanning, enumeration and banner grabbing, and wireless enumeration.

For port scanning, we'll discuss some of the basics of how a port scanner works, why we are performing this activity, and what we're looking for in the results. We'll compare some utilities to see what options and features are out there, to help determine which tools might be better suited to each scenario.

In the second activity, we'll look very briefly at how SNMP operates and some of the things that make it an important service to evaluate for security purposes. We'll get a look at how some network management utilities can be used for security testing purposes, and we'll review other tools designed specifically for evaluating SNMP services, with security in mind.

The basic methods and reasons for performing enumeration are discussed, with the introduction of tools that include manual command-line interface (CLI) testing as well as automated graphical user interface (GUI) utilities. This activity builds off previous activities and takes things farther to discover more information about the target system.

The two most popular tools for performing wireless enumeration are discussed, as is the impact of exposed wireless services. Wireless enumeration has many aspects that must be considered before testing begins, and these should be documented and agreed to with the customer. The most common concerns are introduced, with recommendations on how to address them.

The onsite phase of the IEM relies very heavily on the evaluator's understanding of security concepts and technical issues. This chapter is meant to simply provide a framework for the activities that the IEM expects the evaluator to perform and to facilitate the use of discovered information. Documenting the results of these tests into a single system mapping for the organization's records and the evaluator's process management is covered for each activity. Our goal is to tie the activities together and provide a reference table of activities and results.

Goals and Objectives

The primary goal for the network discovery activities is to learn and document as much of the architecture and system configuration as possible. The two main tasks for mapping the evaluation system are discovery and enumeration. Through the use of automated tools, we want to discover all available resources and services and determine as much information about them as possible. This will help the evaluator to define further detailed testing into suspected exposure areas later in the onsite visit as well as verify that the organization's documentation matches its implementation.

For this methodology to work, the evaluator needs to be able to focus on the system as a whole, at the same time inspecting the smallest configuration details. The IEM requires a customized report, based on the organization's criticality measurements. Although the evaluator is performing each activity, he or she must constantly assess how each weakness may affect the security of the system as well as how a recommended solution may affect that system's operation and the organization's ability to implement it. The strength of the IEM lies in the evaluator performing the work, not any specific tool used to address each required activity.

Notes from the Underground...

System Terminology

One thing to remember while you're reading this chapter is the meaning of the term *system*. In the context of the IAM and IEM, a system is not limited to a single server or IP address but often refers to a collection of devices and data flow. For the purposes of this chapter, the term can be more closely related to the boundaries of the evaluation target.

For example, we might be evaluating two separate systems with hundreds of devices. The first system provides a certain business function and house-specific data sets. This system is limited across a few servers that provide front-end client services and back-end data management. These servers are clustered into a single major application (MA), and the boundary for the system crosses all the servers within. A second system might be the local area network (LAN) and all the client personal computers (PCs). This system can be classified as a general support system (GSS) and include routers, switches, etc.

When speaking about a specific device, we use more detailed terms such as *server, router*, or *resource*. The term *system* should be construed at the target evaluation boundaries.

The classifications GSS and MA are taken from the National Institute of Standards and Technology (NIST) documentation. You can find more information regarding NIST security guidance and standards at the NIST Computer Security Resource Center (CSRC), http://csrc.nist.gov/. The IAM and IEM map very well to NIST practices.

Results as Findings and Evaluation Task Attributes

During the network discovery, most concerns or findings are not usually true vulnerabilities. More often than not, those findings come from tools or manual investigations later in the onsite evaluation phase. The results or findings from the network discovery activities primarily fall into two categories, misconfigurations and differences in documentation, as well security exposures.

The IAM focuses mostly on the documentation of the system and the overriding organizational goals, whereas the IEM is meant to verify that those objectives are met and discover technical vulnerabilities. Part of the requirement for the IEM is to report all inconsistencies between the system mappings created from the network discovery activities and the organization's system documentation. This is where we either validate the organization's perception of the system or adjust that perception to match reality.

As discussed in a previous chapter, there is an important difference between a vulnerability and an exposure. During later IEM baseline activities, the focus of the evaluation shifts more to the discovery of weaknesses, whereas in the network discovery stage, the focus is predominantly on exposures. One of the things to keep in mind is that during the IAM processes, the evaluators should have learned detailed information regarding the purpose and function of the system. Discovered processes operating on the system that aren't required for operation are not technically vulnerabilities; they can, however, be considered exposures and should be reported as findings, with the recommendation of disabling those processes.

Services that are required for operation that present an exposure should also be reported, with a recommendation for an alternate solution. A common example would be the discovery of the telnet service running on a host. Considering that telnet transmits all data in clear text, including logins and passwords, the service inherently presents an exposure. The recommendation of migrating to SSH might be an acceptable solution to the customer, ensuring that all data is encrypted between the host and clients.

This is an area in the IEM baseline activities that requires a great amount of evaluator expertise. Unlike many vulnerability scanning tools that do the work for you, during the network discovery stage the evaluator must have a solid understanding of many common protocols and services. It is up to the evaluator to notice possible exposures and identify how they could affect the system.

System Mapping

A system mapping is not a required aspect of the NSA IEM; however, it is an excellent tool for documenting the work performed during the network discovery activities (see Table 8.1). By combining all the information gathered during these activities into a single document, you will create a mapping of a system's technical resources and services that most organizations do not have.

This document can then be used to verify much of the system configuration documentation that was reviewed during the IAM process. This allows you to trace back unknown or rogue services and resources that might be running against system policy. This helps the organization catch default services that often sneak past an administrator when he or she is hardening a server. It also helps provide a system baseline for the customer, which is often hard to find.

A system mapping can also assist the evaluator in determining where extra attention should be concentrated. From the completed document and even a partially completed mapping, it is usually easy to see where notoriously weak services are waiting for an attacker. This is the first step in identifying the "low-hanging fruit," or easily exploited vulnerabilities.

Table 8.1 IEM System Mapping

ABC123 IEM System Mapping					10/29/2004
XYZ Consulting			POC: Johnny Reboot		(555) 123.4567
Active Hosts:			Address Ranges:		192.168.1.0/24 172.16.2.0/24
IP Address/Device Name	Ports		Identified Services	Detected OS	Notes
WiFi MAC Address	Type	Crypt	SSID	Discovered IP Address	Notes

Tool Basics

The variety of tools covered in this chapter range from incredibly simple and easy to the complex and advanced. Though most of the tools can be used with little experience, it is not recommended that an evaluator use these tools without experience and a solid knowledge of the tools, what they are trying to accomplish, and what the results mean. This chapter is meant to give a simple introduction to many of the more common available options, with the expectation that the reader has some knowledge of networking and TCP/IP.

It is highly recommended that readers download and review the tools that interest them, reading the included documentation and testing results to get a better understanding of how the tools operate and how they could affect an organization's systems. All the tools discussed in this chapter are referenced in Appendix A, with links to the Web sites where you can research or download them.

Obviously, not everyone runs the same base operating system for their security evaluation devices, so we're included tools for both the Microsoft Windows and UNIX platforms for all baseline activities. Most UNIX platform utilities also work on the new Mac OS X with minor adjusting, and , with just a little Internet searching you'll find guides for most tools. It is common practice, however, for many evaluators to use multiple platforms for their work so as not to limit themselves to a smaller set of options. The IEM does not make this a requirement, but as a business practice, Security Horizon requires all evaluators to be experienced in both the Windows and UNIX platforms, to maximize efficiency and customer results. In fact, Security Horizon standardizes on multiple toolkits per evaluator, to increase evaluator efficiency by allowing time-consuming evaluation tools to run on one unit. This allows the evaluator to perform checks, reporting, validation, and shorter testing from an available device.

The number of security tools available to perform these and other activities is much too large to include them all in this book. We chose tools based primarily on their prevalence in the industry. Some are rather new, and some are rather old, but the important thing is they get the job done.

Expected Usage and Requirements

The IEM expectations for the tools used are rather simple. At least one tool must be used within each of the baseline activities. Manual configuration checks can be considered a tool, depending on the evaluator and the organization's needs, although automated tools normally make things faster, with manual checks performed for more sensitive concerns.

Many activities justify the need to use more than one tool, either for different testing methods and test databases or to assist in validating the results reported each tool. Beyond the need to address each baseline activity, there are no other requirements. It is recommended that evaluators understand a wide variety of tools so that they can match the organization's needs to the tool that performs the best in that environment.

At the same time, one tool might cover multiple baseline activities. As discussed in this chapter, several port-scanning tools also have options that enable the evaluator to incorporate enumeration activities. This is an acceptable use of tools, as long as they are configured and run to support both activities.

Most tools offer differing levels of testing and reporting options. The evaluator's expertise is critical in determining the tools that fit the organization's environment. If an organization has banned the use of SNMP, there might not be a need for extensive SNMP evaluation; a quick scan to test for SNMP could be sufficient. At that point, any devices with SNMP enabled are automatically considered a finding because its mere presence is unacceptable to the organization. Conversely, if an organization is concerned about a new wireless networking implementation and security threats it could represent, a more detailed evaluation, including testing encryption strength, might be warranted. The IEM relies on the evaluator's knowledge and experience to make the call as to which tools best support each activity in any given scenario.

WARNING

Many automated tools are discussed in this book; however, the NSA does *not* officially support or endorse *any* specific products, brands, or platforms. Discussions and examples using several different mainstream INFOSEC tools are used here to help explain in greater detail the actions and expectations for the 10 IEM baseline activities.

Port Scanning

For port scanning, we use a variety of automated tools to discover the open ports responding on each of the resources in a system. In this, the first of the IEM baseline activities, what we are really trying to do is just determine "what's out there." By this point in the methodology, you should have already read several documents explaining the function of the system, the services it uses to perform those functions, the management services in place, or any number of configuration documents referring to the system's technical implementation. With port scanning, we start the network discovery portion of activities to see whether all those documents are accurate.

In a perfect world, the results of this activity should be exactly in line with the documentation. By not documenting the allowed and required services in the system, the organization could be leaving itself open to exposure. The administrative staff won't have instructions on what is acceptable. If the administrators are not informed that, for example, Telnet is not an acceptable system management tool, you could have logins and passwords floating in cleartext across the network, or even worse, on the Internet.

Port scanning is also a way to identify services that have inherent weaknesses, usually recognized only by experienced INFOSEC professionals. Through port scanning, these questionable services can be documented and marked for further research by either more detailed tools or manual configuration checks. An example is SSH; although SSH is a much better solution than Telnet for command-line management of a device, there are still security concerns with the configuration that a system administrator, whose primary goal is to make things work, might overlook. When this is recognized, the device can be scheduled for manual checks that might include verifying that protocol 1 is not allowed due to weak encryption. Root access login should also be disabled to minimize password attacks against the service as well as for auditing administrator actions. This activity requires experienced evaluators — not to operate the tools but to analyze the results.

Several of the more popular port-scanning utilities, with some of the more common uses and features, are introduced in brief in this section.

TIP

To understand the basics of TCP port scanning and some of the scanning options, it is important to understand the process that takes place in establishing a normal TCP connection. The client system initiates a connection by transmitting a synchronize (SYN) frame to the target; this frame includes connections parameters such as initial sequence numbers and the port to use for communication. The target machine responds with an acknowledgment (ACK) frame accepting the parameters from the SYN frame, as well as a SYN frame that includes its own required parameters (SYN/ACK). If everything is acceptable when the client machine receives the target's SYN, the client responds with an ACK frame of its own, and a full session is established. This process is often referred to as a *three-way hand-shake* (SYN, SYN/ACK, ACK).

Nmap

Nmap is likely the most popular scanning tool currently in use. Written by Fyodor, Nmap's source code has been released under the GNU General Public License (GPL) for free use. Currently at version 3.81, the Nmap tool supports most UNIX-based platforms, such as HP-UX, Linux, BSD, Mac OS X, and the Microsoft Windows platform.

Nmap's strength has always been the very quick port scan of specific targets or a range of targets. Added functionality has enabled Nmap to cross into multiple activities; however, in this section we concentrate on a brief review of the basic functionality of the port scan. The tool itself is capable of many varied tests and uses, but for the purposes of this book, we will review the most popular functions. (For a more detailed review of Nmap features and capabilities, review the man pages.)

Nmap utilizes a CLI. This allows for quick and easy use while making simple scripts easy to write o that you can manage specific tests or functions. The most basic use of Nmap from the CLI is *nmap <target>*. When run as a non-root user, this scan attempts to open a connection on every interesting port on the target machine (TCP Connect method) for scanning, also callable with the *–sT* option. This includes all ports from 1–1024 and any known service ports listed in the Nmap services file. Figure 8.1 is an example output from the command.

Figure 8.1 Nmap Output from the *nmap –st* Command

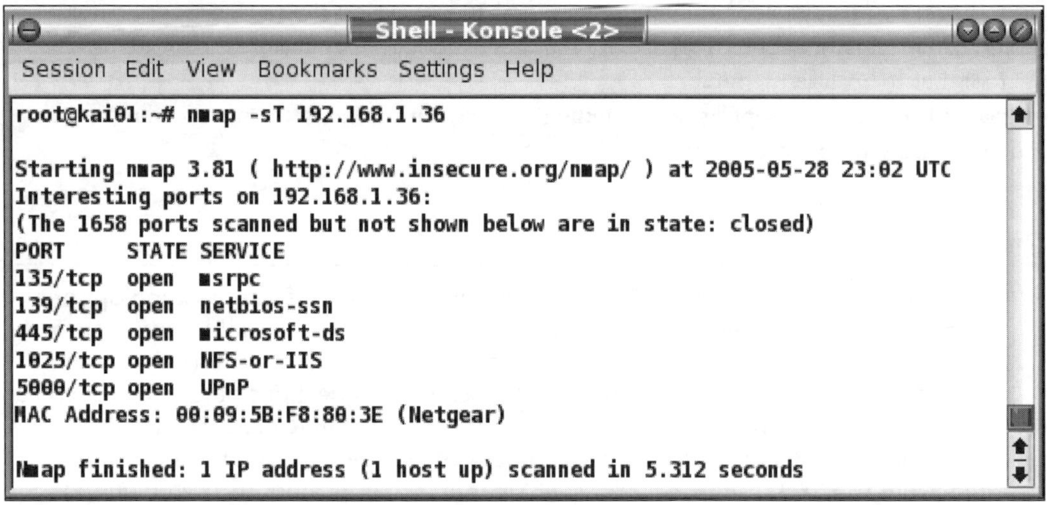
Shell - Konsole <2>
Session Edit View Bookmarks Settings Help
root@kai01:~# nmap -sT 192.168.1.36
Starting nmap 3.81 (http://www.insecure.org/nmap/) at 2005-05-28 23:02 UTC
Interesting ports on 192.168.1.36:
(The 1658 ports scanned but not shown below are in state: closed)
PORT STATE SERVICE
135/tcp open msrpc
139/tcp open netbios-ssn
445/tcp open microsoft-ds
1025/tcp open NFS-or-IIS
5000/tcp open UPnP
MAC Address: 00:09:5B:F8:80:3E (Netgear)
Nmap finished: 1 IP address (1 host up) scanned in 5.312 seconds

As you can see, a total of 1703 ports were scanned on the target machine in just over 5 seconds, and five services were found listening. Those services are defined in the output using the nmap-services list, which is a basic list of "well-known" services and the ports they are associated with. At this point, no testing of the ports is attempted beyond verifying that they are listening.

Usually, it is easier to use the *–v* option when using Nmap, for a more verbose output, which you will see in future examples. By default, Nmap performs a ping scan (either an ICMP request or TCP ping to port 80) and scans only hosts that respond. Adjusting the ping scanning options is discussed in the following section.

NMAP Options

Nmap offers a wide variety of options and features for performing a scan besides the basic TCP Connect option. Not every option is relevant to each scenario (such as internal vs. external scans), and your configurations will be based on the environment to be evaluated and the other tools you use. For these reasons, we cover only a few of the basic, most commonly used functions here.

TCP SYN

Unlike the connect method described previously, a SYN scan does not complete a full TCP connection. A SYN frame is sent, and if a SYN/ACK response is received, the scan responds with a reset (RST) frame rather than actually establishing the connection. This is intended to be a more stealthy approach than performing a full connections scan, since it will not be logged by some resources; however, root privileges are commonly required to perform this scan. The option needed for running this type of scan is −sS. This is also the default scan option when run as root. The −sS scan is shown in Figure 8.2.

Figure 8.2 The −sS Scan

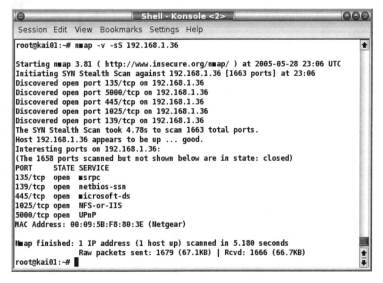

UDP Scanning

Nmap separates the scanning of UDP and TCP ports into separate functions. To perform a UDP scan, you would use the −sU option. Due to the method for this scan, further validation will have to be performed to weed out any possible false positives. The application will send a 0-byte packet to each specified UDP and consider that port open unless an ICMP unreachable message is received. Hence, a firewall or access control list (ACL) blocking these response messages will cause Nmap to report these ports as being open, as shown in Figure 8.3. It can also be a very slow process. It is highly recommended that you consult the man pages before performing this scan so that you know what to expect.

Figure 8.3 Open Port Reports

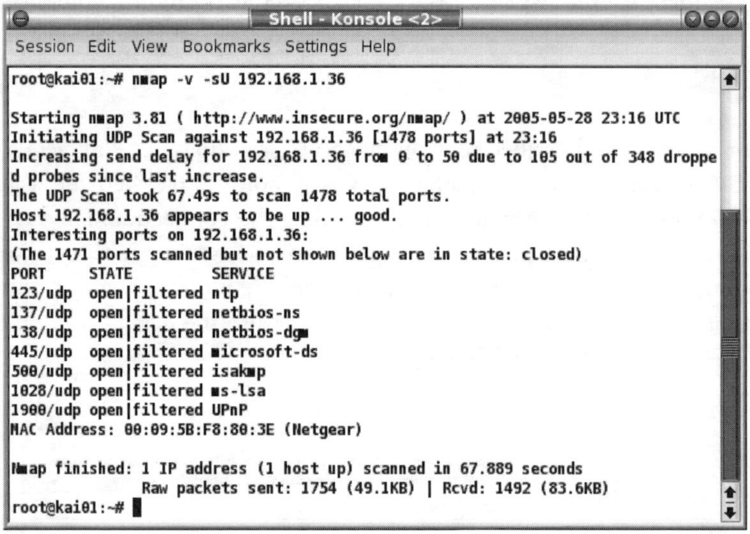

```
                        Shell - Konsole <2>
Session  Edit  View  Bookmarks  Settings  Help

root@kai01:~# nmap -v -sU 192.168.1.36

Starting nmap 3.81 ( http://www.insecure.org/nmap/ ) at 2005-05-28 23:16 UTC
Initiating UDP Scan against 192.168.1.36 [1478 ports] at 23:16
Increasing send delay for 192.168.1.36 from 0 to 50 due to 105 out of 348 droppe
d probes since last increase.
The UDP Scan took 67.49s to scan 1478 total ports.
Host 192.168.1.36 appears to be up ... good.
Interesting ports on 192.168.1.36:
(The 1471 ports scanned but not shown below are in state: closed)
PORT      STATE          SERVICE
123/udp   open|filtered ntp
137/udp   open|filtered netbios-ns
138/udp   open|filtered netbios-dgm
445/udp   open|filtered microsoft-ds
500/udp   open|filtered isakmp
1028/udp  open|filtered ms-lsa
1900/udp open|filtered UPnP
MAC Address: 00:09:5B:F8:80:3E (Netgear)

Nmap finished: 1 IP address (1 host up) scanned in 67.889 seconds
                 Raw packets sent: 1754 (49.1KB) | Rcvd: 1492 (83.6KB)
root@kai01:~# █
```

As you can see, a UDP scan takes a great deal longer to run than a TCP port scan. Remember this when you're performing scans on a large number of systems. You will also notice the introduction of a new state, open|filtered. This means that Nmap did not receive a response and either the port is open or the response was filtered between the service and the scanning device.

Ping Scanning

Often you might simply want to run a quick "ping sweep" to determine what resources are up and responding to ICMP requests. This is likely one of the very first tests you would run once onsite. This type of test performs a ping sweep only and reports back live hosts without actually performing a port scan. The option to use for this type of scan is –sP. Note in Figure 8.4 that the entire 192.168.1.0 network was scanned, and four devices responded. You will also find the MAC address returned and the product vendor displayed, a newer feature of NMAP for all port scans.

Figure 8.4 Ping Scanning

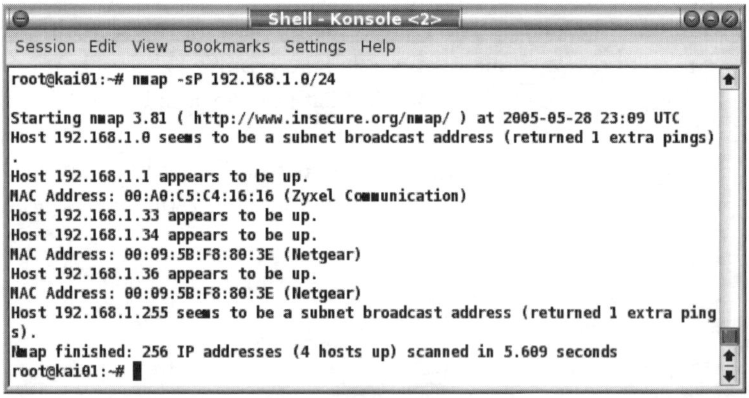

```
                        Shell - Konsole <2>
Session  Edit  View  Bookmarks  Settings  Help

root@kai01:~# nmap -sP 192.168.1.0/24

Starting nmap 3.81 ( http://www.insecure.org/nmap/ ) at 2005-05-28 23:09 UTC
Host 192.168.1.0 seems to be a subnet broadcast address (returned 1 extra pings)
.
Host 192.168.1.1 appears to be up.
MAC Address: 00:A0:C5:C4:16:16 (Zyxel Communication)
Host 192.168.1.33 appears to be up.
Host 192.168.1.34 appears to be up.
MAC Address: 00:09:5B:F8:80:3E (Netgear)
Host 192.168.1.36 appears to be up.
MAC Address: 00:09:5B:F8:80:3E (Netgear)
Host 192.168.1.255 seems to be a subnet broadcast address (returned 1 extra ping
s).
Nmap finished: 256 IP addresses (4 hosts up) scanned in 5.609 seconds
root@kai01:~# █
```

Basic Nmap Options

Nmap has a large list of options beyond those already discussed. For more detailed and specific information, review the documentation provided with the program. These are just a few of the more common options and features that should be remembered when you're using Nmap.

There are several methods for relaying the evaluation target address to the program. As shown in previous examples, the two most common are passing a specific address or a Classless Inter Domain Routing (CIDR) block as an argument. An example is *nmap –v 192.168.3.0/24*. An option that fits well with this targeting is the *exclude* option, which allows you to specify certain addresses to avoid, such as yourself. Starting with the command used previously and specifying a couple of hosts to exclude would result in *nmap –v 192.168.3.0/24 --exclude 192.168.3.12, 192.168.3.65*.

Nmap is very versatile in allowing you to input target arguments in multiple fashion. As shown in the *exclude* function, you can separate targets in any argument using a comma. You can also input non-CIDR block groups using a hyphen. For example, *nmap –v 192.168.3.56-121* will target all IP addresses between 192.168.3.56 and 192.168.3.121. Nmap also supports the use of wildcards in target addressing. Another way to write the command to scan an entire class C CIDR block like the one listed previously is *nmap –v 192.168.3.**. This will effectively scan all addresses in the 192.168.3.0 class C network. The power for address arguments in Nmap is pretty interesting. The following command will work and provides great versatility for specifying targets and possibly sensitive resources to exclude as an example: *nmap –v 192.168.7-18.* —exclude 192.168.*.1-5, 192.168.*.254*.

The last, and more common, target input method is to use a list of hosts in a separate file. These can use all the same methods already mentioned (single addresses, CIDR block addresses, and groupings), separated by tabs, spaces, or new lines. The option for this is *–iL* and would look like *nmap –v –iL <targetfile>*. The *exclude* functionality can be incorporated using a specific host file as well, using the *--exclude* option. Using the previous example, we would end up with *nmap –v –iL <targetfile> --exclude <excludefile>*.

One way to speed up large address range scans is to use the *–n* option, which tells Nmap not to resolve the names of active IP addresses. Conversely, if name resolution is required, you can use the *–R* option, which tells Nmap to attempt to resolve the names of all IP addresses found active.

Sending Nmap output to the screen is pretty convenient for scans with limited addresses, but it's often easier to manage the output when it's directed to a separate log file for parsing as needed. Nmap supports three output formats: a single-line output for simplified parsing, a "human-readable" format, and an XML output. Respectively, those three output command options are *–oG <logfile>, -oN <logfile>, and –oX < logfile>*. A further option, *-oA <logfile>*, tells Nmap to output into all three formats.

SuperScan

SuperScan is a popular port-scanning tool with an easy-to-use Microsoft Windows GUI inter-face. The tool is developed and distributed by Foundstone, free of charge. Although a quick tool to use, it also allows for a decent amount of flexibility through simple configurations.

The tool also offers added benefits beyond the scope of this chapter that could assist you throughout your overall evaluation process. Although not required by the IEM, these tools may be an efficient solution for basic evaluation technical needs:

- Hostname Lookup (DNS Query)
- Ping and Traceroute ICMP Utilities
- DNS Zone Transfer Utilities
- Pre-Configured WHOIS Utilities
- HTTP Banner Grabbing

WARNING

The version of SuperScan discussed here is 4.0. This version supports only Microsoft Windows 2000 and XP and requires administrative privileges to operate. If you need to use the tool on an earlier Microsoft Windows platform or do not have administrative rights, the earlier version, SuperScan 3.0, is still available for download from the Foundstone site.

In the GUI, the second tab allows for the configuration of discovery options. Like Nmap, SuperScan performs a host discovery based on the evaluator's requirements prior to performing the scan using ICMP. ICMP messages are broken down into types. You might find that some types are blocked by a firewall, whereas others are not. The standard ICMP echo request (message type 8) is the default setting for SuperScan. This is the message sent when you perform a ping. Another option is an ICMP timestamp request (message type 13). The last two options are the ICMP address mask request (message type 17) and ICMP information request (message type 15). Many administrators block "pings" at the firewall, unaware that other ICMP message types are available.

On this same page, the evaluator can enable or disable UDP and TCP scanning as well define the specific ports to be checked. Ports can be assigned in ranges and can be read from an external text file. The UDP scan can be configured to require an ICMP destination unreachable (message type 3) to mark a port as closed or consider it open only if a data reply is collected. As with Nmap, be cautious about results when you're performing a UDP scan. The TCP scan can be configured using the same two major scanning approaches described with Nmap: a TCP Connect scan or a TCP SYN scan. All discovery services here can also be set with a user-defined timeout. The default should be satisfactory in most cases, although slower or distant networks (multiple hops) may require a longer timeout.

To bypass simple firewall rules or incorrectly configured devices, there is also an option to use a single source port for all scan attempts, rather than a dynamic port. A user-defined port can be entered for both UDP and TCP scanning. For internal testing purposes, you should rarely need to use this feature (see Figure 8.5).

Figure 8.5 Bypassing Simple Firewall Rules

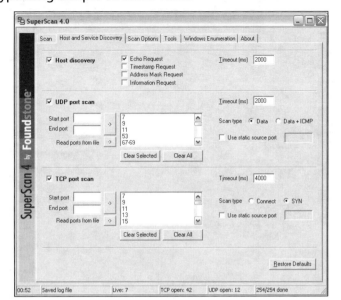

The third tab from the left, Scan Options, provides more options for configuring your scan. Here you can set the number of attempts for both host discovery and actual port scans against discovered hosts. One attempt is the default, and it is not likely that you'll need to increase this number, unless you are on a very slow connection such as dialup. Although running multiple passes across devices will greatly increase the elapsed time, you would probably be better off adjusting a combination of the timeouts from the previous settings page and the speed slider bar. This bar sets the amount of time the tool waits between sending out scan probes. The default setting, 10ms, should be adequate for most connections. If all target devices are on the same LAN (read: not running across 56k ISDN connections), setting the delay between 0ms and 5ms will probably be acceptable and will speed up the overall scan runtime.

You can also choose not to display hosts with no active ports. This is just a simple cleanup feature to remove inactive addresses from you report window, which can fill up very quickly when scanning multiple IP addresses or ranges. An added option is to randomize the order of the hosts scanned and the ports scanned. If you're scanning devices over multiple segments, this can be a beneficial tool for minimizing any bottlenecks that arise and cause slower traffic speeds for users. Some IDS devices are configured to look for successive scans along port ranges as well, which, although not a recommended or appropriate configuration rule, randomization can easily get past.

The last set of options concern banner grabbing (see Figure 8.6), which we address in the next section of this chapter. This is just another example of how some tools can cover multiple IEM baseline activity requirements.

Figure 8.6 Banner Grabbing

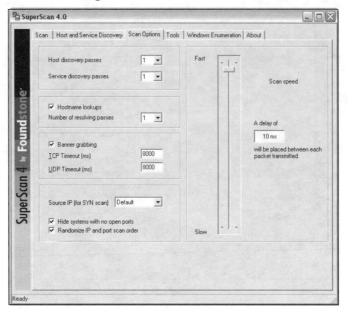

The first tab is the actual scan page. This page is broken down into three basic sections: a target address selection frame, a minimal results window, and a scan status window. In the following image, the scan status window is minimized to give a greater view of the results window.

In the target selection frame, you can enter target addresses one at a time or by range. These addresses are then displayed in the window to the right, allowing for multiple ranges or single address input for a single scan. You can also import addresses from a text file. SuperScan will recognize the same formats discussed earlier, including single IP addresses, CIDR block address ranges, and address groupings (for example, 192.168.6.24-68).

In the results window, the active ports of all discovered hosts, both TCP and UDP, are displayed. If DNS resolution was chosen and is operational, the hostname is displayed as well. After the scan is completed, a total number of hosts and TCP and UDP ports are displayed. In Figure 8.7 you can see the results for three out of seven live IP addresses discovered. For reporting purposes, you can view all the data collected by selecting the **View HTML Results** button at the bottom of the page. This outputs a clear and simple page for reviewing the data, without having to scroll through a small window. An example of this output is displayed in the next section, where the enumeration capabilities of SuperScan 4 are discussed.

Overall, SuperScan 4 is a very simple-to-use Microsoft Windows-based port scanner that takes little time to understand and configure. The speed with which scans are completed, customizable for the scenario, is relatively fast.

Figure 8.7 Discovering Hosts with SuperScan 4.0

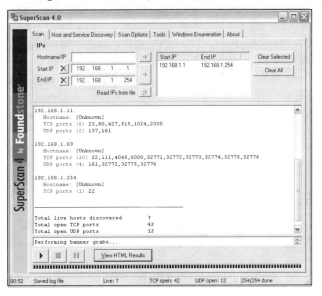

ScanLine

ScanLine is another free tool from the security firm Foundstone. Formerly know as FScan, ScanLine is one of the most popular CLI-based port scanners for the Microsoft Windows platforms. In Figure 8.8 you can see the results of a basic port scan, run with the command *sl 192.168.1.5*.

Figure 8.8 Basic Port Scan Results

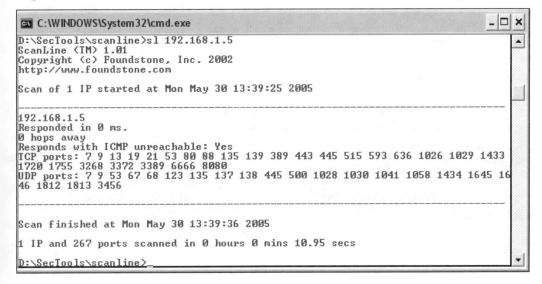

As you can see, by default ScanLine uses an internal list of ports to scan, if none is provided at the command line or in an optional external file. To declare a list of ports or ranges from the command line, the –*t* option can be used, and for UDP, the –*u* option. An example is *sl –t 21-25, 80, 443 –u 20-100 192.168.3.83*. For specifying ports using an external file, you would use the –*l* <*tcpportsfile*> option for TCP scanning and the –*L* <*udpportsfile*> option for UDP scanning. The –*v* option is also beneficial for viewing the tool status while running in verbose mode.

File output with ScanLine is very simple; you use the –*o* <*outputfile*> option to overwrite any data in the current output file or the –*O* <*outputfile*> option to append results to any data in the current output file. For people who predominantly use the Microsoft Windows environment, ScanLine is a great option for creating custom scripts using the argument and output options, as seen often with Nmap in the UNIX environment.

SolarWinds

SolarWinds is the first tool we will look at that was originally designed as, and is mostly still, a resource or network management tool. Over time, added security testing features have been incorporated to make this tool not just a multifunction management utility but also a multifunction security utility. The SolarWinds tools are a Microsoft Windows platform-based set of utilities.

The SolarWinds Network Management Toolset is currently available in version 8.1 and is a pay-for-use commercial product. There are four different pricing options based on the number of utilities in the suite, starting with the Standard Edition and adding more functionality all the way up to the Engineer's Edition. The utilities discussed in this chapter are not all available in the Standard Edition, so whichever tools interest you, make sure to verify that they are included in any edition you research.

The Port Scanner utility within SolarWinds can be configured under the **File | Settings** menu. From here, you can select or deselect specific ports to scan from a prepopulated list. You can also add custom ports not shown. Currently, the utility only supports a full TCP Connect scan, so some of the configuration options for stealth are not available. You can adjust timing configurations such as connection timeouts, maximum concurrent scan connections, and the time allotted between scans, or scan spacing. UDP scanning is not yet available as an option at the time of this writing. Also under the settings are a multitude of graphical display and output options for ease of use.

The main window for the utility is incredibly easy to use and understand. You only have a few options to set. Enter your starting and ending IP addresses, and decide whether you want to use the predefined ports discussed under the Settings menu or manually enter a range or multiple ranges of ports to scan. As you can see in Figure 8.9, the results are then displayed in a grid format in the main window.

The output from the SolarWinds Port Scanner is in HTML format and for manual editing can easily be sent directly to several Microsoft applications, such as Word or Excel, under the **File | Send To** menu.

Figure 8.9 Gridded Port Scanning

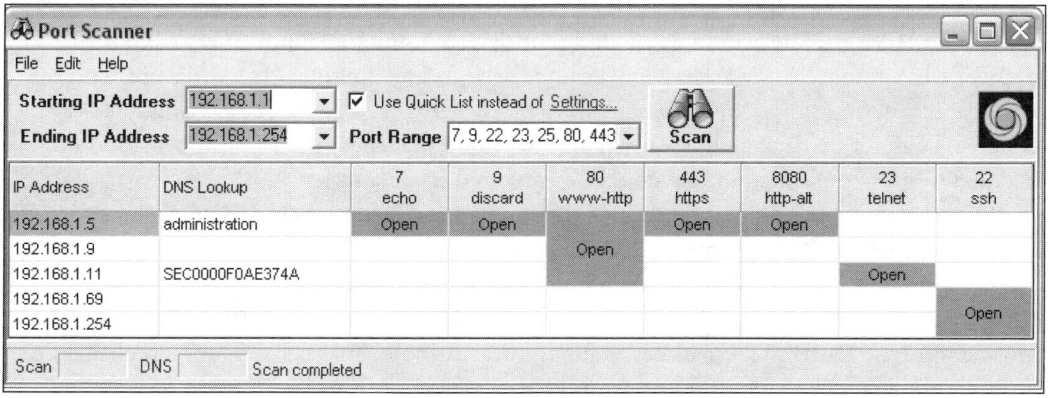

Port Scan System Mapping

At this point, after completing the port scanning of the system, the gathered information needs to be documented. This documentation is considered a business process, and not an NSA IEM process, so we will use the Security Horizon format for putting together a system mapping.

Taking the table displayed earlier in the chapter, we can now start cataloging the data on a detailed resource basis (see Table 8.2). The following table is an example of how our system mapping should look up to this point. This is obviously abbreviated, but should give a better understanding of what is being done. Several devices and ports were left off the list for brevity.

Table 8.2 IEM System Mapping

ABC123 IEM System Mapping					10/29/2004
XYZ Consulting			POC: Johnny Reboot		(555) 123.4567
Active Hosts:		4	Address Ranges:		192.168.1.0/24 172.16.2.0/24
IP Address / Device Name	Ports		Identified Services	Detected OS	Notes
192.168.1.36	TCP	135			
	TCP	5000			
192.168.1.69	TCP	22			
	TCP	898			
172.16.2.5 mohican	UDP	161			
172.16.2.6 navajo	UDP	161			
WiFi MAC Address	Type	Crypt	SSID	Discovered IP Address	Notes

SNMP Scanning

The second IEM baseline activity is scanning for devices using the Simple Network Management Protocol. SNMP has been around for years and continues to evolve but with the core goal of offering simple management services for networked resources. Obviously, since this service is all about management, it only stands to reason that there might be information or weaknesses in its configuration that could be exploited by an attacker.

To understand how SNMP relates to security, we need to understand some of the basics of how SNMP operates. Links to more detailed information can be found in Appendix A, but for now we'll stick to some of the basic terminology and interaction.

SNMP is centered on three main functions: the agent, the manager, and the Management Information Base (MIB). The manager requests information or makes configuration changes to the target resource. The target resource runs an agent-based software application that responds to queries and commands. The MIB is often confused with a database of information on the device. In fact, it is simply a tree mapping that defines the types of information or objects available on that device. Most vendors adhere to a standard SNMP MIB, and then they simply add their own vendor-specific branches.

Each variable information type is a unique object identifier (OID), which is a sometimes-lengthy numerical tag. An example is the System Description variable, for which the OID is 1.3.6.1.2.1.1.1. This OID is from the standard MIB-II tree as defined in the Internet Engineering Task Force (IETF) request for comment (RFC) document 1213 (or simply RFC 1213) and usually contains text information about the device. Many OIDs are vendor specific, and the manager and agent both need to be aware of their existence. This is where the MIB comes into play because it stores the OIDs that are available, not the information variables that may be contained in them.

To actually relay information, SNMP uses five basic messages: *GET*, *GET-NEXT*, *GET-RESPONSE*, *SET*, and *TRAP*. The messages are fairly easy to understand, with *GET* and *GET-NEXT* being queries sent to an agent. The *GET-RESPONSE* message is the returned information requested by the manager device. The *SET* message allows a change in the configuration to be requested by the manager, with the agent responding using the *GET-RESPONSE* message to confirm the change or inform the manager of an error. The *TRAP* message allows the agent to act independently by sending information on an event-based timeframe. Messages to a remote logging device use the *TRAP* message.

SNMP is normally operated over TCP or UDP port 161, with SNMP traps communicating over TCP or UDP port 162. This is not always the case, however. Cisco, for example, uses TCP or UDP 1993. Remember this as you review your system mapping, which should now display port scan results, so that the SNMP scanning activity does not become limited to only the typical ports.

The tools discussed in this section are designed to act as an SNMP manager, requesting information and in some cases making changes on the target resources.

NOTE

SNMPv3 became an official standard in 2002 and incorporates many new security features in the protocol, such as user authentication and encryption. Unfortunately, implementation of these new features has been very limited, with most configurations not enabled. SNMPv3 features are an excellent recommendation for organizations that rely on SNMP for system management, to mitigate some of the inherent flaws with SNMPv2 (such as community strings being transmitted in cleartext).

SolarWinds

With its suite of network management tools, the SolarWinds Engineer's Edition offers a multitude of SNMP utilities. Since the background of SNMP is to manage network, it's no wonder that one of the premier network management tools has a strong showing in the IEM baseline activity of SNMP scanning. To be honest, the tasks that can be performed with SolarWinds and SNMP go way beyond the basic discussions of SNMP that are appropriate for this chapter. Here we briefly discuss three of the utilities, but we recommend testing the free demo version to see what other SNMP capabilities are available.

SNMPSweep

For a very quick pull, SNMPSweep (see Figure 8.10) is a very simple and fast utility for running a quick scan of SNMP-enabled hosts and pulling some basic information. It has only a few settings to configure, since it is meant for a quick, "down and dirty" sweep of the network as it looks for SNMP-enabled devices. Under the **File | Settings** menu are options for adjusting speed setting for ICMP queries (active host detection prior to scan) and SNMP traffic. The defaults should be fine in most instances. You can also configure DNS resolution of active hosts and enter multiple text strings to be transmitted as possible community strings to all devices.

Figure 8.10 Scanning SNMP-Enabled Hosts

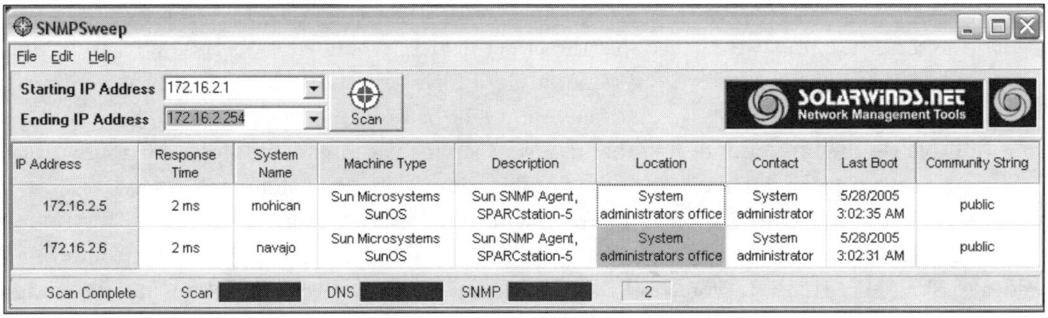

Once started, the scanner attempts to retrieve the information identified by the System branch of the MIB. As stated earlier, this is RFC 1223 OID of 1.3.6.1.2.1.1.1. This utility is excellent for ferreting out resources for more detailed scanning and testing.

MIB Walk

The MIB Walk utility is a great way to pull down all the SNMP-managed information about a device. It reads the device's MIB tree, then requests the information for every OID. This is extremely useful in determining the actual threat an exposed SNMP service presents. Some devices provide little information that's useful to an attacker; others "give away the farm".

The tool is very simple to use, requiring only the selection of the MIB tree to "walk" on the device, the community string configured for that MIB tree, and the IP address of the target. MIB Walk is further illustrated in Figure 8.11.

Figure 8.11 MIB Walk

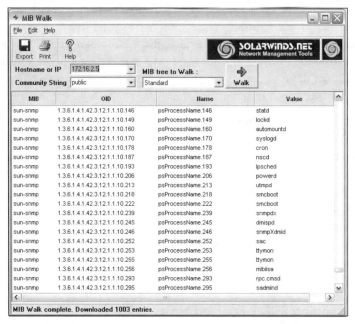

In the screen capture, we can see that the target device responded with 1003 entries. In the image, we have scrolled down to show some of the information available, such as processes currently running on the device. As an attacker, one might be pulled to notice that NFS is probably available on the box, considering that the *lockd* service is running and this is obviously a Solaris platform. One might also notice the combination of the *statd* and *sadmind* services, which have been subject to exploit in the past, with simple scripts available to test.

MIB Walk supports the export of data into myriad formats, including comma-separated values (CSVs), HTML, PDF, Word, and Excel. This makes the tool very useful for incorporating results into customer reports or any "body of evidence" documentation.

MIB Browser

For very detailed SNMP testing needs, the SolarWinds MIB Browser utility is a great resource. The MIB Browser boasts an internal database of over 1,000 standard and proprietary MIBs for interpreting the information from many devices in use.

Simple to configure, MIB Browser has two important settings available under **File | Settings**: the basic speed functions, which can be stepped up or down based on the current connection, and the OID fields. With the MIB Browser, you can configure the information type you want to see and how it is viewed. Some examples beyond those displayed in Figure 8.12 are Type, Raw Value (prior to being interpreted by the internal MIB database), Value (post interpretation), and Description. After configuration, it is a simple matter to identify a target and provide a community string.

Obviously, one important thing you'll notice in Figure 8.12 is the previously discussed interpretation of an OID's acceptable values and what they represent. The raw value for the OID 1.3.6.1.2.1.11.30 can be either a 1 or a 2. Unless you are already very familiar with each OID (both standard and vendor proprietary), many of these OIDs might mean very little to you. In this case, however, you'll notice that MIB Browser has interpreted the meaning of those values and presented them in human-readable fashion. By selecting the OID, more detailed information regarding its purpose is displayed in the lower-left corner, including read and read/write status.

Although out of scope for the purposes of the IEM, you might be interested to see the ease in which an OID setting can be changed on a host. Any value presented in blue can be configured via SNMP. Simply select the field and begin typing away or click the drop-down arrow and select the available option, as shown in Figure 8.12.

Figure 8.12 MIB Browser

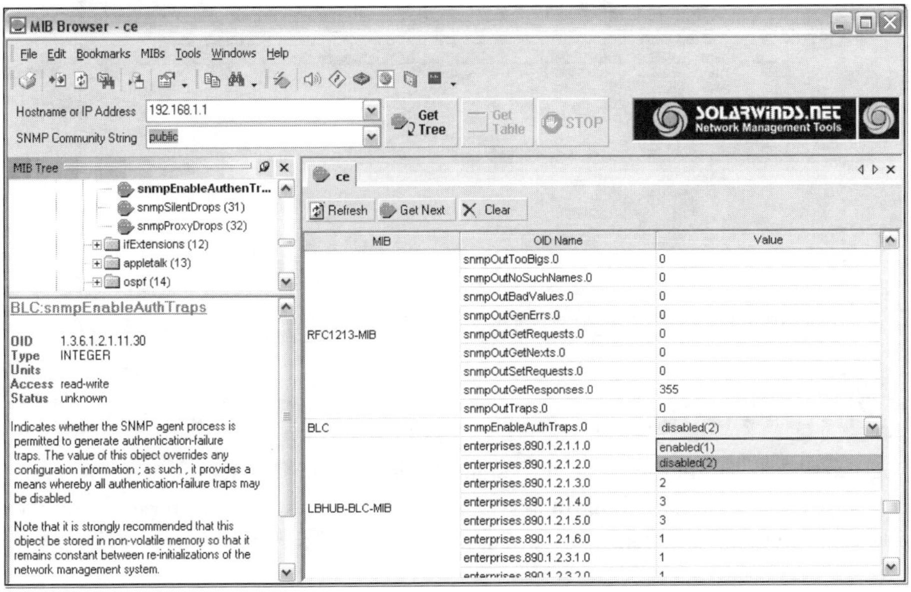

SNScan

Again from the team at Foundstone, SNScan is a free utility that can be used for the detection of SNMP devices. Many of the Foundstone tools are developed to assist administrators search new and serious exploits on their systems. SNScan was originally put out to identify Cisco devices with a potentially serious SNMP flaw. That original version is still available under the name CIScan; added functionality has been added to increase the usability of SNScan for performing basic SNMP detection.

To pop off a really quick scan of the system, simply define the target IP addresses or ranges, select from the predefined SNMP ports available, enter a community string, and go. You can adjust the timeout, but you should have little need to do so unless you encounter a very slow network. You can also use a text file to try multiple community strings, which is a great way to perform a quick dictionary attack against SNMP community strings.

The tool (see Figure 8.13) is great for taking a quick look, but it does not currently offer any data-exporting functionality. For personal use, we find this to be a great tool for discovering SNMP devices, then using the target address information in slower but more detailed utilities.

Figure 8.13 SNScan

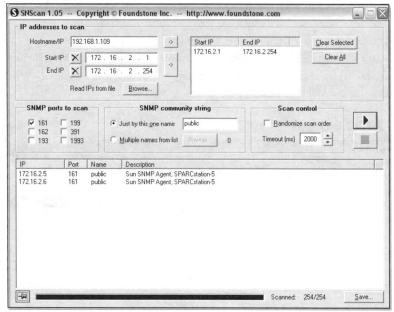

WS_Ping Pro-Pak

WS_Ping Pro-Pak is another set of tools designed originally for IT management purposes, but they have security functionality built in as well. Designed as an information-gathering tool for troubleshooting network problems, the suite also can be used for some network discovery requirements of security evaluations. WS_Ping Pro-Pak (see Figure 8.14) has been developed as a commercial product by Ipswitch.

The main window is very easy to navigate and the SNMP scanning functionality very simple to configure. From the main window, select the **SNMP** tab. You should be presented with the same window as in Figure 8.14. Simply enter the address of a target that you discovered during a port scan, define the community string, determine the OID (labeled **What** in the interface) you want to view, and click **Start**.

You also have the option to define your query. The radio buttons on the left act just as you would expect. By selecting **Get** and clicking **Start**, you will receive a *GET-RESPONSE* with the defined OID. Select *Get Next* and you will receive the next OID in the branch. Select *Get All Subitems*, and the application will return all OID information available under the selected branch of the MIB tree.

Figure 8.14 WS_Pin ProPack

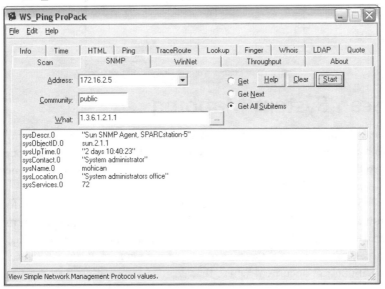

One drawback to the WS_Ping Pro-Pak SNMP utility is that you can query only one host at a time. This might be difficult for detecting SNMP-enabled hosts, but the strength of this utility is in its SNMP Object Selector. If you've detected SNMP devices via port-scanning techniques and you ant to do a fast review of selected hosts, this tool allows you to quickly and easily define the specific information you want.

By clicking the button marked **...** just to the right of the **What** field, you can bring up the SNMP Object Selector, as shown in Figure 8.15. From here, you can easily drill down through the standard MIB tree and select only the specific OIDs you are interested in.

Figure 8.15 SNMP Object Selector

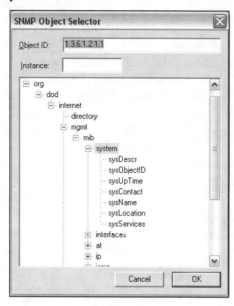

SNMP Scan System Mapping

Now that we have completed the second NSA IEM baseline activity, we can continue adding information to our system mapping. Here we want to add some of the more pertinent information discovered from SNMP scanning, such as discovered community strings, notes for further review, any enumerated information, and reference documentation.

Obviously, with the possibility of retrieving thousands of lines of data by performing a full MIB review, not all the SNMP information can be entered into a simple system mapping. As part of the Security Horizon business process, we deliver all information we collect (including handwritten notes) to the customer as part of a "body of evidence." We can reference SNMP data results by naming the document where that detailed information is stored (see Table 8.3).

Enumeration and Banner Grabbing

Enumeration and banner grabbing is the next activity in the NSA IEM baseline. This activity focuses on going deeper than your basic port scan to learn more about the actual applications listening on any ports discovered as well as learning more about the platform hosting those applications. The more we know about a device, the easier it is to discover possible weaknesses in either its networking applications or actual host processes. It is up to the evaluator to determine whether an information exposure is taking place, based on his or her experience and understanding of the criticality of the system.

Table 8.3 IEM System Mapping

ABC123 IEM System Mapping					10/29/2004
XYZ Consulting			POC: Johnny Reboot		(555) 123.4567
Active Hosts:		4	Address Ranges:		192.168.1.0/24
					172.16.2.0/24
IP Address / Device Name	Ports		Identified Services	Detected OS	Notes
192.168.1.11	TCP	135			
	TCP	139			
	UDP	137			
192.168.1.36	TCP	135			
	TCP	139			
	UDP	137			
172.16.2.5 mohican	UDP	161	Sun SNMP SPARC-5	Sun OS	SNMP String: Public statd and sadmind running 172.16.2.5-SNMP.txt
172.16.2.6 navajo	UDP	161	Sun SNMP SPARC-5	Sun OS	SNMP String: Public 172.16.2.6-SNMP.txt
WiFi MAC Address	Type	Crypt	SSID	Discovered IP Address	Notes

Simply put, in this activity we try to identify target devices through advertisements by responding services about their vendor and, in some more technical methods, gauge how they respond. Many of the tools discussed here operate in different formats. Some are vendor specific, relying on basic platform operations used by different operating systems, such as NetBIOS. Others use basic protocol standard queries to view information advertised about a specific service. Many Internet services such as Web, e-mail, and FTP advertise their version information in responses. Other utilities have an inline description of response methods employed by different vendors and products. A host response can then be compared to these predefined formulas and weighted based on the known type that is more like the received response.

There is a huge variety of utilities and manual checks for this activity, too numerous to account for here. Instead we cover a few of the more commonly used items. The specific tools used to perform this activity, often referred to as *fingerprinting*, should be based on the evaluator's experience with each platform and the environment in which the IEM is being performed. The evaluator's experience with security weaknesses is invaluable at this stage, to recognize common components that have a history of weaknesses and target them for more detailed testing later in the evaluation.

Nmap

As described in an earlier section, by default Nmap uses a table list of services to describe each discovered port. This is a standard list of "well-known" services that run by default over specific ports. For example, any time TCP port 23 is detected, Nmap will display Telnet as the open service on the target, similarly corresponding SNMP with UDP port 161. If all services were locked into specific ports and administrators did not have the capability to change them, this would be a very accurate and fast solution. However, since the term "security through obscurity" has been bandied about, administrators have been moving services across different and varying ports. Running multiple instances of a single service also requires the use of multiple ports, often leading to the use of ports uncommon to that service.

Service detection takes more time than a typical Nmap port scan, yet it is still rather quick and efficient. To enable this option, simply add −sV to the arguments already in use. To include OS detection and service detection, which are discussed later in this section, simply add −A to the arguments passed to Nmap.

Nmap starts out performing the normal port scan, then dumps the results to the service-scanning component for review. The first simple check is a basic banner grab. Nmap opens a full connection and waits for any advertised information. As mentioned earlier, this is a very common practice for many Internet services. The results are compared to a list of service "signatures" within Nmap. This often ends up with the supplied vendor and version information, signaling the end of this test. If vendor information, but not version information, is received, this information is used in the next stage of detection to limit the probe testing performed.

If a full match was not obtained through the simple banner-grabbing technique, specific probes are sent to the host, based on probable matches. The probes begin with the most likely services that would be running on that specific port, such as HTTP signature probes to port 80 and 8080. Also included in this probability is any information gathered earlier, such as vendor information. The probes also include SSL detection, which will cause Nmap to open an SSL connection and then begin sending service detection probes. An example output is displayed in Figure 8.16, showing the services as detected.

Figure 8.16 Nmap Scan Output

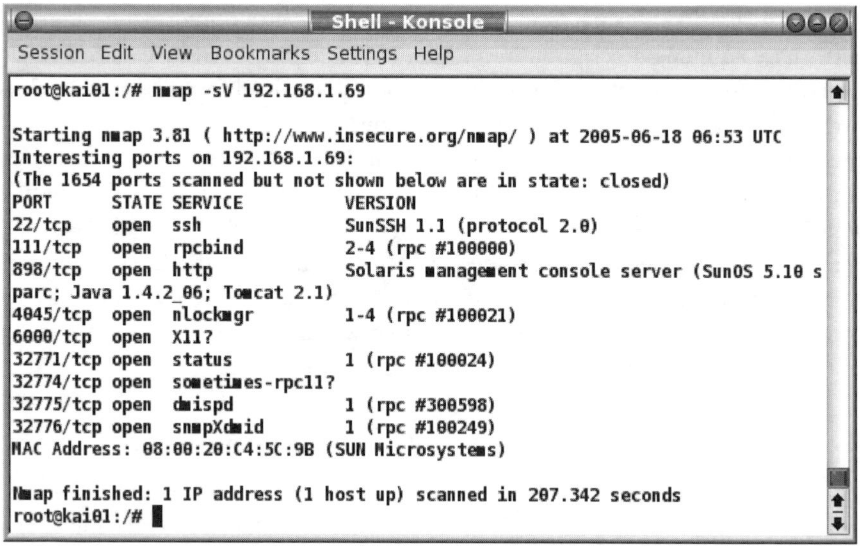

You can see that, when available or identified, version information is included. These are often the exact responses advertised by the service. Although the expected results are similar, the method used for OS detection is different.

For OS detection, Nmap uses a fingerprinting technique that compares the TCP/IP stack implementation of the target to known deviations. Each vendor, and often product version, implements its networking structure differently. Whether it is the way it responds to ICMP requests, performs packet sequencing, generated timestamps, packet fragmentation bits, or myriad other items, each TCP/IP stack is different. The argument required to perform OS detection is *−O*, or, as stated earlier, to perform both OS and service detection, the argument *−A* can be used.

Obviously, generating the signatures for each test and platform required a large amount of testing by Fyodor and his volunteers to create a large list of known "anomalies." Figure 8.17 shows the successful detection of a Sun Solaris host and the normal port scan results. It also helps show the difference between normal port scan results and service detection on those results. Both the OS detection and service detection scans were performed on the same test system, yet only the service detection scan returns captured text from the service.

Figure 8.17 Service Detection Scan Return

```
root@kai01:/# nmap -O 192.168.1.69

Starting nmap 3.81 ( http://www.insecure.org/nmap/ ) at 2005-06-18 07:04 UTC
Interesting ports on 192.168.1.69:
(The 1654 ports scanned but not shown below are in state: closed)
PORT       STATE SERVICE
22/tcp     open  ssh
111/tcp    open  rpcbind
898/tcp    open  sun-manageconsole
4045/tcp   open  lockd
6000/tcp   open  X11
32771/tcp open  sometimes-rpc5
32774/tcp open  sometimes-rpc11
32775/tcp open  sometimes-rpc13
32776/tcp open  sometimes-rpc15
MAC Address: 08:00:20:C4:5C:9B (SUN Microsystems)
Device type: general purpose
Running: Sun Solaris 9
OS details: Sun Solaris 9
Uptime 10.832 days (since Tue Jun  7 11:07:51 2005)

Nmap finished: 1 IP address (1 host up) scanned in 47.658 seconds
```

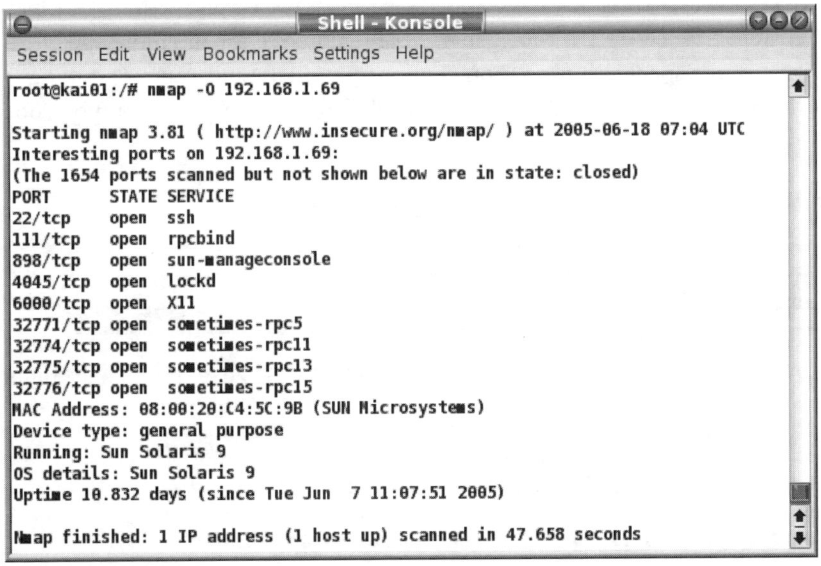

This discussion is meant as just a broad overview of the Nmap OS and service detection features. It does show how multiple techniques for enumeration operate, however. For more information on how Nmap utilizes banner grabbing, response signature comparison, and probe testing to validate discovered services and OSs, refer to the Nmap Web site listed in Appendix A.

THC-Amap

Amap is another tool for security testing and evaluations from the people at The Hacker's Choice (THC). Designed as an "application mapper" (hence the name Amap), it is another utility for the identification of services on a remote target. Amap is another free, command-line tool available with minimum license constraints.

Amap can be used independently with a simple command such as *amap 192.168.1.36 1-65535*. Amap then performs a signature-based test against the selected target and ports, attempting to resolve the host responses against a database of known packet responses. It can also be used in a more efficient method with an Nmap output file to input known targets and open ports to be tested with a command such as *amap –i nmapoutputfile*. This will significantly shorten the time it takes to test multiple targets and ports, due to the fact that Amap will then only test ports and targets already determined active.

In Figure 8.18 you can see a sample run of Amap against what is obviously a Windows device. The *–q* option removes all the extraneous probe information so that you don't have to see the incorrect match attempts. The *–b* option can also be beneficial because it reports the banner collected on that port as well. Some overlapping signatures may result in more than one match for each service. A perfect example is the SSH signature. This is a generic signature and is reported as a match, whereas other more specific signatures are also tested. An OpenSSH service will be matched twice — once for generic SSH and once for the more specific OpenSSH. If the more specific information is not as important and you are looking for fast results, the *–1* option will result in Amap skipping all further testing on each port, once the first match is found.

Figure 8.18 Amap Run Against Windows

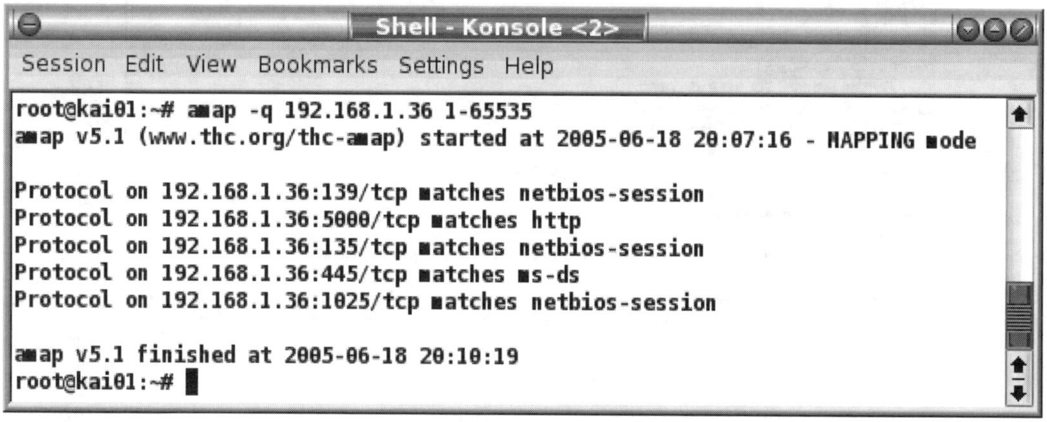
Shell - Konsole <2>
Session Edit View Bookmarks Settings Help
root@kai01:~# amap -q 192.168.1.36 1-65535
amap v5.1 (www.thc.org/thc-amap) started at 2005-06-18 20:07:16 - MAPPING mode
Protocol on 192.168.1.36:139/tcp matches netbios-session
Protocol on 192.168.1.36:5000/tcp matches http
Protocol on 192.168.1.36:135/tcp matches netbios-session
Protocol on 192.168.1.36:445/tcp matches ms-ds
Protocol on 192.168.1.36:1025/tcp matches netbios-session
amap v5.1 finished at 2005-06-18 20:10:19
root@kai01:~#

NBTScan

NBTScan is an open source scanner designed to query Microsoft Windows platform devices for NetBIOS name information. Available for multiple platforms, including Windows and

Linux, it is a very easy-to-use tool specialized for Windows enumeration. It uses a NetBIOS status query over UDP port 137, which results in a very quick response with limited information from the host.

As you can see in Figure 8.19, in the basic run, NBTScan returns the NetBIOS name for the Windows device, the name of the currently logged-in user, and its server option. If the device has available file shares, whether an actual server product or a Windows desktop product with local file sharing enabled, it will display the result *<server>*.

Figure 8.19 NBTScan

```
Command Prompt

D:\SecTools\nbtscan>nbtscan 192.168.1.33
Doing NBT name scan for addresses from 192.168.1.33

IP address       NetBIOS Name     Server    User             MAC address
------------------------------------------------------------------------------
192.168.1.33     KAIMWO03         <server>  JOE              00-0e-35-22-10-19

D:\SecTools\nbtscan>_
```

Another simple NetBIOS service enumeration operation is to use the *–v* option (see Figure 8.20). Combined this with the *–h* option, which formats the results in a more human readable result, and you are rewarded with information regarding the device and its Windows networking configuration. As you can see, the server ADMINISTRATION has multiple services operating in support of its local operations as well as in support of the Windows domain COLORADO.

Figure 8.20 The *–v* Option

```
C:\WINDOWS\System32\cmd.exe
D:\SecTools\nbtscan>nbtscan -vh 192.168.1.5
Doing NBT name scan for addresses from 192.168.1.5


NetBIOS Name Table for Host 192.168.1.5:

Name             Service          Type
----------------------------------------
ADMINISTRATION   Workstation Service
COLORADO         Domain Name
COLORADO         Domain Controllers
ADMINISTRATION   File Server Service
COLORADO         Domain Master Browser
COLORADO         Browser Service Elections
ADMINISTRATION   Messenger Service
COLORADO         Master Browser
☺☻__MSBROWSE__☻  Master Browser
INet~Services    IIS
IS~DMINISTRATIO  Unknown service (code 4e)

Adapter address: 00-04-75-ab-bb-7a
----------------------------------------

D:\SecTools\nbtscan>_
```

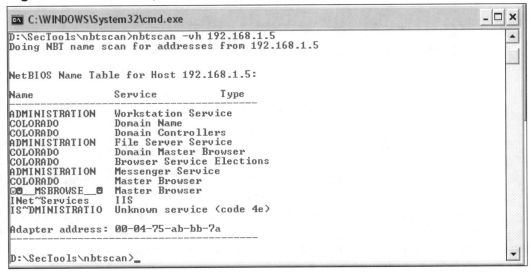

Although a very simple and basic tool to use, NBTScan can present good information specifically oriented around the Windows networking protocol.

SuperScan

By default, SuperScan records any banner information collected during a port scan. In its generated HTML reports, you can see the basic port scan information that the tool discovers at the top of the window. After that, it displays any received information from the target on a per-port basis.

In Figure 8.21, you can see that the IP address 192.168.1.69 has multiple services operating on both UDP and TCP ports. For the first port listed, TCP port 22, you can see the returned information under the **Banner** section. The banner itself has given the exact vendor and version for the service, Sun's SSH version 1.1. The response for the second port found, SunRPC, is also listed. This is just an example of the way one tool can be used to cover multiple IEM baseline activities.

Figure 8.21 A SuperScan Report

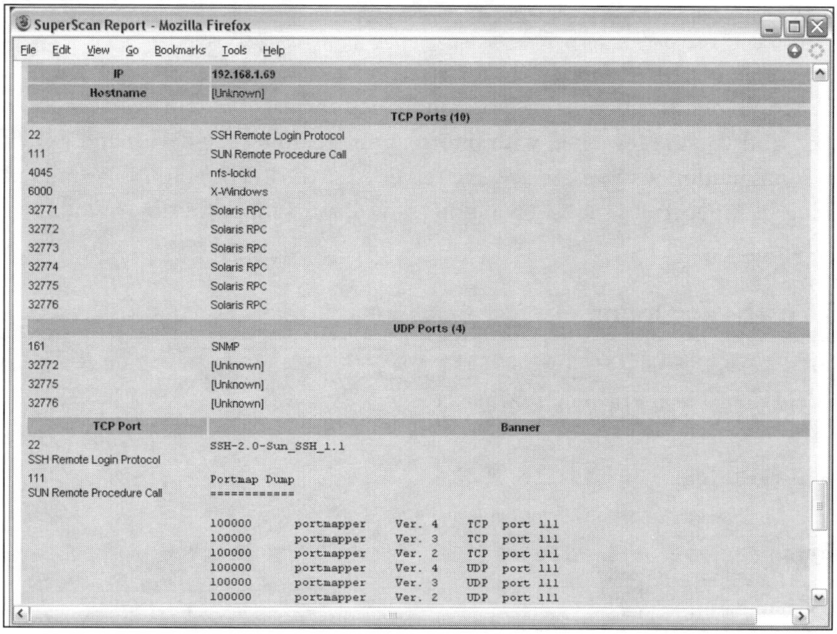

SuperScan also comes with a very easy-to-use Microsoft platform discovery utility. Under the tab **Windows Enumeration**, you will see a screen like the one shown in Figure 8.22. In the left window are optional types of enumeration scans. The very first one performs the same functionality as NBTScan, NetBIOS name retrieval, but in a GUI window. SuperScan automatically connects using a null session if you select that, or under **Options** you can set a specific user account and password to log in with.

WARNING

Be careful when you use an actual account to log in with. The password is not hidden by anonymous characters and is clearly visible even after the Options screen is closed and reopened. Leaving this utility running while away from your PC can expose this account information. The password is not stored anywhere after exit, however, so closing the program immediately after use should be standard procedure.

The amount of information gathered will, of course, depend on the level of privileges on the server, the server version, and whether it is a domain controller. With an inappropriately configured server, you can retrieve user account information, share information, permissions, running services, registry information, domain information and much more. The null session "feature" in Microsoft Windows has been considered a huge exposure, leaking serious amounts of information to unauthorized individuals.

Null sessions are a method of communication for Windows-based file and print services. They ease the administration of services, allowing anonymous queries from clients for resource information on a server. At the same time, they ease the enumeration of possible exposures for people with dishonorable intentions.

Figure 8.22 Null Session Feature

The example here displays only a small portion of what was reported, password policies, file and print shares, and domain information. The results also included users, groups, services, and more, all with only anonymous access.

WS_Ping Pro-Pak

Another utility in the WS_Ping Pro-Pak suite is the HTML tool. Again, the tool was designed from a management perspective to help administrators debug their HTML and discover problems. At the same time, it becomes a useful tool for performing security-based enumeration of a Web site.

The basic options for the HTML tool include a raw or formatted display of results, where the formatted option includes carriage returns. For faster testing, such as pure banner grabbing, you can set the tool to retrieve only the header information transmitted by the target (see Figure 8.23). If you deselect this option, the tool will retrieve the entire HTML document and present it in text form. Depending on the HTML, this may give more information such as literal paths or file information. This can also help identify the system and possible weaknesses, as well as exposures that could result from the HTML code itself.

Figure 8.23 WS_Pin ProPack

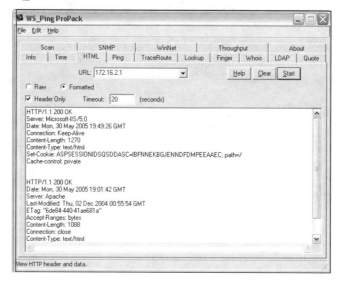

WS_Ping Pro-Pak also includes a GUI utility for performing finger queries as well as a Windows enumeration tool. Both operate similarly to other tools described in this chapter and are fairly simple to operate. One thing to remember about the WinNet Windows enumeration utility is that a null session must be manually created if the target and client are not trusted. This is simple enough to do—enter *net use \\target\IPC$ "" /user:""* from a command line. This will establish an anonymous null session to the target. To connect using a valid account, simply replace the first set of quotation marks with a password and the second set with the username.

UNIX Enumeration

Like Microsoft, UNIX products have enumeration services that enable us to learn more about their configuration. The three most common utilities are *finger, rpcinfo,* and *showmount*. With these three commands, we can collect process information, user accounts, and file mounts on UNIX devices with the services enabled.

In Figure 8.24, you can see the results of a query to a Solaris server with a specific finger vulnerability. When the argument *a b c d e f g h i* is added, the server responds with the entire user list. Normally the *finger* command will respond only with specified users, which makes it a great tool for verifying account information, such as e-mail names.

Figure 8.24 UNIX Enumeration Output

```
root@mercury:~# finger "a b c d e f g h i"@192.168.1.245
[192.168.1.245]
Login       Name              TTY       Idle    When       Where
root        Super-User        console   <Jan  2, 2003> :0
daemon      ???                         < .   .   . >
bin         ???                         < .   .   . >
sys         ???                         < .   .   . >
adm         Admin                       < .   .   . >
lp          Line Printer Admin          < .   .   . >
uucp        uucp Admin                  < .   .   . >
nuucp       uucp Admin                  < .   .   . >
listen      Network Admin               < .   .   . >
nobody      Nobody                      < .   .   . >
noaccess    No Access User              < .   .   . >
nobody4     SunOS 4.x Nobody            < .   .   . >
russr       ???               pts/1     <Jun 16 13:29> 192.168.1.88
tdykstra    ???                         < .   .   . >
rcallow     ???                         < .   .   . >
tpham       ???                         < .   .   . >
sturner     ???                         < .   .   . >
gnotske     ???                         < .   .   . >
ffranks     ???                         < .   .   . >
dbuffo      ???                         < .   .   . >
nking       ???                         < .   .   . >
```

Telnet

Using Telnet or other command-line TCP connection applications such as Netcat is a perfect example of banner grabbing. The simplest way to define this concept is to connect to a host and review the service advertisement it generates, as returned to the client. We assume that this is a rather well-known method, so rather than go into much detail here, we'll just show examples of a few Telnet connections.

To retrieve the header information from a Web server, simply connect to the target using the command *telnet <target port>,* where *target* is the URL or IP address and *port* is the port the Web server is listening on. Once connected, type **HEAD / HTTP/1.0** to retrieve the site header information. An example output might be:

```
HTTP/1.1 200 OK
Content-Type: text/html
Date: Thu, 13 Sep 2007 11:41:03 GMT
Expires: Thu, 26 Oct 1995 00:00:00 GMT
```

```
Last-Modified: Thu, 13 Sep 2007 11:41:03 GMT
Pragma: no-cache
Server: RomPager/4.07 UPnP/1.0
```

An even simpler test is against an FTP server. Simply make the connection with the command *telnet <target> 21*, and you will be rewarded with a banner that normally includes both platform and FTP version information:

```
220 ce FTP version 1.0 ready at Sat Jun 18 11:57:47 2005
```

Similarly, we can gather information about e-mail services as well. Once you're connected via the command *telnet <target> 25*, a banner will be received that by default will display vendor and version information about the running e-mail application:

```
220 mail.testserver.com ESMTP Sendmail 8.12.11/8.12.10; Sun, 19 Jun 2005
07:39:34 -0600
```

Several commands within the simple message transfer mail protocol (SMTP) may help with enumeration as well. The *VRFY* command allows for the verification of e-mail accounts, which often include system accounts of the same name. If the system supports the *HELP* command, try that while connected to see what other tools might be available for enumeration testing. Here's an example response:

```
214-2.0.0 This is sendmail version 8.12.11
214-2.0.0 Topics:
214-2.0.0       HELO     EHLO     MAIL     RCPT     DATA
214-2.0.0       RSET     NOOP     QUIT     HELP     VRFY
214-2.0.0       EXPN     VERB     ETRN     DSN      AUTH
214-2.0.0       STARTTLS
214-2.0.0 For more info use "HELP <topic>".
214-2.0.0 To report bugs in the implementation send email to
214-2.0.0       sendmail-bugs@sendmail.org.
214-2.0.0 For local information send email to Postmaster at your site.
214 2.0.0 End of HELP info
```

Manual connections to services can be a great method for finding out what is running and discovering exposures that could lead to exploitation. This can be done from several applications such as Telnet or Netcat and often allows more investigation capabilities than an automated tool can provide.

DNS Queries

Domain Name System (DNS) enumeration is based on the Internet name to address mapping service. DNS is a rather important tool that supports the translation of named hosts to IP addresses, allowing for simpler network usage. Unfortunately, like any other service, it can be misconfigured to leak more information than is necessary, which assists in the reconnaissance activities of malicious attackers.

Device or service names are often created that match the function they provide, such as ftp.widgets.com or mail.widgets.com. These are required for basic use of e-mail and Web hosting can often include information that an entity really does not want the public to know. For example, any proxy-based firewalls that act as an intermediary to protect and hide the actual server should not be named firewall.widgets.com, although this happens frequently. This type of information can help an attacker determine where an organization's security controls and boundaries reside.

There are also concerns with public and private DNS data. An internal DNS tree often includes names such as hr.widgets.com, payroll.widgets.com, intranet.widgets.com, and many more. This can give an outsider far too much information about internal addressing schemes, as well as information for potential targets to play with if they crack the outer shell and get on the inside network. This information should only be available internally, but DNS hosts are often misconfigured to allow access to this information from the public network.

For basic user operations, DNS works as a basic query system. A client specifies the name of a host, and a DNS server responds with the IP address of the host in question. To replicate this information across multiple DNS servers, a zone transfer request is used. In this instance, a request for a domain is made, and the DNS server responds with all known information for that domain. Although this is not inherently a security violation, it can give too much information to a potential attacker much too easily. Zone transfers should be limited to known DNS peers only.

Multiple utilities already available, some already discussed in this chapter, have built-in functionality for performing DNS queries, including zone transfers. Many are simple Perl or batch scripts; others include a simple-to-navigate GUI. Figure 8.25 is an example of the tool *nslookup* that's available in the basic Windows platform (NT and above). The *ls* query requests basic information from a DNS server. As we can see, the single −*d* options represents a zone transfer, requesting all known information about a specific domain.

Figure 8.25 DNS Queries

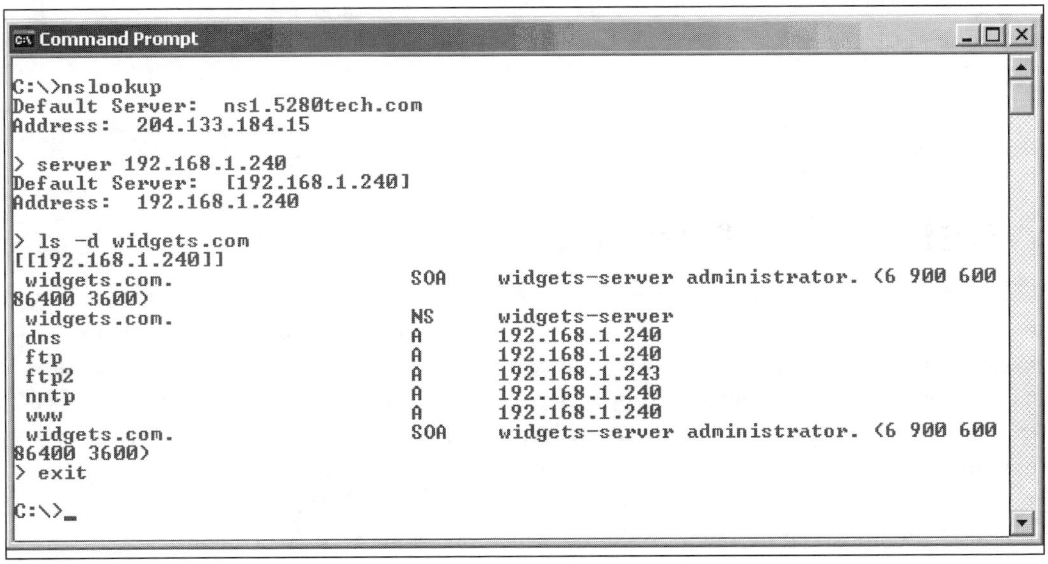

Enumeration and Banner-Grabbing System Mapping

Again, we continue to fill out our system mapping. With the completion of the third IEM baseline activity, we should have a pretty good understanding of most of the exposures to the system in terms of resources available to a remote client.

The system mapping can now be used to assist the fine-tuning of later activities, such as vulnerability detection (see Table 8.4). After the network discovery phase is completed, we can use this mapping to maximize efforts on what to test and how to test it, rather than just throwing everything at the system to see what sticks. The added effort you put in up front in creating the system mapping will pay off in the back end by assisting with validation efforts as well.

Table 8.4 IEM System Mapping

ABC123 IEM System Mapping					10/29/2004
XYZ Consulting			POC: Johnny Reboot		(555) 123.4567
Active Hosts:		4	Address Ranges:		192.168.1.0/24 172.16.2.0/24
IP Address / Device Name	Ports		Identified Services	Detected OS	Notes
192.168.1.36	TCP	135	NetBIOS	Microsoft Windows	Null Session open
	TCP	5000	HTTP		
192.168.1.69	TCP	22	OpenSSH Sun 1.1	Sun Solaris 9	Tomcat running, check for vulnerabilities
	TCP	898	Solaris Management Console Server		
172.16.2.5 mohican	UDP	161	Sun SNMP SPARC-5	Sun OS	SNMP String: Public statd and sadmind running 172.16.2.5-SNMP.txt
172.16.2.6 navajo	UDP	161	Sun SNMP SPARC-5	Sun OS	SNMP String: Public 172.16.2.6-SNMP.txt
WiFi MAC Address	Type	Crypt	SSID	Discovered IP Address	Notes

Wireless Enumeration

Wireless networking has seen a tremendous surge in the last five years. With the incredibly low cost of hardware and the amazing flexibility it allows in terms of network mobility, it's no wonder. Wireless client and gateway devices can be had for as little as $50. The most popular and cheaper devices are manufactured by vendors whose number-one market is the home network. These lean more to the "plug and play" type of solution rather than an appropriately configured secure solution. The price point of this solution also makes it difficult for many organizations to say no. In all honesty, security is really the only drawback to wireless networks in most environments and is often overlooked when reviewing wireless's benefits.

Wireless networks have been popping up in commercial and government arenas like crazy over the last few years. Unfortunately, there are inherent weaknesses in the 802.11 standards as well as client configurations. By default, most vendor products are currently configured without encryption enabled, and most users never bother to change these settings. Last year marked the fourth and final year of the World Wide War Drive (WWWD). The goal of the event's organizer, Chris Hurley, was to raise awareness of wireless security issues. To that effect, people across the globe took to the streets in an effort to discover and catalog as many wireless access points (AP) as possible. The results shown in Table 8.5 were published on the event's Web site:

Table 8.5 Wireless Access Points Tallied by the WWWD

Category	Total	Percent	Percent Change
Total AP Found	228537	100	N/A
WEP Enabled	87647	38.30	+6.04
No WEP Enabled	140890	61.6	-6.04
Default SSID	71805	31.4	+3.57
Default SSID and No WEP	62859	27.5	+2.74

Of over 225,000 APs, less than 40 percent were using encryption. And those aren't all home networks. Over 30 percent were using the default service set identifier (SSID) configured by the manufacturer. In all likelihood, most of those were simply dropped in place and used without any configuration by the user. Many industry insiders are referring to wireless as the new "modem" of IT security concerns because it can very easily leave the network wide open to a remote user. Instead of sitting at home, attackers can now sit in their cars.

Rather than drown this chapter in information regarding the state of wireless security and a discussion of the protocols, we'll cover the two most popular wireless enumeration tools and some of the more important aspects that need to be understood before we perform this activity. For a more detailed account of wireless networking pitfalls and solutions, we recommend you read an in-depth book published by Chris Hurley, Frank Thornton, and others: *War Driving Drive, Detect, Defend: A Guide to Wireless Security*.

Wireless Enumeration Obstacles

Prior to beginning any wireless enumeration, the evaluating team and the customer need to come to an agreement on the extent of that testing. The law regarding wireless network enumeration has been rather vague, although most experts agree that the cataloging of those networks is legal. The problem arises the instant you do anything other than simply discovering and cataloging.

The moment you connect to a wireless network, some experts believe, you break the law. At this point, you are using resources belonging to someone else without authorization and if you're discovered, it could lead to legal disputes. It's recommended that in the TEP, you document that wireless enumeration may include connection to discovered resources by the evaluation team. At the same time, unless there is a true need to connect, an evaluator may simply be better off documenting his or her findings and not connecting. Those discovered connecting might not belong to the target organization at all, but a neighboring entity. No agreement in place between the evaluation team and the customer will be of any use if you trespass on the network of an uninvolved organization.

There are also privacy concerns in regard to wireless enumeration. Any data captured as its transmitted over wireless network is the sole property of that organization, and recording this information can be considered a theft of information. Similar to the activity of network sniffing, this activity must be documented. If it is not required, it will likely be easier not to do it. The level of wireless network security evaluation is up to the customer, and any invasive procedures must be documented, including the return and destruction of private data.

As long as wireless enumeration is thoughtfully planned out and documented and due diligence used in performing the testing, the activity can be pretty straightforward.

Kismet

The first utility we'll cover is Kismet, an open source wireless detection utility designed for Linux. It uses a character-based GUI, ncurses, with the latest stable release being version 2005-04-R1 (the author has decided standardize his releases in dated versioning format). Started from a command line, Kismet's only real trick is getting the configuration operational.

Kismet relies on a passive listening mode, referred to as *rfmon,* to discover active networks. It does not send probes requesting beacon transmissions, and therefore it is completely nonintrusive to target systems. Unfortunately, *rfmon* capabilities are not supported by every vendor, because the client device must have firmware and driver support to use this function. The application documentation and the Web site have an excellent list of supported hardware and specific configurations within Kismet.

Kismet may be a time-consuming effort to get compiled, installed, and configured, but the supporting documentation is excellent and should answer most questions. Some of the added features beyond basic enumeration include wireless intrusion detection functions, logging compatibility with outside applications such as Ethereal and AirSnort, GPS mapping via *gpsmap*, and more. As you can see in Figure 8.26, the utility is fairly simple to use.

In the default display, the SSID of any discovered networks is listed under the name column. The column labeled **T** describes the type of device discovered; in this image all **A**s referring to APs. Client devices probing for available networks would be labeled with a **P**. The **W** column represents the use Wired Equivalent Privacy (WEP), which is an encryption method for 802.11 networks. The **CH** column represents the discovered frequency or channel the device is operating on. The number of packets received and the IP address range of the wireless network, if discovered, are also displayed. The **Flags** column shows current status information about the network. In the example, **U4** notifies us that the IP address range has been discovered up to 4 octets based on UDO traffic. **T3** tells us that the IP address range has been discovered up to 3 octets based on TCP traffic.

The window on the right in Figure 8.26 illustrates statistics regarding discoveries since the application began, such as the number of networks found, the number of cleartext and encrypted packets received, and more. In the bottom Status window you can see the latest information regarding Kismet's discoveries. Kismet definitely provides more functionality than simple wireless enumeration and is a great tool for more advanced security testing that is currently beyond the context of this chapter.

Figure 8.26 Kismet

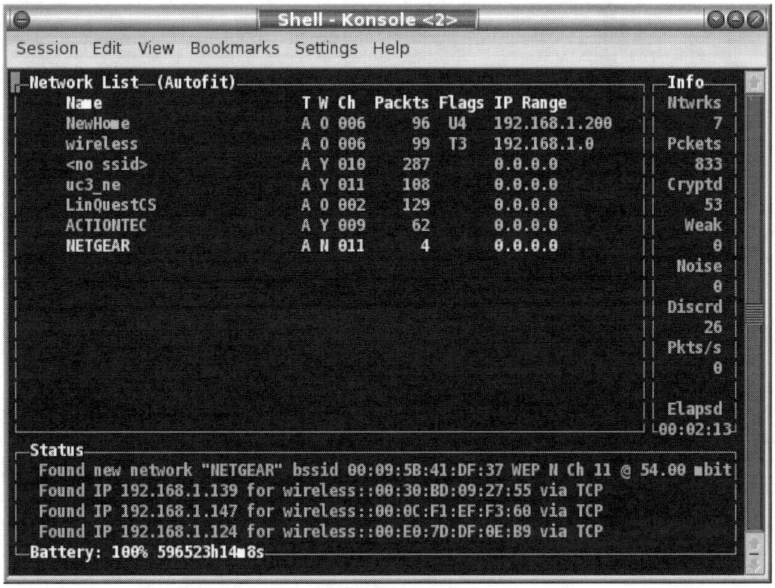

For logging, Kismet supports multiple output formats, including a raw data dump and filtered formats such as XML and CSV that show general discovered network information, a Cisco-specific dump of any Cisco Discovery Protocol (CDP) packets captured, and a dump of weak encryption packets for importing into AirSnort.

NetStumbler

Another widely popular wireless enumeration tool is NetStumbler. Built for the Microsoft Windows platform, NetStumbler is freely available product. The primary difference between Kismet and NetStumbler, besides the OS platform, is that NetStumbler performs active scanning. In this method, NetStumbler sends out beacon requests to determine information about wireless networks. In this mode, an AP configured to *cloak*, or not respond to beacon requests, will not be discovered by NetStumbler.

NetStumbler has an excellent GUI for quick and easy review of discovered networks. The tree view in the left window (see Figure 8.27) allows for basic device view display management, allowing you to group views by the channel they are operating on, their discovered SSID, and some preconfigured filters. For example, by selecting the appropriate filter on the left, the main view window will only display networks with encryption disabled or that are using the default vendor SSID.

Figure 8.27 NetStumbler

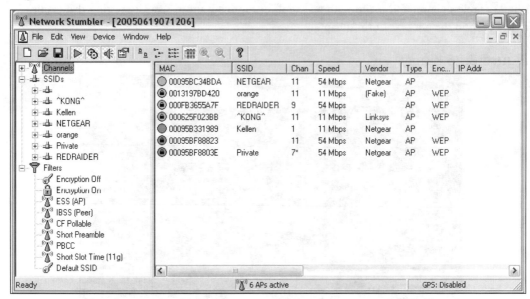

Each column or attribute in the display window is adjustable so that you can move the specific information into the main screen you want to see. NetStumbler reports far too much information per device to be viewed without scrolling. The most common information used for enumeration can easily fit into a single view, as shown. MAC address, SSIDs, channels, speed, vendor information, type of network, encryption, and IP addresses discovered are some of the most useful reporting features for enumeration. NetStumbler includes much more information regarding signal strength, signal-to-noise ratio (SNR), capability flags, and more that are beyond the scope of basic wireless enumeration.

NetStumbler supports a few common reporting formats that have been used in multiple staged projects such as the WWWD. The Wi-scan format has been used by multiple hobbyist competitions as well as groups trying to raise security awareness, because there are scripts available for combining multiple log files into a single aggregate. NetStumbler and Kismet are both GPS enabled, allowing for testing of signal range. This is a great added service for assisting the customer in determining their wireless exposure in terms of area availability. Often an organization will not be aware that its wireless networks are fully available in five levels of the parking garage across the street — an excellent place for the mischievous to hide while experimenting with the organization's network.

Added utilities for this function include gpsmap and GPSDrive, which work well with Kismet, and StumbVerter, which can create informational maps using NetStumbler data and Microsoft MapPoint. Other than MapPoint, which is obviously a commercial product, these are free or open source utilities available for download; you'll find more information in Appendix A.

Wireless Encryption Evaluation

Beyond the scope of the activity but perhaps a concern to the customer requiring additional testing is wireless encryption. The default WEP method has been shown to be vulnerable to key guessing, based on the collection of a certain number of packets. Simple utilities such as AirSnort and WEPCrack have been released that can determine the key in use when provided enough sample packets. Using a tool like Kismet to collect those packets and dump them for use is a trivial matter these days. Another utility call Aircrack has similar functionality but also includes a replay utility, aireplay, that can be used to increase the amount of encrypted traffic generated on the wireless network. This allows for a much faster collection of packets, cutting down the wait time on slower networks.

Vendors began incorporating their own proprietary security techniques, but the incompatibility between devices and vendors has made this a very slowly adopted security technique. Even some of those have already been proven weak, with utilities breaking their encryption. WiFI Protected Access (WPA) encryption technology has been released, but already weaknesses are being exposed, though it is still a much better solution than WEP. Adoption for WPA at this point seems rather slow, since it requires replacing an architecture with new equipment that may have already been put in place.

Again, this type of evaluation is beyond the normal scope of the IEM, but it can be included as added value for the customer if they have concerns in the area. Remember to document in detail any activity such as this in the TEP, so there are no misunderstandings about what will take place. Information about more wireless security-cracking utilities can be found in Appendix A.

Wireless Enumeration System Mapping

Now that we have some information about the customer's wireless networking, we can add that to our system mapping. As a business process, the amount of information you document for the customer might vary, but a minimum should include the SSID of the network, encryptions status, and MAC address (see Table 8.6). In the case of rogue access points, provide as much information as possible that can help the customer identify the device.

Probing client devices should not be ignored, either. Many default PC configurations have the client automatically connect to any wireless network discovered. This means an attacker could host a fake access point, which the client will connect to. This gives the attacker a straight connection to the machine, often only a speed bump to the rest of the network. When you see the startled look on a laptop user's face in the airport, you can guess what just happened. Some networks send pop-up messages to clients, trying to entice them into using the WiFi service. This represents large exposure that can be easily exploited.

Table 8.6 IEM System Mapping

ABC123 IEM System Mapping					10/29/2004
XYZ Consulting			POC: Johnny Reboot		(555) 123.4567
Active Hosts:		9	Address Ranges:		192.168.1.0/24 172.16.2.0/24
IP Address / Device Name	Ports		Identified Services	Detected OS	Notes
192.168.1.36	TCP	135	NetBIOS	Microsoft Windows	Null Session open
	TCP	5000	HTTP		
192.168.1.69	TCP	22	OpenSSH Sun 1.1	Sun Solaris 9	Tomcat running, check for vulnerabilities
	TCP	898	Solaris Management Console Server		
172.16.2.5 mohican	UDP	161	Sun SNMP SPARC-5	Sun OS	SNMP String: Public statd and sadmind running 172.16.2.5-SNMP.txt
172.16.2.6 navajo	UDP	161	Sun SNMP SPARC-5	Sun OS	SNMP String: Public 172.16.2.6-SNMP.txt
WiFi MAC Address	Type	Crypt	SSID	Discovered IP Address	Notes
00:0F:66:03:43:EC	Infra	WPA	NewHome	192.168.1.200	
00:90:4B:37:26:9C	Infra	WPA	Wireless	192.168.1.0	

Summary

We've covered a wide array of available tools for performing the first four IEM baseline activities. There are obviously a lot of options for each IEM activity for both the UNIX and Windows platforms. After reading this chapter, the evaluator should understand the IEM's requirements for the operation of tools and the evaluation goals for each activity. Many of these tools work together very well to provide a flexible and efficient solution. Limited testing can be performed very quickly, allowing the evaluator to perform secondary testing in critical areas based on his or her understanding of the system and common security weaknesses.

Although this chapter focused primarily on the introduction of tools to achieve the goals of each activity, no utility can make up for the knowledge and experience of the evaluator. A successful IEM engagement hinges on the evaluator's ability to recognize potential weaknesses in context with the criticality of the system being evaluated. Getting the most out of each tool's capabilities relies on the strength of the evaluator, both with the tool and in understanding the baseline activity itself.

This chapter also introduced the concept of a system mapping. This is a rather common practice for many INFOSEC professionals and fits very well into the IEM. Although this remains a business process, the benefit it represents to the customer and the evaluation team is hard to ignore. The system mapping introduced here is simply an example and can be modified to fit evaluator and customer needs.

Solutions Fast Track

Goals and Objectives

☑ The network discovery stage is all about determine the actual system implementation and documenting the differences from the customer's perception of that implementation.

☑ Findings from the network discovery activities are normally exposures when following the CVE/CAN definitions of weaknesses. These often relate back to inadequate configuration documentation.

☑ A system mapping or some other form of documented results can assist the evaluation team as a tool to prioritize review and as part of the submitted body of evidence. It can also greatly assist the customer in updating system configuration documentation.

Tool Basics

☑ The NSA does *not* currently endorse or recommend any specific tool or tool platform. These decisions are left entirely up to the evaluators.

☑ Evaluators are expected to use whatever tools fit their experience and the customer's environment, to ensure that each IEM baseline activity is completed.

☑ Some activities justify the use of more than one tool, and one tool may successfully cover more than one activity. Every environment will differ from others in some way, so evaluators should be proficient with multiple tools in each activity.

Port Scanning

☑ Port scanning can be used as a way to begin mapping the system environment to discover what is really there despite what the current documentation leads one to believe.

☑ This activity helps the evaluator determine what focus areas require more additional testing or more detailed review.

☑ Through the use of the port-scanning activity, an experienced INFOSEC professional can find potential weaknesses or exposures based primarily on the history of a protocol or service and the understanding of what the system requires to function.

SNMP Scanning

☑ As its name states, SNMP is a simple protocol intended to ease system management. Unfortunately, *simple* can also be used to describe the security aspects of most implementations of SNMP, making this a dangerous service to use, considering its main role of managing systems.

☑ Like most protocols, SNMP normally rides a specific TCP or UDP port; however, several vendors have implemented proprietary versions with the same base insecurities over different ports.

☑ Most device MIBs operate from a combination of standardized OIDs and proprietary ones. The evaluator needs to understand this and be able to interpret the findings of any given device, whether through automated tools or manual research.

Enumeration and Banner Grabbing

☑ Inherently weak protocols can be discovered through port scanning, but inherently weak applications can also be discovered by enumeration and banner grabbing.

☑ Banner grabbing is the simple enumeration activity of reviewing the banner or service advertisement sent by the target application. Sometimes spoofed, this can still be a great method for determining the types of tests to be run against the target.

☑ Several OS and service detection techniques rely on a signature database provided with a specific tool. Obviously, not all tools use the same signatures, so the use of multiple tools may be of assistance.

Wireless Enumeration

☑ Wireless enumeration presents several possible legal obstacles that should be considered and documented prior to any testing.

☑ Many security tests and evaluations exist for wireless networking, but the main goal for the IEM baseline activity is simply to discover wireless instances and determine exposures based on unobtrusive testing. Methods that go beyond this type of testing can be implemented, depending on customer concerns.

☑ Although awareness of security concerns regarding wireless networking has grown considerably, action to mitigate these concerns has been slow to progress. By performing this IEM baseline activity, you can document many unrealized exposures, with consequences detailed to assist in raising an organization's priorities in securing a highly common security weakness.

Frequently Asked Questions

The following Frequently Asked Questions, answered by the authors of this book, are designed to both measure your understanding of the concepts presented in this chapter and to assist you with real-life implementation of these concepts. To have your questions about this chapter answered by the author, browse to **www.syngress.com/solutions** and click on the **"Ask the Author"** form. You will also gain access to thousands of other FAQs at ITFAQnet.com.

Q: With all the differences in features and options available in different utilities, how do I know which one to use?

A: This will depend on the level of effort you have arranged with your customer. Some of the more detailed utilities require much more time to use, and that needs to be taken into account. In a Security Horizon business process, we normally start with the simplest and quickest of tools, then incorporate more advanced tools depending on what is discovered.

Q: Do I need to create a system mapping to perform an IEM-compliant evaluation?

A: The system mapping is not an IEM requirement; it is simply a best-practice recommendation to help the evaluator stay focused, verify system documentation, and document network discovery activities in a condensed, human-readable form for the customer.

Q: Often I get false positives in regard to enumeration and banner grabbing with my automated tools. Why is that?

A: Some services can be configured to present a false banner. This can be done either in the service itself or by editing the source code and recompiling if available. Automated tools also have a limited number of signatures to work from and may be reporting the closest match, if an exact is not available. The evaluator needs to be aware of these inconsistencies and know how to recognize them.

Q: What should be included in the system mapping?

A: Obviously, system identification such as name or IP address, and both, if known, can help in environments utilizing Dynamic Host Configuration Protocol (DHCP). The system mapping should also include discovered services, wireless information, SNMP exposures, and any other notes from the evaluator that could trigger concern. Exact details are up to the evaluating team based on the customer needs and the environment.

Q: What platform is the best for performing security evaluations?

A: This depends on the expertise of each evaluator and the environment they are walking in to. The NSA does not support any platform over another. As a business process, Security Horizon expects all its evaluators to be proficient in both Windows and a UNIX-based platform to take advantage of the wide array of tools available. In fact, all Security Horizon evaluations include tools run from both platforms.

Chapter 9

Collecting the Majority of Vulnerabilities

Solutions in this chapter:

- **Vulnerability and Attack Trends**
- **Conducting Vulnerability Scans**
- **Conducting Host Evaluations**
- **Validating Findings**
- **Mapping Findings to the IEM Process**

☑ **Summary**

☑ **Solutions Fast Track**

☑ **Frequently Asked Questions**

Introduction

This chapter covers the vulnerability scanning and host evaluation portions of the IEM (see Figure 9.1). Vulnerability scanning is conducted from the network perspective, and host evaluations are conducted directly on the target components or systems. You will more than likely have a different view of the system when you're at the console than when you're evaluating the systems from the network.

Figure 9.1 Phases of the IEM

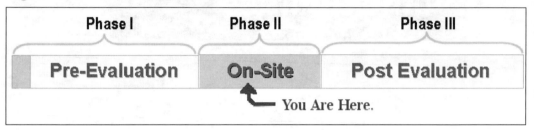

In this chapter we define vulnerability scanning and the goals of these scans in relation to the IEM. We also discuss current vulnerability and attack trends. Then we break out the vulnerability scanning tools (a.k.a. The Fun Part) and gather some findings! Of course, after gathering our findings from the vulnerability scans, we will need to validate and document them (a.k.a. The Not-So-Fun Part). As you can see from Figure 9.2, vulnerabilities play a key role in the management of risk and an organization's INFOSEC posture.

Figure 9.2 The Risk Triangle

The goal of this section of the evaluation is to identify vulnerabilities within the organization. Following the vulnerability-scanning portion of the chapter, we examine host evaluations and define their goals in relation to the IEM. We also discuss what to look for during host evaluations, go over the use of benchmark scripts, and map our host evaluation findings back to the IEM—*after* validating the findings, of course!

Vulnerability and Attack Trends

Computer Emergency Response Team (CERT) was created in November 1988, just after the Morris Worm hit, and has been tracking vulnerability notifications, security bulletins, and INFOSEC incidents ever since. Using the data it gathers, CERT has provided a fairly detailed group of statistics regarding INFOSEC incidents and vulnerability notifications that are released. Some astonishing trends have shown up in the past few years. In fact, the number of incidents reported grew so large that the metrics became essentially useless for meaningful incident tracking. The statistics for 2000–2003 are shown in Table 9.1; you can see the dramatic increase in reported incidents each year.

Table 9.1 Incident Tracking, 2000–2003

Year	2000	2001	2002	2003
Incidents	21,756	52,658	82,094	137,529
% Increase	221%	242%	156%	168%

(Note: According to CERT/CC Statistics 1988–2005 (www.cert.org/stats/cert_stats.html), 9,859 incidents were reported in 1999.)

In 2004, CERT ceased providing the number of reported INFOSEC incidents and is instead focusing on other projects, such as the E-Crime Watch Survey. What changed? Why are there so many incidents occurring each year? Here are some of the trends CERT is noticing:

- There is an increased threat to e-commerce sites.
- The time between vulnerability notification and exploit release (known as *time till exploit*, or TTE) is dramatically decreasing.
- Web-enabled applications are increasing in popularity as an attack vector.
- There is an increase in High and Medium rated vulnerabilities, that are easy to exploit.
- There has been a massive increase in 'bot networks and 'bot network activity (a.k.a. botnets).
- Attackers are becoming more organized and well prepared.

Notes from the Underground...

What Is a Botnet?

The term *botnet* is short for ro*bot net*work. A botnet consists of large numbers of systems that have been compromised (via virus, Trojan horse, and the like) and are commonly used for tasks such as conducting distributed denial of service (DDoS) attacks and sending spam. Hundreds, sometimes thousands, of computers will be part of a single botnet. Most of the time the end users are not even aware that their machine has been subverted and is being used for such dark purposes.

The most common method of compromise being used by botnet controllers and creators is via a Trojan program. The Trojan program is executed on the system, opens up an IRC channel specified by the 'bot creator, and waits for the person controlling the botnet to issue it commands. Many botnets are also for sale to the highest bidder. Lists of compromised computers are sold to spammers and other such unscrupulous people for use in their illicit activities.

CERT attributes the change in reporting to widespread use of attack tools that are becoming increasingly automated and easy to use. CERT also notes that it's become very commonplace for Internet-connected systems to be attacked. Automated attack tools and the short time from vulnerability announcement to exploit release are the two key factors that led CERT to revise its incident reporting. Only time will tell whether this new reporting mechanism will fill the needs of the INFOSEC community; providing better tracking and meaningful statistics.

It's a difficult task to track this information, since it's a fast-moving target. SANS releases a Top 20 list, a consensus list of critical vulnerabilities that require immediate remediation. Organizations use the SANS Top 20 list, shown in Table 9.2 (www.sans.org/top20/), to prioritize their efforts and resources so they can close the most dangerous security holes first. In actuality, the Top 20 list is really two Top 10 lists—the 10 most commonly exploited vulnerable services in Windows and the 10 most commonly exploited elements in UNIX and Linux are shown in Table 9.2.

Table 9.2 SANS Top 20 List for 1Q2005

Top Vulnerabilities to Windows Systems	Top Vulnerabilities to UNIX Systems
W1 – Web Servers & Services	U1 – BIND Domain Name System
W2 – Workstation Service	U2 – Web Server
W3 – Windows Remote Access Services	U3 – Authentication
W4 – Microsoft SQL Server (MSSQL)	U4 –Version Control Systems

Continued

Table 9.2 continued SANS Top 20 List for 1Q2005

Top Vulnerabilities to Windows Systems	Top Vulnerabilities to UNIX Systems
W5 – Windows Authentication	U5 – Mail Transport Service
W6 – Web Browsers	U6 – Simple Network Mgmt Protocol (SNMP)
W7 – File-Sharing Applications	U7 – Open Secure Sockets Layer (SSL)
W8 – LSAS Exposures	U8 – Misconfiguration of Enterprise Services
W9 – Mail Client	U9 – Databases
W10 – Instant Messaging	U10 – Kernel

One interesting trend is that attackers are moving from OS-level attacks to application-level attacks. A favorite within the INFOSEC community seems to be Web-enabled applications, since they are more likely to be susceptible to buffer overflows, errors in boundary checking for variables, or SQL injection attack vectors. Usually these vulnerabilities are not trivial to exploit and require a deeper understanding of the application and its interactions with the underlying operating system. This is where today's more intelligent vulnerability assessment tools tend to shine.

But the security tools are only a portion of the overall INFOSEC evaluation effort. The person doing the evaluation (that would be you) contributes personal experience, knowledge, and the ability to reason. These skills are very important to the evaluation and are useful for weeding out false-positive findings as well as tailoring the evaluation to the organization's infrastructure. False positives are reported vulnerabilities that aren't real. An example of a false positive finding is if the vulnerability scanner notes an IIS-specific finding against an Apache server. The sidebar includes a few helpful URLs for locating INFOSEC mailing lists and tools that can help you keep up to date on vulnerabilities and their impacts.

Notes from the Underground...

Useful Sites: INFOSEC Mailing Lists, Tools, and Information

Here are some rather useful sites for security tools and security mailing lists:

- Tools and mailing lists: www.securityfocus.com
- Tools: packetstormsecurity.nl
- Mailing list: lists.apple.com/mailman/listinfo/security-announce

Continued

- Mailing list archives: seclists.org
- Tools and security advisories: www.frsirt.com/english/index.php
- Tools and security advisories: www.microsoft.com/technet/security/

Vulnerability Scanning's Role in the IEM

As we have mentioned in previous chapters of this book, the IEM process is an evaluation of an organization's INFOSEC posture. The vulnerability assessment portion of the IEM is a more detailed analysis of the components that comprise the organization's critical INFOSEC assets and infrastructure. By identifying potential vulnerabilities or configuration issues with the evaluated components, the organization then has the opportunity to mitigate these findings, based on your recommendations, to better their overall INFOSEC posture. This is an essential element to the security gap analysis, and gap reduction, processes.

Tools & Traps...

Vulnerability Scanning Tools

It's important to know that not every tool or program is perfect. Each tool has a core area that it is better at than other areas. So it is best to conduct vulnerability scans using at least two different tools. Here are some of the more commonly used vulnerability-scanning tools:

- Nessus, www.nessus.org
- eEye Retina, www.eeye.com
- SAINT, www.saintcorporation.com
- GFi Network Security Scanner, www.gfi.com
- HFNetChk, www.shavlik.com
- ISS Internet Scanner, www.iss.net
- NeWT, www.tenablesecurity.com
- Firewalk, www.packetfactory.net/Projects/
- Benchmark scripts and RAT, www.cisecurity.org
- Microsoft Baseline Security Analyzer, www.microsoft.com/mbsa/

The vulnerability-scanning tools used during an IEM should be CVE and CAN compliant, meaning that they should list the appropriate CVE/CAN numbers for findings and give a High, Medium, or Low rating. CVE, or common vulnerabilities and exposures, is "a list of standardized names for vulnerabilities and other information security exposures. CVE aims to standardize the names for all publicly known vulnerabilities and security exposures." A list of CVE compatible products, services, and applications can be found at www.cve.mitre.org/compatible/.

The Mitre Corporation maintains the CVE/CAN list, which is freely available to the public and is sponsored by US-CERT at the U.S. Department of Homeland Security. As of May 2005, over 10,000 unique information security issues were listed, with publicly known names. That's quite a few security issues! And more are discovered daily. You are not "required" to use the CVE/CAN list, but for the IEM process the NSA *highly* recommends that you use a CVE/CAN-compliant resource. What is required is that you use some form of vulnerability rating and identification system that is accessible by the customer. The standardized name and numbering scheme, as well as the mapping of the vulnerabilities to High, Medium, or Low criticality, are essential to the IEM and to correlating the findings to the organization's mission-critical INFOSEC resources. This helps to prioritize the findings so that the evaluation efforts are properly focused on what matters (to the organization). Figures 9.3 and 9.4 are actual CVE and CAN entries, respectively, provided here as an example.

Figure 9.3 A Sample CVE Entry

```
Name: CVE-2004-0121
Reference: IDEFENSE:20040309 Microsoft Outlook "mailto:" Parameter Passing Vulnerability
Reference: BUGTRAQ:20040310 Outlook mailto: URL argument injection vulnerability
Reference: MS:MS04-009
Reference: CERT-VN:VU#305206
Reference: BID:9827
Reference: XF:outlook-mailtourl-execute-code(15414)
Reference: OVAL:OVAL843

Argument injection vulnerability in Microsoft Outlook 2002 does not
sufficiently filter parameters of mailto: URLs when using them as
arguments when calling OUTLOOK.EXE, which allows remote attackers to
use script code in the Local Machine zone and execute arbitrary
programs.
```

Conducting Vulnerability Scans

By this time in the evaluation process, you should have a list of components (workstations, servers, network devices, and/or architecture-level devices) that make up the critical INFOSEC infrastructure for the organization. The critical INFOSEC infrastructure is made up of systems that handle the organization's critical information or that have a direct impact on mission operations.

Figure 9.4 A Sample CAN Entry

```
Candidate: CAN-2005-0047
URL: http://cve.mitre.org/cgi-bin/cvename.cgi?name=CAN-2005-0047
Phase: Assigned (20050111)
Category: SF
Reference: MS:MS05-012
Reference: URL:http://www.microsoft.com/technet/security/bulletin/ms05-012.mspx
Reference: CERT:TA05-039A
Reference: URL:http://www.us-cert.gov/cas/techalerts/TA05-039A.html
Reference: CERT-VN:VU#597889
Reference: URL:http://www.kb.cert.org/vuls/id/597889
Reference: OVAL:OVAL1159
Reference: URL:http://oval.mitre.org/oval/definitions/pseudo/OVAL1159.html
Reference: OVAL:OVAL2351
Reference: URL:http://oval.mitre.org/oval/definitions/pseudo/OVAL2351.html
Reference: OVAL:OVAL2892
Reference: URL:http://oval.mitre.org/oval/definitions/pseudo/OVAL2892.html
Reference: OVAL:OVAL901
Reference: URL:http://oval.mitre.org/oval/definitions/pseudo/OVAL901.html
Reference: XF:win-com-gain-privileges(19105)
Reference: URL:http://xforce.iss.net/xforce/xfdb/19105

Windows 2000, XP, and Server 2003 does not properly "validate the use
of memory regions" for COM structured storage files, which allows
attackers to execute arbitrary code, aka the "COM Structured Storage
Vulnerability."
```

As you may recall, the Technical Evaluation Plan (TEP) is the road map that guides the evaluation efforts and dictates which resources are necessary to properly conduct the evaluation. It also provides us with the "target list" for the evaluation. The list provided in the TEP is intended to include all components, networks, devices, and systems to be evaluated. But occasionally some essential components might not be on the list when they should be. If additional systems and components are discovered during the onsite phase of the evaluation, they should be added to the TEP's "target list" to ensure that they are accounted for, and evaluated, during this process.

NOTE

Vulnerability scanning is typically the portion of the evaluation with which the customer organization is most familiar. It's very important to ensure that the proper expectations are set for activities done during the evaluation and the deliverables.

For example, the customer may request an attack and penetration test (A&P) when what they are actually looking for is a comprehensive vulnerability assessment conducted by an independent third party to measure INFOSEC compliance with the Sarbanes-Oxley Act of 2002.

Breaking Out the Scanning Tools

Before you start scanning for vulnerabilities, let's look at a few points to keep in mind while conducting the scans:

- Depending on the type of scans being conducted and how the information is gathered, these tools can be intrusive and could cause adverse effects on the device being scanned.

- There is a potential for the vulnerability-scanning tools to present false positive findings. Both you, as the evaluator, and the customer should be aware of this. That is why it is so important to validate all findings.

- Some device issues cannot be checked for by a network vulnerability scan; thus we would depend on the information gathered from the device itself (to be obtained during host evaluations).

- In many cases, using the default configuration of these scanning tools will break something in the customer's networks. We'll want to ensure that we're using custom configurations based on our understanding of what the customer has installed and running on their networks.

There are a variety of vulnerability scanners out there, both commercial and freeware. Some work better at scanning Microsoft Windows networks; other scanning tools excel at scanning UNIX networks. That is why it is important to use more than one scanner — to fill the gaps in the evaluation results/findings left by other tools and to validate findings already discovered. NSA only requires that one tool, application, or activity be run to address each of the 10 baseline categories in the IEM, but past history has shown that it's prudent to run at least two different vulnerability scanners to address potential false positives and ensure comprehensive discovery of findings.

Tip

If you are planning to do UDP scanning during your assessments (which you should), be aware that it will significantly increase your scan times. If there is no service running on the UDP port that is being checked, the host will not respond. Since UDP is a connectionless protocol, your scanning tools have to wait for the specified UDP timeout to expire. When there is no service monitoring that UDP port, this will occur for each UDP port you scan.

Vulnerability Scanners: Commercial and Freeware

One of the more popular vulnerability scanners available commercially is Retina Network Security Scanner (see Figure 9.5), developed by eEye Digital Security (www.eeye.com/html/products/retina/).

Figure 9.5 Retina Network Security Scanner

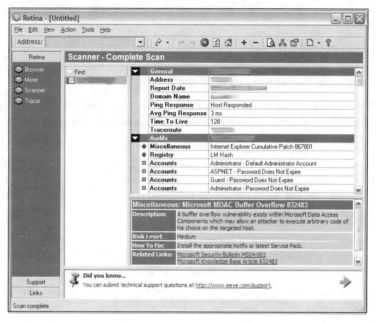

Retina Network Security Scanner has a very detailed vulnerability database that not only provides the vulnerability description, risk level, quick-fix information, and related links (to follow up for further information on the vulnerability)—it also provides the ability to fix many of the vulnerabilities it finds. It is important to note that this tool can only attempt to fix the vulnerabilities it finds on Microsoft Windows platforms, and it requires domain administrator privileges to do so.

Another commercial vulnerability scanner is SAINT, or the Security Administrators Integrated Network Tool (www.saintcorporation.com/saint/). This scanner (see Figures 9.6 and 9.7) runs on only UNIX, Linux, and Mac OS X. However, SAINT does have a remote mode that is available via two methods: add a *-r* on the command line when starting up SAINT or edit *saint.cf* in the SAINT config directory and set *$remote_mode* to *1*. This option allows you to run the SAINT scanner/server on a supported platform and permits you to interface with it via an Internet browser on an unsupported platform (such as Microsoft Windows). Note that the scans will still originate from the host running SAINT, not from the client.

Next is a commercial version of the freeware tool Nessus, called Tenable NeWT (www.tenablesecurity.com). It's Nessus for the Microsoft Windows platform (see Figure 9.8). Normally, the Nessus server runs on only UNIX, Linux, Mac OS X, and other BSD variants; but it doesn't run natively on Microsoft Windows.

Figure 9.6 SAINT Initial Screen

Figure 9.7 SAINT Data Collection

TIP

We were able to get Nessus, version 2.2.4 server and client, to compile and run within a Cygwin environment on Windows XP. It took some manual installation of certain libraries and header files, but it compiles and works! W00t!

There is a client for MS Windows, but not a Nessus server/scanner. This is where Tenable's NeWT comes in to fill the gap by providing a commercially supported, Nessus-based vulnerability scanner that runs on Microsoft Windows.

Figure 9.8 Tenable NeWT Scan in Progress

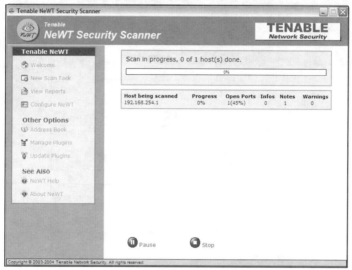

NeWT is somewhat lacking in reporting capabilities, as you can see by the report example in Figure 9.9. Furthermore, it was not able to banner-grab off the open ports to see what services are running on host 192.168.254.1. This resulted in NeWT reporting more false-positive findings than the other vulnerability scanners.

Figure 9.9 A Sample Tenable NeWT Security Report

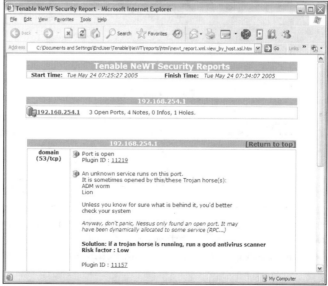

The next vulnerability scanner is also a patch management platform. Shavik HFNetChkPro (www.shavlik.com/hf.aspx) is a tool focused on assessing vulnerabilities on the Microsoft Windows platform and associated applications, which it does well (see Figure 9.10). There are four different versions, or feature sets, of HFNetChk: Basic Edition, Audit Edition, HFNetChkPro, and HFNetChkPro Plus. This tool is useful for discovering patches that are missing from workstations and servers in Microsoft Windows environments.

Figure 9.10 The HFNetChk Starting Screen

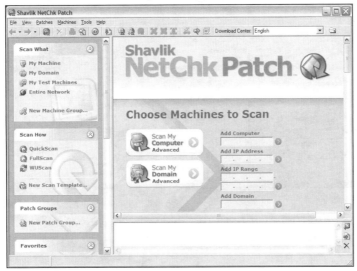

Figure 9.11 is a screen capture of an HFNetChk Pro report. It has a quick summary of the scan results, scan date/time, number of machines scanned, and the overall HFNetChk security assessment (summary) for the devices scanned. This information is very useful. If any critical issues come up on the report, it provides the evidence needed to get the issues resolved quickly.

Another well-known vulnerability scanner is ISS Internet Scanner (www.iss.net), which has been a popular vulnerability scanner for several years and is the preferred scanning tool for many die-hard ISS fans. Like many vulnerability scanners, ISS Internet Scanner has a built-in discovery mode (ISS calls it "Asset Identification"). ISS states that Internet Scanner can identify more than 1,300 types of devices and uses a technology called Dynamic Check Assignment to tailor, in real time, the scanning rules and policies to the environment being scanned. This should help reduce false-positive and false-negative findings. One further note: The reporting functionality in Internet Scanner is fairly comprehensive. It has over 70 report templates by default and the ability to create custom report templates (see Figure 9.12).

Figure 9.11 A HFNetChk Report

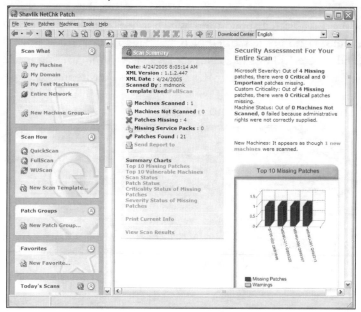

Figure 9.12 ISS Internet Scanner Interface

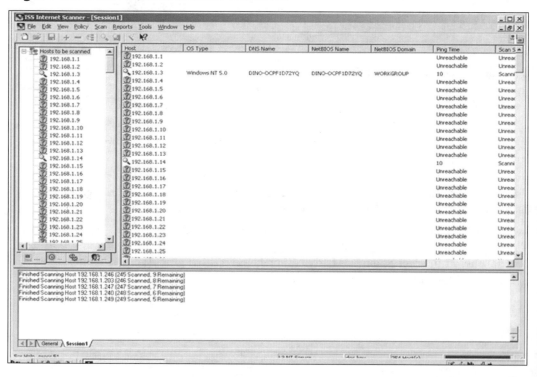

Now we get to nearly everyone's favorite freeware vulnerability scanner, Nessus (www.nessus.org). Nessus, probably the most popular freeware scanner, currently has a very large installed base of devoted followers. It is estimated that the Nessus scanner is being used by over 75,000 organizations worldwide (www.nessus.org/about/). That must mean Nessus is doing something right!

Nessus is highly configurable, able to run scans in multiple threads in parallel, and able to run detached scans and scheduled scans as well as interactive scan sessions. Figure 9.13 shows an example of Nessus running scans in parallel.

Figure 9.13 Nessus Running Scans in Parallel

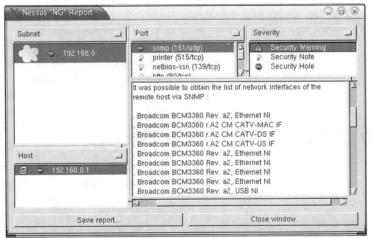

Figure 9.14 is an example of the Nessus reporting interface. Through this interface you can "drill down" into the details of the scan results. Do not forget to validate all findings and remove the false positives.

Figure 9.14 The Nessus Reporting Interface

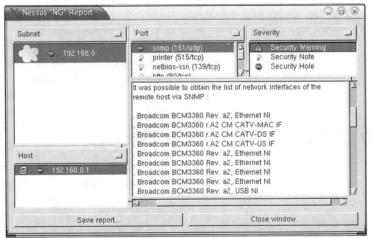

The next vulnerability assessment tool is GFi LANGuard Network Security Scanner (www.gfi.com/lannetscan/), or NSS, which is a Microsoft Windows–only scanner in that it runs on only Microsoft Windows and scans only Microsoft Windows platforms and associated applications or services. It's very selective in comparison to other popular vulnerability scanners. However, it should be noted that what NSS does scan, it scans well. When run locally on Microsoft Windows machines, this tool covers part of the host evaluation requirements for Microsoft Windows platforms (see Figure 9.15).

Figure 9.15 A GFi NSS Report Containing All Vulnerabilities

Notice how granular you can get with the reporting in LANGuard NSS. In addition to drilling down into the information gathered concerning the current scan target(s), GFi provides you with several scan filters to filter through the aggregate information that GFi maintains from each scan. This could provide you with a wealth of information over time. This tool is useful for trending analysis, metrics, and asset tracking/management (see Figure 9.16).

Using the vulnerability scanning tools is only part of the finding-gathering process. Vulnerability scans are conducted from a network perspective; the next part of our evaluation requires that we conduct host evaluations. Due to the host evaluations being conducted "at the console," so to speak, we hope to gain a more detailed view and analysis of the components, devices, servers, workstations, and so on we are evaluating.

Conducting Host Evaluations

Host-based evaluations, or console-level evaluations, are important to the evaluation process in that they provide us with a more detailed, more precise view of the components involved.

Given that host evaluations are conducted on the device itself or via secure console communications to the device, we are able to access more detailed information about the device. The host-based evaluation is the third "perspective" we need for the IEM; the other two are the external and internal perspectives.

Figure 9.16 A GFi NSS High Vulnerability Finding Report

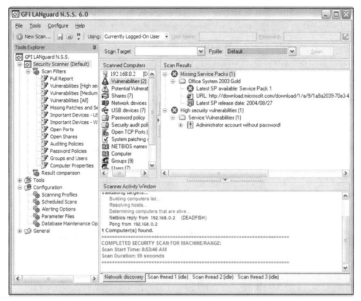

NOTE

According to the methodology, the NSA requires us to test 100 percent of critical systems. You are required to test 100 percent of the servers and critical workstations. But for noncritical workstations, a smaller "representative" subset is tested— approximately 10–15 percent of the workstations. By "representative" we mean that you should test workstations that are typical for the organization, such as the workstations that are similarly built via a common installation image.

Host Evaluation Example Tools and Scripts

Remember the three types of scans/perspectives: external, internal, and host based. Host based is the next perspective we need to cover in our evaluation. The problem with host evaluations is that the tasks can be time consuming, somewhat repetitive, and a bit tedious. Host evaluation tools and benchmark scripts are handy in that they help with the repetitive tasks involved in this type of evaluation.

Since the required checks generally necessitate local access, the bulk of host evaluation tasks are conducted manually, or in some cases via remote domain administrator access or SSH. The exceptions are routers, firewall, and switches where the device configuration is usually analyzed on a different host—for example, using the evaluator's system with RAT installed to check a Cisco router configuration. Firewall rulebases are generally checked manually by an evaluation team member.

Some tools cover more than one of the baseline activities, at least partially (in other words, provide data for vulnerability scanning and host evaluation activities). And some tools focus on certain operating systems or applications. Therefore, depending on the scope of the evaluation, your INFOSEC toolset may vary. No single INFOSEC tool will fulfill all assessment and evaluation needs or requirements. That's why it's recommended that all evaluation team members familiarize themselves with available tools. Since a large part of the host evaluation is more manual than tool oriented, we focus our discussion around the requirements rather than the supporting tools and scripts.

One example of a host evaluation tool that happens to be available for free from Microsoft is the Microsoft Baseline Security Analyzer (MSBA). The latest version of this tool as of this writing is v1.2.1 (see Figure 9.17). This tool is designed to evaluate the baseline security posture of Microsoft Windows platforms. It can scan the local machine as well as an IP network or Windows domain. Even though MSBA has network-scanning capabilities, we include it in this section due to the depth of its host-based evaluation functionality. MSBA provides more information to the host evaluation process than it does to the vulnerability scanning process.

Figure 9.17 Microsoft Baseline Security Analyzer Security Report

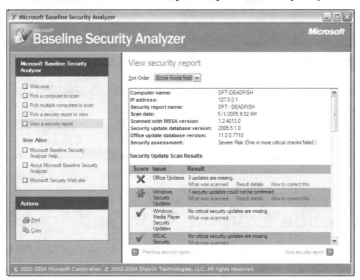

Benchmark Scripts and Custom Scripts

Conducting the host evaluations can be time consuming and tedious work. So what does any geek worth his (or her) salt do? They script it! A general rule of thumb is, "If you have to do it more than twice, script it." Thankfully, the Center for Internet Security (CIS) has put together sets of benchmark scripts and tools to measure a machine's security posture. According to information at www.cisecurity.org/bench.html, the machines are measured against "consensus best-practice security configurations for computers connected to the Internet." This provides you with the required baseline to measure the systems against. A quick note: The benchmark tools and scripts from CIS (see Figure 9.18 and www.cisecurity.org/benchmarks.html) are not free for commercial/consulting use, but they are free for individual users and government users. Commercial users are required to become CIS members to utilize the benchmark tools and scripts.

The following is a list of the operating systems, devices, and applications that CIS provides benchmarks and scripts for. First, the operating systems:

- Windows XP Pro
- Windows 2003 Server
- Windows 2000 Server, Pro
- Windows NT
- FreeBSD
- Solaris 2.5.1 through 10
- Linux
- HP-UX
- AIX
- OS X

The devices:

- Wireless Networks
- Cisco Router IOS
- Cisco PIX

The applications:

- Oracle Database
- Apache Web Server

The CIS benchmarks for Windows have a GUI interface, and the benchmarks for the supported UNIX/Linux platforms are accessed via a command-line interface. Figure 9.19 is an example of the CIS benchmark scoring tool being run on Microsoft Windows. The Windows 2000 Professional security template is shown as selected. The security template contains the "best-practices benchmarks" that the system is to be measured against. The Microsoft Windows templates are stored in *.inf format.

Figure 9.18 The CIS Benchmarks and Tools Listing

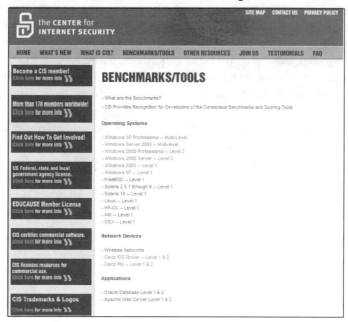

Figure 9.19 The CIS Benchmark Tool Using the Windows 2000 Pro Security Template

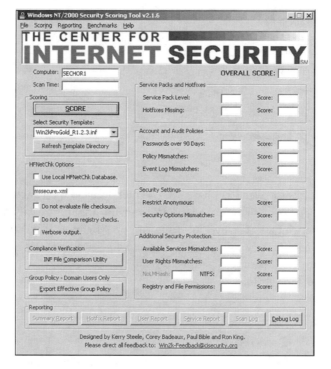

Figure 9.20 is a screen capture of the Solaris CIS benchmark tool being run. As you can tell, it has a command-line interface rather than a GUI interface. Execution of the CIS tool is done via the UNIX shell. Due to what is being checked and where the files are that are being checked, root access is required to run the CIS benchmarks on UNIX.

Figure 9.20 The CIS Benchmark Tool for the Solaris Platform

```
* Lead Developer                             : Jay Beale         *
* Benchmark Coordinator and Gadfly           : Hal Pomeranz      *
*                                                                *
* Copright 2001 - 2003 The Center for Internet Security  www.cisecurity.org *
*                                                                *
* Please send feedback to sol-scan@cisecurity.org.              *
*****************************************************************************

          Investigating system...this will take a few minutes...

                        ******

Now a final check for non-standard world-writable files, Set-UID and Set-GID
programs -- this can take a whole lot of time if you have a large filesystem.
Your score if there are no extra world-writable files or SUID/SGID programs
found will be 3.56 / 10.00 .  If there are extra SUID/SGID programs or
world-writable files, your score could be as low as 3.29 / 10.00 .

          You can hit CTRL-C at any time to stop at this remaining step.

The preliminary log can be found at: ./cis-most-recent-log

                        ******
```

Host Evaluations: What to Look For

Now that we are here at the host, what do we look for? We're glad you asked, since that is what we are going to discuss next. The host evaluation can be broken down into several areas: auditing, file/directory permissions, OS and application services, user rights assignments, and patch management.

Auditing

Auditing is basically security logging, or logging events that are important in terms of security. For example, a Windows domain group policy object (GPO) may require the logging of all accesses of system-critical files. Or every time the registry is modified, a log entry is created. You can imagine how quickly these log files would grow, and it usually turns out that quite a few unimportant events are being logged as well. This serves to make the monitoring of audit logs more difficult, but it's not a task the organization can afford to let slide.

By default, Microsoft Windows does not audit (log) many activities that could be considered detrimental to a system or its data. UNIX systems are better about logging events, but critical systems require more stringent auditing be enabled to be really effective. The organization should enable (better) auditing on these devices so that critical components can be monitored more effectively. It is part of the evaluation to verify that auditing is enabled and that events are being monitored. It's very easy to ignore the audit logs when they start to overflow with logged events; some events are important, though for our evaluation purposes, most are not.

All log events on Microsoft Windows platforms are entered into one of three main logs:

- Application log
- System log
- Security log

On UNIX (or Linux) systems, most logs are stored in /var/log or /var/adm. Some important log files to check are:

- syslog
- messages
- secure
- maillog

Keep in mind that this list is not all-inclusive! There may be additional log files to check, depending on the organization. They may have a "home-brew" application that is doing its own thing logging-wise. It is up to the evaluator (you again) to validate that auditing is enabled and working according to the organization's policies and procedures. Ensure that auditing is being monitored and tracked. You should check to see if critical log events are being tracked and acted on. For example, a syslog entry shows a problem with a drive on one of the Solaris servers. Does the organization create a trouble ticket (or something similar) for the event to track it to resolution? Is the event ignored until data is lost? These are the kinds of things you will be looking for.

NOTE

Something to keep in mind is that even though systems have auditing turned on, it does not necessarily follow that anyone is paying attention to what is logged. Not only should the organization be auditing events (logging), they should be monitoring the logs and acting on events that require attention. The INFOSEC Assessment Methodology (IAM) process examines this piece.

File/Directory Permissions

Certain files and directories should be protected a bit more stringently than the default permissions that are set by the OS/application installation. These files and directories should be restricted to the proper owner and group and should have the proper permissions set.

For example, the following code shows the proper ownership and permissions on the file /etc/passwd:

```
[mdmonk@dotcomd ~]$ ls -lsa /etc/passwd
 4 -rw-r--r--    1 root      root          2308 May 22 21:03 /etc/passwd
```

Notice that the file is owned by user root and group root. Permissions are set to *-rw-r--r--*. This means that the owner has read/write access, the group has read access, and world (everyone on the system) has read access. The initial dash signifies that no sticky bit has been set on the file, and the SUID and/or SGID bits have not been set. The sidebar includes an explanation of the terms *sticky bit, SUID* and *SGID bits* as well as *inode*. These permissions are set properly, since some services/applications need to access the /etc/passwd file to verify that a user is valid for that system but doesn't need to modify the file—read-only access versus read/write access.

Notes from the Underground...

Sticky Bit? SUID? SGID? What Are You Talking About?

When someone mentions those terms, they are talking about permission flags for files and directories in a UNIX file system. Actually, the permission flags are part of the inode and not the file/directory, but it's easier for a person to associate the information with an actual filename, so we'll treat *inode* and *filename* as interchangeable terms (even though they aren't). The inode is a data structure that holds information about the file it references. There is an inode for each file, and this is used to uniquely identify each file by using these two items of information: the file system it resides on and the file's inode number on that system.

An inode contains the following information: device (where the inode is stored), file-locking information, mode of the file, type of file, number of links (*man ln*) to the file, the file owner's user ID and group ID, file size in bytes, file access time, file modification time, inode modification time, and the file's physical location on the system (file system addresses for the file's blocks on disk).

Back to the bits and permission flags: There are 12 bits representing inode/file permissions: set UID; set GID; sticky; read, write, and execute for owner; read, write, and execute for group; and read, write, and execute for world/other. As you can see, they add up to 12.

The Set UID (SUID) bit (the twelfth bit) is set for any application where it has to run as a different user than the one who started the application. For example, /usr/bin/passwd has permissions of *-r-s--x--x*. The *s* represents the SUID bit, meaning that when /usr/bin/passwd is executed, it is executed as though user *root* had executed it, with *root's* privileges.

The set GID (SGID) bit (the eleventh bit) is the same as SUID only it applies to the file's group rather than the file owner.

The sticky bit is the tenth bit. If the sticky bit is set, that tells UNIX systems that once the application is executed, they should keep it in memory. This was used in

Continued

> earlier days to help reduce application start times—back in the days before fast disk access and faster/larger banks of memory were available.

Depending on the UNIX or Linux distribution you are evaluating, key files and directories are in different locations (for example, SSL certificates are stored in /usr/share/ssl rather than /usr/lib/ssl). That's why it's important to have an evaluation team member who is familiar with the UNIX/Linux versions being evaluated. However, scripted solutions can help. With scripted solutions, each distribution's default locations for the various essential files and directories can be stored in a configuration file or separate script. The knowledge of the default locations and basic checks can be scripted to assist the evaluation efforts.

Microsoft Windows key files and directories are generally stored in the C:\Windows or C:\WINNT directories, depending on the version of Windows that's running. Probably the most important directories in C:\Windows and C:\WINNT are the System, System32, Security, and Repair directories. At a minimum, those directories should be secured.

The following list is a sample of essential system files on Microsoft Windows:

- Ntoskrnl.exe
- Ntkrnlpa.exe
- Hal.dll
- Win32k.sys
- Ntdll.dll
- Kernel32.dll
- Advapi32.dll
- User32.dll
- Cdi32.dll
- Ntldr
- Boot.ini

The files listed are important to Microsoft Windows functionality. If they are compromised, the server is potentially compromised.

OS and Application Services

Not every application or service should be installed and running. We know it sounds like fun, but having SMTP, SNMP, HTTP, HTTPS, IMAP, POP3, FTP, SMB, LDAP, and the like all running on a machine not assigned those roles is just asking for trouble. A server (or workstation) should be running only the services and applications necessary to fulfill its operational role(s). The more services running, the more avenues of attack available to a malicious user.

The evaluator should check the list of installed services and applications against the server's assigned role(s). If the server is serving only Web pages (HTTP or HTTPS), it's unlikely that an SMTP service is required to be installed. *If* a service or application is necessary to fulfill the server's role(s), it should be documented, either in the build documentation or where the organization tracks exceptions to policy.

User Rights Assignments

User rights assignments can be a difficult topic to address, because political issues could be involved—for example, additional rights granted to "a buddy" in a different department or admin rights granted to the HR database administrator so that the system administrator doesn't have to be bothered all the time. User rights should be granted based on roles in the organization, not based on individual users. It is much easier for the organization to manage user rights via roles than per individual.

The evaluator should check to ensure that user rights assignments are being granted based on organizational roles. For example, an accountant probably doesn't need domain administrator rights. And the database administrator probably shouldn't have the root password on the Solaris server (that's what *sudo* is for, as we'll see in a moment).

The concept of least privilege is a fundamental tool in managing user rights, whether the rights are assigned or inherited. Briefly, the concept of least privilege is this: Grant the user access to the resources they need, not access to the resources they want. The two usually differ. Let's take the case of a database server in a large organization. Quite often, due to separation of roles and/or duties, the system administrator and database administrator are two different people or teams. The database administrator may require root-level privileges to run certain commands on the server, but giving him or her the root password is normally a breach of security policy (at least one would hope!)—and that person having access to the root password is *way* more privileges than he or she needs.

So a method or facility for providing limited access to privileged commands would come in handy here. On UNIX/Linux/*BSD systems, the command *sudo* is the recommended method for granting limited access to privileged areas and commands on the system. Sudo (*superuser do*) allows a system administrator to grant certain users or user groups the ability to run some or all commands as another user (commonly as root) and log all executed commands and command arguments.

Patch Management

In patch management, we check to see whether the organization has any patch or configuration management in place. Many organizations install a server or workstation and don't follow up with related security or application patches. This leaves the organization very vulnerable to attacks as new vulnerabilities are discovered. An organization cannot safely exist on today's Internet without some form of patch management being used. It's simply not safe.

Something you should keep in mind is that an organization might not be able to apply certain patches or service packs. A very common example is that Service Pack 2 for Windows XP cannot be applied to some systems, because essential applications running on the systems have not been ported to work on XP SP2. If SP2 for XP is installed, those applications cease working. If essential business applications are running on the system (that was upgraded to SP2) and the applications no longer function or are inaccessible due to the upgrade, the organization might get a *bit* irritated. Most organizations tend to frown on downtime. So, if a patch cannot be applied due to restrictions (technical, organizational, or otherwise), note it in the evaluation documentation and look for ways to mitigate or reduce the risk associated with not applying that patch. Looking for additional vulnerability mitigation methods is something you should already be doing so that you can provide more than one recommendation per finding (remember Chapter 8: Cadillac, Chevy, and Yugo).

Mapping the Findings to the IEM Process

It's all well and good to come up with findings, but are the findings valid? Are they even important to the organization's mission or to the evaluation? These are questions you have to ask during the next step of the vulnerability scanning and host evaluation portion of the IEM. Correlating the data/findings, validating the findings, and mapping the findings to the IEM are the tasks ahead of us next.

We need to briefly mention a subject (which will be discussed in more depth later in this text): first-order prioritization of findings. This is a general ranking process used to help focus our efforts on the most important findings that affect critical portions of the organization's INFOSEC infrastructure.

Vulnerability Scans and Host Evaluations: Correlating the Data

In the previous sections, our goal in showing the various vulnerability scanning and host evaluation tools was to introduce you to some of the more familiar and popular tools you could end up using during your own evaluations. Keep in mind that there are more scanning and evaluating tools out there than we have covered here.

Now we will correlate the scan and evaluation data sets, filter out false-positive findings, and map the findings back to the IEM process. To save time, we have summarized some of the findings from the scans conducted for this text. The screen captures are from the actual tools that were used to scan these devices.

Table 9.3 contains a summary of the devices we are evaluating. We prefer to keep a spreadsheet updated with this information so that key information is more readily available for the evaluators. You'll find that this helps identify some findings as false positives right off the bat. For example, if a server is Windows 2000 running an IIS Web server and the finding is only relevant to Apache servers, it's a fairly safe bet that the finding is a false positive.

Table 9.3 A Sample Evaluation Components List

Hostname	IP Address	OS	Component/Device Roles
intgw.evalnet	192.168.0.1	Linux-kernel 2.4, iptables	Firewall
imsohackable.evalnet	192.168.0.2	Windows XP	Developer workstation running various services
ownable.evalnet	192.168.0.3	Windows 2000	File and print sharing

Continued

Table 9.3 continued A Sample Evaluation Components List

Hostname	IP Address	OS	Component/Device Roles
opensun.evalnet	192.168.0.4	Solaris 10	Web, SMTP, SNMP, and database server
securemac.evalnet	192.168.0.5	Apple OS X 10.3	Workstation
lj5.evalnet	192.168.0.50	HP JetDirect	Print server
shnas.evalnet	192.168.0.51	SnapOS	Network attached storage (NAS)

Tables 9.4 and 9.5 show findings and affected IP addresses. The left columns of Tables 9.4 and 9.5 contain the assigned finding number, which we assign for tracking purposes. It isn't a number that will exist outside of our evaluation working documents, but it helps in tracking findings through the evaluation process. A more formal organization of the findings will occur during the post-evaluation phase. By "showing our work," our due diligence is shown, with the discovery of the finding and subsequent analysis of the finding, whether it is valid or a false positive. Documenting your evaluation efforts is key!

Table 9.4 A Sample Findings List

Finding #	Finding	Severity	Exploit Vector	Affected IP Address
F1	OpenSSH may be vulnerable. Multiple issues with OpenSSH ver 3.7.1 and below.	High	Remote	192.168.0.1, 192.168.0.4, 192.168.0.5
F2	SMTP may be a mail relay.	High	Remote	192.168.0.4
F3	Buffer overflow in the ISAPI DLL filter for Macromedia JRun 3.1.	High	Remote	192.168.0.2
F4	Oracle 9i 9.0.x database server allows local users to access restricted data.	High	Local	192.168.0.4
F5	admin.php in PHPGEDVIEW allows remote attackers to obtain sensitive information via *phpinfo* command.	Low	Remote	192.168.0.2
F6	Buffer overflow in Apple iTunes before ver 4.8 allows remote attackers to execute arbitrary code.	High	Remote	192.168.0.5

Continued

Table 9.4 continued A Sample Findings List

Finding #	Finding	Severity	Exploit Vector	Affected IP Address
F7	Vulnerabilities in Microsoft Windows Terminal Server and Remote Desktop could allow a remote attacker to execute arbitrary code or crash the server.	Medium	Remote	192.168.0.2, 192.168.0.3

Table 9.5 Another Sample Findings List

Finding #	Affected OS/App	CVE	CVE/Scanning Tool Recommendation
F1	OpenSSH	CAN-2003-0682, CAN-2003-0786, CAN-2003-0787	Upgrade to the latest version of OpenSSH.
F2	Sendmail 8.9 and below	CAN-1999-0512	Upgrade to the latest version of Sendmail 8.9.x.
F3	Jrun 3.1 and below	CVE 2002-0801	Apply latest patches for JRun 3.x, or upgrade to JRun 4.x.
F4	Oracle 9i 9.0.1 and below	CVE 2002-0571	Apply latest patches for Oracle 9i 9.0.x.
F5	PHPGedView 2.6.1 and below	CVE 2004-0033	Upgrade admin.php and/or PHPGEDVIEW to latest revision.
F6	iTunes 4.8 and below, on Apple and Microsoft Windows	CAN 2005-1248	Upgrade to iTunes 4.8 or higher.
F7	Microsoft Windows 2000 and XP	CVE 2002-0864, CAN 2002-0863	Apply appropriate patch for operating system.

Summarize and Validate Findings

We've said it before, but we'll say it again: All findings must be validated! This is an extremely important point. You do not want to turn in to a client a final report containing false-positive findings or findings that don't even matter to the customer. Take the time to verify that cross-site scripting vulnerability or to verify the SNMP community strings discovered.

Summary

In this chapter we discussed vulnerability scanning and host evaluations in relation to the INFOSEC Evaluation Methodology. As you can now see, this section of the evaluation requires much more thought than perhaps was initially considered. It's not as simple as "Turn on <*insert tool name*> vulnerability scanning tool, have it crank through the subnets, and churn out findings." Modern INFOSEC tools do simplify the task of gathering the suspected vulnerabilities, but the tools do not replace the evaluator's intellect, ability to reason, knowledge, and experience. The evaluator brings his or her skills, technical and nontechnical experience, and appropriate knowledge base to the evaluation efforts. The vulnerability scanning tools provide a tidy list of suspected vulnerabilities, but they are not human and they do not have the ability to reason.

The chapter started with a reminder of which phase of the IEM that vulnerability scanning takes place in. Then we continued on to the subject of vulnerability scanning itself. The risk triangle was introduced to show where vulnerabilities impact an organization's INFOSEC posture and risk profile. Do you recall what the other two sides to the risk triangle were? That's right — threats and asset value. After that we talked about vulnerability and attack trends so that we can be more aware of what we are "up against" when conducting the vulnerability scans. CERT provided us with some eye-opening numbers of incidents reported, but it was a reality check that we needed. The statistics are a subtle reminder that it is not safe "out there" on the Internet.

Then we got to the "Why are we here?" section. We discussed various reasons for conducting an IEM, and we talked about the role vulnerability scans play in your INFOSEC evaluations. Next came the tools section, which listed several vulnerability scanning tools, provided screen captures to familiarize you with the various interfaces to the tools, and briefly noted items of interest regarding each tool.

The vulnerability scanning tools provided us with network-based vulnerabilities, but that isn't the whole picture, is it? We also have to conduct host evaluations to provide a more complete picture of the INFOSEC posture of the organization. Host evaluations are used to gather findings directly from the workstations, servers, network devices, security devices, and the like. You might have different findings based on your perspective to the host/device/component; whether the finding is from an external scan, an internal scan, or a host-based evaluation. These are three different perspectives you can get information from.

Once we gather all our findings, we have to validate them, remove false-positive findings, and map the findings back to the organization's critical INFOSEC systems. By providing multiple recommendations (three per finding is highly suggested) for the mitigation of the critical findings, we hope to present the customer with a viable road map toward the reduction of their organization's security gap and the strengthening of their security posture.

Solutions Fast Track

Vulnerability and Attack Trends

☑ Attacks are becoming increasingly complex and have a much shorter time till exploit (TTE).

☑ Application-level attacks are becoming the attack vector of choice for these network assailants.

☑ 'Bot networks (botnets) are on the rise. The numbers of systems comprising these botnets is staggering. Some computers have been compromised by more than one attacker and end up being part of several botnets.

Conducting Vulnerability Scans

☑ UDP scanning can be *very* time intensive. Remember this when you are conducting your scans.

☑ The vulnerability scanning tools you use should be CVE/CAN compliant. You do not have to use the CVE/CAN list from Mitre.org, but it is required that you use a vulnerability identification and rating system that is accessible by the customer.

☑ The Technical Evaluation Plan (TEP) will provide you with your evaluation target list. The TEP is your road map for the evaluation and helps guide your efforts..

☑ You should tailor the configuration of the tools you will be using to the organization being evaluated. The default configuration for many of the tools is likely to cause more problems than are discovered.

☑ Not all vulnerability scanning tools are the same, nor do they all check vulnerabilities the same way. The evaluation team must do research to find the INFOSEC tools that fit the needs of the evaluation.

☑ Ensure that the proper personnel (network and system admins and the like) are available, either directly or on call, when you are conducting your evaluation efforts. If something breaks, you will want to let the proper folks know as soon as possible. Business continuity should be maintained as much as possible during the evaluation.

Conducting Host Evaluations

☑ Host-based evaluations serve to provide a more detailed picture of the environment being evaluated. They also assist in the findings validation process.

☑ Benchmarks serve to measure the host system's security posture and provide a best-practices baseline to measure against.

☑ The methodology requires that host evaluations be conducted on 100 percent of critical servers and workstations. For standard (noncritical) workstations, a representative sample, approximately 10–15 percent, should be evaluated.

Mapping Findings Back to the IEM Process

☑ Correlate the findings from the vulnerability scans and from the host evaluations. Utilize the results from the differing approaches (external/internal vs. host based) to assist in your finding validation efforts.

☑ At the end of the evaluation, as part of the final deliverables, we include a CD with the raw data from our tests, evaluations, and so on. Don't forget that all findings are considered proprietary to the customer organization—so keep that data, and keep it organized during the evaluation!

☑ Ensure that you are diligent in your efforts to weed out the false-positive findings! It's rather embarrassing to submit a report to an organization and discover that it has false information (findings) in it.

Frequently Asked Questions

The following Frequently Asked Questions, answered by the authors of this book, are designed to both measure your understanding of the concepts presented in this chapter and to assist you with real-life implementation of these concepts. To have your questions about this chapter answered by the author, browse to **www.syngress.com/solutions** and click on the **"Ask the Author"** form. You will also gain access to thousands of other FAQs at ITFAQnet.com.

Q: What is the difference between a vulnerability scan and an attack and penetration (A&P) test?

A: A vulnerability scan is less invasive than an A&P. An A&P attempts to exploit vulnerabilities that are detected, whereas during a vulnerability scan the individual test stops once a vulnerability is found, though the rest of the scan continues. One test finds vulnerabilities, the other (A&P) finds and attempts to exploit vulnerabilities.

Q: Why isn't one vulnerability scanner enough to meet my evaluation requirements?

A: Strictly speaking, you are only required to use one tool for each of the IEM baseline activities. But it is highly recommended that you use two different tools for each of the activities, including vulnerability scanning. It's like getting a second opinion from a doctor. Using two different tools will provide credence to a finding or help prove it to be a false positive.

Q: If my organization has a firewall, we are protected. So I don't need to worry about the findings that are internal only or host based. Right?

A: This is a false assumption. Just because a firewall is in place, that does not mean that the organization is fully protected, and it shouldn't mitigate any of the internal and/or host-based findings. Think of the organization as an M&M candy: hardened outer shell with a soft, sweet center. All it takes is one hole in the "hardened outer shell" and the entire organization is accessible. This is why defense in depth is required.

Q: How many workstations are required to be checked during an evaluation?

A: "A representative sample of the workstation population" is the official answer. I would evaluate approximately 10–15 percent of the workstations if they are all built from the same "image." If differing workstation builds or configurations are to be evaluated, you have to check a sampling from each group.

Q: This report from *<insert vulnerability scanning tool name>* gave me a fix for every issue it found. This is all I need to secure my organization's INFOSEC posture, right?

A: The short answer is No. Every solution that is recommended by the vulnerability scanning tools needs to be verified as a valid finding. Some of the findings may turn out to be false positives or invalid findings. Even if the finding is valid, the recommended solution might not be a fit for your organization. This is where the evaluator's expertise and experience come to the rescue.

Q: What is the difference between external, internal, and host-based evaluations/scans?

A: These are the different perspectives from which an IEM evaluation is conducted:

- An external scan is conducted from outside the organization's environment (in other words, from outside the firewall).

- An internal scan is conducted from inside the environment being evaluated. The device doing the internal scans should have access to all traffic for this environment, so take the network topology into consideration. If everything is connected to a hub, no problem; if it's a switched environment (which is normal), a "spanned port" may be required. A spanned port is configured to receive all network traffic on that specific switch.

- A host-based evaluation is conducted "at the console" of the component (in other words, SSH'd into the firewall, router, or *NIX box or connected via Remote Desktop to Microsoft Windows servers).

Q: What is "least privilege," and why is it important to host-based evaluations?

A: Least privilege is the principle of granting the minimally required amount of access to resources for each user or role. What it boils down to is only give a user the access he or she needs, not what he or she wants. It is part of the host evaluation to verify that least privilege is being applied when granting access to resources or granting system rights.

Q: What are the latest trends in recent incident reports?

A: Reports are showing that application-level vulnerabilities are on the rise as the "attack vector of choice." This is especially true for Web-enabled applications. The operating systems and network devices (firewalls and routers) are becoming more secure. Whereas application vendors historically have lagged behind in providing patches, so more focus has been applied to applications by the "vulnerability finders."

Chapter 10

Fine-Tuning the Evaluation

Solutions in this chapter:

- **Network Device Analysis**
- **Password-Compliance Testing**
- **Application-Specific Scanning**
- **Network Protocol Analysis**
- **Finalizing Your Findings List**
- **Mapping Findings Back to the IEM Process**

☑ **Summary**

☑ **Solutions Fast Track**

☑ **Frequently Asked Questions**

Introduction

This chapter covers the remainder of the scanning, or hands-on, portion of the IEM. As mentioned in the previous chapter, you will more than likely have a different view of the system when you're at the console than when you're evaluating the system from the network. The same can be said of the remaining tasks, in regard to the organization's INFOSEC posture. By conducting network device analysis, password-compliance testing (more commonly known as *password cracking*, but we aren't supposed to call it that anymore), application-specific scanning, and network protocol analysis, we should finally have "the big picture" when it comes to the organization and the status of its INFOSEC resources. It sounds like there is still a lot left to do. And there is; but the tasks go quickly, so don't worry too much.

In this chapter we fine-tune the evaluation. Our goals are to evaluate network devices (routers, firewalls, intrusion detection systems [IDSs], and the like), conduct password-compliance testing, perform application-specific scanning (on Web servers, databases, and e-mail servers), and do a bit of network protocol analysis. All these tasks "flesh out" the evaluation team's understanding of the organization's environment. And unless the evaluation team needs to conduct retesting, these tasks represent the last of the hands-on testing part of the IEM process (see Figure 10.1).

Figure 10.1 Phases of the IEM

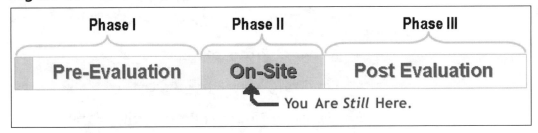

Let's get to work.

Network Device Analysis

The part we refer to as *network device analysis* or *evaluation* is where you examine the border devices or high-assurance devices. When we refer to border devices, think of devices such as routers, firewalls, IDSs, VPN/gateway devices, proxy devices, and the like.

Approaches Used in Network Device Analysis

For the IEM, we use two approaches in our network device analysis/evaluations. The *design approach* is an evaluation of the design of the perimeter and defenses for the organization. The *technical approach* is a technical evaluation of the various perimeter device configurations and settings. The output of these two approaches combine to provide the evaluation team a comprehensive view of the perimeter and perimeter defenses and contribute to a more complete picture of the organization's overall INFOSEC posture.

Evaluating the Perimeter Design and Defenses

When you are evaluating the organization's perimeter and perimeter defenses, the evaluator's experience and knowledge come into play in a big way. For example, let's say that the organization we are evaluating has a firewall in place and a proper ruleset applied and requires all Web traffic to go through a proxy—all good security practices. *But* there is a machine that is dual-homed, with a network interface connected to the outside network (Internet) and a network interface connected to the internal network. That one machine is a hole into the organization's infrastructure; bypassing an otherwise decent security perimeter. That is why the evaluator's experience and knowledge are so important; not everyone could recognize an improperly configured machine or locate holes in perimeter defenses.

TIP

As part of the evaluation team, don't forget why you are there doing the evaluation. You are there to evaluate the organization's INFOSEC posture. The evaluator also has to understand the organization's business processes and what's important to the customer. This information was gathered during the IAM process and plays a key role in your evaluation efforts.

For example, a perceived misconfiguration could in actuality be a requirement for a customer's business-to-business (B2B) connectivity. This is not something you (as part of the evaluation team) would be aware of unless you have the organizational criticality matrix and system criticality matrix(es) as a guide for your efforts. These documentation items are included in the technical evaluation plan (TEP).

We like to use the M&M candy analogy, equating an organization's infrastructure to an M&M—you know, hard candy shell and soft chocolate center. The hard candy shell is the perimeter and perimeter defenses; the soft chocolate center represents the organization's internal infrastructure. When a hole is punched in the hard outer shell (the perimeter), the soft chocolate center (the organizational infrastructure) is vulnerable. It takes only one misconfigured machine to negate the risk mitigation effects a security perimeter provides.

To evaluate the perimeter, you'll initially look for devices that increase the security of the infrastructure—firewalls, routers, IDSs, and the like. The organization should have provided this information to you in the diagrams and documentation you requested earlier in the IEM process. If you have a diagram or documentation of the perimeter and perimeter defenses, you next need to validate those resources. Do they exist? Are they in use (for example, in the rack, but not plugged in)?

Basically, you are examining the design of your customer's perimeter and associated perimeter defenses. We'll talk about examining the security configuration and settings later in this chapter. Questions you might want to answer with the results of this part of the evaluation are:

- Is the perimeter design sound?
- Is the perimeter being circumvented at all (for example, by dual-hosted machines)?

- Is there a Web or e-mail proxy in place? Both?
- Is there an IDS in place? Are the logs being monitored and acted on?
- Is there auditing in place for the perimeter network devices?
- Is there a central syslog server to collect audit logs?
- If so, has that server been hardened and access restricted?

The bulk of the tasks for network device analysis are part of the "evaluating the configuration of network devices" approach, which just happens to be our next topic. Look at the design approach as the way we get our working list of perimeter devices to evaluate the security configuration.

Evaluating Network Device Configurations

To evaluate the perimeter devices and perimeter defenses, a little bit of information goes a long way toward helping our efforts. The following is a list of some useful information or documentation to have regarding the organization for this portion of the evaluation:

- Diagram of the perimeter, including border devices, DMZ hosted machines, and any third-party connectivity coming into the infrastructure
- Documentation of the security device configurations and supporting policies/procedures
- Any contracts for outsourced INFOSEC infrastructure or roles
- Evaluation team members with experience on the device platforms and applications to be evaluated

WARNING

Take special care with the organization's sensitive security device configurations, such as firewall rule sets and router configurations. Considering the sensitivity of the information, some organizations may require the evaluation team to leave such documentation onsite.

If sensitive information or documentation needs to be transferred and it has to leave physical control of either the organization or the evaluation team, the data should be encrypted. If you have to receive the documents via e-mail or some other electronic delivery method, the information should be encrypted with the agreed-on encryption methods. (Issues such as this should be addressed in the TEP.)

What are you looking for when you do this part of the network device analysis? It depends. Though the process is the same for all network devices, you will look for different issues depending on the type of device and/or the vendor of the device being analyzed. Firewalls require you to look at the ruleset or rulebase—to consider whether it is it just a gateway device or whether it handles VPNs too (or even other applications!), whether the underlying OS has been hardened, and so on. Routers require the analysis of the router configuration, a verification of the running IOS version, and other considerations. Considering the number of vendors of security devices and differing versions of devices in use today, this part of the evaluation really requires a specific knowledge base to properly assess them. The knowledge and experience required may differ depending on the technologies in use. This is a subtle reminder to know the environment and tailor the evaluation team to the environment being evaluated.

Table 10.1 lists some of the items that should be checked for each device. They are broken into two broad categories: firewalls and routers/switches. We purposely did not include the other devices in this category, since they will be covered later in this chapter when we get to application-specific scanning. These are devices such as proxies, SMTP gateways, and Web and e-mail servers.

The lists in Table 10.1 are not all-inclusive; they are simply valid examples to get you started.

Table 10.1 Network Device Evaluation Checks

Firewalls:	Routers and Switches:
Check rulesets/rulebases	Check for open ports (check using port scanner)
Any proxy servers configured (as part of the firewall)	Evaluate router/switch configuration
Check for default settings	Check for cleartext protocols in use
Check underlying OS: Has it been hardened? What services are available?	Run vulnerability scanner against device
Patches and firmware updates: Any missing?	Check ACLs
Check for known issues listed on manufacturer's site	Check OS version and patch level (IOS, CatOS, JunOS, etc.)
Check for known or recently discovered issues listed on security portal sites	

Firewalls can be tricky beasts, and some have been known to "flatline" due to improper handling of aggressive vulnerability scans. Keep this in mind when you are checking the perimeter devices and Internet-accessible devices. Not every firewall is made the same. Ensure that you have the proper firewall expertise on your evaluation team. A Cisco PIX admin , might not be well versed in administrating CheckPoint firewalls or vice versa. Also, ensure that you have the administrators of the equipment being evaluated handy to assist if any of the devices stop responding. It's always best to have the organization's administrators on hand or on call when you are conducting your evaluation tasks. If the administrator is able to correct the issue in a timely manner, the end users might not even know there was a problem—it could be fixed quicker than they could say, "Hey! Who broke the Internet!"

On the subject of tools, there are few INFOSEC tools out there to help you with these particular tasks. The tasks are mostly manual processes. But do not despair—a couple of security tools can help you with some of your evaluation tasks.

To assist with the router configuration checks, the Center for Internet Security (CIS) has a tool called Router Audit Tool, or RAT, which is available at www.cisecurity.org/bench_cisco.html. RAT analyzes the router configuration, compares it to its baseline (modifiable by you), and produces a report for the device. The report has a listing of the rules RAT checked and a pass/fail score, the raw score for the device, and the weighted score for the device (on a scale of 1–10). RAT also provides, whenever possible, the IOS/PIX commands necessary to correct the issues it identified.

Another tool that can be very handy in evaluating network devices is SolarWinds (available at www.solarwinds.net/). You probably remember it from the SNMP portion of the evaluation. That's why we bring it in at this point as well. SolarWind's SNMP scanning functionality is pretty nice and will help with the router/switch analysis. It can provide TFTP server functionality as well to assist in the collecting of router/switch configurations.

Password-Compliance Testing

Password-compliance testing, also known as password cracking—it is highly recommended that we refer to the activity by the former term rather than the latter, but we all know what we're talking about: cracking passwords. It's about testing to see how many users are complying with the organization's password policies. Or is it more about the number of passwords that can be cracked in under a minute? Either way, this part of our evaluation tests the organization's compliance with its published password policies and procedures.

Password-Compliance Testing Methods

There are three types of password-checking methods or attacks:

- Brute-force attacks
- Dictionary attacks
- Hybrid attacks (combining dictionary and brute-force methods)

A *brute-force attack* is one in which the password-cracking tool cycles through a specified grouping of characters such as a–z, A–Z, 0–9, or !@#$%^&*()-=+ for a specified password length—say, five to seven characters, encrypting every combination of the characters in the character sets and trying each against the password hash stored in the password file until a collision occurs. A *collision* happens when the string that will be accepted as the password is obtained or guessed. For example, if you tell the password-compliance testing tool to perform a check using passwords between five and seven characters long and using the lower- and upper-case alpha characters and numbers (a–z, A–Z, and 0–9). The tool will cycle through every combination starting with *aaaaa*, then *aaaab*, then . . . well, you get the idea. Obviously, a brute-force password-cracking attempt will take much longer than a dictionary attack. But a brute-force attack could be your only chance to obtain complex passwords. A dictionary attack might not crack the more complex passwords.

For the bulk of user passwords, a dictionary attack is a useful, and quicker, method of password-compliance testing. A *dictionary attack* is one in which the password-cracking tool will go through and encrypt each word in a dictionary and check the encrypted hash against the encrypted hash entries in the password file. Basically, if the hashes are a match, the password has been found. Once again, you have to consider the organization and environment you are evaluating. Passwords come in all shapes and sizes. If you are evaluating a trucking company, you might want to include in your password-cracking attempts a dictionary file containing trucking industry-specific terminology. Or if you are in an area where English isn't the primary language—for instance, Peru—you might want to consider adding to the efforts a dictionary file containing words in the local language or dialect. If you walk by the Windows administrators' cubes and hear Backstreet Boys or similar music playing, you know you should add the boy-band dictionary to your password-compliance tests. Additional dictionary files exist for many languages and a variety of topics, genres, and industries. Tailor your password-compliance testing efforts to the organization. You could find your password-compliance testing will go a bit easier if you do.

The last testing method is called the *hybrid attack method*. Just as you might guess, this is a combination of the brute-force attack and the dictionary attack. This method of password testing is better at getting passwords that are a concatenation of letters and numerics, such as *security01, secretpassword69, imnumber1*, and so on. The dictionary attack gets the dictionary word portion of the password, and the hybrid attack then tries to brute-force the rest of the password. Take the password *security01*, for example—the dictionary attack would catch the word *security*, and then the password-cracking tool would try to brute-force guess the rest of the password by tacking numbers on. This method doesn't always work, but no method will get 100 percent of the passwords in a realistically limited amount of time. But remember that no password is entirely secure.

NOTE

Given the limitations of passwords, one trend in the security industry has been to recommend moving from passwords to *passphrases*. More complexity is involved with passphrases, and they're longer (and so much more difficult to crack) than passwords.

Methods of Obtaining the Password File

Without physical security, there can be no security. How is that important here, in the password-compliance testing world? For one thing, there are more offline password-cracking tools than there are online password-cracking tools. Online password-cracking tools don't work in offline mode, where the password file is given to the tool and it doesn't have to obtain it off the "wire" (the network). So if the organization has a system or component that needs to be protected, restricting physical access to the device is an essential first line of defense. If you can get physical access to a system, it is a trivial task to obtain access to the files you need by popping in a bootable CD and rebooting the system, especially if auditing is not turned on. If auditing is not enabled and it's a Microsoft Windows machine, the fact that the machine was even rebooted, let alone that the password file (a critical file) was copied, will probably go unnoticed.

Notes from the Underground…

Password Paranoia

Some organizations won't want you, an external third party, to have access to their password file(s). There's nothing wrong with that, but since they don't want to grant you access to their password files, the organization will have to conduct the password-compliance evaluation activity and provide you with the general results from the testing.

They don't have to tell you whose password was weak, or anything that detailed. But they *do* have to provide you with enough information to fulfill your evaluation requirements.

How do you get that pesky password file, anyway? We need it for our password evaluation efforts. How you get the password file and what the file name is depend on the operating systems involved. Windows 95/98 differs from Windows NT, which is different from Windows 2000/XP/2003, which in turn is different from *any* UNIX or Linux system. With UNIX, Linux, and BSD systems, it's a bit easier since the password file and shadowed (inaccessible by nonroot users) password file are normally stored in a uniform place (/etc/).

To obtain the password file from a Windows machine, which on Windows is called the Security Accounts Manager (SAM) file, administrator access is required. You should also know whether it is an Active Directory (AD) server, or a workstation, or whatever the role of the system is. Access to the password file, and access to an accurate password file, depends on this information. If the machine is not an AD server, access to the password file is much easier. If it *is* an AD server, you have to run the password-gathering tool as a domain administrator (not only a local administrator account) from the console of the server using a tool such as pwdump3 (pwdump and pwdump2 will not work in that situation). Normally, the SAM file is stored in %SYSTEMROOT%\System32\Config\SAM, and a backup is maintained in %SYSTEMROOT%\Repair\sam.

Access to the password file(s) in UNIX, Linux, or BSD (we'll refer to all OSs in this category as *UNIX*) systems is more uniform, at least in terms of the location of the relevant files. The files needed from a UNIX system are /etc/passwd and /etc/shadow. Example output is shown here. This is from a Solaris 10 system:

```
-bash-3.00$ uname -a
SunOS monstersun 5.10 Generic sun4u sparc SUNW,Ultra-4
-bash-3.00$ ls -lsa /etc/passwd /etc/shadow
   1 -rw-r--r--    1 root            680 May 12 12:25 /etc/passwd
   1 -r--------    1 root            375 May 12 12:26 /etc/shadow
```

Notice that everyone on the system has access to at least read the /etc/passwd file, and read access is granted only to root for the /etc/shadow file. These file permissions are important to note. Nonprivileged processes might need to do a user lookup in /etc/passwd, but all that is stored in the /etc/shadow file are the usernames and passwords. So it's safe to limit access to the /etc/shadow file to root only, which is what the login process runs as. So permissions are set safely and properly on these files. That's why you require administrator or root-level access to conduct some of the evaluation tasks.

Next we get into the password-compliance testing tools in the following section.

Password-Compliance Testing Tools

There are several password-compliance testing tools. Some are commercial, and some are open source. Additionally, some of the tools do more than just crack passwords; some gather the passwords from the local system for you, some get the passwords from the network, and some tools require you to provide the password file. In fact, some password-cracking tools will do all these things.

Let's look at some examples of password-compliance testing tools, but we won't go into the gory details of each tool, since they all basically do the same thing. Some tools are better than others, and some just cost more.

One of best-known "password auditing and recovery applications" (another term for password-cracking utility) is LC5, the latest version of L0phtCrack by @stake (recently acquired by Symantec; www.atstake.com). LC5 is a fast password-cracking tool, with support for scheduled password audits, cracking Windows and UNIX passwords, remote password auditing, international character support, and password quality scoring (see Figure 10.2).

Next is an open source project called ophcrack 2.0 (see Figure 10.3). You can find this project at http://ophcrack.sourceforge.net. It's called the *time-memory tradeoff cracker* because it relies on the precomputed hash tables already being in memory. So, by sacrificing memory, the password-cracking time is drastically decreased. The ophcrack Web site offers the option to submit a Windows password or Windows password hash to be cracked. The speed at which this tool works is pretty awesome. Here are some statistics from the ophcrack Web site:

Figure 10.2 An LC5 Screen Capture

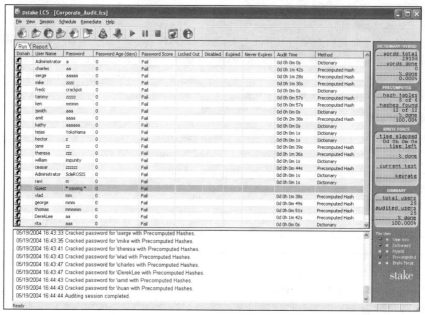

- Average running time for the demo using table set SSTIC04-2.7k (1.1GB)
- Alphanumeric passwords: 1.67 seconds
- Passwords with one nonalphanumeric half: 26.14 seconds
- Passwords with two nonalphanumeric halves (not cracked): 42.14 seconds

Figure 10.3 An ophcrack Screen Capture

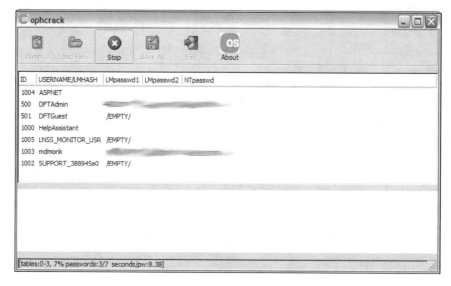

Another popular open source password cracker called John the Ripper is available at www.openwall.com/john/ (see Figure 10.4). John the Ripper is a command-line password cracker that runs on several different architectures. Its primary purpose, according to the John Web site, is to detect weak UNIX passwords. Not only does John the Ripper handle password files from UNIX, it can crack Kerberos AFS passwords and Windows NT/2000/XP/2003 LM hashes. OpenWall also has word lists (dictionary files) available on its site.

Figure 10.4 A John the Ripper Screen Capture

Even though some of the vulnerability scanners on the market will also do password gathering and cracking for you, this is still an activity an evaluation team member should conduct with a dedicated password-cracking tool. You might encounter an organization that doesn't want password cracking conducted, and that is their right to refuse that portion of the evaluation, as long as the reasons are documented and signed off on. But I offer this as a (hopefully) convincing argument if the organization doesn't want you to conduct password-compliance testing: I was part of a team performing an evaluation at an organization in which password-compliance testing was a required task. Of 585 Active Directory accounts, I was able to obtain the password for 174 of the accounts in the first 60 seconds. This isn't an exceptional number, either; it's a fairly accurate representation of end-user password strength (or lack thereof) in most organizations.

Application-Specific Scanning

Application-specific scanning is where we get to more closely analyze some of the network-available applications. Each app scanner is designed to evaluate certain applications, and it usually does that application very well. Unfortunately, no single app scanner will fill all scanning needs. Remember to tailor your INFOSEC tool set to the evaluation requirements. For example, if there are no Oracle instances to be evaluated, you probably wouldn't need to bring in your Oracle database guru.

The DMZ

Previously I mentioned DMZ devices. When I say "DMZ-hosted devices," I am referring to devices or servers that are specifically hosted in the organization's DMZ. Examples of these types of devices are Web servers, e-mail servers, and SMTP gateways. *DMZ* stands for *demilitarized zone* and refers to the area where Internet-facing, trusted servers are hosted. Note that having a DMZ is optional; an organization might not have one. We mention DMZs specifically because there is overlap with these devices. They will be scanned during the vulnerability scanning phase and checked during the host analysis phase, so we should have a very good idea of what these servers are made up of. To complete the picture, we have to run specific checks and scans against the applications themselves—hence the term *application-specific scanning*.

Types of Applications to Be Scanned

Since quite a bit of the work has already been completed (or at least started) during other activities of the IEM, all that's left for the server-side evaluations is to finish with the application checks. During this part of the evaluation, we check out the database instances, e-mail server/services, Web server/services, and any proprietary applications the organization is using. We're looking for vulnerabilities and configuration errors with the applications and services themselves.

The categories of application to be scanned are databases, Web servers, e-mail servers, and proprietary applications. Many of the vulnerability scanners and host evaluation activities have already taken care of most of the required checks, and all that's left are the checks specific to the type of application.

For databases, we check the access and authorization mechanisms, privilege assignments, the access control methods, and the auditing that is enabled. We check database versions and patch levels to ensure that everything is properly patched and up to date. We also verify that default accounts do not have the default passwords still in place. With databases, disasters quickly follow when password management and access controls are lacking. The most used attack vector with databases is SQL injection.

> ## Notes from the Underground...
>
> ### SQL Injection Defined
>
> SQL injection is a hacking technique for exploiting Web-enabled applications that use client-supplied data as input in SQL queries, without doing any taint checking of the input and stripping out potentially harmful characters prior to executing the SQL query.

For e-mail servers, as with most Internet-facing servers, the most common attack vector is buffer overflow attacks. Additionally, with e-mail servers, one of our essential evaluation tasks is to ensure that the e-mail server isn't acting as an open relay. Usually an e-mail server would act as an open relay due to a server misconfiguration. By open relay, we mean an e-mail server that will send e-mail for a client, even if the client isn't authorized to send e-mail via that server. We'll check application versions and patch levels to ensure that the application is properly patched and up to date.

Web servers are probably the most commonly attacked servers; they require us to pay special attention to these devices. Approximately 75 percent of all security incidents are targeted at Web applications. They can be a weak link in the organization's infrastructure and are quite often used by malicious hackers as "jumping-off points" into the organization and to launch network attacks. Web servers are usually attacked using buffer overflow attack, or cross-site scripting attacks, so these are the primary issues we check when evaluating Web servers.

Now let's briefly look at a few of the application-specific scanning tools. The tools are fairly straightforward and generally provide excellent output for your evaluation reports and evidence gathering.

WebInspect, by SPI-Dynamics (www.spidynamics.com/products/webinspect/), is a Web application-scanning tool. It simulates many Web-based application attacks such as cross-site scripting attacks, parameter manipulation, brute-force attacks, and many others (see Figure 10.5). It's a pricey product, but it is *very* good at what it does.

Next up is an open source app called Wikto, which is an extended version of Nikto, written for the .NET environment (see Figure 10.6). Wikto/Nikto can do something other application scanners cannot do: It comes with the Google Hacking Database (GHDB). This allows you to check Google for information it might have concerning the servers you are scanning. This is a very cool, and very useful, feature.

Figure 10.5 A SPI Dynamics WebInspect Screen Capture

Figure 10.6 Wikto in Action

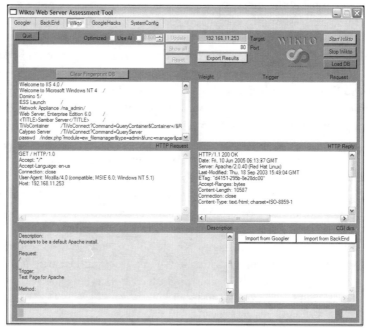

There are many other application-specific scanners, but we're limited on the amount of space we can dedicate to this area. We have given you a brief introduction to the application-scanning tool genre. To ensure that your application-specific scanning needs are met, you'll need to do some research into these various tools yourself.

Network Protocol Analysis

Network protocol analysis is an activity that might not always be conducted during the IEM process due to the privacy issues involved. When you are analyzing network traffic at the protocol level, you are seeing everything (unless it's encrypted). All the cleartext protocols are captured and decoded for you to view. This bothers some organizations. It is something to keep in mind when you're conducting the evaluation. If the organization permits network protocol analysis, you need to ensure that all data you gather and information you see is considered proprietary and subject to your nondisclosure agreement. If you have questions about anything you see during network scanning, consult your team lead. The NSA IEM urges organizations to consider conducting the network analysis during an evaluation, and for that reason it is considered one of the 10 baseline activities.

Why Perform Network Protocol Analysis?

As an evaluation activity, network analysis is important for validation of previously gathered results, for locating potential "hot spots" in the organization's network, and for detecting cleartext protocols in use (such as Telnet, FTP, IMAP, and POP3). "Hot spots" are areas of a network that are highly congested or under a heavy network traffic load. Network "hot spots" are issues that an organization should be aware of but might not be. The help desk could get calls from end users saying "E-mail is slow" or "The Internet is slow," and other signs of network congestion may pop up. But without looking at the network traffic and mapping the traffic patterns, it would be very difficult for an organization to diagnose the network problems. They would appear as somewhat random network outages/events. A network protocol analyzer can provide evidence needed to resolve network issues. Therefore, that can be a good selling point when you encounter organizations that are being difficult about having network-level protocol analysis done as part of the IEM.

Introducing Network Protocol Analyzers

Prior to starting up your network traffic analyzer, check to see if it is a switched environment. What we mean by "switched environment" is one in which network switches are used rather than network hubs. A switched network is more efficient, but it also foils our network analysis activities. You will have to get the network administrator to set up a "spanned port" for you. This will permit your network analyzer to see all the network traffic crossing that switch.

> **NOTE**
>
> Ensure that the port configuration is returned to normal (not spanned) or disabled after you are finished with the network protocol capture and analysis. Usually it's a good idea to notify the customer POC and team lead when you are finished.

We mention only a few of the available network protocol analyzers here, since most accomplish the same activities and tasks in similar fashions. We briefly introduce you to some of the popular protocol analyzers (you'll thank us later for not going over them all).

The first network analyzer we'll mention is Ethereal (http://ethereal.com/). This is a very popular open source network protocol analysis tool. Even though it's free, Ethereal has all the standard features you would see in a commercial-grade protocol analyzer (see Figure 10.7), and some features you won't find in the commercial ones. Personally, we use Ethereal quite often. It's a reliable network analysis tool and very feature-rich—and arguably the best open source protocol analyzers available today.

Figure 10.7 The Ethereal Packet Decode Window

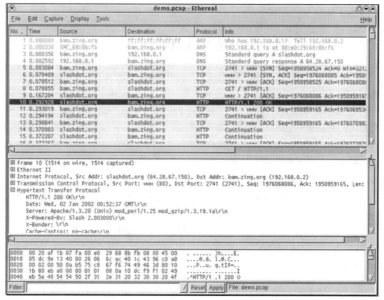

Another protocol analyzer is EtherPeek NX from WildPackets (www.wildpackets.com/products/etherpeek_nx). EtherPeek NX claims to be the first protocol analyzer to offer both frame decoding and expert analysis in real time during packet capture. Figure 10.8 is a screen capture showing EtherPeek NX during a packet capture; Figure 10.9 shows EtherPeek NX offering its expert analysis.

As you can probably see just from these few screen captures, protocol analyzers share a fairly common interface or look and have a common feature set. Protocol analysis has been around for quite a while and isn't a very lively technology area; it's seen no really new innovations in recent times. Nearly any protocol analyzer should fit your needs as long as it provides the standard protocol analyzer functionality. Oh yeah, and it has to have cool colorful gauges, too. (Not really.)

Figure 10.8 An EtherPeek NX Sample Packet Capture

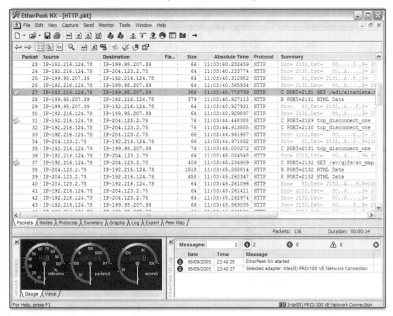

Figure 10.9 EtherPeek NX Expert Analysis and Problem Detection

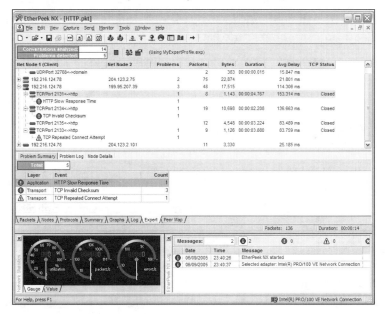

Summary

In this chapter we completed the technical portion of the INFOSEC Evaluation Methodology. We did an evaluation/analysis of all network devices, including firewalls, routers, and IDSs. We conducted password-compliance testing, also known as password cracking. We discussed application-specific scanning and how it supplements the results from our vulnerability scans and host evaluations. Finally we examined network protocol analysis and its role in the IEM. We covered quite a bit of material and concepts, but it was a fun ride.

It's important for you to remember that all these tasks are in support of the IEM process. Nothing is standalone; all tasks have a purpose. As mentioned in the previous chapter, this section requires more thought and interaction than you perhaps initially thought. It can be an eye-opener once you see the amount of manual work ahead of you during an evaluation.

Solutions Fast Track

Network Device Analysis

☑ Not all firewalls are created equal. Some are stateful firewalls, some are packet-filtering firewalls, and some are application-proxy firewalls. Each type may react differently to your scans and evaluation efforts.

☑ Border routers with lots of ACLs and packet filtering in place do not take the place of a proper firewall—no matter what the resident router jock says.

☑ To get a more complete view of the organization's perimeter and INFOSEC posture, you must conduct the network device analysis using two approaches: the design approach and the technical approach.

Password-Compliance Testing

☑ There are three types of password-compliance testing methods or attacks: dictionary, brute-force, and hybrid.

☑ You are testing the organization's compliance with its password policies and procedures. It's not a race to see how many passwords you can crack.

☑ Different password file-retrieval methods are used depending on whether a Microsoft Windows machine is an Active Directory server or a normal Windows server. AD servers store the Active Directory tree in a secure portion of memory and require a tool such as pwdump3 to extract the information you need for your password-compliance testing.

Application-Specific Scanning

☑ The host operating system might be secured, but if the application is unpatched or has security holes, the server is still vulnerable.

☑ Application-specific scanners are brought in for the evaluation because they do their job well. Each is designed to scan its own niche of applications and scan them well. Stock your INFOSEC toolbox accordingly.

☑ Not all application issues can be patched or solved with the application itself. Sometimes other risk-mitigation techniques must be utilized to ensure that the organization's infrastructure is protected.

Network Protocol Analysis

☑ Check to see whether you are evaluating components on a switched network. If you are, get a spanned port set up on the switch for your network analysis activities.

☑ Look for network "hot spots," or points of network congestion.

☑ Look for cleartext protocols such as Telnet, FTP, SMTP, and SNMP.

Frequently Asked Questions

The following Frequently Asked Questions, answered by the authors of this book, are designed to both measure your understanding of the concepts presented in this chapter and to assist you with real-life implementation of these concepts. To have your questions about this chapter answered by the author, browse to **www.syngress.com/solutions** and click on the **"Ask the Author"** form. You will also gain access to thousands of other FAQs at ITFAQnet.com.

Q: How many approaches are there in the evaluation of network devices?

A: For the INFOSEC Evaluation Methodology, we use two approaches to network device analysis: the design approach and the technical approach. The design approach evaluates the design of an organization's perimeter and defenses. The technical approach evaluates the security configuration and settings of network devices.

Q: Briefly, what are the differences between a stateful inspection firewall, a packet-filtering firewall, and application proxies?

A: A stateful inspection firewall can look at the entire packet to make (firewall) policy decisions based on packet contents and the packet context. The firewall tracks active connections in a "state table." A packet-filtering firewall screens all network traffic at the network and transport layers of the TCP/IP stack. Application proxies act as "middlemen" for connectivity between clients and servers. They take the connection requests from the clients and make the connection to the appropriate server/application on the client's behalf.

Q: How long should I let the password-compliance tool run? How many cracked passwords are required?

A: There is no requirement for a certain number of cracked passwords. At least, the methodology does not require a certain number or percentage of cracked passwords. Twelve hours is an average amount of time to let your password-cracking tool run. If a password holds up after 12 hours, it can probably be assumed to be a decent password. Plus, by the end of 12 hours, you will likely have a large percentage of the password file cracked.

Q: What is the best way to view and locate network "hot spots" when using a network protocol analyzer?

A: With most network protocol analyzers, a matrix view is available. This view permits you to see all active "conversations" as lines between hosts. This will allow you to see which hosts are the top talkers and which are slowing the network down.

Q: For all the baseline activities, you recommend two tools be used per activity. Does this hold true in all cases?

A: Actually, no. For the password-compliance testing activity, only one tool is required and recommended.

Q: Are there other activities not on the baseline activities list that I can do for an evaluation?

A: Of course! The baseline activities list is just that—a list of the baseline, or minimum required, activities necessary for the IEM. Some activities come with warning labels, though. The following three activities are available but not part of the baseline due to the activities' invasiveness: penetration testing, war dialing, and denial-of-service (DoS) tests.

Chapter 11

The Onsite Closing Meeting

Solutions in this chapter:

- **Organizing the Meeting**
- **TEP Overview**
- **Setting Timelines**
- **Overview of Critical Findings**
- **Points of Immediate Resolution**
- **What Do You Do with the Information You Have Collected?**

☑ **Summary**

☑ **Solutions Fast Track**

☑ **Frequently Asked Questions**

Introduction

You have been working side by side with many individuals from your customer organization and performing multiple technical tests. Now it's time to close out the onsite phase of the IEM. These individuals are curious and possibly nervous about what the evaluation team has been doing and the types of things being discovered. In this chapter we discuss the *out-brief meeting* that you'll hold with the customer. The purpose of the out-brief is to present an overview of critical findings that you identified during the onsite activity, provide immediate resolution for the findings, address any customer concerns, and communicate the timelines and status to the customer. You will gain some valuable insight into ways to successfully organize and conduct the out-brief meeting and demonstrate the IEM's business value to the customer.

Organizing the Meeting

"Begin with the end in mind" is a truism that captures the essence of the planning process for the customer out-brief meeting. It is important that you look at the TEP to check the onsite schedule and start preparing for the out-brief meeting ahead of time. Planning ahead for the meeting is essential to having a successful out-brief. Take the time to determine when the meeting will be held, where it will be held, who will attend, what information will be presented, and how the meeting will be conducted.

TIP

To allow you and your team enough time to prepare a successful out-brief meeting, we recommend that you start preparing three to five days ahead of the scheduled meeting.

Time and Location

You will find that it can be a challenge to set the final time and location for the out-brief meeting. The size and scope of the evaluation tends to determine the number of people who need to be involved in the out-brief. In bringing a group of people together, you must take many factors into account. Work closely with the organization POC to help select a day and time that will accommodate all attendees' work schedules. Most of the time, the in-brief meeting attendees will also be involved with the out-brief meeting and should be forewarned. Depending on the number of findings, the meeting typically is one to two hours in length. Having breaks and refreshments during the meeting can help create a successful and comfortable meeting.

The meeting location should be central and convenient for the most important attendees. Most organizations require that conference rooms be reserved ahead of time. The room should be able to accommodate all attendees as well as provide conferencing capabilities for remote attendees. Try to visit the scheduled room several days before the meeting to see its layout and identify any equipment and special needs for the meeting.

WARNING

During the out-brief meeting, you will be discussing critical security findings that should be considered sensitive and be protected. We once had a customer who scheduled the out-brief in their company lunchroom during lunch hour! Not only was the noise level unbearable, it was difficult to be discreet about our findings from the evaluation.

Evaluation Team and Customer Involvement

During the evaluation, you will work with many different individuals from the customer organization. Work closely with your POC to identify the individuals who need to be invited to the out-brief meeting and the ones it might be best to avoid inviting. Not only is the out-brief the time to share the evaluation findings and recommendations—it is also the time to close any remaining items or issues that were brought up during the onsite activities. Each company that offers the IEM will go about managing engagement in its own way. The following sections highlight the individuals who should attend the meeting.

The Customer

You might not have input into who should be involved with the out-brief, but it is important to try to get as many people from the customer side, to ensure that there are no surprises at the end of the evaluation. Sometimes final evaluation outcomes are not presented to the people who need them the most to make the necessary security improvements. The out-brief can provide a great forum for knowledge transfer of valuable security information from the evaluation team to the customer team. You will want the following people at the meeting:

- The **POC** is the person who represents the organization and who interfaces with the evaluation team from start to completion of the IEM evaluation.

- **Upper management** representatives can help gauge company risk tolerances on presented critical findings and can provide management guidance on following the evaluation recommendations to the rest of the organization. Having at least one upper-management representative involved in your out-brief ensures that all disputes will be resolved and all recommendations approved and managed by a business owner.

- Key **security management and staff** will need to know the outcome of the evaluation and be able to continue to support other organization staff members in resolving the evaluation findings.

- Key **network management and engineers** for all network-related findings need to attend.

- Key **system management and administrators** for all platforms and systems targeted during the evaluation need to attend.

- **Contract personnel** ensure that all deliverables up to this point have been met.

The Evaluation Team

Although it's not required, it is recommended that you never have more people from your organization than the customer has present. You don't want to intimidate and/or overwhelm the customer. You will want the following people from your company at the meeting:

- The **evaluation team** that performed the evaluation. If not all members are available, we recommend that you have the evaluation team lead there to represent the team.

- The **sales contact** who routinely interfaces with the customer and was the one who sold them the evaluation. By having this person involved, you can provide additional training for future sales opportunities as well as provide a "check and balance" to keep the sales process clean and honest. We're not saying that salespeople are dishonest, but we have seen instances where more was promised initially than was or could be delivered. The involvement of the salesperson helps build trust and furthers the relationship with the customer by providing a level of comfort that the evaluation was performed and controlled as expected.

Presentation Needs

How your message is received relies on he way it is delivered. Studies have shown that people remember 50 percent of what they see and hear. To successfully get your message across in your meeting, you should use several visual tools:

- **PowerPoint** This is a great visual aid for enhancing a presentation, but it can negatively impact the message you are trying to convey if it's not used correctly. Be sure to create a backup copy of your presentation on a CD, disk, or Flash drive!

- **Whiteboard or flip chart** These are great tools for highlighting and illustrating key points of your presentation, especially for drawing recommended network architectural changes. Be sure in advance that all markers work and that you have an eraser for the whiteboard.

- **Handouts** These are ideal for allowing people to follow along with your presentation. Print your PowerPoint slides using the Handout format with three slides per page. This will allow enough room on the right side of each slide for note taking, and it condenses the amount of paper needed for copies.

If you plan to use a PowerPoint presentation, you might need to provide one or more of the following types of equipment:

- **Laptop** For running the presentation. A fully charged battery should be able to get you through most meetings.

- **Overhead projector** Might be provided by the customer. As you plan for the out-brief meeting, check with the organization POC, if one will be available. You might have to provide the projector yourself. Additionally, check that the scheduled room has a projection screen or, at a minimum, a blank wall.

- **Laptop wireless remote** This is not required but is recommended. We have been in rooms where the presentation laptop was in the back of the room while the presenter was at the front of the room. Additionally, some remotes have a laser pointer that can be used to highlight key points in the slides.

TIP

Use the following presentation tips to "professionalize" and visually enhance your presentation. Be careful not to include too many types of visuals in your presentation. You want your message, not the visuals, to be the focus of your presentation:

1. Be consistent from slide to slide by using the same font size and format.
2. Make each slide easy to read. The title of the page should summarize your message with a maximum of bulleted key items.
3. Use color to emphasize facts and ideas.
4. Choose the right font size. We've attended too many presentations that could not be seen by the majority of the audience.
5. Avoid using too many animations and graphics in your presentation. They should be used to help convey and emphasize your message, not distract the audience from it.

The Agenda

Preparing an agenda for the out-brief is no different from doing so for any other business meeting. The out-brief cannot be everything to everyone, but you should know who will be attending the meeting, since that information will be helpful in preparing your agenda. Having a clear agenda provides an outline for the meeting and can be used as a checklist to make sure that all areas of the TEP are covered. Key things to focus on in creating the agenda are assigning a time limit for each discussion item (and sticking to it), the types of topics you plan to cover, and start and stop times for the meeting. Once the agenda is complete, have the organization POC distribute copies to all attendees at least a day in advance. The agenda items will include:

- Reviewing the TEP and how the overall evaluation was accomplished
- Reviewing critical findings and immediate resolutions

- Reviewing timelines and expectations for the rest of the evaluation process
- Question and answer session

TEP Overview

You began the onsite activities with an in-brief meeting, where the Technical Evaluation Plan (TEP) was reviewed with the organization's staff and the evaluation team. The TEP is a living document that is used as a key management tool for the entire evaluation process. It contains the objectives and goals of the evaluation, boundaries of testing, and customer concerns and constraints that should be addressed during the evaluation. Reviewing the TEP during the out-brief meeting can ensure that the evaluation team addressed all fundamental areas of the TEP and will help communicate the overall comprehensiveness of the evaluation process.

The Evaluation Process

The IEM is a structured, flexible, yet repeatable process for performing technical evaluations for any organization. Many of the attendees of the out-brief have probably never been exposed to a technical evaluation. If they have been involved with a security audit or vulnerability assessment, it is more than likely that they have not been involved with the IEM process. It is important that you spend enough time educating your audience about the process that they come away with an understanding of the way information was collected and analyzed.

How Was Information Collected?

It is important to cover the 10 baseline activities of the IEM for collecting technical information and discuss what each activity is trying to accomplish. Some customers will ask for additional activities outside the 10 baseline IEM activities; be sure to cover those as well. This is also a good time to discuss any technical testing constraints that occurred during the evaluation as well as established network and system boundaries defined in the TEP.

The Tools

For various reasons, some people think it is taboo to discuss the tools that were used during technical testing. Let's face it—this is not rocket science! Many Internet sites and reference books explain how to use the majority of testing tools. The out-brief provides a great opportunity to demonstrate your expertise with these tools to your customer. Give a brief explanation of each tool used, in what phase of the process the tool was used, and how the tool was used.

While we are on this topic, it is imperative that you know how each tool works. That does not mean that you have to understand each switch that can be passed to the tool, though that's important; we mean that you should understand how the tool elicits and evaluates responses from systems and applications. Does the tool make assumptions? Are there any technical limitations that can cause unreliable results for the tool? When no switches are used for the tool, what default settings are used? Will the tool work on a subnet or just a single host? Rely on your experience as a tester; don't always rely on the output of your tools. They can sometimes mislead you in how they interpret responses from systems. How do you know whether the host that you are testing remotely is responding? Maybe it is a router or a firewall response.

Customer Documentation

All customer documentation that was collected during the evaluation should be briefly discussed in terms of the way the information was used during the onsite activities and how it will be used during the post-evaluation phase. In some situations, the evaluation team could receive new or supporting documents as late as this meeting. This is the case when an individual has forgotten to provide documentation to the evaluation team in support of a finding that is presented during the meeting. It is recommended that you have all customer documentation present during the meeting, in case it needs to be used as a reference or if the customer needs to verify version information. We have received older versions of customer documentation in organizations that lack version control. The types of documentation that you might have collected could include, but is not limited to:

- INFOSEC policies, procedures, and standards for implementing security at the organization
- Customer inventory sheets to help identify rogue systems and critical components
- Architectural diagrams illustrating firewall, IDS, router, switch, wireless, and DMZ layouts for identification of physical and logical boundaries, critical paths, and architectural weaknesses
- System configurations for networking equipment (router, switch, wireless, etc.)
- Firewall rules (host and network), proxy rules, router ACLs
- Password files for password-compliance testing
- Application-specific configuration files (Web server, DNS, SMTP, etc.)
- Organizational and system criticality documentation, if the customer has been through an IAM

Customer Concerns

Managing customer expectations and concerns is critical during the out-brief meeting. Have the customer concerns been met, or will the evaluation results conflict with the organization's goals, expectations, and concerns? The TEP will provide initial concerns and expectations from the customer perspective as well as the evaluation team's. Keep notes on additional concerns that arise during the evaluation activities and during the out-brief meeting. They should be addressed during the meeting and in your final report.

What Is Driving the Evaluation?

It is imperative that the entire evaluation team understand the reason the customer wants the evaluation. Don't assume that organizations in the same industry have identical concerns. Each organization is unique, with different strategies, tactics, and risk tolerances. The following are some concerns that we have seen in past evaluation experiences:

- Regulation and standards compliance (Sarbanes-Oxley [SOX], HIPAA, GLBA, FISMA)
- The organization had a recent security incident
- A competitor had a recent security incident
- Meeting security objectives
- Insurance requirements
- Partner requirements
- The organization is starting to build a security practice and will use the evaluation findings as a road map

Customer Constraints

For a number of reasons, the evaluation team will not be allowed to perform various types of testing, or testing may be limited to specific dates and times that have limited impact on the customer mission. This can make it difficult to gather the information required to perform a comprehensive evaluation. Not all participants in the meeting will be aware of the constraints. It is recommended that in the out-brief meeting, the presenter cover these constraints as well as the impact of those restrictions on the evaluation. One example is when the evaluation team is able to identify a finding but not validate it because of constraints that the customer has placed on the evaluation.

Protecting Testing Data

Customer information gathered during the IEM process should be protected at all times. The last thing you and the customer want is to have information about their vulnerabilities leaked into the public forum because you didn't protect the information. Not only does it expose the customer to potential malicious activity, it could bring a lawsuit against you and the company you work for. The following recommendations provide guidance on how to ensure protection of your customer's sensitive and proprietary data:

- Encrypt all communications between your firm and the customer that could contain sensitive information regarding the evaluation activities.
- Keep all communications about the client internal to the evaluation team and your customer POC.

- Use encryption on all systems to protect customer data that is collected during the evaluation.

- Keep all paper documents locked in a secure location.

Setting Timelines

As with any engagement, we need to identify timelines and keep track of milestones during the evaluation. Keeping the customer updated on your progress during the evaluation can help you manage customer expectations and adds a level of professionalism to the evaluation team efforts. During the out-brief meeting, you want to present an outline of the timelines that have been established for the evaluation. Cover all major milestones that have been accomplished, as well as ones that you've failed to meet, and what the customer should expect during the post-evaluation phase.

Important Events During Testing

Covering important events that occurred during testing allows you to communicate the comprehensiveness of the IEM process to the customer without "tooting your own horn." The customer wants to know that work was performed and what they are paying for. Services are less tangible than products and are based on status reports and the final deliverable. Communicating details about the process ensures that the organization appreciates the value of the evaluation service. The larger the evaluation, the more events you will have. Some key events that should be covered are:

- When the onsite phase began and ended

- Onsite visits, if multiple sites are being evaluated

- When key interviews were performed

- When each of the 10 baseline activities began and ended

- When specific goals and concerns were met—for example, incident response to scanning activities

Final Report Delivery

The out-brief meeting is used wrap up the onsite activities and to communicate critical findings discovered during this phase. It is important to discuss the timelines for the post-evaluation process and the point at which the customer should expect delivery of the final report. In most cases, the customer can expect to receive the report within two to six weeks after the out-brief meeting. This delivery date varies based on the size of the evaluation that is being performed and the amount of information that needs to be analyzed.

Briefly outline the document structure of the final report. Most organizations expect to see an executive summary that will not contain a lot of technical detail as well as a technical section that can be used by the organization's technical staff members. Find out how detailed should the report be. When making recommendations, can you summarize, or does it have to be a step by step? How will the customer expect to receive raw tool output? Will there be a CD? Will the customer want to know which tool was used to identify the finding for validation after the recommended fix has been implemented?

Overview of Critical Findings

Up to this point in the out-brief, you have provided a brief summary of the IEM process, discussed customer concerns and expectations, and covered important events that happened during the onsite evaluation. Now it is time to specifically discuss the critical findings discovered during the evaluation. Show the customer what you have found and discuss why each finding is considered a critical finding for the organization. For each finding, offer multiple recommendations to either mitigate or minimize the impact of the vulnerability on the organization. The majority of the time allocated for the out-brief meeting should be spent discussing the findings and recommendations.

You might be asking, "What is a critical finding?" In the following chapters, you will find detailed information on organizing and analyzing all the data you collected as well as creating the system vulnerability criticality matrix (SVCM) and the overall vulnerability criticality matrix (OVCM). The SVCM and OVCM will be used to provide a detailed analysis of the information security posture of each system based on the technical rating of each vulnerability and the organizational and system criticality rankings defined during the IAM process.

In the out-brief, you will not offer this type of detailed analysis. Each vulnerability will be given a risk rating, with a High, Medium, or Low label, using industry standards for technical vulnerabilities. You will find that most vulnerability scanners have in their signature databases predefined ratings for every vulnerability. Make sure you understand how the vendor of each tool has decided on these ratings. It is recommended that you use multiple vulnerability scanners. You will sometimes find that each scanner has a different rating for the same vulnerability. This is where your expertise as a security professional comes into play to offer a final technical rating. Some things to consider when you have to perform a rating analysis are discussed in the following sections.

How Does the Vulnerability Impact the System?

Vulnerability impacts more than just the system itself—it is about how a vulnerability can affect the way the system supports the organization's mission and objectives. The initial impact of a vulnerability will affect the system or the data on the system in one of three ways:

- Loss of confidentiality
- Loss of integrity
- Loss of availability

What Is the Likelihood That a Threat Will Exploit the Vulnerability?

What type of skill would a threat need to have to take advantage of the vulnerability? Has exploit or proof-of-concept code been published for the vulnerability? Are any worms or viruses in existence that use the vulnerability as an attack vector? Is the system Internet facing? Does the vulnerability exist on an operational system that could directly impact the customer mission? These key questions can help provide insight into the characteristics associated with each threat and the threat's likelihood of success in exploiting the vulnerability.

Mapping to Business Mission and Objectives

Many companies today follow the old principle of "consulting by the pound," whereby the more information they can throw at the customer, the more value the customer will receive. We have worked with customers for which evaluations were performed in this manner. The organization POC gets a call from the receptionist to pick up a package from her because it will not fit into his mailbox. He stops by the receptionist to find a three- to five-inch-thick report. He starts to review the report, starting at page one and slowly going through each page. As he reaches about page 10 or 15, he starts to speed up. By the time he ends at the last page, he can't recall what he just read because the majority of the report was tool output. Overwhelmed by the report, the POC ends up stashing it on a shelf to be used as a bookend, never to be used for its intended purpose. Sound familiar?

After gaining some experience by performing multiple IEM evaluations, you will find common vulnerabilities across many organizations and multiple systems in each organization. Yet each finding will have varying influences on the security posture and risk to the organization. The IEM takes into account the mission function of each system and the way the loss of confidentiality, integrity, or availability of the system would affect the organization's mission. This is one of the main factors differentiating the IEM from other technical methodologies and is the real business value-add of the IEM. To say to a customer, "We discovered 10 High vulnerabilities in your environment" is not as practical as saying "We discovered 10 High vulnerabilities, and eight of those were identified on eight mission-critical systems." We recommend that you present each finding in this manner because it provides a much stronger frame of reference for the customer.

Positive vs. Negative Findings

To this point, we have been discussing findings that have a negative impact on the organization. Be wary of merely presenting negative findings in the out-brief. You could get someone in the meeting asking, "Geez, are we doing anything positive?!" You also don't want to make individuals look bad. This can cause tension and hostility in the meeting, and if you're invited back, you will not receive any cooperation from these individuals. You are there to help the organization, and presenting positive findings, in addition to the negative findings, will help convey the nonattribution characteristics of the IEM.

Points of Immediate Resolution

For every finding you present, you should provide multiple recommendations to help minimize the impact of or mitigate the finding. These recommendations should be based on the organization's security policy, industry best practices, industry standards, and any regulations that the organization must comply with. Providing multiple remediation solutions to the organization will assist them in determining the best way to deal with the risk of the finding. Take into account any customer constraints, such as cost, that will impact the types of solutions you will introduce. Presenting recommendations that fly in the face of known constraints provides no value to the customer.

Short Term vs. Long Term

When a report is generated by a vulnerability scanner, you will find the recommended fixes are geared toward "quick-fix" solutions: "Implement patch from vendor"; "Change this registry setting"; "Limit access to this port." We all know what happens when we apply "Band-Aid" fixes to problems—you might stop the bleeding but not fix the symptom!

Identifying the same technical finding across multiple systems in an environment can be indicative of a weakness in a policy or procedure or that someone failed to follow a process. For example, installing a patch across multiple systems is a great short-term fix, but a long-term fix is to review the organization's patch management process (if they have one) to look for any weaknesses. Maybe you are seeing the same configuration management issue across multiple systems. Tie your solutions into the organization's information security policy. By doing so, you will assist the organization in dealing with each findings immediately as well as identify long-term solutions that will ultimately assist the organization in reducing risk. Remember, many of these organizational types of findings will be discovered during the IAM process, allowing the IEM process to verify whether the system really works as documented or intended.

What Do You Do With the Information That You Have Collected?

Your out-brief meeting was successful, and it is time for you to go back to the office to start the post-evaluation process. Be sure that you have all the documentation you need from the organization and that you have all the technical raw output from each tool that was used during the evaluation. The next step is to protect all the customer information before you leave the site. Encrypt all data on testing systems and removable media. All customer documentation that is considered sensitive should be stored in a lockbox. Make backups of encrypted data. The last thing that you would want is that you show up at the office to find that your testing system will not boot!

Summary

We have covered a lot of topics in this chapter. Please remember that the out-brief is usually only one to two hours long, depending on the size of the assessment. The out-brief provides the evaluation team with a way to communicate what has been done up to this point in the evaluation, the types of critical findings identified, the way each finding impacts the customer, the type of solutions that can be implemented to minimize the impact or mitigate each finding, and when to expect the final report from the evaluation. You don't want to leave the customer site with unanswered questions or surprises.

Solutions Fast Track

Organizing the Meeting

- ☑ Select a time and location that will be convenient for all out-brief meeting attendees.
- ☑ Work closely with your POC to identify who should be invited to attend the meeting as well as who should not.
- ☑ Know your presentation needs before you schedule the meeting, to ensure that all needs can be accommodated.
- ☑ Create an agenda for the meeting and send it to all invitees to help monitor and control expectations.

TEP Overview

- ☑ Understand the true value of the TEP as a key management tool for the IEM process.
- ☑ Communicate what information was collected, how was it collected, and how it will be analyzed.
- ☑ Managing customer expectations and concerns is critical to providing a successful evaluation.

Setting Timelines

- ☑ Covering important events that occurred during testing allows you to communicate the comprehensiveness of the IEM process.
- ☑ Be sure to communicate the points at which major milestones were or were not accomplished .
- ☑ When milestones are not met, it is critical that supporting details about the failure be documented.

Overview of Critical Findings

☑ Show the customer what you have found and discuss why each finding is considered a critical finding for the organization.

☑ The majority of the time allocated for the out-brief meeting should be spent discussing your findings and recommendations.

☑ For each finding, offer multiple recommendations to either mitigate or minimize the impact of the vulnerability to the organization.

☑ You are there to help the organization, and presenting positive findings, in addition to the negative findings, will help convey the nonattribution characteristics of the IEM.

☑ You don't want to leave the customer with unanswered questions or surprises.

Points of Immediate Resolution

☑ Recommendations should be based on the organization's security policy, industry best practices, industry standards, and any regulations that the organization must comply with. Offering both short-term and long-term solutions will ultimately assist the customer in reducing risk in their organization.

☑ Take into account any customer constraints, such as cost, that will impact the types of solutions you will introduce.

What Do You Do with the Information You Have Collected?

☑ Protect all customer information before you leave the site.

☑ Encrypt all data on testing systems and removable media.

☑ Make backups of all collected data.

Frequently Asked Questions

The following Frequently Asked Questions, answered by the authors of this book, are designed to both measure your understanding of the concepts presented in this chapter and to assist you with real-life implementation of these concepts. To have your questions about this chapter answered by the author, browse to **www.syngress.com/solutions** and click on the **"Ask the Author"** form. You will also gain access to thousands of other FAQs at ITFAQnet.com.

Q: Can the out-brief meeting be performed remotely?

A: We have found the out-brief meeting to be more effective if performed onsite because at times you will have to be able to read the body language of individuals to deduce whether they are fully comprehending the presentation.

Q: How do you handle a person who does not understand or agree with one of the evaluation findings?

A: Never get argumentative or defensive when this situation occurs. And it *will* happen to you. Stay calm and discuss the issue with all the attendees in the room. It is your responsibility to stayed unbiased and communicate all findings, with recommendations, to the organization. It is the customer's responsibility to make a decision as to how they want to manage the finding. All reported findings should be based on industry recommendations and standards, which should keep this scenario from happening.

Q: During an evaluation, we found that a system contained pornographic material. How do you communicate this finding without revealing the individual responsible for the activity?

A: This situation must be handled with kid gloves. The nonattribution characteristic of the IEM must be adhered to so that you foster trust and collaboration among all participants. In this situation, or one with a similar outcome, it is best to address it with management only and let them handle the situation according to their company policies.

Q: A customer is asking about a concern that was not addressed during the onsite activities. What should I do?

A: Managing scope creep can be challenging for the evaluation team. What is the individual's role in the organization? Were they involved in the initial evaluation initiation process where scope, concerns, and expectations were defined? Was this concern already documented in the TEP? Due to the comprehensive nature of the IEM, an experienced evaluation team should be able to address additional concerns using the data collected during the evaluation.

Q: We have a small evaluation team that is constantly busy. Is it practical to have all members of the evaluation team present at this meeting?

A: Yes. The out-brief meeting should have been planned and effectively scheduled during the sales and contract process to meet the needs of the customer and the evaluation team. The customer is paying for the expertise of all evaluation members and would like to have access to them during the entire evaluation. When that's not possible, use your creativity to involve all participants in the meeting.

Part III
Post-Evaluation

Chapter 12

Post-Evaluation Analysis

Solutions in this chapter:

- **Getting Organized**
- **Categorization, Consolidation, Correlation, and Consultation**
- **Conducting Additional Research**
- **Analyzing Customer Documentation**
- **Developing Practical Recommendations**

Introduction

If you have been involved in conducting any type of technical assessment or evaluation in the past, you know that such processes can often produce a large amount of data that can take a significant amount of time to organize, analyze, and correlate. You must be able to analyze the data in an efficient amount of time but still be able to provide an accurate and high-quality final report to the customer. Organizing the data collected during the evaluation is a critical component of the post-evaluation phase of the IEM.

The variety of tools used during the evaluation produce raw data in diverse formats. You must be able to organize the evaluation data in ways that make sense to you or are meaningful to the person who will analyze the data so that it can be turned into usable information. The final deliverable is dependent on how you break down the complex raw data collected during the onsite activities into its most basic elements and relationships, then how you are able analyze the data, through the process of categorizing, consolidating, correlating, and consulting, to develop practical and effective solutions for the customer. This chapter walks you through this process.

Getting Organized

At this point, we need to discuss what to do with the data that has been collected. Throughout the onsite evaluation process, the evaluation team identified and verified potential vulnerabilities and weaknesses of the customer's systems. Organizing the raw data that has been collected can be either simple or complicated, depending on the number of people involved in collecting data during the evaluation. The way you organize your data will be up to you or the person who will be performing the final analysis. Each person has different tools and techniques for correlating, analyzing, and understanding the associations between the various evaluation tool results and the evaluation goals. To better understand the various approaches to data organization, let's first look at the types of analysis and reporting needs you have.

Analysis Needs

The first and foremost analysis need is knowledge. Knowledge is not about how much training or how many certifications a person has. Knowledge is individualistic. It is inherent to individuals and is acquired through the natural process of experience and learning. The competence, often referred to as *expertise*, of each evaluation team member is essential to successfully analyze captured data and apply critical problem-solving techniques to guide the customer in making important decisions concerning their information security.

The logical approach to analyzing data depends on a systematic way of organizing the raw results produced by your security tools. The security tools that are most commonly used for evaluations generate a log or report of their findings, typically to a flat file of some format type such as ASCII, PDF, HTML, XML, binary, or RTF. This can be problematic during the analysis process, since these files are frequently viewed and searched. The first step is to organize these data files into a practical structure that will allow you to discern where different types of IEM evaluation data can be found. Once you've amassed all the evaluation raw data, you might consider categorizing the data and utilizing a tree structure for organization, as shown in Figure 12.1.

Figure 12.1 A Tree File Structure for Two Baseline Activities

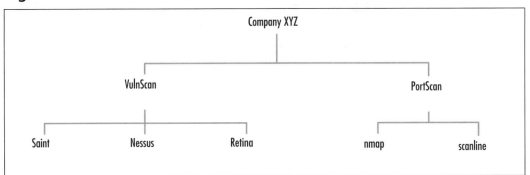

As illustrated, the parent directory is named after the organization for which the evaluation was conducted. Under the parent directory are subdirectories that are mapped to the 10 baseline activities of the IEM. Each baseline directory includes subdirectories that contain the results of each tool employed for that activity during the evaluation. It is recommended that you follow a naming standard for your raw data files for easier identification of their contents. For example, the nmap security tool offers a number of port-scanning types and features. You might name the results file of an nmap TCP SYN scan against a single network something like *SYN_Scan* using the *−oA* nmap switch. When multiple networks are scanned, such as 192.168.1.0/24, 192.168.2.0/24, and 192.168.3.0/24, you might use the following naming standard: *SYN_Scan_Net_1*, *SYN_Scan_Net_2*, *SYN_Scan_Net_3* for each respective scan result. The nomenclature for your raw data files may include perspective and/or boundary information, which we cover later in this chapter.

TIP

To keep from having to change filenames during the analysis process, we advise establishing a naming standard prior to the evaluation so that all members on the evaluation team are utilizing the same standard. It is best to follow the same standard for each evaluation that you perform, to limit any confusion for yourself or any of your team members.

Once your data is organized, you need a way to correlate data among your evaluation tools. Unfortunately, there are no known "point and click" solutions for this task. You will be spending a considerable amount of time reviewing the evaluation raw data and need a means of documenting your findings. Evaluation teams have used the following three approaches to achieve this goal:

- **Spreadsheet approach** Using spreadsheets for data organization, correlation, and tracking is the most common approach used not only by evaluation teams but by companies in general. We have seen Internet service providers (ISPs) use spreadsheets like a database to document and track thousands of pieces of critical customer network connectivity information. Why not? Spreadsheets are easy to use and have minimal training requirements for users. If used properly, they can be used not only to track multiple types of data but also when quantification of data and the creation of graphs are needed. In the following chapters, you will create a system vulnerability criticality matrix (SVCM) and the overall vulnerability criticality matrix (OVCM), which have the appearance and layout of a spreadsheet. It may be only natural to utilize the spreadsheet approach for your data analysis needs. Most spreadsheet packages, like Microsoft Excel, provide a tabular worksheet design, which you can use to document and correlate findings identified for each IP address. It is recommended that you devise a spreadsheet template that will be used to document common evaluation information. A person who has mastered the full features offered by most spreadsheets will be able to create a full template workbook that will be able to calculate all your IEM quantification needs. Using a centralized spreadsheet could cause problems when multiple team members need to access and modify data in the workbook.

- **Database approach** Databases are powerful in this respect: Once you get data into them, you can manipulate the data in multiple ways. The problem you will have is finding a commercial product that will fulfill your IEM analysis needs. The key to a good database is its design. If you are to design your own database, you must understand the types of records and fields that are needed and understand the relationships between them. How will the database be accessed? Is there a requirement to offer this database to the customer? How will the data in the database be protected? You have to evaluate the true ROI of creating such a database.

- **Document approach** This approach uses templates to correlate and document findings for each IP address. This approach is similar to the spreadsheet approach uses of a word-processing package such as Microsoft Word.

Most evaluation teams are composed of several individuals. The team lead should coordinate the collection and consolidation of information during the analysis phase. The team lead will set and manage timelines to increase team productivity and keep the effort on track. This responsibility includes organizing team meetings and assigning individual responsibilities for the successful execution of the project. Responsibilities include:

- Technical writing assignments
- Host evaluation analysis
- Network evaluation analysis
- Application-specific analysis

An initial team kickoff meeting should be conducted to start the analysis process. Ongoing meetings will be conducted to manage the progress of each member and for review of findings from the evaluation, discussing impact of the findings to the customer, and brainstorming recommendations that will be presented to the customer.

Reporting Needs

The team lead will delegate and track writing assignments. It is critical that the technical findings be translated into information that will be easily understood by and usable to the customer. Some key responsibilities have been identified in providing a quality final deliverable to the customer:

- **Team lead** The lead delegates and manages all analysis and reporting responsibilities and needs and interfaces with the customer when needed.

- **Technical writer** Technical writers are a great asset that can aid in the process of turning the technical information into common language that is understandable to nontechnical people.

- **Quality assurance** It always helps to have a third set of eyes to review the document and make sure that all expectations have been met.

Categorization, Consolidation, Correlation, and Consultation

Now that you have a general idea of your analysis and reporting needs, it is time to begin taking action. It is the moment to begin making sense of all the evaluation data using the "4 C's": categorization, consolidation, correlation, and consultation. If you have never done this before, it might seem like a daunting task. Relax! Don't let yourself be inundated by the process or the details that some tools create. You have been provided with some ways to consolidate and categorize the data. First, there are several points worth keeping in mind while you're analyzing the raw data.

False Positives and False Negatives

In the previous chapter, we talked about knowing how your evaluation tools elicit responses and how they interpret responses from systems and applications. During the analysis process, you will consolidate and compare data to eliminate two common issues that are known to most security tools: false positives and false negatives.

When a security tool reports the existence of a finding that does not actually exist, the reading is known as a *false positive*. This occurs because security vulnerability scanners use a signature database that contains logic for the identification of known vulnerabilities. Sometimes the vulnerability check relies on the banner information that the service provides. This can be troublesome when vendors do not change the application banner during upgrades or when the organization that is using the application purposely changes the banner to throw off "script kiddies" and malicious mobile code. The Apache Web server is a good example of an application that is known to generate false positives for this reason.

Often, vulnerability checks expect specific types of responses and will make assumptions when the criteria have not been met. For example, Nessus ID 11875 checks for the existence of the OpenSSL ASN.1 Parsing vulnerability by sending an invalid client SSL certificate, which can lead to a denial of service if exploited by an attacker. We have seen this reported on many evaluations against systems that are running the latest version of OpenSSL. Reviewing the Nessus plug-in that performs this check, we find that the plug-in is expecting an error code (0x0A or 0x2a) from the application to determine whether the vulnerability exists. If the service replies with any other response, such as a TCP RST or a TCP FIN, the author of the plug-in concludes that this is not the expected response from the application and reports the existence of the vulnerability.

Another type of false positive occurs when a vulnerability is reported for a specific application, but the application is not running on the system. This is caused by the vulnerability check being created for a specific application but being found in multiple applications. So, the vulnerability may exist on the system, but it is not being reported for the correct application.

By now, you probably have guessed what a *false negative* is. It is a security vulnerability that affects the OS or application but that has not been identified. This can be caused by a security tool not having the appropriate checks, the person running the tool configuring the tool with specific checks disabled, or some type of filtering device denying some part of the vulnerability check communication.

We can reduce the number of false positives and negatives by comparing the output from multiple tools and relying on not only your security expertise but your network and system administration expertise. Later, we will discuss what to do when you do not have the experience or knowledge to effectively evaluate a finding.

NOTE

One of the values of following a comprehensive technical evaluation methodology is reducing the number of false positives and false negatives. This is a point that should be communicated to the customer during the sales process and during the out-brief meeting. But remember, the IEM is not the panacea for false positives or false negatives. You must rely on your evaluation experience, too.

Evaluation Perspectives

The approach that was used for the evaluation data collection activities must be kept in mind during the analysis process. The evaluation might involve more than one type of perspective in the scope of work. When we speak of *perspective*, we base it on the location of the person performing the evaluation when the vulnerability was identified. This is usually based on physical location, but it can be a logical location. For example, say that the customer wants an external evaluation but wants the evaluation team to be physically at the customer office. This is accomplished by connecting the testing systems "outside" of the customer internal network via a logical segmentation or through a network port on an external networking device. Although the evaluation team is physically onsite, the testing is performed from an external perspective, and all findings will be presented in that light. In the IEM, you can use three approaches during the evaluation: external exposures, ,internal exposures, and system boundaries.

External Exposures

External exposures are findings that were identified from outside the organization, typically from an Internet perspective. The 2004 Computer Crime and Security Survey, conducted by the Computer Security Institute (CSI), illustrates that the most likely source of an attack is an external threat source. The mainstream of Internet threats are not targeting specific companies but are searching the Internet for known vulnerabilities to gain unauthorized access to systems and information. Most organizations, particularly those that have never had an evaluation performed, do not know where they are at risk from external threats and usually want to start the evaluation from this perspective.

Internal Exposures

"Eggshell" security is a term used to describe the security posture of most organizations across all industries. This is a product of the way people have viewed and implemented security throughout history. Think of castles surrounded by high and impenetrable stone walls and a drawbridge to allow trusted travelers to cross over crocodile-infested moats. In the epic movie *Lord of the Rings: The Two Towers*, the people of Rohan take refuge in the great fortress of Helm's Deep, consisting of several layers of stone walls and caverns behind to protect its occupants from external threats. We have always been concerned with external threats and tend to be less attentive to protecting ourselves from internal threats. Yet internal security incidents have been shown to have a greater negative impact on organizations.

Insiders know more than outsiders about where your "keys to the kingdom" are and the inherent weaknesses of the security mechanisms and controls that protect them. Organizations tend to have fewer security controls internally and a propensity to monitor less for unauthorized access on mission-critical systems. When performing technical testing, it is important to keep detailed information on where inside the company you were performing the technical evaluation when you identified the internal exposures. This information, which typically consists of IP address and segment information, can aid in identifying not only host vulnerabilities but weaknesses in network access controls as well.

NOTE

When an external threat breaches an organization's perimeter security controls, it has the same visibility and access to internal exposures as an internal threat and should be considered an internal threat.

System Boundaries

Here it is important to revisit the definition of a system. A *system* is something that transmits, stores, or processes critical information within a customer organization. We defined system boundaries during the scoping phase of the IEM and documented them in the TEP. When we refer to system boundaries, we are alluding to one of the following attributes: the *physical* boundary of the system or the *logical* path the information traverses from one entrusted entity to another.

It is fairly simple to get a mental grasp on physical boundaries, because they are tangible. We deal with physical boundaries every day. When it comes to understanding logical boundaries, however, it is best to have an up-to-date architectural diagram that illustrates where each logical "zone" exists.

Conducting Additional Research

During your analysis, you will come across findings that will inevitably need additional research, for one of several reasons. The reported findings from a tool might not contain sufficient detail for you to perform an accurate analysis. Maybe you do not have enough experience or have limited or no knowledge on the product about which the finding is reported. You cannot be an expert at everything (regardless of what your sales guy is saying). What you can be, though, is resourceful. When you don't understand a finding or you need an answer to something that you cannot answer yourself, it is essential that you know where to find the answer. It is said that "Information is power," and we live in the Information Age. If you want to know something, go find it. The Internet has made information and people accessible at our fingertips. This openness does not come without caveats. Let's review some additional research resources that you may need to rely on during your analysis.

Resources

A multitude of Internet resources can provide information you need for your research on findings discovered during your evaluations. Not all the resources at your disposal will provide accurate or reliable information. You may be looking for technical information about a finding to match customer expectations on finding deliverables. Maybe you are looking for threat information to understand the likelihood and probability of the finding being abused. Or you could be looking for version information of a potentially affected product for which a finding is being reported. Here is a brief list of some resources that you can use for your research:

- **Search engines** Although Google has a large following, you might prefer another search engine. It is advised to learn some of the advanced search capabilities of the search engine of your choosing. As with a vulnerability scanner, it is recommended that you use several search engines due to their various capabilities. Search engines such as Dogpile (www.dogpile.com) provide the ability to perform searches by simultaneously using multiple search engines.

- **Security Web sites** At several trusted security Web sites you can find information on vulnerabilities and exploits:

  - Packet Storm, http://packetstormsecurity.com

  - Securiteam, www.securiteam.com

  - Linux Security, www.linuxsecurity.com

  - INFOSYSSEC, www.infosyssec.com

  - Security Focus, www.securityfocus.com

- **Mailing lists** Multiple security mailing lists provide information pertaining to vulnerabilities, threats, and practices. Since you are performing an evaluation, you might be more focused on vulnerability disclosure and research lists. But beware. The information posted on lists frequently provides vague vulnerability information and every now and then is erroneous because the information could be theoretical and untested. You will sometimes find a "bug finder" who does not fully understand the technical issues of a vulnerability and posts inaccurate information. In cases such as this, some lists provide an obfuscated e-mail address of the poster, which can be useful in putting you in contact with the bug finder. It is recommended that you use a list archive site such as Neohapsis (http://archives.neohapsis.com), which provides a search feature for current and archives security list postings.

- **Vulnerability databases** A *vulnerability database* is a centralized database of information on security vulnerabilities. This information can include vulnerability description, impact of vulnerability, references on vulnerability, solutions and workarounds, and exploit information. We say "can provide" because not all databases are built the same way. Lack of standards, attempts to stay updated, and providing accurate, dependable, and complete information plague users of current vulnerability databases. Are we saying not to use them? Not at all. Just as you should not fully rely on the output of your tools, you need to understand the weaknesses of vulnerability databases and work with them. Here is a list of the major vulnerability databases that exist on the Internet today:

  - OSVDB, www.osvdb.org/

  - BID, www.securityfocus.com/bid/

  - ISS X-Force, http://xforce.iss.net/

  - Secunia, www.secunia.com/

  - Security Tracker, www.securitytracker.com/

  - ICAT, http://icat.nist.gov/icat.cfm

  - CVE, http://cve.mitre.org/

- **Vulnerability notification services** Vulnerability notification services disseminate technical security information, warnings, and advice to the Internet community. They are commonly known as Computer Emergency Response Team (CERT); most organizations are familiar with the US-CERT at Carnegie Mellon University. Other countries have their own versions of the US-CERT. The Computer Incident Advisory Capability (CIAC) is another vulnerability notification service that releases technical security vulnerability bulletins to the general public.

- **Vendor Web sites** Most vendors are starting to jump on the security wagon by providing security information and fixes for their products. In some instances, a vendor denied a vulnerability existed in its product, even though a proof-of-concept exploit exists for the vulnerability. We have also seen cases in which a vendor acknowledges a vulnerability but gives it a lower security risk rating than it perhaps should have.

Consulting Subject Matter Experts

It's not what you know but who you know. This truism pertains to many aspects of our lives, including evaluations. Having access to subject matter experts (SME) will prove valuable when you're researching abstract security findings. At times during your research, you will have a difficult time finding the details needed to complete a full impact analysis on a finding. It could be that the vulnerability is new and the original security advisory was released with unclear information or the finding is an older vulnerability that has not been kept up to date in the vulnerability databases. Perhaps you are searching for a tailored and practical solution to mitigate a finding. Unless you have the resources and expertise to deploy a vulnerable test system on which to perform your own analysis, you will have to resort to consulting a trusted SME.

Other Team Members

The first place to look for trusted SMEs should be within your evaluation team and then within your organization. Security people have a wide range of IT experience that was acquired in previous "lives," before they entered the dark side of the security world. Arguably, what sets a security professional apart from other IT personnel is mindset. When you can't find an SME on the evaluation team, look within your organization's IT department. Usually, every company has a team of network and system administrators who are responsible for the mission-critical systems of that company. Many times, these individuals are a wealth of knowledge and have experience that surpasses the skills needed for their specific job functions. Where they don't have the knowledge, they usually have a friend or two who does.

External Resources

Networking with other security professionals is where you will glean the biggest value for attending security conferences and events. You will find that most security specialists are open to sharing their knowledge in areas in which they are known to have expertise. You must take care when dealing with external resources, however. You must maintain the confidentiality of your customer and not leak detailed information about where the security finding was discovered. All that you need to tell an external resource is an adequate amount of technical information about the finding to help you get the information that you need for your research. Consulting external resources can also involve reading previous posts or posting a general question to specific mailing lists. Chances are that you have a question that some other researcher is investigating!

NOTE

Check all your contractual agreements between the evaluation team and the customer to verify that you are permitted to contact external resources for research purposes. We have had customers who want to know up front the individuals who will be involved with the entire evaluation and might want background investigations performed on them. You should review the legal section of this book for additional legal guidance.

Analyzing Customer Documentation

Throughout the evaluation process, the evaluation team accumulates different types of documentation that support the way the customer organization's security is designed, implemented, and maintained. This information can range from INFOSEC policy and procedures, security technical implementation guides (STIGs), network architectural diagrams, access controls, and host configurations to past security assessment results. During the analysis process, you will use these types of documents as references in understanding the customer's security paradigm and mapping findings and solutions to their security culture. At times you will have to ask the customer POC for documentation that was either overlooked or never delivered to the evaluation team.

INFOSEC Policies and Procedures

Security policies are the foundation of a successful information security program within an organization. Policies provide a framework for defining a desired posture that the organization is working toward attaining through best operational security practices and will be used when formulating your recommendations. You will find purpose and strategy of the information security program, guidelines for everyday operational security practices, regulatory and industry compliance standards, appropriate ways to respond to security incidents, and references to additional complementary security documents.

During your analysis, among all the findings you could find a common theme that points to a weakness with a security practice. Maybe the company needs a patch management process or already has one that needs to be updated. Perhaps the company policy is not being implemented and individuals need to be educated on the information security policy. If it is found that the information security policy needs to be updated or added to, we recommend you follow industry best practices and standards to keep your recommendations subjective.

Knowing up front how the organization implements technical security controls on hosts is important when you're performing host evaluations. Most companies are still maturing their information security program and have not implemented standard host configurations, commonly referred to as a STIG. Sometimes you will find that STIGs have been documented but were put together by an individual who had no security background. It is also common to find that OS STIGs exist within an organization, but STIGs for mission-critical applications do not. Where STIGs are not found, it is recommended to go along with one of the following known standards:

- Center for Internet Security (CIS), www.cis.org

- National Institute of Standards and Technology (NIST), http://csrc.nist.gov

- National Security Agency (NSA), www.nsa.gov/snac/

- Defense Information Systems Agency (DISA) STIGs, http://csrc.nist.gov/pcig/cig.html

WARNING

Be careful when you're following or recommending a STIG standard, especially on operational systems. If the standard is fully implemented, your customer could end up with a system that might not operate properly or functions but nothing else can be done on it. We have seen situations in which customers started to apply STIG configurations and crashed the system. If you're not familiar with a STIG setting and the way it could impact the system, refer to the additional research section of this chapter.

Previous Evaluations/VA/Penetration–Testing Results

The evaluation team may or may not get access to the results of any prior testing that has been performed against the organization. It's helpful for the evaluation team to know what findings were previously identified and how the organization dealt with the risk of the findings. Were the findings accepted, fixed, or not addressed? You do not want to create noise in your final deliverable with findings that have been acknowledged and accepted by the organization. This is not to say that these findings should not be revisited. The risk from a vulnerability can change over time.

If you discover issues that were assumed to be fixed, it's possible that either the finding is a false positive or the issue was not resolved properly. You must carry out further investigation with the customer to accurately report the finding to them. You should never make an assumption about identified findings.

Be prepared to answer the question as to why previous tests did not identify findings that the IEM process has uncovered. This could occur due to the type of security test that was performed, the lack of a comprehensive methodology being utilized, or maybe the finding was discovered but not properly analyzed. This is not the time to bash your competitor; instead, educate the customer on the value of the IEM and why it can be more effective than conventional approaches in discovering security issues.

Developing Practical Recommendations

Up to this point we have been discussing analysis issues and the process of evaluating and correlating the evaluation raw data. You have trudged your way through volumes of raw data and are on the verge of losing your sanity. The data has been categorized, consolidated, and correlated. So now what? You have uncovered problems that have varying degrees of impact on the organization's mission-critical systems, and you now need to document practical and effective solutions. It is recommended that you provide multiple solutions per finding to give the customer some flexibility in selecting the best solution for them. Take into account that an identified recommendation may address a single finding or multiple findings, and there could be multiple solutions that mitigate one finding. The recommendations that you present will entail operational, managerial, and/or technical improvements to the organization's information security way of life.

So, you might be asking, "What is a practical recommendation?" This is best determined by understanding the appropriate level of security for the organization to accomplish its mission objectives and to do it securely. What is the organization's risk tolerance? How will the finding impact the organization? Will new risks be introduced into the customer's environment if they follow the evaluation recommendations? What types of threats are likely to exploit the identified findings? Will there be sacrifices that the customer will have to accept to be protected from the identified risks? The answers to these questions will start the process of guiding you toward completing the IEM analysis process and improving your customers' overall security posture.

Level of Detail

In the Coordination Agreements section of the TEP, you will find particulars about the level of detail the customer expects with reference to the recommendations in the final report. As an evaluator, you want to make sure that you understand these requirements before you start your analysis and research. They will help determine the level of effort required to collect details about each finding. What follows are recommended details that you will want to document for each finding that will be useful during the formation of your final recommendations. It is advised to create a template that you'll use during your evaluation research—something like the one shown in Table 12.1 and described in the following subsections.

Table 12.1 An Example of a Finding Research Template

Finding	Description	References	Threat Likelihood	Business Impact Criticality Rating	Recommendations

Finding

Use a short yet descriptive title for the finding—usually only one sentence in length and containing enough detail to communicate the finding. For example, let's say that a host is found to be vulnerable to a format sting attack against the *ssl_log* function in the Apache *mod_ssl* module. A title could be written as follows: "Apache *mod_ssl-2.8.18 - 1.3.31 mod_ssl ssl_log* function format string." In this example, the finding is seen to include the product name, affected version information, and a brief description of the vulnerability.

Description

The description section is a technical description of the finding and usually a short paragraph in length. An example description of the previously mentioned Apache finding may be written as follows: "The *mod_ssl ssl_log* function in Apache contains a flaw that may allow an attacker to execute arbitrary messages. The issue is triggered due to a *ssl_log()* format string error within the *mod_proxy* hook functions."

References

It is recommended that you use reputable references when presenting a finding. The IEM is partial to using CVE identifiers as a reference. You may think about documenting additional references that provide detailed information about the finding. Usually, we find it valuable to document three references. You might not use all of this information in the final report, but it's worth having in case you need to provide additional sources.

Criticality Rating

Depending on the scope and complexity of the organization's environment, the criticality rating of the vulnerability in relation to risk can be challenging. This is likely due to the subjective nature of deciding on the criticality rating of a finding. The ultimate goal of the criticality rating is to provide a description of the vulnerability in terms of how it relates to the customer's environment, which will eventually be linked to asset criticality for prioritization of short- and long-term remediation efforts.

Criticality ratings are categorized as High, Medium, or Low to convey the overall risk impact on the system the vulnerability signifies to the organization. The rating will consider such factors as the exposure perspective of the finding, business impact of the vulnerability (loss of confidentiality, integrity, or availability), threat likelihood analysis, and remediation effort. As you can see, you will have to rely not only on the information uncovered during your research but also on your experiences as a security professional. It is recommended that you articulate the definitions of your criticality ratings so that your customer is aware of the risk impact of the vulnerability. Here we provide an example definition for each rating:

- **High** A High risk finding is usually assigned to vulnerabilities that will have a high threat or impact potential and allow unauthorized privileged access, allow execution of code, or grant the ability to alter the system in some way. It's recommended that you correct these types of findings immediately.

- **Medium** A Medium risk finding is representative of a vulnerability that poses a medium level of risk to the organization and will allow a threat immediate access to the system with unprivileged access. The risk gives a threat the opportunity to continue to attempt gaining privileged access on the system.

- **Low** A Low risk finding is defined as one that provides sensitive information that could lead to further attempts to impact the confidentiality, integrity, or availability of the system.

Business Impact

It is common information security language to express impact in terms of the loss of confidentiality, integrity, or availability. Eventually, a vulnerability could pilot the way to the loss of all three impact attributes. It is advised to report on the initial impact of the finding against a system. Briefly describe the type of attack and how it can be carried out by a threat. For those of you who are new to information security, we provide brief definitions for each impact attribute:

- **Loss of confidentiality** This is the result of the information being read or copied by an unauthorized individual.

- **Loss of integrity** This is the result of the unauthorized or unintentional alteration of data.

- **Loss of availability** This is the inaccessibility of information or services to authorized persons.

Here is an example business impact statement for the Apache *mod_ssl* finding we discussed earlier: "It is possible that the flaw may allow a remote attacker to execute arbitrary messages via format string specifiers in certain log messages for HTTPS, resulting in a loss of integrity."

Threat Likelihood

Standard mainstream security assessments offered by "run-of-the-mill" companies focus only on vulnerabilities. By now, you should understand that not all vulnerabilities are created equal. A vulnerability that exists internally may be ranked with a lower risk rating than if it were exposed to external threats.

To fully understand the risk of a finding, you must consider the value of the asset to the organization, the threat likelihood, and the business impact and rating of the vulnerability. You should already understand the nature of the vulnerability through your research efforts and have been provided the business value of the asset through the system criticality matrix developed during the IAM process.

It is important to fully comprehend threat sources, motivations, and capabilities that could abuse the identified finding. Vulnerabilities may be the focal point for multiple threats, and threats may appear from the existence of multiple vulnerabilities. Are there any known threats exploiting the vulnerability? What type of skill level is required to exploit the finding? Is there publicly available exploit code? What is the visibility of the finding to the identified threats?

Threat likelihood can increase the overall criticality rating of a finding. Every day, the changing "threatscape" of the Internet can increase or decrease an organization's external risk exposure. The types of Internet threats that you identify for your customer could include:

- Organized crime

- Governments

- Terrorists

- Competitors

- Insiders

- Professional hackers

- Script kiddies

- Worms, viruses, and malware

Recommendations

Providing the customer with multiple recommendations to deal with a negative finding allows them to make an informed decision on the level of protection that is acceptable to the organization. Each problem will almost always have multiple solutions. Many organizations look to the IEM to gain better insight into their security posture. On the other hand, the results of the IEM will trigger the start of establishing a comprehensive security program.

One of the greatest challenges you will face as an evaluator is translating all the findings into practical solutions to reduce the organization's security exposures. Depending on the evaluation testing perspectives and your understanding of the customer's environment, you might not consider security mechanisms in the context of the entire environment. Effective security solutions should be built on layered security strategies and include both preventative and detection security measures. In time, preventative measures will fail, and organizations need the ability detect malicious activity for prompt response.

The recommendations must be cost-effective for the customer so that they are not spending thousands of dollars to protect resources that do not support the organization's mission. The likelihood of the evaluation team knowing the customer's budgetary capabilities and limits is slim to none. Your recommendations should include a best-of-breed solution, a midlevel solution, and a low-level solution. This flexibility provides options for the customer that will empower them to choose a customized solution that matches all their monetary, operational, technical, and human resources. Vulnerability remediation should not be based solely on the ease or low cost of implementing the recommended solution. Furthermore, it should not be assumed that the most complex vulnerabilities should be addressed immediately or with long-term solutions. The next chapter addresses the way the IEM approach in defining a prioritized road map will guide the customer in focusing their remediation efforts.

Keep in mind the entire life-cycle costs for all solutions that you recommend. We have seen companies that focused only on the initial purchase costs of a security solution and did not properly plan for ongoing maintenance and training expenses. The cost of fixing a finding can have a significant influence on how it is rectified.

Customer expectations, scope of findings, and constraints may have an impact on scheduling a selected recommendation in a customer environment. For example, you might have discovered a finding that involves implementing a vendor patch for the mitigation of a security hole across 50 servers. What OS is involved? Does the customer have an automated method to deploy the patch? How much time is needed to test the patch before deployment? How often are change control requests reviewed and scheduled in the customer environment? Will personnel be available to perform the recommendation? Are there physical or logical limitations? Does the customer have an automated way of validating the patch application?

Tying in Regulations, Legislation, Organizational Policies, and Industry Best Practices

Due to the flexibility and comprehensiveness of the IEM, you may be performing an evaluation to fulfill regulatory or legislative requirements. As an evaluator, you must be conscious of any regulations and/or legislative responsibilities that are applicable to your customer. This could be a challenge for the evaluation team when the customer organization crosses regional and national boundaries. You will usually find the details of these requirements in the TEP document. Be aware, though, that some customers are not aware of their compliance responsibilities or are not fully aware of the compliance requirements.

Summary

The IEM process is a culmination of many activities resulting in the identification of security findings and recommendations that reflect the overall business mission, desired security posture, and the risk to the company. The chapter discussed strategic approaches for the organization and analysis of the raw data that was collected during the onsite evaluation process. We discussed how to determine risk through fully understanding the impact of a finding by not only looking at the security vulnerability but providing real business value to the IEM process, combining the threat likelihood, the value of the asset, and the criticality of the finding. You learned how to conduct additional research to formulate remedial recommendations that provide the customer with practical immediate and long-term recommendations to eliminate identified risks and meet business goals. In the next few chapters, we discuss how to use this information to provide a prioritized road map of the evaluation findings and create the final evaluation report.

Solutions Fast Track

Getting Organized

- ☑ Understand your analysis and reporting needs.
- ☑ Devise a systematic approach of organizing the raw data collected from the onsite activities.
- ☑ Decide on the approach you will take to correlate data between your evaluation tools.

Categorization, Consolidation, Correlation, and Consultation

- ☑ Relax and don't be inundated by the post-evaluation phase.
- ☑ Understand that people, not tools, perform analysis. Tools are used for the collection of data to be transformed into usable information.
- ☑ Defining a naming standard for raw data files will assist you in the identification of files and their contents. Be able to identify, understand, and eliminate false positives and false negatives.
- ☑ Know the evaluation perspective that was prominent when the data was collected.

Conducting Additional Research

☑ You cannot be an expert at everything. You can be resourceful, however.

☑ Understand the value of each available resource and know when to use it.

☑ Be aware of any contractual limitations on your research capabilities.

Analyzing Customer Documentation

☑ Understand the value of customer INFOSEC documentation during the evaluation.

☑ Become familiar with industry standards and guidelines.

☑ Has the customer had a previous information security evaluation or assessment?

☑ Reviewing the customer INFOSEC documentation can reveal the maturity of their security program.

Developing Practical Recommendations

☑ Recommendations should involve operational, managerial, and technical considerations.

☑ Understand the level of detail the customer is expecting for recommendations.

☑ Risk involves the value of the asset, the threat likelihood, and the business impact of a vulnerability.

☑ Your recommendations must be practical and based on effective security strategies.

☑ Recommendations must take into account any regulatory or legislative requirements, organizational policies, and industry best practices.

Frequently Asked Questions

The following Frequently Asked Questions, answered by the authors of this book, are designed to both measure your understanding of the concepts presented in this chapter and to assist you with real-life implementation of these concepts. To have your questions about this chapter answered by the author, browse to **www.syngress.com/solutions** and click on the **"Ask the Author"** form. You will also gain access to thousands of other FAQs at ITFAQnet.com.

Q. How involved is the customer POC in the post-evaluation phase?

A. The evaluation team lead should stay in contact with the customer POC. At times, additional information is needed, such as finding out the patch level of a specific application or requesting a document from the customer. Weekly updates are recommended to inform the customer of the evaluation team's progress and to address any other issues that crop up during this phase.

Q. Do you always need to analyze the customer documentation?

A. Yes. Not only is doing so a requirement of the IEM, it is also provides value to the customer when the evaluation team links recommendations to the organization's information security program. A vulnerability scanner can only report on technical issues; it cannot correlate a technical finding to an organizational or managerial issue.

Q. Do you list all findings individually or do you group them together?

A. We have seen and done it both ways. It depends on the level of detail required for the final document, size and scope of the evaluation, and the number of reported findings. For larger evaluations, it is convenient for the customer to review a finding, understand the impact to them, and know where the finding exists within their organization. This is accomplished through grouping. For smaller evaluations, it might be harder to group findings and you will have to resort to reporting findings to individual systems.

Q. How do I handle a finding that I cannot determine to be a false positive or false negative?

A. If the onsite data gathering is performed correctly by following the 10 baseline activities, you should not be faced with this issue. The evaluation team's expertise of knowing what tool to use, when to use it, and how to use it, in accordance with a comprehensive methodology, will play a big role in eliminating this problem.

At times, though, a TCP port could be interrogated and the service or application on the listening port cannot be determined. We say "listening" because a traffic analyzer is utilized to verify a full TCP handshake to the port. The listening port must be reported to the customer so that source of the listening port on the server can be researched in more detail. Once the source has been identified, the testing perspective and business justification of the identified application and how it should be accessed will be accounted for in the customer's decision process.

Q. Is it practical to gather detailed information about each finding?

A. Yes. This information will be used for the preparation of recommendations and will be useful when completing the final report. The evaluator, as well as the customer, must be able to understand the full risk of a finding. A poorly researched finding may lead to security breach of the customer environment, and the evaluation team could find themselves involved in a lawsuit.

Chapter 13

Creating Measurements and Trending Results

Solutions in this chapter:

- **The Purpose and Goal of the Matrixes**
- **Information Types**
- **Common Vulnerabilities and Exposures**
- **NIST ICAT**
- **Developing System Vulnerability Criticality Matrixes**
- **Developing Overall Vulnerability Criticality Matrixes**
- **Using the OVCM and SVCM**

☑ Summary

☑ Solutions Fast Track

☑ Frequently Asked Questions

Introduction

Now that you have the findings and you know why they are an issue for your customer, it is time to present them to the customer management. The biggest issue that we have seen in our years of doing evaluations is the standardization of reporting formats. In this chapter we cover the sources of findings information and how this information can be put into a single chart that the customer can use as a road map to improving their security posture.

We all know that the findings or results of your evaluation are important information to the customer; the problem we run into is how to present the information in an understandable manner. The findings are usually reported in three levels of understanding: executive, management, and technical. This chapter focuses on the executive and management portions, along with developing a simple graphic table that will provide prioritization of the findings at a glance for senior management. This table will allow senior management to readily track the work being accomplished and how that work directly impacts the security posture of the organization.

Keep in mind as you read this chapter, and again as you develop these matrixes for the first time, that they are meant to provide a detailed picture of findings and the organization's security posture for the executive and senior levels of management. With each successive evaluation, management can compare the findings to see how the security posture has been improved. This becomes a repeatable process that can be used over and over again. Another secondary benefit is the ability to see repeat findings that may have been reported as closed and now are reopened or simply have not been addressed.

The Purpose and Goal of the Matrixes

As mentioned in the previous chapter, you should have no expectation that all the findings will be closed when you and your team do follow-on evaluations. In the theoretical world, it is easy to see that all findings should be closed, but reality sets in when you realize that's not the case. Some findings are not worth the effort or cost to close. This topic could lead into a full-blown discussion of risk management, but at this point we will leave it in this simple state. You should have mitigated all findings from previous evaluations through risk management by doing one of three things:

- Close the exposure (elimination).
- Insure or budget for the exposure loss (mitigation).
- Take the risk (acceptance).

Notes from the Underground

Risk Management

Every organization has a job or mission. Because organizations use automated IT systems to process their information to support their missions, risk management is critical to protecting information assets from IT-related risk. The principal goal of a risk management process is to protect the organization and its ability to perform its mission, not just its IT assets. Although the IEM is not a risk management methodology, it is a tool that can be used to gather the information needed to perform risk management. You can obtain a good foundation for understanding risk management by reading and understanding NIST SP 800-30, "Risk Management Guide for Information Technology Systems," a publication that can be found at http://csrc.nist.gov/publications/nistpubs/800-30/sp800-30.pdf.

The matrixes do not provide any finding details or recommendations for the technicians and administrators, although these individuals can still use the matrixes as a road map. The primary targets for the matrixes are the organization's management and executives. The matrixes are a snapshot of the posture and prioritization of the findings based on the technical and management weighting. Before we go into the development of the matrixes, let's look at the information that you will need to put this all together.

Simply put, the three things you need are the information types impacted, industry standard ratings, and evaluation team expertise. As we begin this process, keep in mind that it is built on the work we did in the organizational assessment, which was a top-down approach. We will use some of that top-down approach and then go bottom-up to build the final product, the overall vulnerability criticality matrix.

Information Types

The impacted information types are pulled directly from the organizational information criticality matrix (OICM) or system information criticality matrix (SICM) that we developed during the pre-assessment phase of the organizational assessment (the IAM). If the assessment and the evaluation are accomplished concurrently (at the same time), you will still have the IAM as it is developed by your team. If you are trying to do the evaluation without having accomplished the organizational assessment, then stop right here, because you will not be able to create these final reporting matrixes. The IEM final products are directly dependent on input from the organizational pre-assessment. Failure to use or draw the information from the organizational assessment will mean that the evaluation is not IEM compliant.

If you attended the NSA Information Security (INFOSEC) Assessment Methodology (IAM) and NSA INFOSEC Evaluation Methodology (IEM) classes, you will remember the matrix shown in Table 13.1. It was the first criticality matrix we developed during the IAM.

Table 13.1 shows how there are four critical information topics for the organization called COPS. Each information topic is a rollup of probably several subelements each. For the purposes of this book, we won't go into the development of this matrix; instead we'll consider it one of the input variables from the organizational assessment that is unique to each and every organization.

Table 13.1 The COPS OICM

COPS OICM	Confidentiality	Integrity	Availability
Criminal Records	M	H	M
Informants	H	M	M
Investigations	M	M	M
Warrants	L	H	H

What we want to consider here is that there is some prioritization by impact value, not by information topic. Each of the information topics is a rollup of multiple subtopics. The information topics reflect the "50,000-foot view" of what management considers the important information. All of these were determined to be of equal value when the OICM was developed. To prioritize the impact values, let's first assign a number to each of the rows (see Table 13.2). Assigning the number will help ensure that we can properly track the rows later on as they are broken down into the system criticality matrixes.

Table 13.2 The Numbered OICM for COPS

COPS OICM	Confidentiality	Integrity	Availability
Criminal Records (1)	M	H	M
Informants (2)	H	M	M
Investigations (3)	M	M	M
Warrants (4)	L	H	H

Once the numbers are assigned, we can pass the numbering down to the system criticality matrixes. Again we will use matrixes that were used in the IAM class for the examples. Table 13.3 shows that three of the critical information topics—criminal records, investigations, and warrants—are used (in other words, the process transmitted or stored) on the Federal Agents Comprehensive Tracking System (FACTS).

Table 13.3 The FACTS SICM

FACTS	Confidentiality	Integrity	Availability
Criminal Records (1)	M	H	M
Investigations (3)	M	M	M
Warrants (4)	L	H	H

In Table 13.4 you can see that two critical information topics, informants and warrants, are used on the Secret Network of Operational Programs (SNOOP) system. The main reason we number the information topics is to ensure that we transfer the rows correctly as we develop the system vulnerability matrixes and that we have the ability to map backward to the OICM. This will be important as you develop multiple vulnerability criticality matrixes.

Table 13.4 The SNOOP SICM

SNOOP	Confidentiality	Integrity	Availability
Informants (2)	H	M	M
Warrants (4)	L	H	H

With this part completed, we can now transfer the information from the information criticality matrixes to the vulnerability criticality matrixes. A vulnerability criticality matrix is a simple chart or table that shows the importance of the customer findings in a format that is easy to understand. The most significant finding is always at the top left of the matrix; the least important finding is always at the bottom right, as depicted in Table 13.5.

Table 13.5 An Example of an Early SVCM

		HIGH			Medium			Low	
		IC1	IC2	IC3	IC4	IC5	IC6	IC7	IC8
High	V1								
	V2								
	V3								
Medium	V4								
	V5								
	V6								
Low	V7								
	V8								

The top row of this chart shows information categories (IC) in order of severity, beginning with the highs and then the mediums and then the lows. The left column of the chart is the findings (V) in order of the highest to lowest. If you were to start with the FACTS SICM and transfer the information categories, it would look like Table 13.6.

As you can see, the method of transferring the critical information topics is to start with the top row of the SICM. Scan across each row, from left to right, and as you find a high-impact attribute, put that impact attribute in the row. There is no prioritization of these impact attributes at this point. They are placed in the order found. Continue this process for all the highs, and then start over doing the same thing for each of the medium-impact attributes and then the low-impact attributes. Once you have all the impact attributes accounted for, you can arrange the High values in any order you feel is appropriate based on your expertise. Do the same thing with your Medium values and then your Low values.

Table 13.6 The Top Row of the FACTS Vulnerability Criticality Matrix

FACTS Vulnerability Criticality Matrix	Finding Number	Severity	High				Medium				Low
			Criminal Records Integrity	Warrants Integrity	Warrants Availability	Criminal Records Confidentiality	Criminal Records Availability	Investigations Confidentiality	Investigations Integrity	Investigations Availability	Warrants Confidentiality

Once this process is complete, we'll need to look at the findings themselves. Since you already completed the order of precedence identification in the last chapter, we will only look at the impact rating and a possibly very good source for them.

Common Vulnerabilities and Exposures

To quote the Mitre Web page defining the Common Vulnerabilities and Exposures (CVE), it is "A list of standardized names for vulnerabilities and other information security exposures— CVE aims to standardize the names for all publicly known vulnerabilities and security exposures." Further defined, "the CVE is a dictionary, *not* a database. The goal of CVE is to make it easier to share data across separate vulnerability databases and security tools. While CVE may make it easier to search for information in other databases, CVE should not be considered as a vulnerability database on its own merit."

We strongly encourage you to utilize CVE-compliant tools. They are continuously updated to ensure that the findings identified during an evaluation are traceable through the use of different tools. The benefit of using CVE tools is that the customer will have a common identification that can be used for research and tracking. Also, your team and other security consultants will be able to track and correlate previous findings.

Currently, once a finding or vulnerability is submitted to Mitre for inclusion in the dictionary listing, it goes through a stringent process of review. Initially, each submitted finding is listed as a "candidate" (CAN). CVE candidates are those vulnerabilities or exposures under consideration for acceptance into CVE. Candidates are assigned special numbers to distinguish them from CVE entries. Each candidate has three primary items associated with it:

- Number (also referred to as a *name*)
- Description
- References

The number, also referred to as a *name*, is an encoding of the year that the candidate number was assigned and a unique number N for the Nth candidate assigned that year— for example, CAN-1999-0067.

Established practices are followed when a candidate is created. If the Editorial Board accepts the candidate, an official CVE entry is created that includes the description and references.

The candidate number is converted into a CVE name by replacing the *CAN* with *CVE*. For example, when the Editorial Board accepted the candidate CAN-1999-0067, the candidate number was converted to CVE-1999-0067, and the resulting new entry was added to CVE.

Starting October 19, 2005, CAN entries will no longer be created or maintained. All the current CAN entries will be migrated to a CVE number. There should be no significant effect for end users of the CVE system. If you enter an old CAN number, the system will still retrieve the information and show you the new CVE number. The big difference will be the addition of a "status" line to the CVE information. That status line will be the only indication of whether or not a CVE is Candidate, Entry, or Deprecated.

The issue that we have seen is that the CVE process does not assist in identifying the impact value to an organization. Though that was never the intended function of the CVE, having an initial or recommended impact value would be nice. That is where the National Institute of Standards and Technology stepped in to help the community. You can find more information about the CVE at www.cve.mitre.org/.

NIST ICAT

The National Institute of Standards and Technology (NIST) developed ICAT. (The ICAT name does not officially stand for anything today; initially the ICAT project was intended as a database of Internet attacks used by malicious hackers, and ICAT was its acronym. As the project changed its focus to a searchable database of all system findings, what ICAT stood for became obsolete but the name ICAT was kept.) Today ICAT is a searchable index of information on computer vulnerabilities. It provides search capability at a fine granularity and links users to vulnerability and patch information.

One of the nice things about using the ICAT search capabilities is the simple process of inputting the CVE or CAN number and getting more information than is available in the CVE dictionary. ICAT allows you to search by vendor, product, version, keyword, or severity. The ICAT database, as shown in Figure 13.1, is a filterable search engine that allows you to quickly locate findings in the database and identify their initial or recommend severity level.

As with any input tool used in developing and implementing the reporting portion, the ICAT is not meant as the last or only word in the severity level. ICAT is a starting point for which you, with your expertise and the input of the customer, will determine the final severity level. You can find more information on the ICAT at http://icat.nist.gov/icat.cfm.

Figure 13.1 A NIST ICAT Screen

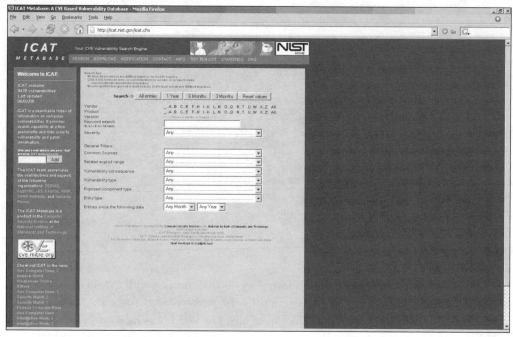

Developing System Vulnerability Criticality Matrixes

Starting with FACTS system that we use in the COPS example during the NSA courses, let's look at how the system vulnerability criticality matrix (SVCM) is developed. Now we have the impact attributes and the findings transferred to the chart, as depicted in Tables 13.7 and 13.8.

Table 13.7 The Initial FACTS SVCM Chart

FACTS Vulnerability Criticality Matrix	Finding Number	Severity	High			Medium					Low
			Criminal Records Integrity	Warrants Integrity	Warrants Availability	Criminal Records Confidentiality	Criminal Records Availability	Investigations Confidentiality	Investigations Integrity	Investigations Availability	Warrants Confidentiality
CVE 2001-0013	2	H									
Organizational	3	H									
CVE 2002-0571	4	H									
Organizational	5	M									
CVE 2002-1024	7	M									
Operational	8	L									
CVE 2002-1025	9	L									

Table 13.8 The Initial SNOOP SVCM

SNOOP Vulnerability Criticality Matrix	Finding Number	Severity	High			Medium						Low
			Criminal Records Integrity	Warrants Integrity	Warrants Availability	Criminal Records Confidentiality	Criminal Records Availability	Investigations Confidentiality	Investigations Integrity	Investigations Availability	Warrants Confidentiality
CVE 2002-0801	1	H									
Organizational	3	H									
CVE 2002-0571	4	H									
Organizational	5	M									
CVE 2002-1060	6	M									
Operational	8	L									
CVE 2004-0033	10	L									

Take a good look at these charts. You should notice some things right off the bat. No finding number 1, 6, or 10 is showing in the FACTS matrix, and numbers 2, 7, and 9 are missing from the SNOOP matrix. There are also three findings that do not have a CVE number. But don't panic. First, the missing findings are findings that do not apply to this system. Not every finding applies to all systems. As for the findings that don't have CVE numbers, as we said before, a lot of findings are organizational or common end-user configuration issues and so they will not have a CVE number.

You can actually see now why we number the findings and the critical information topics. When you went from the OICM, you had to map each information criticality topic to the appropriate system. Not all information topics will apply to all systems, nor will all the findings discovered during the evaluation apply to every system. Initially you might think that you should just list all of them and then put a "Not Applicable" (N/A) for the findings, but that would create a rather large and unwieldy chart for each system. To enable the customer to use these charts, we strongly recommend that you put only the findings that are applicable to each system on the appropriate chart.

As for the non-CVE findings, let's face it—some findings are so new that they might not have gone through the CVE process yet. Some findings you will come across will affect a system but will not be technical in nature. Consider the finding "weak passwords." You *could* search the ICAT for the keywords *weak passwords* and severity *high*, and you would get 12 matching findings. But none of those CVE findings would cover the fact that there is no enforcement of strong passwords. So, the result is that you have ended up identifying an organizational or operational finding that has no related CVE number, even though this is a common finding in many organizations. The CVE system does not address configuration issues or administrator error.

Don't skip, hide, or ignore nontechnical findings identified during the evaluation. There is a place for them in the chart, and they are just as valuable to the customer. Also, this is the place where you would incorporate the organizational findings that were identified during the IAM assessment portion.

The next portion becomes a little more difficult for junior security analysts. This is where you identify the applicability of a finding to the impact attributes. You say, "Huh?" Well, think about the differences in what various findings do when exploited. Some findings affect the confidentiality of information; others affect availability or integrity. Some findings can and will affect all the impact attributes.

Again, a good starting point if you have not done this before is to use the ICAT database. When you input a CVE in the keyword search, you can use the output as your starting reference. For example, if you were to use finding number 2 from FACTS, CVE 2001-0013, you would get the information shown in Table 13.9.

Table 13.9 ICAT CVE-2001-0013 Output

Vulnerability Name:	CVE-2001-0013
Published Before:	2/12/2001
Summary:	Format string vulnerability in nslookupComplain function in BIND 4 allows remote attackers to gain root privileges.
Severity:	High
Vulnerability type	Input Validation Error
Exploitable Range:	Remote
Loss type:	Security Protection (Gain super user access)
Reference 1:	Source: CERT Type: General and Patch Name: CA-2001-02 www.cert.org/advisories/CA-2001-02.html#http://www.cert.org/advisories/CA-2001-02.html
Reference 2:	Source: PGP Security Type: General and Patch Name: Vulnerabilities in BIND 4 and 8 www.pgp.com/research/covert/advisories/047.asp#http://www.pgp.com/research/covert/advisories/047.asp
Vulnerable software and versions:	ISC, BIND, 4.9.3 ISC, BIND, 4.9.5-P1

From reading this table you should be able to determine that this finding would affect all the impact attributes due to the fact that as a superuser, the attacker can view, modify, change, and delete anything they want on that box. But this is not necessarily the same for all findings. If you take a look at FACTS finding number 4, CVE 2002-0571, you would see that the output from ICAT, listed in Table 13.10, is not the same.

From this output in ICAT we see that the impact to the organization is still significant, High, but the affected impact attribute is confidentiality and not integrity or availability. There have been many discussions and heated debates about how a finding affects impact attributes, but we are not going to go into that area here. This book is meant to give you the basic information to do this work yourself. Your expertise and experience will determine whether you add more impact attributes to a particular finding. For the examples we are using, we decided to use the default output from ICAT for the identification of affected impact attributes.

Table 13.10 ICAT CVE-2002-0571 Output

Vulnerability Name:	CVE-2002-0571
Published before:	7/3/2002
Summary:	Oracle Oracle9i database server 9.0.1.x allows local users to access restricted data via a SQL query using ANSI outer join syntax.
Severity:	High
Vulnerability type:	Design Error
Exploitable range:	Remote
Loss type:	Security Protection (Gain other access) Confidentiality
Reference 1:	Source: Neohapsis Type: General Name: ansi outer join syntax in Oracle allows access to any data archives.neohapsis.com/archives/bugtraq/2002-04/0175.html
Reference 2:	Source: Ciac Type: General Name: Oracle9i User Privileges Vulnerability www.ciac.org/ciac/bulletins/m-071.shtml
Reference 3:	Source: ISS X-Force Type: General and Patch Name: oracle-ansi-sql-bypass-acl(8855) www.iss.net/security_center/static/8855.php
Reference 4:	Source: Security Focus Type: General and Patch Name: bid 4523 www.securityfocus.com/bid/4523
Vulnerable software and versions:	Oracle, Oracle9i, 9.0 Oracle, Oracle9i, 9.0.1

Once you have done your analysis and identified the affected impact attributes for each finding, you need to show which ones are *not* affected. For this we will use the simple N/A for each block that is not an affected impact attribute, as shown in Tables 13.11 and 13.12.

Table 13.11 The FACTS SVCM with Some Attributes Marked "Not Applicable"

FACTS Vulnerability Criticality Matrix	Finding Number	Severity	High — Criminal Records Integrity	High — Warrants Integrity	High — Warrants Availability	Medium — Criminal Records Confidentiality	Medium — Criminal Records Availability	Medium — Investigations Confidentiality	Medium — Investigations Integrity	Medium — Investigations Availability	Low — Warrants Confidentiality
CVE 2001-0013	2	H									
Organizational	3	H									
CVE 2002-0571	4	H	N/A	N/A	N/A		N/A		N/A	N/A	
Organizational	5	M									
CVE 2002-1024	7	M	N/A	N/A		N/A		N/A	N/A		N/A
Operational	8	L									
CVE 2002-1025	9	L	N/A	N/A	N/A		N/A		N/A	N/A	

Table 13.12 The SNOOP SVCM with Some Attributes Marked "Not Applicable"

SNOOP Vulnerability Criticality Matrix	Finding Number	Severity	High			Medium					Low
			Criminal Records Integrity	Warrants Integrity	Warrants Availability	Criminal Records Confidentiality	Criminal Records Availability	Investigations Confidentiality	Investigations Integrity	Investigations Availability	Warrants Confidentiality
CVE 2002-0801	1	H									
Organizational	3	H									
CVE 2002-0571	4	H	N/A	N/A	N/A		N/A		N/A	N/A	
Organizational	5	M									
CVE 2002-1060	6	M			N/A	N/A	N/A	N/A		N/A	N/A
Operational	8	L									
CVE 2004-0033	10	L	N/A	N/A	N/A		N/A		N/A	N/A	

NOTE

We want to emphasize that although the information displayed here is based on the output of ICAT, you should use your personal expertise to determine the appropriate applicability. What we really don't want to see is analysts simply using the defaults from any tools. This would result in as poor a quality as though you were merely cutting and pasting the findings from a default tool output—or worse, just printing it and handing it to your customer as the deliverable.

Now the hard part is done. Let's look at the easy part: calculating the value of the findings. The first part of this task can be negotiated with your customer. When determining the value for each block in the matrix, you want to ensure that you use some standardization. For this task we decided to use the information shown in Table 13.13, which is based on the most common impact attribute weights: High, Medium, and Low.

Table 13.13 Finding Weights

Technical Finding	High	Moderate	Low
Information Criticality Impact	3	2	1
Vulnerability Severity	6	4	2
Organizational Finding	**High**	**Moderate**	**Low**
Information Criticality Impact	4.5	3	1.5
Vulnerability Severity	4.5	3	1.5

The calculation is simple and based on the idea that a finding of High = 9, Medium = 6, Low = 3. These values are the same without regard to the source of the finding being organizational or CVE. The difference is use of the initial value weights. For technical findings, we have given two-thirds of the weight to the vulnerability severity value and one-third of the weight to the information criticality impact value. For the organizational findings we have split the weights 50-50.

After a few years of debating the numerical value of various formulas used to do this calculation, we decided that we needed something that is easy for customer comprehension and yet provides a mapping to the IAM. You'll recall that in the IAM the values that are most consistently used by customers are High, Medium, and Low. Most organizational findings will probably come from the organizational assessment that was, or is, concurrently being done. For the weighting we looked at various methods and formulas being used and decided that we needed to put the weight on the factor that the INFOSEC industry has recognized—vulnerability severity. Let's face it, information criticality impact values change with each customer and even with each time the process is repeated, even with the same customer.

Now that you understand that technical finding weights are based on an industry standard impact value and that information criticality weights are based on customer opinions, you should see why we give two-thirds of the weight to industry standards and one-third to customer opinions. This, if you think about it, is the same logic that was used with the organizational findings. Because there are no industry standards for organizational findings, we have to agree that the end result is that both are opinions.

The customer's opinion is important; do not fool yourself into thinking that your opinion is more important. Yes, you might have the expertise and background to say to yourself that more weight should be given to your opinion since that is what the customer is paying for. Consider that you will be trying to justify how your opinion is more important than what the customer has already documented in the OICM definitions. We do not recommend getting into that discussion or debate with your customer, and we strongly recommend that you give the customer's opinion equal value to your own opinion.

Does this mean that you are limited to using three impact levels? No. Does this mean that you cannot use a different weighting? No. Does this mean that you are limited to using the values of 9, 6, and 3? No. This is still *your* evaluation of the customer. You can use as many impact levels as fit the customer. We have occasionally seen four levels, but that is a rarity. What is important for you to understand is that you should start simple using the model we have just shown you and then expand and tailor it to fit to your customer. At the same time, keep in mind that to be most effective for the customer, you need to ensure that the process is repeatable—not just the activities but in the reporting phase—to allow the customer to compare the reports from different evaluations.

Notes from the Underground

FIPS Pub 199

Yes, some industries do provide a starting block for organizations to work with. These are not intended to be the ultimate answer, just the minimum standards by which you can work. One of the better standards to work with if you have never worked with a customer to develop any yourself is from the NIST Federal Information Processing Standards (FIPS) Publication 199 (FIPS Pub 199), "Standards for Security Categorization of Federal Information and Information Systems." FIPS Pub 199 defines three levels of potential organizational impact, should your customer incur a loss of confidentiality, integrity, or availability:

- The potential impact is Low if the loss of CIA could be expected to have a limited adverse effect on organizational operations, organizational assets, or individuals. A limited adverse effect means that, for example, the loss of CIA might (1) cause a degradation in mission capability to an extent and duration that the organization is able to perform its primary functions but the effectiveness of the functions is noticeably reduced; (2) result in minor damage to organizational assets; (3) result in minor financial loss; or (4) result in minor harm to individuals.

- The potential impact is Moderate if the loss of CIA could be expected to have a serious adverse effect on organizational operations, organizational assets, or individuals. A serious adverse effect means that, for example, the loss of CIA might (1) cause a significant degradation in mission capability to an extent and duration that the organization is able to perform its primary functions but the effectiveness of the functions is significantly reduced; (2) result in significant damage to organizational assets; (3) result in significant financial loss; or (4) result in significant harm to individuals that does not involve loss of life or serious life-threatening injuries. Adverse effects on individuals may include, but are not limited to, loss of the privacy to which individuals are entitled under law.

- The potential impact is High if the loss of CIA could be expected to have a severe or catastrophic adverse effect on organizational operations, organizational assets, or individuals. A severe or catastrophic adverse effect means that, for example, the loss of CIA might (1) cause a severe degradation in or loss of mission capability to an extent and duration that the organization is not able to perform one or more of its primary functions; (2) result in major damage to organizational assets; (3) result in major financial loss; or (4) result in severe or catastrophic harm to individuals involving loss of life or serious life-threatening injuries.

Continued

So you are probably wondering why we quoted these definitions from NIST FIPS Pub 199 instead of just referencing them. There are two reasons: (1) to show you how even definitions like these tend to be so generalized that they provide a lot of latitude for customer interpretation, and (2) to ensure that all of you reading this book but who have not taken one of our classes have a good foundation to start with when working with customer definitions.

Now that you have defined values to input into the charts that we have been developing, it is a simple process to add the values together where they intersect. Once you have done this for all blocks that are not N/A, your charts should look something like Tables 13.14 and 13.15.

Table 13.14 FACTS with Values Added

| FACTS Vulnerability Criticality Matrix | Finding Number | Severity | High | | | Medium | | | | | Low |
			Criminal Records Integrity	Warrants Integrity	Warrants Availability	Criminal Records Confidentiality	Criminal Records Availability	Investigations Confidentiality	Investigations Integrity	Investigations Availability	Warrants Confidentiality
CVE 2001-0013	2	H	9	9	9	8	8	8	8	8	7
Organizational	3	H	9	9	9	7.5	7.5	7.5	7.5	7.5	6
CVE 2002-0571	4	H	N/A	N/A	N/A	8	N/A	8	N/A	N/A	7
Organizational	5	M	7.5	7.5	7.5	6	6	6	6	6	4.5
CVE 2002-1024	7	M	N/A	N/A	7	N/A	6	N/A	N/A	6	N/A
Operational	8	L	6	6	6	4.5	4.5	4.5	4.5	4.5	3
CVE 2002-1025	9	L	N/A	N/A	N/A	4	N/A	4	N/A	N/A	3

Table 13.15 SNOOP with Values Added

| SNOOP Vulnerability Criticality Matrix | Finding Number | Severity | High | | | Medium | | | | | Low |
			Criminal Records Integrity	Warrants Integrity	Warrants Availability	Criminal Records Confidentiality	Criminal Records Availability	Investigations Confidentiality	Investigations Integrity	Investigations Availability	Warrants Confidentiality
CVE 2002-0801	1	H	9	9	9	8	8	8	8	8	7
Organizational	3	H	9	9	9	7.5	7.5	7.5	7.5	7.5	6
CVE 2002-0571	4	H	N/A	N/A	N/A	8	N/A	8	N/A	N/A	7
Organizational	5	M	7.5	7.5	7.5	6	6	6	6	6	4.5
CVE 2002-1060	6	M	7	7	N/A	N/A	N/A	N/A	6	N/A	N/A
Operational	8	L	6	6	6	4.5	4.5	4.5	4.5	4.5	3
CVE 2004-0033	10	L	N/A	N/A	N/A	4	N/A	4	N/A	N/A	3

There is one last step in developing these system vulnerability criticality matrixes: adding color to the charts. To do this we need to decide which vulnerability criticality weight values in the chart define what is high, medium, or low. Right now as you read this you are saying, "That's easy, right?" Well, yes. We use a scale from 3 to 9. Then we add color based on what value in the block. Table 13.16 shows the scale that we have used.

Table 13.16 Vulnerability Criticality Weight

HIGH = 8 - 9
MEDIUM = 5 – 7.5
LOW = 3 – 4.5

In the NSA IEM classes it is taught that the weights used are Low (covering 3.0 to 4.5), Medium covering 5.0 to 7.5), and High (covering 8.0 to 9.0). This, combined with the coloring of Red for high, Yellow for medium, and Green for low, does add to the goal of showing that the more critical a finding to an organization, the higher in the chart it should be.

We would show you what the colorized version of the charts would be at this point but as you might have noticed, all our diagrams are in black and white for printing purposes. So you will have to make your own charts and add color to see how this part works and what it looks like.

Notes from the Underground...

Changing Impact Attributes

On occasions, the customer has wanted to change the impact attributes at this point. We strongly encourage you to dissuade the customer from changing them. Changing any impact attributes, even adding new ones, would mean starting over with the OICM. This would require stepping back and redoing several days' worth of work. Changing the values or adding a new value can cause the impact definitions to change, possibly resulting in greater cost for the customer and a feeling of wasted time for your team members.

Developing Overall Vulnerability Criticality Matrixes

Once you have all the system vulnerability criticality matrixes completed, it is time to move on to the overall vulnerability criticality matrix (OVCM). Keep in mind that every system that was included in the scope of the evaluation will require a separate SVCM. At this point, it's also a good practice to compare each of the SVCMs for consistency. By this we mean that you should ensure that the critical information topics that you have mapped directly from the OICM did not get mixed up when you mapped them to each individual system.

Now comes what is probably the easiest part of the process: merging the SVCMs into the OVCM. Again, we want to emphasize that there are multiple SVCMs for each system, but only one OVCM. The first step is to add a new column to the chart to allow for tracking of the findings to the applicable system, as shown in Table 13.17.

Table 13.17 COPS OVCM Header

COPS Overall Vulnerability Criticality Matrix	Finding Number	Systems Affected	Severity	High			Medium						Low
				Criminal Records Integrity	Warrants Integrity	Warrants Availability	Criminal Records Confidentiality	Criminal Records Availability	Investigations Confidentiality	Investigations Integrity	Investigations Availability		Warrants Confidentiality

As you look at this chart header, keep in mind that you will need to decide on a simple but effective method to identify which systems are which. In the example we've been using in this chapter, it is fairly easy to identify each system. We can identify the FACTS system by *F* and the SNOOP system by *S*. As a result, all we need to add to the Systems Affected column is an *F* or *S* to allow the customer to see if a finding affects more than one system. Table 13.18 shows the entire OVCM for the COPS organization with the Systems Affected column filled in.

Table 13.18 The COPS OVCM with Systems Affected

COPS Overall Vulnerability Criticality Matrix	Finding Number	Systems Affected	Severity	High			Medium						Low
				Criminal Records Integrity	Warrants Integrity	Warrants Availability	Criminal Records Confidentiality	Criminal Records Availability	Investigations Confidentiality	Investigations Integrity	Investigations Availability		Warrants Confidentiality
CVE 2002-0801	1	S	H	9	9	9	8	8	8	8	8		7
CVE 2001-0013	2	F	H	9	9	9	8	8	8	8	8		7
Organizational	3	F,S	H	9	9	9	7.5	7.5	7.5	7.5	7.5		6
CVE 2002-0571	4	F,S	H	N/A	N/A	N/A	8	N/A	8	N/A	N/A		7
Organizational	5	F,S	M	7.5	7.5	7.5	6	6	6	6	6		4.5
CVE 2002-1060	6	S	M	7	7	N/A	N/A	N/A	N/A	6	N/A		N/A
CVE 2002-1024	7	F	M	N/A	N/A	7	N/A	6	N/A	N/A	6		N/A
Operational	8	F,S	L	6	6	6	4.5	4.5	4.5	4.5	4.5		3
CVE 2002-1025	9	F	L	N/A	N/A	N/A	4	N/A	4	N/A	N/A		3
CVE 2004-0033	10	S	L	N/A	N/A	N/A	4	N/A	4	N/A	N/A		3

One of the benefits of merging the charts is that the customer can quickly see how many systems a particular finding affects. It is very common that a single finding will affect multiple systems, and this greatly reduces the repetition in the chart. Consider from the chart in Table 13.18 that finding number 4, CVE-2002-0571, is applicable to both the FACTS system and the SNOOP system. This finding is a design error in the Oracle 9.0.1.x database server that is mitigated by installing a patch, but this should not be shown in the OVCM as two findings. Putting the finding as one and showing that it is applicable to both systems allows management to easily see that there is one finding that needs to be addressed.

Keep in mind that this chapter has used a fairly simple organization that has only two systems. The total OVCM had only 10 findings, four critical information topics, and a total of nine impact attributes. This makes for a fairly small chart. Imagine if you had a much larger organization. It is not uncommon for organizations to have as many as 10 or 15 critical information topics.

Add to that the fact that the customer might want to use more impact attributes beyond the CIA. If they added nonrepudiation and accountability, you would have 15 impact attributes. And we all know that there are usually more than 10 findings. Consider if there were 45 findings—that would make for a very large OVCM.

Using the OVCM and SVCM

So now you have created the SVCMs and the OVCM. What are you going to do with them? As with any output related to the evaluation, you should have a purpose and a user group that the charts are intended for. Each chart has a use and an intended target audience. None of the charts is intended for use by the system administrators.

The SVCMs are system specific. Each of these charts should be intended for the system mangers of that particular system. Each chart contains the specific findings for that particular system. Consider the political atmosphere of many organizations. The system managers do not want to have their peers knowing the findings related to their systems. The system managers don't need to know the findings for systems that they have no responsibility for or management of. Keeping the SVCM system specific also makes for a usable size chart for each manager to track the work that needs to be done.

The OVCM is intended for senior or executive management; it contains the rollup of all the findings. This chart is intended to give the senior or executive management the "big picture" of the findings that need to be addressed.

Summary

In this chapter, you learned how to present the evaluation findings in a standardized reporting format. This report format is not intended as a working tool for the system administrators but rather as a single chart that the customer can use as a road map to improving their security posture.

The intended audience for the SVCMs is the system managers. The intended audience for the OVCM is the senior or executive-level management. The development of the matrixes is a bottom-up approach versus the top-down approach that was used during the assessment. Beginning with the SICMs, you map the each of the impact attributes by order of severity. Each finding's severity is based on two factors: the common vulnerability and exposures (CVE) value and the impact attribute value. If a finding does not have a CVE value, the weighted value that is used is 50/50. An excellent source for the finding weights is the NIST ICAT if the finding is technical in nature and has been entered into the CVE process.

Not all findings will normally be found on all systems, and not all findings will affect every impact attribute. You will need to use your expertise to decide which impact attributes are affected. Once you have added the values used for each weighting, you will be able to add color to the charts for ease of identification.

When all of the SVCMs, are completed you will be able to create an OVCM. This chart is a rollup or merger of all the SVCMs into one chart.

Now it is time to move on to Chapter 14 and the development of a numeric value for your customer's security posture.

Solutions Fast Track

The Purpose and Goal of the Matrixes

☑ The final matrixes can be used to assist in good risk management.

☑ The matrixes are designed for managers, not the administrators.

☑ You need three pieces to create matrixes: information types that are impacted, industry standard ratings, and evaluation team expertise.

Information Types

☑ Information types that are impacted are drawn from the organizational assessment.

☑ If the organizational assessment was not accomplished, your team will have to develop the information criticality matrixes before proceeding.

☑ Not all information topics will apply to all systems.

☑ Number the information topics to keep from getting confused when you're developing multiple matrixes.

Common Vulnerabilities and Exposures

☑ CVE is an industry standard you should use.

☑ CVE is a dictionary for technical findings, not a database.

☑ CVE contain no nontechnical findings.

☑ To be considered IEM compliant, you need to use CVE-compliant tools.

NIST ICAT

☑ ICAT provides a great starting point for beginning evaluators.

☑ ICAT is a searchable index of vulnerabilities.

☑ ICAT provides more information about vulnerabilities than CVE.

Developing System Vulnerability Criticality Matrixes

☑ SVCM is developed for each system that is evaluated.

☑ Numbering the findings will help you not forget any or prevent you from attributing a finding to a system that it does not apply to.

☑ If a finding is not applicable to an impact attribute, it should be marked with *N/A*.

☑ Technical findings have a weighting of two-thirds industry standard and one-third organizational impact value.

☑ Nontechnical findings have a weighting of one-half evaluator expertise and one-half organizational impact value.

Developing Overall Vulnerability Criticality Matrixes

☑ The OVCM is a compilation of all the SVCMs.

☑ There is only one OVCM per organization or evaluation.

☑ Add a column to track the systems that were affected by a particular finding.

Using the OVCM and SVCM

☑ The OVCM is intended for the executive level that has oversight for all the systems included on the OVCM.

☑ The SVCM is intended for the system owner or manager responsible for the system.

Frequently Asked Questions

The following Frequently Asked Questions, answered by the authors of this book, are designed to both measure your understanding of the concepts presented in this chapter and to assist you with real-life implementation of these concepts. To have your questions about this chapter answered by the author, browse to **www.syngress.com/solutions** and click on the **"Ask the Author"** form. You will also gain access to thousands of other FAQs at ITFAQnet.com.

Q: Is the IEM a risk management methodology?

A: No. It is a tool that can help an organization make good risk management decisions.

Q: Can administrators use these charts?

A: Yes, as a tracking tool, maybe even for prioritizing work, but the charts do not contain enough information for administrators, and there should be a detailed section in the final report that gives the administrators what they need.

Q: Can you do an evaluation without input from the organizational assessment?

A: Yes, companies do that all the time. But doing so does not provide the value that can be gained by drawing from the organizational assessment, and that evaluation will not be IEM compliant.

Q: Is there any other benefit in making an OVCM other than having an executive tracking chart?

A: Yes, the OVCM allows management to see where a single finding affects multiple systems. This can lead to justification for a single fix that mitigates the finding across the organization.

Q: How does FIPS Pub 200 fit into this?

A: FIPS Pub 200 contains 17 minimum security requirements for federal information and information systems. The 17 requirements, expressed at a very high level of abstraction, correspond to the 17 families of security controls in NIST SP 800-53. FIPS 200 points to the security controls in 800-53 and makes those controls mandatory.

Chapter 14

Trending Metrics

Solutions in this chapter:

- Metrics and Their Usefulness
- The INFOSEC Posture Profile
- The INFOSEC Posture Rating
- Value-Added Trending

☑ Summary

☑ Solutions Fast Track

☑ Frequently Asked Questions

Introduction

You now know how to build the executive and senior management charts for tracking the vulnerabilities that have been identified. This is good, but does it answer the customer's question, "How are we doing?" No, it doesn't. Although the charts provide a means for seeing what work needs to be done, they do not provide a description of the overall security posture of the organization. For that we need some kind of metrics that will readily identify the current security posture.

Metrics and Their Usefulness

Why do we want metrics? The answer to that question is really in two responses. First, executive management wants to know whether their expenditures on security have met their expectations for security protection. Second, executive and senior management want to know at a glance just what their security status is. You have probably heard the question, "So what is the bottom line; how are we doing?" or "So how do we compare to our competitors?" To answer these questions, you need to understand why managers ask them.

Return on Investment

Security has been and will continue to be an overhead expense for all organizations, much like payroll and other administrative tasks that are required to keep an organization running. The question that seems to pop up every few months in the security industry is, What is the value of all the security work that takes place in an organization? Organizations want to see what the return on investment (ROI) for the security budget is now and what it's expected to be in the future. Making such an estimate is a very difficult task. After all, if the security team is doing its job, the organization will likely not see a measurable impact from security problems.

When we're talking about IT security, ROI has historically focused on returning actual organizational payback where implementing tools, devices, or training should reduce operating costs. This is almost never the case. Since security acts as a version of insurance for your data or information, any return provided by required security should focus on this aspect.

Over the years there have been many attempts to define the ROI for security. There is by no means only one way to determine ROI for security. Currently, several projects are under way that are still working to determine this magic formula. More information on this topic can be found by doing a simple search on the Internet for *security ROI*.

For our purposes, we use a simplified formula that is based on the annual loss expectancy. Simply put, how much do you expect to lose from a single security incident each year? The annual loss expectancy of a single security breach that costs $1 million and has a 35 percent probability of occurring would be reflected as:

Incident Cost x Probability = Annual Loss Expectancy

$1,000,000 x 0.35 = $350,000

This is good, but it does not take into account the factor of mitigation, so we add this factor by multiplying the probability by the mitigation factor. Consider the impact that computer worms have had over the past few years or even the various Sober virus variants. If you have installed up-to-date antivirus software, you could expect to have mitigated about 50 percent of the probability. Or if you implemented strong user awareness training, you could mitigate about 80 percent of the probability of occurrence. (Can anybody say customer choices?) This makes the formula slightly different, as follows:

Incident Cost x (Probability x Mitigation) = Annual Loss Expectancy

$1,000,000 x (0.35 x 0.5) = $1,000,000 x 0.175 = $175,000 (Antivirus Software Mitigation)

$1,000,000 x (0.35 x 0.2) = $1,000,000 x 0.07 = $70,000 (User Awareness Training Mitigation)

If the cost of implementation is known—antivirus $75,000, user awareness program $10,000—you can show a simple ROI by demonstrating that the cost of mitigation is less than the cost of loss. Now, this does not take many factors into account and is not meant as an introduction or tutorial on determining ROI.

How Do We Compare?

If you can't prove ROI on security, how do you know you are making any progress? This can be shown to the customer as a simple numeric value. We'll show you how to calculate two numeric values. The first one is the INFOSEC Posture Profile (IPP); the second is the INFOSEC Posture Rating (IPR). They are designed to be flexible enough that you can utilize either one for your customers.

Each numeric value will show the customer their security posture. This is especially useful when you have a parent/child relationship in an organization. Consider the situation of a large university, where all the colleges within the university might not be able to conduct the evaluation at the same time. The standards to which they are held do not change from college to college. Conducting the evaluation and creating the IPP or IPR for each college allows the university to see how the colleges' security postures compare.

The concept used here is to provide the customer the ability to do trend analysis of vulnerabilities and mitigations over a period of time, to show the progress toward improving their security posture. Each of these numeric values, IPP and IPR, is designed to bring together both the IAM and IEM findings, to give an overall snapshot of an organization's security posture. Whether you use the IPP or the IPR, you should understand that it is generated for a specific customer at a specific time and thus cannot be legitimately compared among organizations. That said, continuous use of the IEM and this metric at the same organization can provide the ability to trend the organization's security posture and show improvements or declines in security posture.

The INFOSEC Posture Profile

The INFOSEC Posture Profile (IPP) was developed by the NSA and is focused on the DoD. The IPP is based on the DoD concept of Computer Network Defense (CND). CND is the application of security and operations to support the concept of defense in depth (DiD), first developed by the DoD and published in a white paper you can download from http://nsa1.www.conxion.com/support/guides/sd-1.pdf.

Defense in Depth

To understand how to use the IPP, you need to understand how CND is applied to meet the goals of the DiD strategy. This chapter is not meant as a tutorial in DiD or CND, but it is important we review the high points. DiD is a layered security strategy designed to provide protection for the information data.

The concept is that you and your customer can use a practical strategy for achieving information assurance in your computing environments. The concepts of DiD are based on the utilization of "best practices" to fit the computing environment. Good DiD requires a strategy that relies on the intelligent application of techniques and technologies that exist today. These techniques and technologies will change as advances are made. The bottom line here is that no single solution will work for every organization, so you must provide the best mixture of techniques and technologies that fits your customer's environment based on their underlying requirements for security.

CND and DiD both recommend a balance among your customer's protection capability, cost, performance, and operational considerations. Implementation of the DiD strategy is based on focusing on the four areas of CND: *Defend* the network and infrastructure, *Protect* the local and wide area communications networks, *Provide* protection for data transmitted over these networks, and *Defend* the enclave boundaries. As you look at each of these areas you need to consider the technologies and techniques that will best fit your customer's environment, and consider the following factors and how they apply to the decisions that you make.

Adversaries or Threats

Every organization has adversaries or threats. Therefore, each organization needs to identify, in advance, who or what is the threat, what is their reason for attacking (motivation), and the possible ways that they can attack. Adversaries can be anything from a script kiddie who wants to make a name for him or herself in the underground up to and including nation-states that want to weaken another country or economy. In between these significantly different threats are things like corporate espionage and criminals who attack to make a profit at your customer's expense. These are malicious adversaries that receive the most publicity in the news, but don't forget the nonmalicious threats such as fire, water, power failures, and the most common threat, user error.

Once you have identified the appropriate threats, you can look at the current protection schema by considering confidentiality, integrity, and availability. Think of these as protection services that you are providing for your organization or customer. These services are always included in the CND concepts of Protect, Detect, Respond, and Sustain. Organizations should expect attacks; they would not be in business if they did not have something important that needs protection. Organizations should employ tools and procedures that allow them to react to and recover from attacks.

Protect

Protect is based on the hardening or securing of the system and components. In the commonly used CND, this is proper system configuration management and remediation management. If you don't know what you have and how it is "supposed" to be used, how can you protect the system? If you don't have a defined approach to fixing problems that pop up, how will you fix those problems? Unfortunately, in many organizations this is an ad hoc process and is the reason that *Protect* is difficult to implement and maintain.

Detect

Detect is based on the ability to identify anomalous activity. Simply put, this is the implementation of an audit. If you don't monitor the activities that are occurring on the network, how will you know if something unusual is happening? This means that you will have to identify normal activity to be able to identify abnormal activity.

Respond

Respond is the ability to report and react to anomalous activity. This definitely builds on *Detect*. Once you have identified an abnormal activity, you must determine whether it is malicious or nonmalicious. Then what do you do? How will the activity be reported, and to whom? Are there defined processes for reacting to the abnormal activity?

Sustain

Sustain is the ability to maintain the proper level of security through a mature process. This can be the normal day-to-day activity known as network management. Network management can be a nightmare for some organizations because they have not implemented *Protect, Detect*, or *Respond*. This creates an organization that is continuously in "fire-fighting mode," dealing with issues over and over again based on what is going wrong today.

As we are all aware, to implement these principles and create a sound DiD strategy, you must have three elements: people, technology, and operations. These must be balanced to provide the best coverage for the price. Relying too much on one element will result in exposure to attacks.

People

People represent the beginning of a complete information security package, starting with senior management. The senior management must have a commitment to protecting the information based on a clear understanding of the threats. Senior management provides the policy and procedures needed for effective information security. Senior management must provide the resources needed to implement the policies and procedures, with clear understanding of roles and responsibilities and personal accountability. Training must be included in this resource assignment for all personnel, especially critical personnel. Having the senior management commitment includes the establishment of both physical and personnel security, allowing the organization to monitor and control access to facilities, information, and critical elements of the IT environment.

Technology

Technology is available in a variety of components and services. Technology can be used to detect attacks, malicious activity, or even nonmalicious activity. But what technology should be used? Every organization should employ its defined policies and processes for technology acquisition. These are normally based on the information security architecture and standards found in the security policy. The organization should have defined criteria for selecting and procuring products. These products should be implemented with defined and standardized configuration guidance. Prior to implementation there should be a process to assess the risk that could be introduced to the system by implementing the technology. When you implement technology in the DiD strategy, you should look at the following information security principles: defense in multiple places, layered defenses, security robustness, robust key management, and event correlation.

Defense in Multiple Places

Adversaries can and will attack from multiple angles. Your organization or customer must employ protection mechanisms at different locations to be resistant to all classes of attack. Defensive locations, called *focus areas*, include networks and infrastructure, enclave boundaries, and computing environment:

- Defending the network and infrastructure provides protection of the LAN and WAN by ensuring confidentiality and integrity of the data transmitted.

- Defending the enclave boundaries provides resistance to active network attacks.

- Defending the computing environment provides access controls on hosts and servers to resist insider or distributed attacks.

Layered Defenses

No single product or service is a cure-all for the inherent weaknesses of a network. Given enough time and resources, an adversary will find an exploitable vulnerability. The best method to mitigate this threat is through the use of multiple countermeasures that present different obstacles to the adversary. These countermeasures should include both protection and detection measures. This strategy will increase the adversary's risk of detection and reduce his or her chance of success. A common example in large networks is perimeter firewalls in conjunction with intrusion detection and implementation of more granular firewalls and controls on the internal network.

Specify the Security Robustness

Specifying the security robustness involves understanding the value of what you are protecting and placing appropriate technical controls in the appropriate place. One example is the deployment of strong perimeter defenses and implementation of security templates for workstations and servers. This makes sense because it is usually operationally effective and suitable to deploy stronger mechanisms at the network boundary than at the user desktop.

Robust Key Management

Infrastructures are lucrative targets. Deploying robust key management and public key infrastructures, such as PKI or PGP, that support all the information assurance technology that is deployed will ensure that your systems are resistant to attack.

Event Correlation

Deployed infrastructures should be able to detect intrusions, analyze them, and correlate the results to provide enough information to react accordingly. This will allow the operations staff to answer the following questions: Am I under attack? Who is the source? What is the target? Who else is under attack? What are my options?

Operations

Operations focus on all the activities required in maintaining and sustaining the organization or customer's security posture on a daily basis. Operations will always include:

- Maintaining the security policy and ensuring that all personnel are aware of and following the policy.

- Certifying and accrediting systems to ensure that good risk management decisions can be made.

- Managing the security posture by keeping patches and virus definitions and access control lists updated.

- Providing key management services.

- Performing security readiness reviews, commonly called *assessments,* to ensure that the controls are functioning correctly.

- Monitoring and reacting to threats or attacks as they occur.

- Recovery and resumption of operations from attacks or nonmalicious events such as fire or flood.

DiD is simply a means of using multiple controls to implement a more complete security posture based on perceived threats or adversaries. We know that we cannot achieve a 100 percent secure stance, because that would leave us with 0 percent usability. For example, we could deny all inbound or outbound connections to the Internet, but in today's computing environment the network usability would suffer greatly. We want to avoid weak links through the balance of people, technology, and operations. Each of these elements is used to maintain the organization or customer's ability to *Protect, Detect, Respond*, and *Sustain* their information assurance.

Developing the INFOSEC Posture Profile

As we stated earlier in this chapter, the greatest value of using these metrics is the ability to utilize all the organizational and technology findings to create a value-added numeric value. To bring these findings together, you first need to understand the mappings of the findings to the areas of *Protect, Detect, Respond*, and *Sustain*. First let's look at the categories of information from the IAM:

- **Management**
    1. INFOSEC Documentation
    2. INFOSEC Roles and Responsibilities
    3. Contingency Planning
- **Technical**
    4. Identification and Authentication
    5. Account Management
    6. Session Controls
    7. Auditing
    8. Malicious Code Protection
    9. Maintenance
    10. System Assurance
    11. Networking/Connectivity
    12. Communications Security
- **Operational**
    13. Media Controls
    14. Labeling
    15. Physical Environment
    16. Personnel Security
    17. Education Training and Awareness

Each of these baseline INFOSEC categories is mapped to one of the four pillars of DiD: *Protect, Detect, Respond*, and *Sustain*, as shown in Table 14.1.

Table 14.1 IAM Mapping for IPP

Protect	Detect
• Identification and Authentication	• Auditing
• Session Controls	**Respond**
• System Assurance	• Contingency Planning
• Networking / Connectivity	**Sustain**
• Malicious Code Protection	• INFOSEC Documentation
• Communications Security	• INFOSEC Roles and Responsibilities
• Media Controls	• Configuration Management
• Labeling	• Account Management
• Physical Environment	• Maintenance
• Personnel Security	• Education Training and Awareness

Then we need to look at the 10 baseline activities from the IEM and the way they map to the four pillars of CND (see Table 14.2).

Table 14.2 The IEM Baseline Activities

Port Scanning	Host Evaluation
SNMP Scanning	Network Device Analysis
Enumeration & Banner Grabbing	Password Compliance Testing
Wireless Enumeration	Application Specific Scanning
Vulnerability Scanning	Network Sniffing

Now as you look at these you should be thinking that it is not that easy to map the activities. The IEM was much simpler because it uses topics, not activities. So we need to determine exactly what information is being derived from the IEM activities. The easy answer is findings. But that is not very useful information if we do not know what that information applies to. So, what is the purpose and defined information output of each of the activities? To recap the information previously covered in other chapters, the goal of each activity is as follows:

- **Port scanning**
    - Identify enabled network services on systems
    - Look for unauthorized or unnecessary services
    - Look for back doors
- **SNMP scanners**
    - Enumerate systems on the network

- Identify community strings
- **Wireless enumeration tools**
  - Identify access points and potential exposures
- **Enumeration and banner grabbing**
  - Verification of operating system
- **Vulnerability Scanners**
  - Identify well-known vulnerabilities on systems
- **Network device analysis**
  - Analyze security architecture for well-known vulnerabilities and insecure configurations
- **Host evaluation**
  - Analyze configuration, discretionary access control, and policies against accepted standards (NSA, DISA, NIST, etc.)
- **Password-compliance testing**
  - Evaluate adherence to password policy and determine whether password filters are being effectively implemented
- **Application-specific scanning**
  - Evaluate security configuration of critical applications
- **Network sniffing**
  - Identifies sensitive information traversing the network (login, passwords, server configurations via Telnet, etc.)

Each of these activities provides valuable output, and if we look at the output we can see that basic information types can be mapped as shown in Figure 14.3.

Table 14.3 IEM Mapping for IPP

Detect
- **Auditing Implementation**
  - IDS
  - Firewalls
  - Host Based

Protect
- **Remediation Managment**
  - Patches
  - Hotfixes
  - Virus Signature Updates
- **System Configuration**
  - Permissions
  - ACL
  - Privileges
  - Passwords
  - System Services

Respond
- **Reactive Measures**
  - Incident Response
  - Incident Alerting

Sustain
- **Network Management**
  - Patch Management Processes
  - Group Policy Administration
  - Role-based Policies
  - Mandatory Access Control

Now that we know the mapping, the next step is to determine the applicability of each finding to each of the CND areas: *Protect, Detect, Respond*, and *Sustain*. Each finding affects one area only. Though you could argue that some findings could directly affect more than one topic, such as INFOSEC documentation, each finding maps to only one pillar of the CND. Evaluator expertise is needed here to determine which area or aspect of the CND each finding applies to (see Table 14.4).

Table 14.4 The COPS OVCM

COPS Overall Vulnerability Criticality Matrix	Finding Number	Systems Affected	Computer Network Defense	Severity	High			Medium					Low
					Criminal Records Integrity	Warrants Integrity	Warrants Availability	Criminal Records Confidentiality	Criminal Records Availability	Investigations Confidentiality	Investigations Integrity	Investigations Availability	Warrants Confidentiality
CVE 2002-0801	1	S	D	H	9	9	9	8	8	8	8	8	7
CVE 2001-0013	2	F	P	H	9	9	9	8	8	8	8	8	7
Organizational	3	F,S	S	H	9	9	9	7.5	7.5	7.5	7.5	7.5	6
CVE 2002-0571	4	F,S	R	H	N/A	N/A	N/A	8	N/A	8	N/A	N/A	7
Organizational	5	F,S	S	M	7.5	7.5	7.5	6	6	6	6	6	4.5
CVE 2002-1060	6	S	P	M	7	7	N/A	N/A	N/A	N/A	6	N/A	N/A
CVE 2002-1024	7	F	P	M	N/A	N/A	7	N/A	6	N/A	N/A	6	N/A
Operational	8	F,S	S	L	6	6	6	4.5	4.5	4.5	4.5	4.5	3
CVE 2002-1025	9	F	P	L	N/A	N/A	N/A	4	N/A	4	N/A	N/A	3
CVE 2004-0033	10	S	R	L	N/A	N/A	N/A	4	N/A	4	N/A	N/A	3

Going back to the COPS overall vulnerability criticality matrix (OVCM), we now can see that we need to add another column to the chart, to apply the mapping of the CND pillars. We have labeled the column *Computer Network Defense* and used *P* for *Protect, D* for *Detect, R* for *Respond*, and *S* for *Sustain*. Now we need to calculate the IPP for this customer. First we will determine the number of High, Medium, and Low findings for each of the CND aspects. This is done by adding up each severity independently for each aspect (see Figure 14.5).

Table 14.5 Computer Network Defense Summary by Severity

```
Protect            Respond
High = 1           High = 1
Medium = 2         Medium = 0
Low = 1            Low = 1

Detect             Sustain
High = 1           High = 1
Medium = 0         Medium = 1
Low = 0            Low = 1
```

Once you have added the number of findings by severity and CND aspect, you can calculate the value of each area. To do this we use the model that we have used throughout this book: High is worth 3, Medium is worth 2, and Low is worth 1. Now let's multiply the total findings for each severity by the assigned value. When you have all the values for each severity, sum each CND aspect for the rating value (see Figure 14.6).

Figure 14.6 INFOSEC Posture Profile Calculation

```
Protect                         Respond
High:      1 x 3 = 3            High:      1 x 3 = 3
Medium:    2 x 2 = 4            Medium:    0 x 2 = 0
Low:       1 x 1 = 1            Low:       1 x 1 = 1
           Total = 8                       Total = 4

Detect                          Sustain
High:      1 x 3 = 3            High:      1 x 3 = 3
Medium:    0 x 2 = 0            Medium:    1 x 2 = 2
Low:       0 x 1 = 0            Low:       1 x 1 = 1
           Total = 3                       Total = 6
```

With these totals or rating values, we can insert the values into the COPS OVCM and easily show the customer their current IPP (see Table 14.7). Once again we want to point out that we have used a very simple organization with only a few findings spanning two systems. The results for a large organization with multiple systems and many findings will significantly increase the values for each aspect.

Table 14.7 The COPS OVCM with IPP

COPS Overall Vulnerability Criticality Matrix / INFOSEC Posture Protect = 8 Detect = 3 Respond = 4 Sustain = 6	Finding Number	Systems Affected	Computer Network Defense	Severity	High						Medium					Low
					Criminal Records Integrity	Warrants Integrity	Warrants Availability	Criminal Records Confidentiality	Criminal Records Availability	Investigations Confidentiality	Investigations Integrity	Investigations Availability	Warrants Confidentiality	
CVE 2002-0801	1	S	D	H	9	9	9	8	8	8	8	8	7
CVE 2001-0013	2	F	P	H	9	9	9	8	8	8	8	8	7
Organizational	3	F,S	S	H	9	9	9	7.5	7.5	7.5	7.5	7.5	6
CVE 2002-0571	4	F,S	R	H	N/A	N/A	N/A	8	N/A	8	N/A	N/A	7
Organizational	5	F,S	S	M	7.5	7.5	7.5	6	6	6	6	6	4.5
CVE 2002-1060	6	S	P	M	7	7	N/A	N/A	N/A	N/A	6	N/A	N/A
CVE 2002-1024	7	F	P	M	N/A	N/A	7	N/A	6	N/A	N/A	6	N/A
Operational	8	F,S	S	L	6	6	6	4.5	4.5	4.5	4.5	4.5	3
CVE 2002-1025	9	F	P	L	N/A	N/A	N/A	4	N/A	4	N/A	N/A	3
CVE 2004-0033	10	S	R	L	N/A	N/A	N/A	4	N/A	4	N/A	N/A	3

So now you have the rating profile for COPS. Is this a good profile or a bad profile? Only time will tell. This value is applicable to this organization at this time and provides the baseline of where the organization stands as far as its current security posture. The profile tells the organization which of the four aspects of the CND is the weakest by the highest number, but it does not provide any comparison to any other organization. The main reason that there is no way to compare the DoD organizations that utilize the IPP is that there is insufficient empirical data to define what a good rating profile should be. At this time we recommend that you utilize the profile and develop a trend analysis for the security posture. With each successive evaluation, the customer can compare the profiles obtained and determine whether they are meeting their security requirements.

The INFOSEC Posture Rating

The INFOSEC Posture Rating (IPR) was developed for organizations that do not utilize or might not even understand the DiD and CND concepts. This is not to say that these organizations are less informed. Each has a different objective and usually much different requirements to meet, as discussed in previous chapters.

The IPR works well for commercial and federal organizations that do not have a DoD requirement to meet. This numeric rating is intended to provide a number value of the current security posture of a specific organization. The IPR is customized for each customer for which you utilize it and should not be used to compare organizations. The value to the customer is that the continuous use of the metric at the same organization will provide the customer the ability to do trend analysis of the organizational security posture.

The concept behind using the IRP is that it is based on the average of all findings, with weighting applied based on the severity of the findings. Using the OVCM that we developed in the last chapter, we can see how the weighting has already been applied (see Table 14.8).

Now to determine the IPR, we add all the severity values and divide that total by the number of values that were added together:

(Sum All Values Not "N/A") / (Number of Values Added Together) = INFOSEC Posture Rating

In this case, this would be:

403 / 60 = 6.72

The IPR is susceptible to skewing by excessive low findings, but we believe that it is probably 95 percent accurate. You can validate this accuracy by repeating the process with the same customer and trending the change in their security posture. There is a bonus in using this simple method: It is simple enough for any customer to quickly understand the mathematics behind the number without a lot of discussion on how it was developed.

Now that you have a numeric value, what does that mean? Recall from Chapter 13 that we have already set a scale for the customer to identify the severity of the numeric value calculated for each finding (see Table 14.9). We can use that value already defined for the customer and now tell them their security posture.

Table 14.8 The COPS OVCM

COPS Overall Vulnerability Criticality Matrix	Finding Number	Systems Affected	Computer Network Defense	Severity	High			Medium					Low
					Criminal Records Integrity	Warrants Integrity	Warrants Availability	Criminal Records Confidentiality	Criminal Records Availability	Investigations Confidentiality	Investigations Integrity	Investigations Availability	Warrants Confidentiality
CVE 2002-0801	1	S	D	H	9	9	9	8	8	8	8	8	7
CVE 2001-0013	2	F	P	H	9	9	9	8	8	8	8	8	7
Organizational	3	F,S	S	H	9	9	9	7.5	7.5	7.5	7.5	7.5	6
CVE 2002-0571	4	F,S	R	H	N/A	N/A	N/A	8	N/A	8	N/A	N/A	7
Organizational	5	F,S	S	M	7.5	7.5	7.5	6	6	6	6	6	4.5
CVE 2002-1060	6	S	P	M	7	7	N/A	N/A	N/A	N/A	6	N/A	N/A
CVE 2002-1024	7	F	P	M	N/A	N/A	7	N/A	6	N/A	N/A	6	N/A
Operational	8	F,S	S	L	6	6	6	4.5	4.5	4.5	4.5	4.5	3
CVE 2002-1025	9	F	P	L	N/A	N/A	N/A	4	N/A	4	N/A	N/A	3
CVE 2004-0033	10	S	R	L	N/A	N/A	N/A	4	N/A	4	N/A	N/A	3

Table 14.9 The IPR Scale

> **High = 8.0 to 9.0**
> **Medium = 5.0 to 7.5**
> **Low = 3.0 to 4.5**

Using this scale, we can say that the customer has a Medium overall security posture, because their IRP is 6.72. This could even be used in a briefing graphic to allow for better visualization of a customer's status. An IPR Graphic can be seen in Figure 14.1.

Figure 14.1 An IPR Graphic

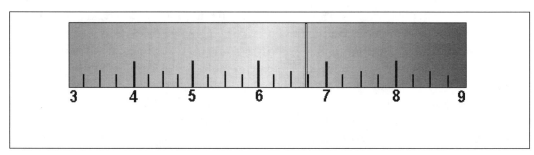

Value-Added Trending

What does trending do for each level of an organization? That is a good question that is probably drawing a few groans from some of the readers of this book. But in fact, value-added trending (VAT) of the security posture has benefits for every level of the organization.

Executive management is always looking for some standard or measurement of how their security posture is meeting requirements. Many would call this *due diligence,* and they would not be wrong. Executive-level management needs the "warm and fuzzy" feeling that they have done all that is required and possibly be able to show that they have exceeded the requirements. VAT also allows the executive level to see the effectiveness of the security program and budget.

Middle to senior management needs a tracking mechanism that allows them to see what progress is being made. This progress is usable for budget justifications and prioritization of work assignments. Without any tracking and a viable picture of the security posture, middle management is unable to focus on long-term goals and objectives. Instead, middle management will stay in the "fire-fighting mode" of operation.

Administrators and technicians can use trending to see what progress has been made. Though when rolled up, the numbers usually don't mean much to this level, it is easy to give them a numeric value based on their systems only. This allows them to see what significant improvements can be made easily and which mitigations will take time and probably out-year budgeting to accomplish.

Summary

In this chapter you have seem the "why and how" of building an effective metric for your customer that allows for trending of the security posture. This metric allows the senior or executive level to answer the questions "How are we doing?" and "Was it worth the cost?" Although there are many projects under way that are trying to determine the return on investment (ROI) for security, there is no industry standard for answering that question.

What *can* be answered is the "How are we doing?" question. To answer this question, you need a simple but effective method to calculate a numeric value. We showed you how to build two different versions of a security metric: the INFOSEC posture profile (IPP) and the INFOSEC posture rating (IPR). Each is designed to be flexible enough to be used in any industry. The factor that will normally drive the choice of metric is the customer. From experience we have seen that the IPP is a DoD preference or requirement, whereas the IPR is for all other customers. This quite possibly won't be the case all the time, but we believe that there is more usability and flexibility in the IPR.

The IPP is based on the implementation of CND to meet the DiD strategy. DiD requires that you use a layered strategy to provide protection for data. To implement the CND, you need to intelligently implement the techniques and technologies that are current and that fit your customer organization. The implementation of the CND is based on four aspects: *Protect, Detect, Respond*, and *Sustain*. Each of these aspects provides for a layered defense aimed at four areas: defend the network and infrastructure, protect the local and wide area communications networks, provide protection for the data transmitted over these networks, and defend the enclave boundaries. Development of the IPP requires you to map the 18 IAM information topics and the 10 IEM activities to the four aspects of the CND. Though there is a viable argument that some topics could directly affect more than one topic, such as INFOSEC documentation, each finding maps to only one pillar of the CND. Once all the findings are mapped, you will be able to do some simple math and give your customer a snapshot in time of their security posture. This is not something that could be used to compare different organizations, but it is very effective when doing the trend analysis of the security posture of one organization.

The IPR was developed for organizations that do not utilize or might not even understand the DiD and CND concepts. The IPR works well for commercial and federal organizations that do not have a DoD requirement. This numeric rating is intended to provide a number value of the current security posture of a specific organization. The IPR is customized for each customer and should not be used to compare organizations. The value to the customer is that the continuous use of the metric at the same organization will provide the customer the ability to do trend analysis of the organizational security posture. The IPR is developed by determining the average of all the findings, including organizational and technical, with weighting applied based on the severity of the findings. There is a mathematical susceptibility to skewing of the value by having an excessively large number of low findings, we have found that counting duplicate findings only once will reduce any possibility of skewing. One of the nice benefits of using the IPR is that it is a numeric value that lends itself to a briefing graphic that is easily understood by executive management.

Administrators and technicians are not the prime target for developing any trending metrics, but there is benefit to be gained at all levels of an organization by trending the security posture. Executive-level management can see their status and how much improvement has been made. Middle management can look at the trends to prioritize and justify budgets to improve the security posture. Both of the metrics, the IPP and the IPR, can be drilled down to show administrators or technicians the posture of the systems they are responsible for. This will help them understand the organizational security goals and what they can do to meet those goals.

Solutions Fast Track

Metrics and Their Usefulness

- ☑ Metrics provide management with the answer to the question, "How are we doing?"
- ☑ Security is an overhead expense that cannot be easily quantified by calculating a return on investment, or ROI.
- ☑ Two very usable metrics are available for use: the INFOSEC Posture Profile (IPP) and the INFOSEC Posture Rating (IPR).

The INFOSEC Posture Profile

☑ The IPP was developed by the NSA for the Department of Defense (DoD).

☑ The IPP requires an understanding of defense in depth (DiD).

☑ DiD is a strategy implemented through Computer Network Defense (CND).

☑ CND has four areas: defend the network and infrastructure, protect the LAN and WAN, provide protection for the data transmitted, and defend the enclave boundaries.

☑ The four input factors for deciding what techniques and technologies to use are adversaries or threats, people, technology, and operations.

☑ All areas and input factors are applied to the four aspects of CND: *Protect, Detect, Respond*, and *Sustain*.

☑ All 18 information topics from the IAM are mapped to the four aspects of the CND.

☑ All 10 activities from the IEM are mapped to the four aspects of the CND.

☑ The information topics and activities that are mapped to the CND are only mapped to a single aspect and not shared.

☑ The final rating is not valid for comparison between organizations.

The INFOSEC Posture Rating

☑ The IPR was developed for organizations that do not utilize the IPP.

☑ The IPR is based on the average of all findings, with weighting applied based on the severity of the findings.

☑ The IPR is susceptible to skewing by excessive low findings.

☑ The IPR lends itself to being used in an executive-level briefing graphic.

Value-Added Trending

☑ Metrics provide senior management with a snapshot of the status of the security posture.

☑ Trending allows the executive level to see the effectiveness of the security program and budget.

☑ Trending allows middle management to monitor the progress of the security program.

☑ Trending is useful for budget justifications and prioritization of work assignments.

☑ Trending can provide administrators and technicians with prioritization of work.

Frequently Asked Questions

The following Frequently Asked Questions, answered by the authors of this book, are designed to both measure your understanding of the concepts presented in this chapter and to assist you with real-life implementation of these concepts. To have your questions about this chapter answered by the author, browse to **www.syngress.com/solutions** and click on the **"Ask the Author"** form. You will also gain access to thousands of other FAQs at ITFAQnet.com.

Q: Are any metrics developed for a specific industry such as health care?

A: Not yet. Over time, as these metrics are used throughout various industries, there will be. This is still a fairly new concept for most organizations. If you want to contribute to developing an industry standard, feel free to contact Ed Fuller at <ed@securityhorizon.com>.

Q: If we use these metrics in the parent/child relationship that you explained, would that not just cause more political in-fighting over who is better?

A: Yes, it can. The thing to remember here is that as you help the organization understand where they really are, creating a little competition between divisions of the organization can be a good thing.

Q: Does anybody really use the INFOSEC posture profile (IPP)?

A: Yes, the NSA is a proponent of the IPP for DoD. Should the NSA Inspector General's Office (IG) start pushing the standardization of assessments and evaluations, the result could and will affect organizations that have to meet DoD requirements.

Q: How stringent is the mapping of the IAM topics and IEM activities to the IPP?

A: Right now it fairly strict, but that can change. The deciding factor will be the consensus of the security professionals using these metrics and the consistency of application by those same professionals. As with any methodology, there will be changes over time as the methodology is refined.

Chapter 15

Final Reporting

Solutions in this chapter:

- **Pulling All the Information Together**
- **Making Recommendations**
- **Creating the Final Report**
- **Presenting the Final Report**

☑ **Summary**

☑ **Solutions Fast Track**

☑ **Frequently Asked Questions**

Introduction

Your team has completed the onsite technical evaluation of your client, and now it's time to review all the information you gathered, create the final report in a clear, understandable format, and present it to the customer. The final report will contain many things and provide your customer with more than just recommendations and options. The final report should ensure that not only does it bring added value but that it will help the organization create a plan, or road map, to a better, more secure information security posture.

Part of the value-add for the customer is the followup after you present all the documentation and the evaluation is complete. You've probably seen or heard of that information security company that simply runs a tool and hands in a report. You want to show the organization that you honestly want to improve the company's security posture. You want to relay to the organization that you will be there while they are incorporating your recommendations and will be there in the future, not only for the next evaluation but for information and ideas on how to apply the recommendations to the findings you and your team have uncovered. You should be a partner in the process with your customer, as much as you can.

Regarding the information security company that simply runs a tool and hands in a report: Do you think this company will be asked back to do another evaluation? Will the organization receiving this report recommend that company to another organization? The answer to both questions should be obvious: *No!* Of course you must make money, but a better way to increase you client base is to become known as an information security company that cares about its customers' information security and will be there when a customer needs help.

The other thing you'll want to cover here is the fact that, because this information is so sensitive, you will only store it for a certain period of time (30–45 days is typical). For that reason, you'll want to perform the followup during that window of time, ensuring that the customer has all questions answered. After all, a final report that the customer can't use is worthless. After the 30–45 days, you will typically destroy the information because you're probably not set up to act as a secure storage facility. This clause is usually mentioned in the contract with the customer before the engagement begins.

Pulling All the Information Together

You and your team have spent a great deal of time and effort evaluating the information security posture of your customer organization. In the process of doing the evaluation, you have collected information that now needs not only further review but to be organized in a way that is beneficial to your client. Before you are able to collect all the data and coalesce it into a useful document for the customer, the following tasks should be conducted:

- A team meeting
- Research
- SVCM and OVCM
- Review

The Team Meeting

Many things that go into having a successful meeting: reserving a room of the right size, supplying pens and pencils, deciding who will facilitate. The purpose of the team meeting is to get everyone refocused. Many of us are working on multiple projects, and we need to set aside time to bring all the material together in an organized manner. This would be the time to:

- **Set up the agenda** Discuss the objectives, who has done what, and what needs to be done to complete the evaluation and turn in the final report on time.

- **Bring up questions about your findings** In the initial meetings following the onsite evaluation, a lot of the time is used to discuss your findings, how they could affect your client, and what would be the best solution for the organization.

- **Assign work** Review where everyone is with their responsibilities and assign any work that needs to be completed.

- **Create an action plan and deadlines** The action plan should contain a list of tasks that need to be done, with names attached and deadlines.

- **Consult any additional expertise that might be needed** With so many advancements in technology and the different ways organizations do business, it could be possible that you will need to bring in additional expertise to complete the evaluation.

- **Any other applicable information** Make sure everyone is on the same page, and utilize good communication to ensure a quality product.

NOTE

Writing the final report does not have to be the responsibility of one person. In many cases, multiple team members will contribute to the actual writing of the final report. Assign the writing responsibility according to the abilities of individual team members.

Research

Further research will probably be necessary to confirm or refute many of the vulnerabilities that you and your team uncovered during your evaluation. During this phase, you and your team should do research into the vulnerabilities that you have found and discover the latest fix or patch for each vulnerability, taking into consideration the effect your recommendation could have on the applications your client is running. This is another great place to add value to your evaluation by helping your customer understand how these vulnerabilities can impact their organization. Remember, during your research your goal is to analyze your data, keeping in mind your customer's information security so you can make the appropriate recommendations that will advance the organization's information security posture.

Research has been underrated in the information security field. This activity should be something that an information security professional does on a regular basis.

The SVCM and OVCM

You create two matrixes during the IEM to help your customer understand their vulnerabilities and the risks they represent to the organization. The system vulnerability criticality matrix (SVCM) and the overall vulnerability criticality matrix (OVCM) are created using the information criticality matrixes that were developed in the IAM; these are used during the IEM to aid the customer. This type of information is created during the IAM, but with the IEM we start at the system level and move to the organizational level. The purpose of the SVCM is to provide a detailed snapshot of the customer's security posture at a very high level. We call this a *first-order prioritization* of the customer's findings.

To create these matrixes, you must base them not only on your findings and knowledge of information security, but also on the customer's input. Customer input refers to the information provided by the customer that gives you and your team insight as to how a particular vulnerability could directly impact your client. This step is normally performed in the NSA IAM pre-assessment phase. This snapshot not only assists the customer in prioritizing their vulnerabilities but also assists you in tracking vulnerabilities through successive evaluations. For more in-depth discussion on the SVCM and OVCM, refer to Chapter 13, "Creating Measurements and Trending Results."

Review

In pulling your information together after the onsite evaluation phase, with the amount of information that you and your team have collected it is important to continue to work together to make sure that your information is accurate and that you take the time to determine the vulnerabilities that are present within the organization. During this review process, it is important to review not only your notes and findings, but those of your evaluation team. We cannot emphasize enough how vital it is for you and your team to work together during this review process. Remember to share not only the information from your scans, but any interviews or conversations you had with members of the organization and any notes you took, no matter how insignificant you thought they were at the time. At this point in the review, your team should have a conversation on all the information you have gathered, including the findings, good and bad, as well as best practices that could help the organization.

NOTE

Examples of good and bad findings:
- **Good findings** Findings that you and your team come across during your evaluation that reveal good security practices.
- **Bad findings** Findings that reveal poor configurations (of firewall, default passwords, or the like) or other technical security issues.

Making Recommendations

The Recommendations section of your final report is critical when it comes to adding value to your evaluation. Now you have finished your technical evaluation of your client, reviewed the information that you have collected, used your own expertise and possibly brought in other experts who might be able to add insight on specific platforms and/or business models, you need to review your data. It is time to organize a list of your findings from high to low criticality or however the client requested the information. Findings should be discussed in direct relation to their impact on the customer organization, based on three things: customer input, industry ratings (CVE/CAN/ICAT), and your professional experience.

TIP

The information security professional who works for the organization that you are evaluating might already feel angry, disturbed, or anxious that you and your team are in his or her network poking around. They probably think, no matter what your team has explained in the in-brief, that you are there to point out what they are doing wrong. You need to assure these professionals that you are not there to show their managers what hasn't been done or who didn't secure what, but instead to show the organization the gaps that currently exist in their organization.

One way to improve this situation is to remember, when discussing findings and vulnerabilities in your final report, that the individuals who maintain the systems security will be directly affected by not only your findings but your recommendations. Chances are that you will find critical security concerns during your evaluation. It is a good idea to add positive findings and comments in your final report so it doesn't seem as though you're attacking the individuals concerned. Without these positive findings, the individuals within the organization could take your report as a personal insult, which in turn could make it difficult for them to accept and implement your recommendations.

These positive findings could also give the organization as well as the individual(s) an idea of what they are doing well and what security practices they can build on. An example of a positive comment is something like, "Our evaluation determined that the organization's network and IT systems were configured with security in mind."

Other examples of good or positive findings could look something like these:

During the INFOSEC evaluation, many good findings were documented, indicating that your security team included security within the development life cycle. The good findings included:

- Enforcement of strong password policies
- Evidence that the IDS team reviews logs on a regular basis
- Disabling of finger service

Findings

Findings are security concerns that you uncovered during your evaluation. This section of the report should be broken into three sections: High, Medium, and Low. You should have developed the definitions for the criticality findings with the customer, through interviews and conversations. Use these definitions to assign the risk impact levels to each of the vulnerabilities. Examples of what these definitions might look like are:

- **High criticality findings** Loss could result in the unauthorized release of information that could have a significant impact on the organization's mission or financial assets or result in loss of life.

- **Medium criticality findings** Loss could result in the unauthorized release of information that could have an impact on the organization's mission or financial assets or result in harm to an individual.

- **Low criticality findings** Loss could result in the unauthorized release of information that could have some degree of impact on the organization's mission or financial assets or result in harm to an individual.

Defining what is a **High**, **Medium**, or **Low** criticality finding depends on the impact to the customer. There are many ways to determine factors at each level of criticality, but the bottom line is how the finding impacts the organization. These definitions are not something the evaluation team can come up with on their own, and normally we prefer that the customer create them completely on their own while the evaluation team acts in the role of facilitator to the process. Again, this is a task that should have been conducted in the NSA IAM process and migrated over to the evaluation. For technical findings, we see that most standard definitions for High, Medium, and Low have been developed already by various organizations and will require only minor modifications by the evaluation team.

TIP

Remember, when we deal in organizational findings from the IAM, it is up to the organization to develop definitions for High, Medium, and Low criticality specific to their organizations. For the IEM, vulnerabilities are rated High, Medium, and Low according to industry rating (CVE/CAN/ICAT), your professional experience, and the customer's input. (The industry ratings are discussed in more detail in Chapter 7 of this book.)

When listing the findings in your report, discuss the most critical findings first, medium second, and if appropriate, list the low findings last. Write your findings so that first you categorize them in relation to whether they represent external exposures, internal exposures, or systems boundary issues. Clearly explain each vulnerability using language your client will understand, but try to limit your definition to about two to three sentences.

Your report should also list finding name, the corresponding common vulnerabilities and exposures (CVE/CAN) number where applicable at a level of detail that is appropriate to your audience, severity rating, and recommendations. When possible, use the Cadillac, Chevy, and Yugo model.

Notes from the Underground…

Cadillac, Chevy, and Yugo

If you have been working in the security arena and/or mitigating vulnerabilities, you might be familiar with the Cadillac, Chevy, and Yugo model. This is simply a way of providing recommendations to your customer that allows them to have options. After all, if we only provide the customer with the best possible solution, what are the chances that they will be capable of implementing it across the entire organization? Financial and resource constraints will limit their abilities to do that. By providing multiple levels of recommendation, where available, you give the customer options and allow them to have a greater positive impact on their security posture. Here are the three parts of the model:

- **Cadillac** This is not always the best solution for the organization, but it is, for sure, the top of the line. This solution is probably the most expensive and time consuming, but it offers the highest level of protection.

- **Chevy** This is the middle-of-the-road solution for your client. This solution offers to reduce the risk to the organization, but not as much as the Cadillac. Of course, this solution will cost less than the Cadillac and require fewer resources to implement.

- **Yugo** As you have already realized, this solution is the cheapest for your client. It provides some elimination of risk immediately, with very little cost to the organization. This can be a great temporary patch until your client has the resources to implement the Cadillac or Chevy.

NOTE

If you or your organization do not use the CVE, it is strongly suggested that you use something similar that will provide your client with the definitions and information needed to fully understand a vulnerability. The use of this type of standard allows you and the customer to cross-reference specific vulnerabilities and weaknesses across different platforms, databases, and tools. The CVE provides users free services and databases that can strengthen an organization's information security.

The importance of using the CVE standard is that you and your team can determine a standard rating for each of the vulnerabilities that you discovered. This process will gain value as your team completes annual evaluations and can use the CVE scores to compare the current security posture of the organization to past evaluations.

Recommendations

Knowing the security issues is only half the battle. Providing your customer recommendations in the form of options for your findings is critical. As we mentioned earlier in this section, it is very important to create or provide your client with a specific way to resolve a finding. Your recommendations should be specific to your client while taking into consideration any concerns or constraints the client has. Following the results from the SVCM and the OVCM will assist you in determining the findings you uncovered that are critical and will help you prioritize them in the report.

When considering recommendations, you should use what we call the *multiple-solution path*. This path consists of offering multiple solutions such as patches, upgrades, filters, and enhancements. Your recommendations should talks about how your findings are important to your client, the risk (see Figure 15.1), and how might they affect the mission of the organization. Unfortunately, it is not always easy to know the concerns and constraints relating to politics and finances. Sometimes the most common solution will not always work for your client. Some of the concerns and constraints you could come across when dealing with customers are:

- Time
- Finances
- Personnel
- Government requirements/restrictions

Knowing your customer's concerns and constraints will allow you to make the appropriate recommendations that are exclusive to your customer.

Each component of the risk triangle—threat, asset value, and vulnerability—must be present for there to be risk (see Figure 15.1). Removing one of the components eliminates the risk to the organization. In most cases, if you are able to minimize the vulnerability, which may be the easiest of the components, you will minimize the risk.

Creating the Final Report

This section presents a collection of proven and established strategies that are effective in preparing a final report. It will take more than following these simple practices to create a great report, but use these as a guide in helping you produce a quality final report that will add value and assist your customer in developing a stronger security posture.

Figure 15.1 The Risk Triangle

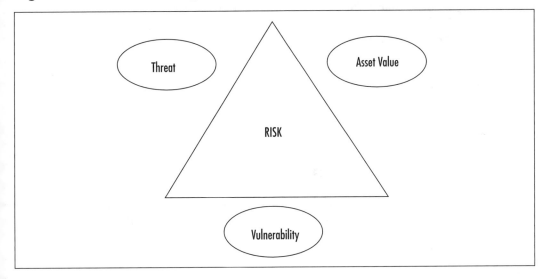

Organizing the Data

Begin the process of organizing and discussing the data you have collected as soon as possible after the onsite evaluation.

- Utilize all your team's notes because you could have missed something important.
- Set goals and assign responsibilities to ensure a high-quality report that's delivered on time.

Discussion of Findings

Review the definitions for High, Medium, and Low criticalities that you and your team developed from the discussions and interviews with the client.

- Provide more than one solution for the customer, to allow them to have some control over the remediation process.
- Determining the appropriate discussion of a finding should be done individually, as well as including all the notes taken by the team.
- Determine the risk to your customer while developing discussion of the findings.

Final Report Delivery Date

Depending on the size of the organization, the vulnerabilities found, and the required detail, the final report is usually delivered to the customer two to eight weeks after the onsite evaluations. It is customary to provide your client with a draft of the final report for review before delivery of the final product. If any new high-criticality findings are discovered during this phase, you should notify your client before you complete the report.

The Cover Letter

The cover letter should include who you are, your business process, and the appropriate contact information for a responsible person at your organization. This person will be responsible for providing answers to customer questions and performing followup with the customer. The cover letter should also give a very brief summary of what the customer can expect to find in the final report.

The Executive Summary

The executive summary is a brief description and high-level overview of what is in the final report. When writing the executive summary, keep in mind that your goal is to summarize what you and your team have done and what you've found during the evaluation. Your audience is the customer organization's management team, so now is not the time to get overly technical. Save the technical language for the final report.

Some of the items you should cover in the executive summary are:

- **Organization synopsis** This includes a description of the customer organization and what they do. Are they part of a larger organization? Include the organization mission, vision, focus, location, size, and organizational structure.

- **Purpose for the evaluation** This should include why you and your team were asked to do the evaluation and by whom. What benefit is the organization hoping to gain from your efforts?

- **System description** Describe the system or systems within the customer organization and which, if not all, systems were part of the evaluation. Include specific servers, high-assurance devices such as routers, switches, and firewalls, and IP-address ranges.

- **Summary of evaluation** Briefly describe what was done during the evaluation process and include a timeline of important events. Also include a brief description of the IEM, what it consists of, and where it came from.

- **Major findings and recommendations** List the most critical vulnerabilities to the organization that you and your team discovered and how they were uncovered in your evaluation. Following the vulnerabilities should be at least two options or recommendations to resolve your findings. Remember, not all findings in the executive summary need to be negative in nature. (Refer to the Cadillac, Chevy, and Yugo definitions of recommendations.)

- **System vulnerability criticality matrix** The SVCM is included here so the management can have a snapshot of vulnerabilities in their organization as well as a picture of their organization's security posture. Include one SVCM for each system.

- **Overall vulnerability criticality matrix** The OVCM gives an overall security posture of the organization and is often too large to include in this section. If that is the case, include just the upper-left portion of the matrix.

The INFOSEC Profile

This section of the report identifies the organization's vulnerabilities and allows the organization to assess its security posture. As discussed earlier, you can report vulnerabilities using the NIST SP 800-53, which identifies the 17 baseline information security classes, or simply organize the vulnerabilities from High to Low according to the ways they might affect the organization.

The Introduction

The information in the introduction is similar to the executive summary but with a greater amount of detail. You want your audience to have a complete understanding of who you are and what you and your team have done as well as information about the process and methodology that you used. This section should include information about your organization and where you are located as well as your mission statement. Explain why your organization was asked to do the evaluation, when the evaluation was conducted, why your team uses the IEM, and what background and expertise your team brings to the evaluation. Reiterate that what you and your team are doing is an evaluation and not an audit, inspection, certification, or risk analysis. Explain what you and your team expect to accomplish during the evaluation. In the introduction you should include the background information.

The background information should include the name and address of the organization that you are evaluating as well as the scope of the evaluation, including when the work was done as well as dates and locations of the evaluation. A table of IP addresses that were provided and used in the evaluation could also be included here.

You should also discuss why the evaluation was done, and reiterate the fact that you and your team did an information security evaluation and not any type of certification or accreditation.

Within the Background Information section, address the following points:

- **Organization's mission** By stating or elaborating on the organization's mission, this section helps the reader understand why the evaluation was done and why the organization's information is critical.

- **Purpose of the evaluation** Why was the evaluation done? What was the driving force behind having someone do an information security evaluation? How is the organization going to use the results of your evaluation?

- **Organization's information criticality**

- **System criticality (from the IAM pre-assessment)**

- **The technical evaluation plan (TEP)**
    - Concerns
    - Constraints

Also include:

- The system vulnerability criticality matrix (SVCM)
- The overall vulnerability criticality matrix (OVCM)
- Technical data (CD)
- Rules of engagement (ROI) as predetermined by your team and the customer

INFOSEC Analysis

The purpose of the INFOSEC Analysis section of the final report is to give clarity to your customer's information security posture. To accomplish this clarity, identify the vulnerabilities and specifically outline how these vulnerabilities could affect the organization. At this point in the evaluation, you should know how your client would like you to present the vulnerabilities you found during your evaluation.

The following are some sample outlines for presenting your analysis.

TIP

The most common way to present your findings is to list them according to the client's predefined High, Medium, and Low criticality levels.

Technical Areas

- External Exposures
- Internal Exposures
- System Boundaries

High-Criticality Findings

- **Finding:** SNMP set public community

  Finding ID #: 1

  CVE/CAN: CAN-1999-0517

  Category: Identification and Authentication (External Exposure)

  Location: *xxx.xxx.xxx, xxx.xxx.xxx*

  Severity: High

  Discussion: The SNMP default public community name is specified, allowing anyone the ability to change the computer's system information if they use this default value. An attacker can use SNMP to obtain valuable information about the system, such as information on network devices and current open connections. In this case, the ability exists to actually change information, because the SNMP Set password is set to Public.

Recommendations:

Option 1: If the SNMP Service is not necessary, disable or remove the it.

Option 2: If your organization requires the use of the SNMP Service, you should take steps to secure the SNMP community names and the community strings.

■ **Finding:** Telnet default account accessible

Finding ID #: 2

CVE/CAN: No common corresponding vulnerability

Category: Technical Finding (System Boundary)

Location: *xxx.xxx.xxx, xxx.xxx.xxx, xxx.xxx.xxx*

Severity: High

Discussion: An accessible default account was detected through Telnet. Default accounts through Telnet allow attackers easy access to remote systems by providing a network-accessible service on the server or printer.

Recommendations:

Option 1: Disable the Telnet account/service on each network.

Option 2: Change the password for the account to something difficult to guess.

Medium-Criticality Findings

■ **Finding:** Access Validation Error

Finding ID #: 3

CVE/CAN: (CVE-2000-0475)

Category: Technical Finding (Internal Exposure)

Location: *xxx.xxx.xxx, xxx.xxx.xxx, xxx.xxx.xxx*

Severity: Medium

Discussion: A local user or attacker could gain access and/or additional privileges to another user's desktop. Microsoft Windows 2000 could allow an attacker to gain increased privileges on the local system. The Windows 2000 security architecture restricts processes through a system of sessions, Windows stations, and desktops. A local attacker could create a process that runs in a higher-privilege context ("desktop") than the local user. This would give the attacker access to certain input devices available to the higher-privilege desktop, for instance, allowing the user to monitor local logins to record usernames and passwords.

Recommendation: Install the appropriate Microsoft patch for your systems. Reference: ww.microsoft.com/technet/security/bulletin/fq00-020.mspx.

■ **Finding:** IisVirtualUncShare: IIS virtual UNC share source read

Finding ID #: 4

CVE/CAN: (CVE-2000-0246)

Category: Technical Finding

Location: *xxx.xxx.xxx, xxx.xxx.xxx, xxx.xxx.xxx*

Severity: Medium

Discussion: Microsoft Internet Information Server (IIS) could reveal the source code of files that reside on a UNC network share. A remote attacker could request a file from the Web server that resides on a network share and append specific characters to the end of the URL to cause the Web server to return the text source of the file to the browser. An attacker could send your source code to him- or herself, thus stealing your source code.

Recommendation: Install the appropriate Microsoft patch for your system. Reference: http://support.microsoft.com/support/contact/default.asp.

Low-Criticality Findings

■ **Finding:** Design Error

Finding ID #: 5

CVE/CAN: (CVE-2003-0007)

Category: Technical Finding (Internal Exposure)

Location: *xxx.xxx.xxx, xxx.xxx.xxx, xxx.xxx.xxx*

Severity: Low

Discussion: Microsoft Outlook 2002 does not properly handle requests to encrypt e-mail messages with V1 Exchange Server Security certificates, which causes Outlook to send the e-mail in plaintext, aka "Flaw in how Outlook 2002 handles V1 Exchange Server Security Certificates could lead to Information Disclosure."

Recommendation: Install the appropriate Microsoft patch for your system. Reference: http://microsoft.com/technet/security/bulletin/ms03-003.mspx.

- **Finding:** Access Validation Error

  Finding ID #: 6

  CVE/CAN: (CVE-2002-1186)

  Category: Technical Finding (Internal Exposure

  Location: *xxx.xxx.xxx, xxx.xxx.xxx, xxx.xxx.xxx*

  Severity: Low

  Discussion: Internet Explorer 5.01 through 6.0 does not properly perform security checks on certain encoded characters within a URL, which allows a remote attacker to steal potentially sensitive information from a user by redirecting the user to another site that has that information, aka "Encoded Characters Information Disclosure."

  Recommendation: Install the appropriate Microsoft patch for your system. Reference: http://microsoft.com/technet/security/bulletin/ms02-066.mspx.

TIP

Do not use a default finding write-up from a commercial tool. You and your customer want your discussions to be original.

The Conclusion

In the same way that we open with an introduction section that introduces the final report, we close with a conclusion section that concludes it. The conclusion basically summarizes your report, bringing all the main ideas together and stressing anything that might be important to your customer.

Impress on your client a sense urgency and that they should give the vulnerabilities you and your team have discovered immediate attention. Follow up with a brief statement discussing the majority of the findings and an idea of how your client can get started on the remediation.

Talk about what good INFOSEC security is and how it can benefit the organization. Include a short paragraph on good policies, training, and implementation. Reiterate that the recommendations in the final report are not requirements but simply guidance that will help your client reduce risk and improve their INFOSEC security posture.

Include positive statements about the organization and its people and a willingness to work with the organization in the future. Finally, include your contact information and the contact information of a responsible party in your organization.

> **TIP**
>
> It is always nice to point out or reiterate a good or positive finding in the conclu-
> sion.

Three other areas that should be mentioned are posture description, posture profile, and security practices.

Posture Description

Now that you are familiar with the organization and have the data and information from your evaluation, you are in a position to make an educated statement about the customer's security posture. You are also in a position to stress to the customer the changes the customer needs to make to better their security posture.

Posture Profile

The overall INFOSEC Posture Profile (IPP) is fairly brief and to the point while showing the organization a score that directly relates to the vulnerabilities that you and your team found during the evaluation. The IPP is based on the four aspects of the DOD Computer Network Defense (CND):

- **Protect** Systems configuration and remediation management
- **Detect** Audit implementation
- **Respond** Reactive measures
- **Sustain** Network management

After calculating each of these areas based on the average of all your findings, you can determine the IPP. The IPP can then be used to provide your team the ability to trend vulnerabilities and develop countermeasures over time. This will allow the organization to track progress and improve their security posture. The higher the IPP score, the greater the risk to the organization.

> **NOTE**
>
> The IPP has limited value if it is only used once and should not be used to com-
> pare various organizations.

Security Practices

In addition to the findings and recommendation that you have provided to the client, it is also a good idea to provide your client with some good security practices. These security practices should be those practices that are generally accepted in the information security field. They could be suggestions or guidelines for the organization you are evaluating that will help them improve their security posture. Some security practices that you can recommend might be more in-depth, such as these:

- **Performing annual evaluations and penetration tests** IT systems in organizations are constantly changing and new vulnerabilities are being discovered at a very rapid rate. Annual evaluations and penetration tests allow an organization to assess its security posture and the state of its IT security.

- **Include IT security within the life cycle of all your systems and applications** Too often, organizations develop applications and systems and then think about their security. Security should be considered in all phases of the development life cycle, from design and development to implementation and maintenance.

- **Configuration management process** This is an important part of controlling and maintaining a secure environment through tracking and documenting the mechanisms used on your systems.

You can also include some good security practices that are brief and to the point, such as:

- Remove default passwords
- Reevaluate the configuration of your security tools
- Develop an IT security policy

Presenting the Final Report

The final report is what you leave with the customer; in the end it will be all that is left to represent you when you have left the customer's site. The first thing you need to remember when you present the final report is the deadline. Don't be late with it! An organized, well-written final report that is delivered on time or ahead of schedule will leave a lasting positive impression of your organization. A final report that is thrown together and does not take into consideration the customer's expectations will not only make you and your team look bad but could give the organization an impression that the work you did was poor and unprofessional. Before you present the customer with any information, make sure you are clear on their expectations.

Summary

You and your team have just completed an INFOSEC evaluation of an organization. You are almost done, but you know you need to analyze the information and organize it in a way that is useful to your client. To do this, you need to put together a final report that talks about and defines the vulnerabilities that could impact your client. Included in you report should be recommendations specific to your client so that they can begin to start the required implementation.

Pulling everything together in the form of team meetings will help your team focus on what needs to be done to deliver a quality final report. During this time you will bring up any questions about the evaluation and findings, assign work to the team members, create action plans, and discuss deadlines.

The most important part of pulling your information together will be your findings and how you organize them in a way that is valuable to your customer. During this time you will discuss in detail the findings and how they could impact your client and create recommendation so your client can develop a road map to secure their information.

As you and your team discuss the findings, continue to keep in mind how they affect your customer and the customer's risk from the vulnerability.

In the end you are leaving your client a final report that will be the lasting impression of the work you and your team performed.

Solutions Fast Track

Pulling All the Information Together

- ☑ Conduct team meetings soon after the onsite evaluation to evaluate and discuss the information that you and your team collected.

- ☑ Do your research on your team's findings in an effort to provide your client with the best options to reduce vulnerability.

- ☑ Review not only the information that you have gathered but all the information that your team has collected to ensure you have a complete picture of the organization and its positive and negative findings.

Making Recommendations

- ☑ Provide multiple recommendations for each finding, to give your client options.

- ☑ Do not use generic recommendations, but use language in your recommendations that makes them specific to your client.

- ☑ Take into consideration your client's concerns and constraints when providing your recommendations.

Presenting the Final Report

☑ The final report will leave a lasting impression of your team with the customer.

☑ Do not be late with your final report.

☑ Know what your client expects from the final report.

Frequently Asked Questions

The following Frequently Asked Questions, answered by the authors of this book, are designed to both measure your understanding of the concepts presented in this chapter and to assist you with real-life implementation of these concepts. To have your questions about this chapter answered by the author, browse to **www.syngress.com/solutions** and click on the **"Ask the Author"** form. You will also gain access to thousands of other FAQs at ITFAQnet.com.

Q: How long should it take to write and present the final report?

A: The final report should take about 2–8 weeks to put together, depending on the size of the organization that you are evaluating. Do not underestimate your final report delivery time to your client. Remember that you and your team not only need to review and analyze the information that you have collected but put together a final report that reflects the quality of work that you have done. Another thing to consider is the amount of detail that will be required.

Q: Is there an official or required format used for the final report?

A: No. There are only recommendations for formatting the final report. Take your time and include the elements discussed in this chapter and you will be fine.

Q: Why should you include multiple recommendations for your findings?

A: Multiple recommendations give your client control over the resolution of the vulnerability and give them flexibility as well. We cannot always be sure what is driving the customer; referring back to the customer's constraints, it could be finances, available resources, politics, or something else. Making multiple recommendations will give your client the flexibility they might need to implement your recommendations.

Q: How long are you required to keep your documentation?

A: This is something that you should cover in your contract with the customer. It would be appropriate to hold on to the information for 30–45 days after delivering the final report.

Q: In the threat triangle, there are three elements of risk: threat, asset value, and vulnerability. Which area would be the most effective one for our client to focus on?

A: Your client should focus on its vulnerabilities. We have little control over asset value and the threats against us. Mitigating by implementing the recommendations will be the best solution to reducing the risk to the organization.

Chapter 16

Summing Up

Introduction

Throughout this text, you've learned about a methodology that is attempting to lay out a standard baseline for technical evaluations. If you've been in the business a while, it's likely that none of the information was truly new to you. If you're just getting into this type of work, you'll want to keep in mind that all we've done is give you a new tool for your toolbox. Once the majority of information security consultants are beginning from the same square on the playing board, it will be easier for customers to understand what to expect when they request this type of work. All we're doing here is building a common starting point for technical evaluations.

One thing we'd like to reiterate is that there is simply no replacement for valid experience in this arena. Unlike the occupations of old, such as blacksmiths, there is no apprentice program. Any individual who is enterprising enough can walk out to the sidewalk and hang up their shingle, proclaiming themselves *security consultants*. In all likelihood, this is normally done from a desire to capitalize on the increasing information security marketplace, but it can have a detrimental effect on customer organizations that are trying to legitimately secure their information assets.

Nearly everyone has read the stories of the young man who becomes an apprentice to the local blacksmith. He spends years learning the trade and how to do the work professionally and correctly. After an investment of 10–15 years, the now older man is considered a professional. But that's not the end of our scenario. This same young man is enrolled in a guild, which acts as a governing body for the education of new blacksmiths. The guild ensures that each man in the program has achieved a level of knowledge deemed appropriate before allowing him to call himself a blacksmith. The key is that the community accepts the guild's word as to who is reliable and knowledgeable. The public directs requests for service to only those individuals who were certified or deemed appropriate.

We don't have any of that in the current world of information security. There are no strict guidelines about who can be considered a reliable practitioner of the "black art" of INFOSEC. Attempts to create something like a guild system have been either centralized around a specific industry or have been watered down by loopholes in the founding organizations.

One example is the ISC(2) Certified Information System Security Professional, or CISSP, program. Although a valiant effort has been made to control the quality of individuals receiving the certification, it's often impossible to verify this type of thing. Let's face it—people can easily lie on their certification applications. And a test, no matter how extensive, can always be studied for rather than passed based on actual experience. The beginning of every successful control mechanism has been to develop a set of acceptable performance criteria that can be followed by professionals within the industry. As the industry grows and matures, new people come into that profession and are introduced to these basics.

The INFOSEC Evaluation Methodology (IEM) is an example of that. The NSA has recognized a need in the marketplace to standardize our practices. In the NSA's opinion, the IEM is strictly the minimum baseline of activities that must take place if one is to conduct a truly valuable and comprehensive technical evaluation. With that in mind, remember that you're not locked into doing *only* these things. Nor are you stuck with the report formats, tool selections, or metrics we've shown you in this book. These are simply tools for your toolbox. You can expand and extend the IEM to fit the needs of both your own organization and your customers.

The Pre-Evaluation Phase

The pre-evaluation phase can be said to start as soon as you have initial contact with the customer. This is the point at which you can guide the customer and provide advice on what may be needed to help improve their security posture. For instance, if you get a call from someone requiring a *penetration test*, it's easy enough to agree because the work sounds like fun. But is it what the customer needs? Will it honestly improve their security posture, or will it leave them with a false sense of security?

We're also setting the scope and the rules of engagement and laying out the evaluation plan that we'll follow during the evaluation. Customers need to understand what will happen during the evaluation, that their concerns have been taken into account, and that they can track everything that is occurring.

Many of the requests for evaluations we receive have been based primarily on compliance. What regulations is the organization liable for adhering to? Is it a financial institution concerned with meeting Gramm-Leach-Bliley guidelines? Is it a university or college that needs to comply with the Family Education Rights and Privacy Act (FERPA)? Some organizations need to comply with multiple regulations. You'll need the knowledge of these documents and understanding of specific ways they can impact the customer.

As opposed to the NSA IAM, where we only had a single point of contact, the IEM requires multiple points of contact, both administrative and technical. Whereas the administrative contacts will be primarily concerned with setting up our meetings with important personnel, assigning us appropriate workspace, and maintaining a schedule for the evaluation; the technical points of contact will provide us with more detailed information. This could include anything from concerns about existing systems we will be evaluating and windows of opportunity for the evaluation activities to network connections or addresses from which to conduct our activities.

Rules of engagement (ROE) are developed in concert with the customer. This is the customer's evaluation and we want to ensure that it is done according to their specifications. Items of interest include the activities that are allowed, when they are allowed, and on what systems they are allowed. ROE also lists the opposite for each of these things. What systems are considered out of scope? When are we *not* allowed to conduct evaluation activities? What activities should be excluded from the evaluation due to appropriate customer concerns?

Never forget that legal representation during the entire evaluation process is recommended as a protective measure. Although honest security professionals never go into these types of arrangements with malicious intent, misunderstandings and accidents do occur. We want to ensure that the customer has given us full license to conduct the agreed-on activities. And in most cases, utilizing legal counsel as a conduit for this line of business can provide client/attorney privilege that protects the sensitive findings in court cases.

All this information is placed into the technical evaluation plan (TEP) that will serve as a guide for all activities related to this evaluation. The information in the TEP should never be a surprise to the customer. We often ensure customer approval by requesting their signature and date on the TEP itself, prior to beginning any of the onsite evaluation activities. The signature helps reinforce management buy-in of this process and serves as documentation that the customer agrees with our understanding of the evaluation activities.

The Onsite Evaluation

In the onsite evaluation phase, the proverbial rubber meets the road. Here we address the 10 baseline activities that NSA requires for a comprehensive evaluation. As you saw in earlier chapters, we've tried to establish a repeatable and simple process that will provide value to the customer organization. Assuming that the customer is serious about information security, you provide experience-driven recommendations that are viable solutions for the customer, and they implement some or many of your recommendations; the security posture of the customer organization is thus improved.

The first thing we do in the IEM is conduct the opening meeting, called an *in-brief*. This is where we reinforce the management buy-in and let all associated customer employees know how the evaluation will be conducted. In the in-brief, we'll explain the IEM, where it came from, and what areas we'll be looking at while we evaluate their systems. We really want the customer to walk away from this meeting with a clear and comfortable understanding of the evaluation team and the evaluation process.

As we begin the evaluation activities, it's important to understand the difference between an organizational finding and a technical finding. Whereas the organizational finding is normally discovered during the IAM and revolves around policies, process, or procedures, the IEM findings are more technical and are based on the technical implementation or configuration of technical systems. Both of these findings are used later in the final road map that we deliver to the customer organization.

The first general area of activities in the IEM centers around information gathering. We're looking to enumerate all the systems, machines, devices, services, and more that are used in or using the customer network. This activity includes running port scans to locate and identify all the hosts, services, and devices on the network. We're also looking to gain information about those items. For example, the banner-grabbing activity of the IEM tries to identify specifically what service or application is running on a certain port. All the information we gain from these activities will help us narrow our search for findings within the customer organization.

The next set of activities—the automated vulnerability scans and the host evaluations that are conducted on critical servers and workstations—often creates the bulk of technical findings. Each of these activities generates a number of important findings. Your experience comes into play when you need to determine which findings are real and which ones are false positives. This can be a time-intensive activity, but if it's handled and interpreted correctly, the customer will gain tremendous value from this piece of the IEM.

In the final set of activities, we bring the evaluation down to a point where we are gaining greater detail about the security posture of the customer's technical systems. For example, we can gauge the effectiveness of the customer's password policy by performing password-compliance testing. The configuration of high-assurance devices such as firewalls, routers, and switches will provide clues to the ways that network traffic is allowed to move in and out of the customer network and points at which there could be issues.

The last activity performed during the onsite evaluation phase is the out-brief. If there were critical findings, we want to ensure that the customer understands what they are. We're not out to impress the customer by giving them a final report full of surprises and critical findings. In fact, if we locate critical findings during the onsite phase, we want to notify our contacts immediately. The out-brief is your chance to show the customer how the work has been progressing, what you've found thus far, and when they can expect further information.

The Post-Evaluation Phase

The post-evaluation phase of any evaluation tends to be the most tedious. It conjures images of techies sitting at their desks rummaging through tons of data collected during the onsite phase, looking for problem areas. In fact, this is often the case. A big problem with many security companies is their tendency to run a piece of software, dump out the default report, and send it to their customer with the logo replaced with their own. The true value in any evaluation comes down to the quality analysis performed by the security experts. Without proper analysis, the results have very little value to your customer.

But even if you conduct the best analysis possible, you still need a means by which to communicate those findings to the customer. What does it all mean to them? What is the *real* impact to the customer?

To help answer these questions and aid you in communicating the big picture back to the customer, NSA created a set of matrixes. These matrixes provide a clear picture of findings that have the biggest impact to the organization, based on information gained during the IAM and the IEM processes.

Along with the matrixes comes the introduction of two metrics that can be used to trend security posture over time. Depending on your requirements, the customer might choose to use one or the other of the two metrics. One was intended specifically for Department of Defense systems; the other one has more commercial value. That's not to say that are not interchangeable; they are. Again, use what works for your customer.

Finally, we arrive at the point at which we create the final report and deliver it to the customer. Your final report should reflect the attitude and personality of the customer organization while still conveying the important facts. And don't think your work is through once the customer has the report in hand. You still have a responsibility to follow up with your customer and ensure that they understand the findings your team located and the recommendations you made to eliminate or mitigate those findings. The actual format of the final report depends heavily on your own business processes, but we've made suggestions on what areas are important to include.

As a final reminder, remember that it's important for every security professional to have a plethora of tools in their toolkits. The NSA INFOSEC Evaluation Methodology should be one of those tools. When the information security industry begins to standardize on those things that professionals consider acceptable, we can not only begin controlling the quality of the individuals who are performing this type of work, but the customers themselves will benefit. Imagine a world where a customer calls you up asking for a security evaluation and they have a pretty good idea of what they should expect.

Examples of INFOSEC Tools by Baseline Activity

Solutions in this chapter:

- Port Scanning

- SNMP Scanning

- Enumeration and Banner Grabbing

- Wireless Enumeration

- Vulnerability Scanning

- Host Evaluation

- Network Device Analysis

- Password-Compliance Testing

- Application-Specific Scanning

- Network Protocol Analysis

NOTE

No specific tools are implied or endorsed.
No specific brands are implied or endorsed.
CVE/CAN relation is strongly recommended.
Tool versions are current as of the writing of this book.

Port Scanning

Tool Name: Nmap (v.3.81)

Developer: Fyodor (Insecure.org)

Platform/OS: UNIX, Linux, FreeBSD, NetBSD, OpenBSD, Solaris, OS X, Microsoft Windows, HP-UX, AIX, DigUX, Cray UNICOS

Commercial or Freeware? Freeware (GPL)

URL: www.insecure.org/nmap/

Notes: Microsoft Windows XP SP2 disabled the ability to use RAW sockets, it throttled the number of permitted outbound TCP connections, and disabled the ability to send spoofed UDP packets. This is "fixed" in Nmap version 3.55 and newer. Nmap is a tool that fits into more than one baseline activity. It can provide a wealth of information.

Tool Name: ScanLine (v.1.01)

Developer: McAfee (formerly FoundStone)

Platform/OS: Microsoft Windows

Commercial or Freeware? Freeware

URL: www.foundstone.com/resources/proddesc/scanline.htm

Notes: ScanLine is the replacement for Fscan. This is a command-line scanner for the MS Windows platform; it can handle scanning in a highly parallel fashion and provides more scanning capabilities than Fscan did.

Tool Name: Scanrand (part of paketto v.2.0p3)

Developer: Dan Kaminsky

Platform/OS: Compiles on Linux (RedHat, Mandrake, and Debian), FreeBSD, MinGW (on MS Windows)

Commercial or Freeware? Freeware

URL: www.doxpara.com

Notes: Libnet (v1.0.2) and libpcap are *required*.

Tool Name: SuperScan (v.4.0)

Developer: McAfee (formerly FoundStone)

Platform/OS: Microsoft Windows

Commercial or Freeware? Freeware

URL: www.foundstone.com/resources/proddesc/superscan4.htm

Notes: SuperScan v3.0 and v4.0 are available from this site. Version 4.0 provides more functionality but doesn't seem as fast as version 3.0.

Tool Name: MingSweeper (v.1.0alpha5, build 130)

Developer: HooBie

Platform/OS: Microsoft Windows NT/2000/XP

Commercial or Freeware? Freeware

URL: www.hoobie.net/mingsweeper/index.html

Notes: MingSweeper is a network reconnaissance tool. It is designed for scanning large address spaces and for high-speed node discovery and identification. It is capable of doing ping sweeps, reverse DNS sweeps, TCP scans, and UDP scans as well as OS and application identification.

SNMP Scanning

Tool Name: SolarWinds Network Management Toolset

Developer: SolarWinds.net Network Management

Platform/OS: Microsoft Windows

Commercial or Freeware? Commercial

URL: www.solarwinds.net/Toolsets.htm

Notes: SolarWinds toolset is much more than a simple SNMP scanner. Considering how much functionality this application suite provides, it could be considered a one-stop shop when it comes to network management and troubleshooting.

Tool Name: Snscan (v.1.05)

Developer: McAfee (formerly FoundStone)

Platform/OS: Microsoft Windows

Commercial or Freeware? Freeware

URL: www.foundstone.com/resources/proddesc/snscan.htm

Notes: Snscan is a decent SNMP scanning tool but limited in its capabilities and information it provides.

Tool Name: GetIF (v.2.3.1)

Developer: Philippe Simonet

Platform/OS: Microsoft Windows

Commercial or Freeware? Freeware

URL: www.wtcs.org/snmp4tpc/getif.htm

Notes: This is an excellent freeware SNMP tool for MS Windows. Very handy and easy to use.

Tool Name: Braa (v.0.8)

Developer: Mateusz "mteg" Golicz

Platform/OS: Linux, FreeBSD, OpenBSD

Commercial or Freeware? Freeware

URL: http://s-tech.elsat.net.pl/braa/

Notes: Braa is a mass SNMP scanner. What separates this tool from the rest is the way it handles multiple queries simultaneously. According to the author of this tool, it is able to scan dozens or even hundreds of hosts simultaneously, in a single process. Braa implements its own SNMP stack and requires a system that implements BSD sockets and supports POSIX syscalls.

Enumeration and Banner Grabbing

Tool Name: Winfingerprint (v.0.6.2)

Developer: Vacuum

Platform/OS: Microsoft Windows

Commercial or Freeware? Freeware

URL: http://winfingerprint.sourceforge.net

Notes: Winfingerprint is a host/network enumeration and scanning tool. It is capable of the following scan types: TCP, UDP, ICMP, RPC, SMB, and SNMP. If you ant to do TCP SYN scans, you must have WinPcap installed as well. Otherwise the scans will be nonblocking connect() based.

Tool Name: NBTScan (v.1.5.1)

Developer: Alla Bezroutchko (Inetcat.org)

Platform/OS: Microsoft Windows NT/2000/XP, OS X, Linux, Solaris, FreeBSD, OpenBSD, HP-UX, AIX

Commercial or Freeware? Freeware

URL: www.inetcat.org/software/nbtscan.html

Notes: This is an easy-to-use NetBIOS scanner. It is used for enumerating resources available via NetBIOS on the network.

Tool Name: Xprobe2 (v.0.2.2)

Developer: Fyodor Yarochkin and Ofir Arkin

Platform/OS: Linux, Solaris, FreeBSD, OpenBSD, NetBSD

Commercial or Freeware? Freeware

URL: http://sys-security.com/index.php?page=xprobe

Notes: Xprobe2 is a remote active OS fingerprinting tool. It does its OS fingerprinting a bit differently than other tools. Xprobe2 relies on fuzzy fingerprint matching, guesswork (based on probabilities), simultaneous multiple matches, and a signature database.

Tool Name: hping2 (v.2.0.0-rc3)

Developer: Lead Maintainer: Salvatore Sanfilippo (see www.hping.org/authors.html for additional contributors)

Platform/OS: Linux, OS X, Solaris, FreeBSD, OpenBSD, NetBSD

Commercial or Freeware? Freeware

URL: www.hping.org

Notes: hping2 is a command-line-oriented TCP/IP packet assembler and analyzer. Hping2 supports the following protocols: ICMP, TCP, UDP, and RAW-IP. Additionally, it has a *traceroute* mode. Hping2 has so many features, it would take up too much space to list them all. Note: at press time hping3 was still in development.

Tool Name: Netcat (*NIX: v1.10, Windows: v1.11)

Developer: Hobbit

Platform/OS: Linux, Solaris, SunOS, OS X, AIX, HP-UX, Irix, Ultrix, BSDi, FreeBSD, NetBSD, OpenBSD, UnixWare, NeXT, Microsoft Windows

Commercial or Freeware? Freeware

URL: www.vulnwatch.org/netcat/

Notes: Netcat is *essential* for every INFOSEC toolbox. There's a reason people call it the "Swiss army knife of TCP/IP"—it can do so much. Read up on this tool and you will see how useful it is. Simply put, Netcat is a UNIX utility for reading and writing data across network connections, using TCP or UDP for its protocol. Netcat can act as a client *or* a server and can be used directly or accessed via programs or scripts. Flexibility is the best word to describe Netcat.

Wireless Enumeration

NOTE

Wireless Ennumeration has privacy concerns/issues, as well as potential "theft of service." Be aware!

Tool Name: Kismet

Developer: Kismetwireless.net

Platform/OS: Linux (preferred), OS X, FreeBSD, OpenBSD, NetBSD, and limited support on Microsoft Windows

Commercial or Freeware? Freeware

URL: www.kismetwireless.net/

Notes: Kismet is a passive wireless network detector, protocol analyzer, and intrusion detection system. Kismet works with any wireless card that supports raw monitoring mode (rfmon). Kismet can capture and analyze 802.11a, 802.11b, and 802.11g traffic. Kismet on Windows works only with remote captures, since there are no public rfmon drivers for Windows (win32). Furthermore, Kismet on Windows requires Cygwin to provide the necessary POSIX layer.

Tool Name: Netstumbler

Developer: Marius Milner

Platform/OS: Microsoft Windows 2000/XP/2003, PocketPC 2002, 2003

Commercial or Freeware? Freeware (not open source)

URL: www.stumbler.net (Netstumbler forums: http://www.netstumbler.net)

Notes: Netstumbler is a Microsoft Windows-only wireless network detector. It is free but not open source. It's a very popular freeware wireless network detector and does its job pretty well. But unlike Kismet, Netstumbler isn't passive. It uses active probing to detect wireless networks.

Tool Name: Airsnort

Developer: Snax

Platform/OS: Linux, Microsoft Windows

Commercial or Freeware? Freeware

URL: http://airsnort.shmoo.com/

Notes: Airsnort is a wireless network tool designed to recover wireless encryption keys. Airsnort passively monitors for wireless transmissions, and when it has enough packets gathered, it computes the encryption key (in less than a second!). Airsnort requires approximately 5–10 million encrypted packets to guess the encryption key.

Tool Name: AiroPeek NX

Developer: WildPackets

Platform/OS: Microsoft Windows XP (SP1), 2000 (SP3)

Commercial or Freeware? Commercial

URL: www.wildpackets.com/products/airopeek/airopeek_nx/overview

Notes: AiroPeek NX is an expert wireless network analyzer that provides expert diagnostic tools for troubleshooting and managing your wireless infrastructure. AiroPeak can do site surveys, wireless LAN analysis, wireless LAN monitoring, and application layer protocol analysis.

Vulnerability Scanning

Tool Name: Nessus (v.2.2.4)

Developer: Renaud Deraison

Platform/OS: n/a

Commercial or Freeware? Freeware

URL: www.nessus.org

Notes: Nessus is probably the most popular open source vulnerability scanner in use today. It is used for remote vulnerability scanning and can be used for local host scanning too. It has an up-to-date CVS/CAN-compliant vulnerability database and built-in scripting capabilities (via NASL), and each security test is written as a plug-in in NASL, so you are able to view the code being executed and modify it to fit your needs or the needs of the organization you are evaluating. There are over 6000 plug-ins (vulnerability checks) available with the default install of Nessus.

Tool Name: NeWT (v.2.1)

Developer: Tenable

Platform/OS: Microsoft Windows

Commercial or Freeware? Commercial

URL: www.tenablesecurity.com

Notes: NeWT stands for *Nessus Windows Technology*. As the name states, this is a version of Nessus built to run on Microsoft Windows platforms. It has the same capabilities and checks as Nessus.

Tool Name: Retina (v5.2.12)

Developer: eEye

Platform/OS: Microsoft Windows

Commercial or Freeware? Commercial

URL: www.eeye.com/html/products/retina/

Notes: Retina is a really good vulnerability scanner, but it is commercial and somewhat pricey. It has an excellent vulnerability database, and the reporting capabilities are much more flexible than in previous versions.

Tool Name: SAINT (v.5.8.4)

Developer: Saint Corporation

Platform/OS: UNIX, Linux, OS X, FreeBSD, Solaris, HP-UX 11

Commercial or Freeware? Commercial

URL: www.saintcorporation.com/saint/

Notes: SAINT stands for *Security Administrators Integrated Network Tool*. SAINT is a vulnerability assessment tool that is also CVE/CAN compliant (as well as IAVA). This tool is excellent for measuring compliance (for example, for GLBA, SOX, and HIPAA), and the reporting capabilities are quite good.

Tool Name: VLAD the Scanner (v.0.9.2)

Developer: BindView

Platform/OS: Linux, OpenBSD, FreeBSD, OS X

Commercial or Freeware? Freeware

URL: www.bindview.com/Services/RAZOR/Utilities/Unix_Linux/vlad.cfm

Notes: VLAD is an open source vulnerability scanner that tests for the SANS Top 10 vulnerabilities (http://www.sans.org/top20/top10.php). VLAD requires several Perl modules: LWP::UserAgent, HTTP::Request, HTTP::Response, Net::DNS::Resolver, IO::Socket, IO::Pty, IO::Stty, Socket, Net::SNMP, Net::Telnet, Expect, File::Spec, and Time::HiRes.

Tool Name: LANGuard Network Security Scanner (v6.0).

Developer: GFi

Platform/OS: Microsoft Windows

Commercial or Freeware? Commercial

URL: www.gfi.com/lannetscan/

Notes: LANGuard NSS is primarily a Microsoft Windows vulnerability scanner, but GFi recently added some Linux checks/scans to the product. LANGuard NSS is an excellent vulnerability scanner and enumeration tool for Microsoft Windows platforms. Not only does it do vulnerability scanning and enumeration activities, but it can handle patch management as well.

Tool Name: Typhoon III

Developer: NGS Software

Platform/OS: Microsoft Windows NT/2000/XP

Commercial or Freeware? Commercial

URL: www.nextgenss.com/typhon.htm

Notes: Typhoon is another vulnerability scanner that provides much of the same information as other scanners, but it goes about it differently; using NGS's spidering technique. Typhoon is a high-speed scanner and can do application-level checks as well (such as cross-site scripting attack checks and SQL injection checks).

Host Evaluation

Tool Name: CIS Benchmark Tools/Scripts

Developer: Center for Internet Security (CIS)

Platform/OS: Microsoft Windows NT, 2000, 2000 Pro, 2000 Server, 2003 Server, and XP Pro; OS X, FreeBSD, Solaris 2.5.1-10, Linux, HP-UX, AIX, wireless networks, Cisco IOS Router, Cisco PIX, Oracle Database 8a, 9a, and 10g, and Apache Web Server

Commercial or Freeware? Free for noncommercial use

URL: www.cisecurity.org/benchmarks/

Notes: The CIS Benchmark Tools measure the assessed system or application against widely accepted security benchmarks and best-practice security configuration for computers connected to the Internet.

Tool Name: Microsoft Security Baseline Analyzer (v.1.2.1)

Developer: Microsoft

Platform/OS: Microsoft Windows 2000, XP and 2003

Commercial or Freeware? Freeware

URL: www.microsoft.com/technet/security/tools/mbsahome.mspx

Notes: The Microsoft Baseline Security Analyzer (MSBA) is an easy-to-use tool that helps determine the security state of the evaluated machine, in accordance with Microsoft security recommendations, and offers remediation guidance.

Tool Name: HFNetChk / HFNetChkPro (v.5.0)

Developer: Shavlik

Platform/OS: Microsoft Windows 2000, XP and 2003

Commercial or Freeware? Commercial (demo available)

URL: www.shavlik.com/hf.aspx

Notes: Though HFNetChkPro is listed as a patch management solution, it is also very good at checking for vulnerabilities and missing patches and security updates and provides a method for mitigating many issues remotely. That's why we listed this tool in the Host Analysis section—it covers more baseline activities in this section.

Network Device Analysis

Tool Name: Firewalk (v5.0)

Developer: Mike Schiffman

Platform/OS: n/a

Commercial or Freeware? Freeware

URL: www.packetfactory.net/firewalk/

Notes: Firewalk is an active reconnaissance network security tool that attempts to determine what layer 4 protocols an IP forwarding device will allow to pass through. Firewalk is designed for testing firewalls and other IP forwarding devices. Building Firewalk requires libnet 1.1.x, libpcap, and libdnet.

Tool Name: RAT (Router Audit Tool)

Developer: CIS (Center for Internet Security)

Platform/OS: Microsoft Windows, UNIX, Linux

Commercial or Freeware? Free for noncommercial use

URL: www.cisecurity.org/rat/

Notes: The Router Audit Tool from CIS can download the configuration from the device to be evaluated (router, PIX firewall) and check the configuration against the settings defined in the provided benchmarks. RAT provides a list of all the rules to be checked, along with a pass/fail score for each, the raw overall score, the weighted score (scale of 1–10), and a list of IOS/PIX commands that will correct the issues identified.

Password-Compliance Testing

Tool Name: Brutus (v.AET2)

Developer: HooBie

Platform/OS: Microsoft Windows

Commercial or Freeware? Freeware

URL: www.hoobie.net/brutus/

Notes: Application still is in development. It's a remote password cracker.

Tool Name: L0phtCrack (v.5.0)

Developer: Symantec (formerly @Stake)

Platform/OS: Microsoft Windows

Commercial or Freeware? Commercial

URL: www.atstake.com/lc/

Notes: L0phtCrack (LC5) has been around for quite some time and is very well known. LC5 can test the password strength of Windows and UNIX passwords. Now LC5 comes with tables of precomputed password hashes, which makes the password-testing phase go quicker.

Tool Name: OPHCrack (v.2.0)

Developer: Philippe Oechslin

Platform/OS: Microsoft Windows, Linux

Commercial or Freeware? Freeware

URL: http://ophcrack.sourceforge.net/

Notes: OPHCrack is also referred to as the "time-memory tradeoff cracker." It uses precomputed hash tables loaded into memory to dramatically speed the password-cracking process. OPHCrack can obtain the password hash in any one of three ways: through the encrypted SAM file, through the local SAM file, and through the remote SAM file.

Tool Name: John the Ripper (v.1.6)

Developer: Openwall Project

Platform/OS: UNIX (11 flavors), Microsoft Windows, OS X, Linux, BeOS, FreeBSD, OpenBSD, NetBSD

Commercial or Freeware? Freeware

URL: www.openwall.com/john/

Notes: John the Ripper is a fast password cracker that was developed for the task of detecting weak UNIX passwords. Since then, John the Ripper has expanded to test not only UNIX passwords (several of the most common crypt() password hash types) but Kerberos AFS and Microsoft Windows NT/2000/XP/2003 LM hashes as well. Contributors to the project have submitted patches to test the password strength of several applications and services.

Application-Specific Scanning

Tool Name: WebInspect

Developer: SPI Dynamics

Platform/OS: Microsoft Windows 2000/XP/2003

Commercial or Freeware? Commercial

URL: www.spidynamics.com/products/webinspect/

Notes: WebInspect is an application security assessment tool. It identifies vulnerabilities at the Web application layer. WebInspect is great for measuring compliance, making Web application vulnerability assessments, or checking the configuration of a Web application. SPI Dynamics provides the industry's largest Web application vulnerability database with WebInspect.

Tool Name: AppDetective

Developer: Application Security Inc.

Platform/OS: Microsoft Windows 2000/XP/2003

Commercial or Freeware? Commercial

URL: www.appsecinc.com/products/appdetective/

Notes: AppDetective is a network-based vulnerability scanner for database applications. It supports the scanning of MySQL, Oracle, Sybase, IBM DB2, MSSQL, Oracle Application Server, and Lotus Notes/Domino. AppDetective allows you to assess the three primary application tiers: Web front-end, application/middleware, and back-end database. AppDetective locates, examines, reports, and fixes security holes and configuration issues.

Tool Name: Wikto (v.1.6)

Developer: SensePost

Platform/OS: Microsoft Windows

Commercial or Freeware? Freeware

URL: www.sensepost.com/research/wikto/

Notes: Wikto is a port to Microsoft Windows of the tool Nikto (www.cirt.net/code/nikto.shtml). Wikto has three main sections of functionality: back-end miner, Nikto-like functionality, and Googler. It is a Web server scanner that performs comprehensive tests against Web servers for multiple issues. Including over 3,200 potentially dangerous files/CGI/scripts, it obtains the versions on over 625 servers and version-specific problems on over 230 servers.

Something to keep in mind: Neither Nikto or Wikto are stealthy at all.

Tool Name: Achilles

Developer: Robert Cardona of Systegra

Platform/OS: Microsoft Windows

Commercial or Freeware? Freeware

URL: www.mavensecurity.com/achilles

Notes: Achilles is a general-purpose Web application security assessment tool. Achilles acts as a HTTP/HTTPS proxy that permits the user to intercept, log, and modify Web traffic on the fly.

Tool Name: IKE-Scan (v.1.7)

Developer: NTA Monitor Limited

Platform/OS: Linux, FreeBSD, OpenBSD, NetBSD, Solaris, OS X, HP-UX, Microsoft Windows (via Cygwin)

Commercial or Freeware? Freeware

URL: www.nta-monitor.com/ike-scan/

Notes: The IKE-scan tool scans IP addresses for VPN servers by sending a specially crafted IKE packet to each host within a network. Most hosts running IKE will respond, identifying their presence. The tool then remains silent and monitors retransmission packets. These retransmission responses are recorded, displayed, and matched against a known set of VPN product fingerprints.

Tool Name: k0ld (v.1.9)

Developer: FX

Platform/OS: Requires the OpenLDAP libraries

Commercial or Freeware? Freeware

URL: www.phenoelit.de/kold/

Notes: k0ld, or Knocking 0n LDAP's Door, is a dictionary attack against an LDAP server. It queries the LDAP server, dumps all users from a given DN, and tries to find the password for each user account. The newest version includes Windows 2000 AD attacks and a list of default DNs to attack.

Tool Name: SPIKE Proxy (v.1.4.8)

Developer: Immunity

Platform/OS: Linux, Microsoft Windows

Commercial or Freeware? Freeware

URL: www.immunitysec.com/resources-freesoftware.shtml

Notes: SPIKE Proxy is a tool for looking at application-level vulnerabilities in Web applications. It covers such things as SQL injection and cross-site-scripting attacks, but it's written in a completely open Python infrastructure, so it's customizable for Web applications that other tools break on.

Network Protocol Analysis[1]

Tool Name: Ethereal (v.0.10.11)

Developer: Gerald Combs and the Ethereal dev community

Platform/OS: Microsoft Windows 98/ME/2000/XP/2003, Linux, Solaris, OS X, BeOS, FreeBSD, OpenBSD, NetBSD, AIX, HP-UX

Commercial or Freeware? Freeware

URL: http://ethereal.com/

Notes: Ethereal is probably the most popular open source network protocol analyzer. It can dissect over 680 protocols and has a very comprehensive feature-set. Ethereal is the network protocol analyzer of choice for many folks.

Tool Name: Ettercap (v.NG-0.7.3)

Developer: Alberto Ornaghi and Marco Valleri

Platform/OS: Linux, OS X, Solaris, FreeBSD, OpenBSD, NetBSD, Microsoft Windows 2000/XP/2003

Commercial or Freeware? Freeware

URL: http://ettercap.sourceforge.net/

Notes: Ettercap is a suite for conducting man-in-the-middle attacks on local area networks (LANs). Ettercap provides for the capture of live connections, content filtering on the fly, and several other interesting features. It supports active and passive protocol dissection and has many features that contribute to the network and host analysis portions of evaluation efforts.

Tool Name: Sniffer (v.4.7.5)

Developer: Network General

Platform/OS: Microsoft Windows NT, 2000, XP

Commercial or Freeware? Commercial

URL: www.networkgeneral.com

[1] Network sniffing has privacy issues in that all cleartext protocols are visible. The organization might not want you to see their data "up close and personal."

Notes: Network General's Sniffer is one of the more well-known commercial network protocol analyzers. This product has been around for a long time and provides excellent expert decodes and analysis. The Network General Sniffer product line consists of Sniffer Distributed, Sniffer Portable, Sniffer Mobile, Sniffer Voice, and Sniffer Wireless.

Tool Name: EtherPeek NX (v.3.0.1)

Developer: WildPackets

Platform/OS: Microsoft Windows 2000, XP

Commercial or Freeware? Commercial

URL: www.wildpackets.com/products/etherpeek/etherpeek_nx/overview

Notes: EtherPeek NX claims to be the first network protocol analyzer to offer both expert diagnostics and frame decoding in real time during packet capture. It is fast and accurate, and the interface is easy to navigate. WildPackets offers four different protocol analyzers: EtherPeek NX, EtherPeek SE, EtherPeek VX, and EtherPeek for Mac.

Tool Name: Snoop

Developer: Sun Microsystems

Platform/OS: SunOS, Solaris

Commercial or Freeware? Freeware (comes with the OS)

URL: N/A

Notes: Snoop is a network analysis tool that comes with the Solaris operating system. Snoop captures packets from the network and displays their contents. If you are working on a Solaris machine, Snoop is essential.

Tool Name: Tcpdump (v.3.8.3)

Developer: Originally Lawrence Berkeley National Lab (LBNL); now maintained at Tcpdump.org

Platform/OS: UNIX, Linux, *BSD, OS X, Microsoft Windows

Commercial or Freeware? Freeware

URL: www.tcpdump.org

Notes: Tcpdump, simply put, dumps traffic from the network. It prints out the packet headers on the monitored network interface. You can also match on Boolean expressions or pipe the output to "grep." It is a very flexible and easy-to-use network troubleshooting tool.

Technical Evaluation Plan Outline and Sample

Solutions in this chapter:

- Sample Technical Evaluation Plan
- Important Evaluation Points of Contact
- Methodology Overview
- Organizational and System Criticality Information
- Detailed Network Information
- Customer Concerns
- Customer Constraints
- Rules of Engagement
- Coordination Agreements
- Letter of Authorization
- Timeline of Events

Introduction

The Technical Evaluation Plan (TEP) plays a critical role in meeting a customer's needs and expectations. The TEP should be organized as a logical document to provide the greatest value to the customer.

The following outline introduces the TEP format and is intended to provide a guide for the development of a flexible evaluation plan. It can be tailored and formatted to meet your or your customer's needs.

I. **Important Evaluation Points of Contact** POC name, phone number, and e-mail address.

II. **Methodology Overview** Describe the methodology to be used to conduct the evaluation, and identify the specific evaluation tools to be used during the evaluation process.

III. **Organizational and System Criticality Information** A representation of the information criticality for each organizational system, determined by discussion with the customer. Utilize information from the IAM where applicable. Include organizational criticality matrix, system criticality matrix, impact value definitions, and system descriptions.

IV. **Detailed Network Information** Include physical boundaries, identified subnets and IP ranges, detailed network diagrams, and contact information for system owners and administrators.

V. **Customer Concerns** Include applicable customer concerns from the IAM and additional technical customer concerns.

VI. **Customer Constraints** Include applicable customer constraints from the IAM and additional technical customer constraints.

VII. **Rules of Engagement** This section provides the agreed-on approach and limitations related to the execution of the evaluation

VIII. **Internal and External Customer Requirements** Evaluation team's scanning IP addresses, immediate contact information for assessment team, notification of personnel on assessment activities, CIRT coordination for test purposes.

IX. **Coordination Agreements** This is a catchall area. How detailed does the customer want the recommendations to be? Will the standard low level for the executive summary and the midlevel for technical staff be acceptable, or will more detail be required? What are the deliverables? Discuss other agreements not yet addressed.

X. **Letter of Authorization** Include the approved letter of authorization.

XI. **Timeline of Events** This is a sequence of important events and their associated dates, such as the date of the receipt of the request letter, date of proposal or contract, customer coordination dates, planned internal and external dates, and report delivery date.

> **NOTE**
>
> The document included in this appendix is only a *sample* and should not be considered a complete or comprehensive template.

Sample Technical Evaluation Plan

Technical Evaluation Plan (TEP)
Prepared for
Organized Union for Critical Healthcare

June 4, 2005 (V3.2)
Prepared by:
Security Rocks

Anywhere, USA

I. Evaluation Points of Contact

The individuals in Table B.1 are the primary points of contact for the evaluation effort with OUCH.

Table B.1 Points of Contact

Name	Position	Phone	E-Mail Address	Organization
Ima Hungry	Team Leader	555-1111 x6543	ima.hungry@srocks.com	Security Rocks
Bob Smith	Team Member	555-1111 x6511	bob.smith@srocks.com	Security Rocks
Wilma Flintstone	Team Member	555-1111 x6522	stoneages@srocks.com	Security Rocks
Bean Counter	CIO	555-1212 x1234	dstove@ouch.com	OUCH
Penny Frugal	MIS Manager	555-1212 x1412	pfrugal@ouch.com	OUCH

Continued

Table B.1 continued Points of Contact

Name	Position	Phone	E-Mail Address	Organization
Shirley Secure	Risk/Security Specialist	555-1212 x1321	sbutto@ouch.com	OUCH
Mia Trusta	ISP Contact	555-3456	trustmia@3rdparty.com	Third party

II. Methodology Overview

The methodology used to conduct this evaluation is the National Security Agency's INFOSEC Evaluation Methodology (IEM). The IEM is an internationally recognized methodology for which the application is not dependent on a specific industry or type of client. This methodology incorporates a customer's requirements and needs along with regulatory requirements for the specific client. The IEM is technically focused and provides 10 IEM baseline activities that should be included as part of any evaluation. Ultimately, after completion of the 10 baseline activities, the customer is provided with an understandable and usable set of recommendations that, when implemented, will improve the overall security of the organization. The technical tools that are used to collect INFOSEC information will be a combination of commercial, freeware, and shareware tools. These tools will assist in gaining a larger cross-section of the system/network status and provide a means to identify and eliminate false positives throughout the evaluation process. The 10 IEM baseline activities used to collect the information about the organization's current technical security posture are:

- Port scanning
- SNMP scanning
- Enumeration and banner grabbing
- Wireless enumeration
- Vulnerability scanning
- Host evaluation
- Network device analysis
- Password compliance testing
- Application-specific training
- Network sniffing

III. Organizational and System Criticality Information

The organizational and system criticality information is gained from either a previously conducted INFOSEC assessment utilizing the IAM or during the pre-evaluation phase of the IEM. In our case, this information came from an IAM conducted in June 2004. The information was reviewed with the OUCH staff to ensure its currency.

The OUCH Mission

The Organized Union for Critical Healthcare (OUCH) has been contracted by Our Lady of Perpetual Pain Memorial Hospital to handle their information processing. The facility can house up to 5000 patients at a time. The day-to-day operations require automated information systems support for tracking and controlling information that includes admitting/releasing patients, administering medications, scheduling surgeries, feeding patients, tracking traffic to and from the hospital morgue, and various other information for doctors, nurses, and staff. OUCH has developed a single networked system that allows all the functions to be performed from terminals throughout the facility. The connectivity includes all databases and applications so that the information is readily available no matter where in the facility it is needed.

OUCH Impact Definitions

The following are OUCH's definitions for the impact to their organization should they lose confidentiality, integrity, and/or availability (CIA) of their critical information:

- **High** Loss of public trust, preventable significant patient injury or death or loss of patient for greater than 30 minutes, or regulatory takeover and fines in excess of $10,000 per day.

- **Medium** Loss of some public confidence, preventable minor patient injury or loss of patient for greater than 10 minutes but less than 30 minutes, or regulatory fines in excess of $5,000 but less than $10,000 per day.

- **Low** Minor bad press, loss of patient for less than 10 minutes, or regulatory fines less than $5,000 per day.

NOTE

These impact definitions are overly simplified for the purpose of providing an example and should not be used as serious definitions. Real-world examples encompass much greater detail than these and focus on setting levels and thresholds for occasions when certain criteria are met to move to the next higher or lower level of impact.

OUCH Organizational Criticality

OUCH has identified four primary areas of critical information the organization is concerned about in terms of protecting and safeguarding their customers, employees, and the OUCH business. These four areas of critical information are scheduling, monitoring, patient information, and corporate information. Based on meetings with OUCH key staff, Security Rocks developed the OUCH organizational information criticality matrix (OICM) shown in Table B.2, which was approved by OUCH staff. This matrix takes into account the OUCH impact definitions mapped against the critical information in relationship to CIA.

Table B.2 The OUCH OICM

Critical Information Area	Confidentiality	Integrity	Availability
Scheduling	Medium	High	Medium
Monitoring	High	High	High
Patient Information	High	High	Medium
Corporate Information	High	High	Medium

Overall	Confidentiality	Integrity	Availability
OUCH Information Criticality	High	High	High

System Information Criticality

OUCH identified only one system that processes, transmits, or stores the critical information identified during this process. OUCH has developed a single networked system that allows all the functions to be performed from terminals throughout the facility. The connectivity includes all databases and applications so that the information is readily available no matter where in the facility it is accessed. The system information criticality matrix (SICM) in this case will exactly match the OICM (see Table B.3). If another system were to be identified that processes any one or more pieces of critical information, another SICM would be created to reflect this situation.

Table B.3 The OUCH SICM

Critical Information Area	Confidentiality	Integrity	Availability
Scheduling	Medium	High	Medium
Monitoring	High	High	High
Patient Information	High	High	Medium
Corporate Information	High	High	Medium

IV. Detailed Network Information

The OUCH day-to-day operations require automated information systems support for tracking and controlling information that includes admitting/releasing patients, administering medications, scheduling surgeries, feeding patients, tracking traffic to and from the hospital morgue, and various other information for doctors, nurses, and staff. The network diagram in Figure B.1 provides the logical layout of the existing network at OUCH. This information has been confirmed with OUCH as being current.

Figure B.1 The OUCH Network Diagram

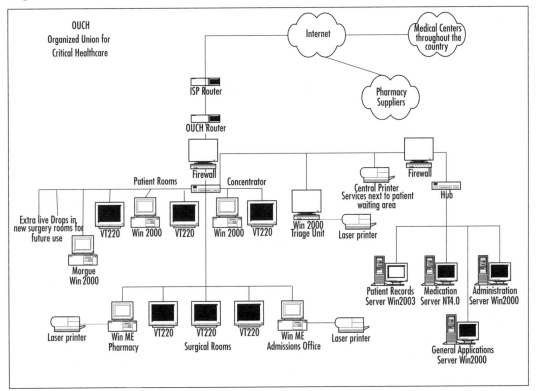

V. Customer Concerns

OUCH has expressed the following concerns related to the organization's security operations:

- Being compliant with new regulatory requirements such as the Health Information Portability and Accountability Act (HIPAA)

- Contract renewal with Our Lady of Perpetual Pain is 12 months away

- Avoid bad publicity related to security incidents

- Wireless networking security (just installed the system)

- Management of user accounts
- Training of medical staff on need for security (they say it's inconvenient)

VI. Customer Constraints

OUCH has identified the following constraints related to the evaluation:

- Hardware and network owned by Our Lady of Perpetual Pain; OUCH only provides the management
- Hardware located across three buildings but on one campus
- OUCH needs 24/7 operations, cannot lose connectivity while the evaluation is under way

VII. Rules of Engagement

This section provides the agreed-on approach and limitations related to the execution of the evaluation.

- OUCH will provide Security Rocks with a cubicle, phone access, fax access, printer access, and network access for the internal portion of the evaluation.
- OUCH will provide Security Rocks with internal static IP addresses for the duration of the internal evaluation.
- Security Rocks will do external scanning from the following IP addresses: 10.10.10.10 and 10.10.10.100.
- OUCH documentation is allowed to leave the OUCH site as long as it remains under reasonable protection.
- Security Rocks may only scan during nonpeak operating hours, which have been identified as Monday through Friday from 6:00 P.M. to 6:00 A.M. and on weekends.
- OUCH will notify the OUCH Computer Incident Response Team (CIRT) of the testing schedule to avoid issues with false identification of malicious activity. (This is not a penetration test; prior notice to CIRT will occur.)
- The team lead (Ima Hungry) will be Security Rocks' primary point of contact at all times. Her cell phone number is 555-1234. This contact should be used if there is an emergency or if questions arise.
- Shirley Security will be OUCH's primary emergency point of contact (cell 555-1212) for any issues while the testing is under way.
- OUCH has approved the following tools for use in the evaluation: SAINT, Nessus, Whisker, SPIDynamics WebInspect, Ethereal, and LC5. Configurations will disable all denial-of-service testing and shall limit active strings to no more than five on any

given IP to avoid system impact. OUCH has not excluded any specific tools from the scanning process but has asked to be notified prior to running a tool not on the approved list.

VIII. Internal and External Customer Requirements

Evaluation team's scanning IP addresses, immediate contact information for assessment team, notification of personnel on assessment activities, CIRT coordination for test purposes. This section describes network connections and IP addresses, facilities, scan windows, relevant IP addresses or subnets to access, and immediate administrator contact information for the customer.

IX. Coordination Agreements

This section provides additional detail not previously covered by any other TEP section.

Level of Detail of Recommendations

OUCH has a competent technical staff that can implement recommendations without a step-by-step "how to" provided in the final report. Therefore, the standard medium level of detail will be used in the recommendations.

Deliverables

OUCH and Security Rocks have agreed to the following deliverables:

- Technical Evaluation Plan Draft
- Technical Evaluation Plan Final
- Weekly Status Report
- Preliminary Findings Presentation (PowerPoint)
- Final Report Draft
- Final Report Final

Other Agreements

No other evaluation agreements have been requested or implied.

X. Letter of Authorization

Attached is the OUCH signed letter of authorization. A copy of this document will be in the possession of all Security Rocks staff while the evaluation is being conducted.

XI. Timeline of Evaluation Events

OUCH and Security Rocks have identified the following timeframes for completion of the evaluation effort:

- **Initial Engagement Agreement** May 15, 2005 – Complete
- **Pre-Evaluation Begins** May 24, 2005 – Complete
- **TEP Prepared and Approved** June 4, 2005 – Complete
- **Onsite Evaluation** June 15, 2005–June 30, 2005
- **Post-Evaluation** July 1, 2005–July 23, 2005
- **Final Report Draft Delivered** July 24, 2005
- **OUCH Comment on Final Report Draft** Due NLT July 31, 2005
- **Final Report Delivered** August 7, 2005

Index

A

Achilles tool, 414
adversaries. See threats
"advice of counsel" defense, 133
agreements, formal
  about, 33
  amendment process, 128
  approval process, 44, 47
  composition, 34–40
  contracting parties, 120–123
  handling potential conflicts, 126–128
  minimum contents, 34–36
  pitfalls, 40–43
  poorly written, 42–43
  pricing options, 36–38, 46
  restricting scope slippage, 75
  specifying cost elements, 125–126
  TEPs as, 149–150
  what to cover, 117–130
Aircrack tool, 239
AiroPeek tool, 407
Airsnort tool, 407
AppDetective tool, 413
application proxies, 295
application-specific scanning
  about, 287–288
  Achilles tool, 414
  AppDetective tool, 413
  as IEM baseline activity, 186, 365, 366
  IKE-Scan tool, 414
  k0ld tool, 414
  SPIKE Proxy tool, 414–415
  tools, 289–290, 413–415
  types to be scanned, 288–289
  WebInspect tool, 289, 290, 413
  Wikto tool, 289, 290, 413
applications
  evaluating services, 268
  vulnerabilities, 276
assessment, defined, 30, 167. See also IAM
      (INFOSEC Assessment Methodology)
assumptions, making, 42, 76–77, 87
attack trends, 247–251
attorney-client privilege, 132–133
attorneys. See lawyers
auditing, evaluating, 265–266
audits, vs. INFOSEC Evaluation
      Methodology (IEM), 15–16

B

border devices, defined, 278
botnets, 248
boundaries, system, 82–84, 322
Braa tool, 404
brute-force password attacks, 282–283
Brutus tool, 411
budgets, 57
buy-in, obtaining, 61–65

C

Cadillac, Chevy, and Yugo model, 381
California Database Protection Act, 55
CAN (candidates), 187–188, 340, 341. See
      also CVE/CAN numbers
candidates. See CAN (candidates)
Cardholder Information Security Program
      (CISP), 55
Center for Internet Security (CIS), 263–265,
      282, 410
CERT (Computer Emergency Response
      Team), 247, 323–324
certification, and IEM, 18, 47
CFAA (Computer Fraud and Abuse Act),
      107–108
ChoicePoint, 111
CIP (Critical Infrastructure Protection)
      standards, 26
CIS (Center for Internet Security), 263–265,
      282, 410
CISP (Cardholder Information Security
      Program), 55
Clarke, Richard, 102
CND (Computer Network Defense), 360
commercial contracting, 37
common vulnerabilities and exposures. See
      CVE (common vulnerabilities and
      exposures)
Computer Emergency Response Team
      (CERT), 247, 323–324
Computer Fraud and Abuse Act (CFAA),
      107–108

427

Computer Network Defense (CND), 360
consultants
  customer interactions, 16
  and expertise, 17–18
  matching to customers, 93–94
  what IEM contracts should cover, 117–130
"consulting by the pound" principle, 307
contracts
  about, 33
  amendment process, 128
  approval process, 44, 47
  combining for IAM and IEM, 46
  composition, 34–40
  fixed price vs. hourly rate, 37–38
  government vs. commercial, 36–37
  handling potential conflicts, 126–128
  minimum contents, 34–36
  overbidding, 43
  parties to agreement, 120–123
  pitfalls, 40–43
  poorly written, 42–43, 77–78
  pricing options, 36–38, 46
  restricting scope slippage, 75
  role in defining rights and protecting
    information, 114
  specifying cost elements, 125–126
  underbidding, 43
  what to cover, 117–130
cost estimating, 43, 78
critical components, 84
critical findings
  discussion in out-brief meeting, 306–307
  final report examples, 386–389
  points of immediate resolution, 308
  positive vs. negative, 307
Critical Infrastructure Protection (CIP)
    standards, 26
critical path, 84
criticality matrices, 155–156, 190, 336, 337,
    421–422. See also organizational
    information criticality matrix
    (OICM); overall vulnerability
    criticality matrix (OVCM); system
    information criticality matrix (SICM);
    system vulnerability criticality matrix
    (SVCM)
cultural sensitivity, 192–193
customer-required third-party independent
    reviews, 28

customers
  collecting and analyzing their
    documentation, 303, 325–327, 334
  concerns and expectations, 72–74, 97, 158,
    190, 303, 423–424
  constraints, 79–82, 158–159, 190, 304,
    423–424
  contract approval, 44, 47
  desired level of report detail, 81–82,
    327–331
  and formal engagement agreements, 33–43
  identifying times for scanning and tests, 79
  obtaining TEP approval, 163
  protecting their data, 304–305
  publicly available information about, 32
  reasons for requesting evaluations, 24–29,
    54–61, 78–79, 304
  role in out-brief meeting, 299–300
  as source of scoping information, 85–91
  specifying concerns in TEPs, 158, 190,
    423–424
  specifying constraints in TEPs, 158–159,
    190, 424
  specifying contacts in TEPs, 153, 189,
    419–420
  specifying rules of engagement in TEPs,
    159–160, 190, 424–425
  treatment of their customers, 130
  understanding requests by, 30–33
  ways of making requests, 29–30
CVE/CAN numbers, 250, 251, 381
CVE (common vulnerabilities and
    exposures), 187–188, 251, 340–341,
    343, 381–382
cyber attacks, 100–104, 140
cyber-insurance, 58

D

databases, for data analysis, 318
deceptive trade practices, 108
defense in depth (DiD), 5, 360, 364
Defense Information Assurance Certification
    and Accreditation Process (DIACAP),
    25, 60
Defense Information Systems Agency
    (DISA), 1
deliverables, specifying in TEPs, 160

Syngress: *The Definition of a Serious Security Library*

Syn·gress (sin-gres): *noun, sing.* Freedom from risk or danger; safety. See *security*.

AVAILABLE NOW
order @
www.syngress.com

Security Assessment: Case Studies for Implementing the NSA IAM

Russ Rogers, Greg Miles, Ed Fuller, Ted Dykstra

The National Security Agency's INFOSEC Assessment Methodology (IAM) provides guidelines for performing an analysis of how information is handled within an organization: looking at the systems that store, transfer, and process information. It also analyzes the impact to an organization if there is a loss of integrity, confidentiality, or availability. This book shows how to do a complete security assessment based on the NSA's guidelines.

ISBN: 1-932266-96-8
Price: $69.95 US $89.95 CAN

Hacking a Terror Network: The Silent Threat of Covert Channels

Russ Rogers, Matthew G. Devost

AVAILABLE NOW
order @
www.syngress.com

Written by a certified Arabic linguist from the Defense Language Institute with extensive background in decoding encrypted communications, this cyber-thriller uses a fictional narrative to provide a fascinating and realistic "insider's look" into technically sophisticated covert terrorist communications over the Internet. The accompanying CD-ROM allows readers to "hack along" with the story line, by viewing the same Web sites described in the book containing encrypted, covert communications.

ISBN: 1-928994-98-9
Price: $39.95 US $57.95 CAN

AVAILABLE NOW
order @
www.syngress.com

Microsoft Log Parser Toolkit

Gabriele Giuseppini and Mark Burnett

Do you want to find Brute Force Attacks against your Exchange Server? Would you like to know who is spamming you? Do you need to monitor the performance of your IIS Server? Are there intruders out there you would like to find? Would you like to build user logon reports from your Windows Server? Would you like working scripts to automate all of these tasks and many more for you? If so, *Microsoft Log Parser Toolkit* is the book for you...

ISBN: 1-932266-52-6
Price: $39.95 U.S. $57.95 CAN

SYNGRE